Eddie James

TOPICAL BIBLE

KING JAMES VERSION

EDDIE JAMES DEVOTIONAL TOPICAL BIBLE

KING JAMES VERSION

Scripture quotations marked (AMP) are taken from The Amplified Bible, Old Testament copyright © 1965, 1987, by The Zondervan Corporation. The Amplified New Testament copyright © 1958, 1987, by The Lockman Foundation. Used by permission.

Scripture quotations marked (NIV) are taken from The Holy Bible, New International Version copyright © 1973, 1978, 1984 by International Bible Society. Used by permission of Zondervan Bible Publishers.

Grateful acknowledgment is hereby expressed to the following publishers who have granted permission to include copyrighted materials in this book. Any inadvertent omission of credit will be gladly corrected in future editions. Christian Publications: *Born After Midnight, The Dwelling Place of God, Of God and Men, Roots of the Righteous,* and *That Incredible Christian* by A. W. Tozer. Used by permission. Baker Book House: *The Vance Havner Quote Book* by Dennis J. Hester copyright © 1986. *3,000 Quotations on Christian Themes* by Carroll E. Simcox copyright © 1975. *12,000 Religious Quotations* by Frank S. Mead copyright © 1965.

All rights reserved. Written permission must be secured from the publisher to use or reproduce any part of this book, except for brief quotations in critical reviews or articles.

Copyright ©2025 Eddie James
Copyright © 1998 - Scripture Compilation Licensed by Pneuma Life, Inc.
Printed in the United States of America
Eddie James Devotional Topical Bible– King James Version
ISBN: 978-1-56229-879-1

Pneuma Life Publishing
12138 Central Ave, Suite 251, Mitchellville, MD 20721
1-469-481-3896
Website: http://www.pneumalife.com

BIO

Eddie James was born in Phoenix, Arizona, and raised in the Church of God in Christ. He accepted Christ as his personal Lord and Savior at the age of eight and began pursuing music ministry the following year. This early start shaped his lifelong passion for reaching young people and those in need through music and ministry.

Music Ministry and Achievements

James founded Eddie James Ministries in 1993, launching several influential musical groups, including the Phoenix Mass Choir, ColourBlind, Asaph, Tab, and Ultimate Call. His national debut came in 1995 with the Phoenix Mass Choir's album Higher, which reached No. 3 on the Billboard Gospel Albums chart. He followed this with solo projects such as Grace and Psalm 23, and continued to innovate with groups like ColourBlind, whose musical drama Break the Walls addressed issues facing youth, including drugs, violence, and racism.

James's songwriting and worship leading have made him a sought-after figure in the gospel and worship community. His songs, including "Freedom," "I Am," "Psalm 23," and "You've Been So Faithful," have been performed by artists and ministries such as Judy Jacobs, Helen Baylor, Brooklyn Tabernacle Choir, Mississippi Mass Choir, Joel Osteen's Lakewood Church, and universities like Lee and Liberty. He has toured extensively in the United States and internationally, ministering alongside leaders like Bishop TD Jakes, Karen Wheaton, and Kirk Franklin.

Ministry and Outreach

Beyond music, Eddie James is deeply committed to youth outreach and restoration. He established DreamLife, a recovery and discipleship program for high school and college-aged youth struggling with addiction, abuse, and other life-controlling issues. DreamLife operates in Tennessee and Georgia, helping young people find hope and transformation.

James also serves as the Music and Performing Arts Director for Karen Wheaton Ministries' youth ministry, Chosen, and is active at The Ramp, a youth center in Hamilton, Alabama. He frequently appears on Christian television networks such as TBN and Daystar, and his work has been featured in various media outlets.

Legacy and Influence

Eddie James is recognized for his dynamic worship leadership, impactful songwriting, and dedication to mentoring the next generation of Christian leaders. His music and ministry continue to inspire and influence churches, choirs, and worship teams around the world.

Personal Mission

Eddie James's life and work are driven by a desire to bring healing and revival, especially to young people, through the power of worship and the message of Christ.

Table of Contents

God Your Father
Who is God? 9
Who is Jesus? 12
The Trinity (The Father, The Son, and The Holy Ghost) 16
How to Reach God 18
How to Love and Please God 19
Communicating With God 19
Praising God 20
Worshipping God 24
Fear of the Lord 26
Trusting God 27
Faith in God and His Word 29
The Will of God 35

God's Word
The Integrity of God's Word 39
God's Word is Spiritual Food 41
The Word of God in the Heart 43
Meditating on God's Word 46
How to Obtain Promises from God's Word 47
The Cleansing of the Word of God 49
Memorizing the Word of God 49
Guidance from God's Word 50
The Spoken Word of God 51

The Holy Spirit
Respecting the Holy Spirit 53
Receiving the Baptism of the Holy Spirit 53
The Benefits of Praying in the Holy Spirit 54
Examples of Believers Being Filled With the Holy Spirit 54
The Holy Spirit is the Teacher, Leader, Revealer, Guide and Counselor 55
The Holy Spirit Living Inside the Believer 56
Sealed by the Holy Spirit 57
The Power of the Holy Spirit 57
The Gifts of the Holy Spirit 58

The Name of Jesus
The Different Names of Jesus 59
The Name Above All Names 62

Praying in the Name of Jesus 62
Power in the Name of Jesus 63
Believing in the Name of Jesus 64
Serving in the Name of Jesus 64
Suffering for the Name of Jesus 65

CONSECRATION
Seeking God 67
Obeying the Word of God 70
Submitting to the Correction of God 73
Dying to Self 74
Following Christ and Carrying Your Cross 75
Being a True Representative of God 76
Fasting 79

LEARNING TO LOVE
Characteristics of Love 81
God's Love 82
Loving God 83
Loving Others 84

OVERCOMING SIN
Sin 87
Secret Sins 88
Deliberate and Willful Sin 89
Sowing Sin and Reaping the Consequences of Sin 90
Sin Gives satan Entrance Into Your Life 90
A Life of Sin is Hard 91
What Should I Do When I Sin? 92
Deliverance from Sin 95
Curses 96

GOD'S FORGIVENESS
Sins Cleansed by the Blood of Jesus 99
God Will Forgive Your Sins 99
God Will Not Remember Your Sins 100
God Will Blot Out Your Sins 101
Overcoming Guilt 101
Overcoming Condemnation 103

SALVATION
Believing in Jesus Christ 105
Plan of Salvation 106
Saved by Grace 108
Sanctification 109

Righteousness 110
Justification 112
Remaining in the Kingdom of God 113
The Return of Christ 114
Eternal Life 116
Backslider 117
Compromising Christian 118
A Warning for the Backslider or Compromising Christian 120

ETERNITY
Heaven 123
Hell 126

PRAYER
Praying in the Name of Jesus 133
The Lord's Prayer 134
God Hears Your Prayers 134
Hindrances to Prayer 135
Praying With the Right Attitude and Motives 135
Different Kinds of Prayer 136
Prayer of Agreement 137
Praying in Faith 137
Waiting on God in Prayer 137
Praying in the Holy Spirit 137
Intercessory Prayer 138
Examples of Prayer Warriors 139
Praying Continuously 139

LIFE'S CHALLENGES
Fear 141
Enemies 142
Revenge 145
Persecution 146
Loneliness 147
Temptation 149
Stress and Depression 150
Anxiety and Worry 153

YOUR MIND
Renewing Your Mind 155
Focusing Your Mind on the Word of God 155
Focusing Your Mind on Jesus 156
Controlling Imaginations and Thoughts 156
Controlling Lust 157
Television, Movies and Music 159

Your Body
Your Body
The Temple of the Holy Spirit 163
Sex Before Marriage 163
The Consequences of Fornication 164
Adultery 165
The Consequences of Adultery 165
Homosexuality and Lesbianism 165
Gluttony 166
Biblical Diet 167
Healing 167

Maturing in Christ
Forgiveness 171
Patience 172
Living in Holiness 174
Fruitful Living 176
Peacemaker 177
Overcoming Covetousness 178
Overcoming the Fear of Man 179
Becoming Bold in Christ 179

Character
Honesty 181
Being Honest With Yourself 182
Keeping Your Word (Promises, Vows, and Commitments) 183
Accepting Advice and Positive Criticism 183
Learning to Control the Words that You Speak 184

Positive Attitude
Humility 191
Meekness 193
Overcoming Pride 195
Controlling Anger 198
Overcoming an Envious Heart 199
Overcoming a Judgmental Attitude 200
Overcoming the Tendency to Gossip or Slander 202
Building Your Self-Confidence Through Christ 204
Building Your Self-Image Through God's Word 205

Attributes of a Proverbs 31 Woman
Proverbs 31 207
Wisdom 208
Knowledge 212
Understanding 215
Direction 218

Favor from God 221
Decisions 222
Diligence 222
Faithfulness 223
Work 225
Good Works 227

Relationships
Marriage 231
Divorce 233
Unsaved Marriage Partner 234
Child-Parent Relationship 235
Children and Teenagers 237
Dating and Engagements 238
Friends 240
Avoiding or Breaking Bad Relationships 241

Spiritual Warfare
The Superior Power and Authority of Christ 245
You Have Power Over the devil and his demons 246
Spiritual Warfare 247
The Weapons of the Spiritual Realm 247
Binding and Loosing 249
God's End-Time Army 249
Spiritual Enemies 249
Attacking the Enemy 250

Spiritual Discernment
Discerning Good and Evil 251
Discernment From God's Word 251
Spiritual Eyes and Ears 252
Deception 253
The Strategies of satan (the devil) 256
Laying on of Hands 261
False Brothers 263
False Prophets 266
Casting Out devils 269
Occult, Witchcraft and Idolatry 273

Biblical Economics
Tithes and Offerings 275
Sowing Seeds 276
Reaping the Harvest 277
The End-Time Transfer of Wealth to Christians 277
Loans 278

Co-Signing for Others 279
God Wants You to Prosper Financially 279
Giving in the Right Attitude 281
True Riches 282
Do Not Put Your Trust or Hope in Money 282
Contentment 283
Spreading the Gospel of Jesus Christ 284
Helping the Poor 285

The Provisions of Christ

Love 287
Hope 288
Joy 290
Mercy 292
Peace 295
Comfort 298
Deliverance 299
Perseverance 300

Deep Waters Devotional 316

God Your Father

Who is God?

God is love; and he that dwelleth in love dwelleth in God, and God in him. 1 John 4:16

God is a Spirit: and they that worship him must worship him in spirit and in truth. John 4:24

Shall we not much rather be in subjection to the Father of spirits, and live? Hebrews 12:9

O God, the God of the spirits of all flesh. Numbers 16:22

Let the Lord; the God of the spirits of all flesh. Numbers 27:16

1. God is the Creator of Heaven and Earth

In the beginning God created the heaven and the earth. Genesis 1:1

Thus saith God the Lord, he that created the heavens, and stretched them out; he that spread forth the earth, and that which cometh out of it; he that giveth breath unto the people upon it, and spirit to them that walk therein. Isaiah 42:5

For thus saith the Lord that created the heavens; God himself that formed the earth and made it; he hath established it, he created it not in vain, he formed it to be inhabited: I am the Lord; and there is none else.
Isaiah 45:18

2. God is Sovereign and Omnipotent

For his eyes are upon the ways of man, and he seeth all his goings.
Job 34:21

Behold, God is great, and we know him not, neither can the number of his years be searched out. Job 36:26

Dost thou know the balancings of the clouds, the wondrous works of him which is perfect in knowledge? Job 37:16

Nature is the art of God. - Thomas Browne

He ruleth by his power for ever; his eyes behold the nations: let not the rebellious exalt themselves. Selah. Psalms 66:7

Lord, thou hast been our dwelling place in all generations. Before the mountains were brought forth, or ever thou hadst formed the earth and the world, even from everlasting to everlasting, thou art God. Thou turnest man to destruction; and sayest, Return, ye children of men. For a thousand years in thy sight are but as yesterday when it is past, and as a watch in the night. Psalms 90:1-4

He causeth the vapours to ascend from the ends of the earth; he maketh lightnings for the rain; he bringeth the wind out of his treasuries.
Psalms 135:7

When he uttereth his voice, there is a multitude of waters in the heavens, and he causeth the vapours to ascend from the ends of the earth; he maketh lightnings with rain, and bringeth forth the wind out of his treasures.
Jeremiah 10:13

Thy kingdom is an everlasting kingdom, and thy dominion endureth throughout all generations. Psalms 145:13

Great is our Lord, and of great power: his understanding is infinite.
Psalms 147:5

For the ways of man are before the eyes of the Lord, and he pondereth all his goings. Proverbs 5:21

The eyes of the Lord are in every place, beholding the evil and the good.
Proverbs 15:3

The king's heart is in the hand of the Lord, as the rivers of water: he turneth it whithersoever he will. Proverbs 21:1

Who hath ascended up into heaven, or descended? who hath gathered the wind in his fists? who hath bound the waters in a garment? who hath established all the ends of the earth? what is his name, and what is his son's name, if thou canst tell? Proverbs 30:4

All nations before him are as nothing; and they are counted to him less than nothing, and vanity. To whom then will ye liken God? or what likeness will ye compare unto him? Isaiah 40:17-18

For my thoughts are not your thoughts, neither are your ways my ways, saith the Lord. For as the heavens are higher than the earth, so are my ways higher than your ways, and my thoughts than your thoughts.
Isaiah 55:8-9

Thus saith the Lord, The heaven is my throne, and the earth is my footstool: where is the house that ye build unto me? and where is the place of my rest? Isaiah 66:1

Am I a God at hand, saith the Lord, and not a God afar off? Can any hide himself in secret places that I shall not see him? saith the Lord. Do not I fill heaven and earth? saith the Lord. Jeremiah 23:23-24

For with God nothing shall be impossible. Luke 1:37

O the depth of the riches both of the wisdom and knowledge of God! how unsearchable are his judgments, and his ways past finding out!
Romans 11:33

Because the foolishness of God is wiser than men; and the weakness of God is stronger than men. 1 Corinthians 1:25

For when God made promise to Abraham, because he could swear by no greater, he sware by himself. Hebrews 6:13

Wherefore we receiving a kingdom which cannot be moved, let us have grace, whereby we may serve God acceptably with reverence and godly fear: For our God is a consuming fire. Hebrews 12:28-29

And when I saw him, I fell at his feet as dead. And he laid his right hand upon me, saying unto me, Fear not; I am the first and the last: I am he that liveth, and was dead; and, behold, I am alive for evermore, Amen; and have the keys of hell and of death. Revelation 1:17-18

And I heard as it were the voice of a great multitude, and as the voice of many waters, and as the voice of mighty thunderings, saying, Alleluia: for the Lord God omnipotent reigneth. Revelation 19:6

And he said unto me, It is done. I am Alpha and Omega, the beginning and the end. I will give unto him that is athirst of the fountain of the water of life freely. Revelation 21:6

I am Alpha and Omega, the beginning and the end, the first and the last.
Revelation 22:13

3. God is the Creator of Mankind

And God said, Let us make man in our image, after our likeness.
Genesis 1:26

So God created man in his own image, in the image of God created he him; male and female created he them. Genesis 1:27

And the Lord God formed man of the dust of the ground, and breathed into his nostrils the breath of life; and man became a living soul.
Genesis 2:7

And the Lord God said, It is not good that the man should be alone; I will make him an help meet for him. Genesis 2:18

And the Lord God caused a deep sleep to fall upon Adam and he slept: and he took one of his ribs, and closed up the flesh instead thereof; And the rib, which the Lord God had taken from man, made he a woman, and brought her unto the man. And Adam said, This is now bone of my bones, and flesh of my flesh: she shall be called Woman, because she was taken out of Man. Therefore shall a man leave his father and his mother, and shall cleave unto his wife: and they shall be one flesh.
Genesis 2:21-24

The Lord, which stretcheth forth the heavens, and layeth the foundation of the earth, and formeth the spirit of man within him. Zechariah 12:1

As thou knowest not what is the way of the spirit, nor how the bones do grow in the womb of her that is with child: even so thou knowest not the works of God who maketh all. Ecclesiastes 11:5

He hath made the earth by his power, he hath established the world by his wisdom, and hath stretched out the heavens by his discretion.
Jeremiah 10:12

Who is Jesus?

Who is the image of the invisible God, the firstborn of every creature:
Colossians 1:15

For by him were all things created, that are in heaven, and that are in earth, visible and invisible, whether they be thrones, or dominions, or principalities, or powers: all things were created by him, and for him: And he is before all things, and by him all things consist. And he is the head of the body, the church: who is the beginning, the firstborn from the dead; that in all things he might have the preeminence. For it pleased the Father that in him should all fulness dwell; Colossians 1:16-19

He was in the world, and the world was made by him, and the world knew him not. John 1:10

1. Jesus is the Mediator Between God and Man

For there is one God, and one mediator between God and men, the man Christ Jesus. 1 Timothy 2:5

Jesus saith unto him, I am the way, the truth, and the life: no man cometh unto the Father, but by me. John 14:6

Whosoever denieth the Son, the same hath not the Father: (but) he that acknowledgeth the Son hath the Father also. 1 John 2:23

And, having made peace through the blood of his cross, by him to reconcile all things unto himself; by him, I say, whether they be things in earth, or things in heaven. Colossians 1:20

All things are delivered unto me of my Father: and no man knoweth the Son, but the Father; neither knoweth any man the Father, save the Son, and he to whomsoever the Son will reveal him. Matthew 11:27

All that the Father giveth me shall come to me; and him that cometh to me I will in no wise cast out. For I came down from heaven, not to do mine own will, but the will of him that sent me. And this is the Father's will which hath sent me, that of all which he hath given me I should lose nothing, but should raise it up again at the last day. And this is the will of him that sent me, that every one which seeth the Son, and believeth on him, may have everlasting life: and I will raise him up at the last day.
John 6:37-40

2. Jesus is the Son of God

Which were born, not of blood, nor of the will of the flesh, nor of the will of man, but of God. John 1:13

For he whom God hath sent speaketh the words of God: for God giveth not the Spirit by measure unto him. John 3:34

I came forth from the Father, and am come into the world: again, I leave the world, and go to the Father. John 16:28

And declared to be the Son of God with power, according to the spirit of holiness, by the resurrection from the dead. Romans 1:4

3. Jesus is God

I and my Father are one. John 10:30

And without controversy great is the mystery of godliness: God was manifest in the flesh, justified in the Spirit, seen of angels, preached unto the Gentiles, believed on in the world, received up into glory.

1 Timothy 3:16

But whosoever drinketh of the water that I shall give him shall never thirst; but the water that I shall give him shall be in him a well of water springing up into everlasting life. John 4:14

Therefore the Jews sought the more to kill him, because he not only had broken the sabbath, but said also that God was his Father, making himself equal with God. John 5:18

And he that seeth me seeth him that sent me. John 12:45

And Jesus said unto them, I am the bread of life: he that cometh to me shall never hunger; and he that believeth on me shall never thirst.

John 6:35

But if I do, though ye believe not me, believe the works: that ye may know, and believe, that the Father is in me, and I in him. John 10:38

Hath in these last days spoken unto us by his Son, whom he hath appointed heir of all things, by whom also he made the worlds; Who being the brightness of his glory, and the express image of his person, and upholding all things by the word of his power, when he had by himself purges our sins, sat down on the right hand of the Majesty on high;

Hebrews 1:2-3

4. Jesus Existed as God Before He Came to Earth

John bare witness of him, and cried, saying, This was he of whom I spake, He that cometh after me is preferred before me: for he was before me. John 1:15

He that cometh from above is above all: he that is of the earth is earthly, and speaketh of the earth: he that cometh from heaven is above all.

John 3:31

Who, being in the form of God, thought it not robbery to be equal with God: But made himself of no reputation, and took upon him the form of a servant, and was made in the likeness of men: And being found in fashion as a man, he humbled himself, and became obedient unto death, even the death of the cross. Wherefore God also hath highly exalted him, and given him a name which is above every name. Philippians 2:6-9

And God said, Let us make man in our image, after our likeness: and let them have dominion over the fish of the sea, and over the fowl of the air, and over the cattle, and over all the earth, and over every creeping thing that creepeth upon the earth. Genesis 1:26

But thou art the same, and thy years shall have no end. Psalms 102:27

In the beginning was the Word, and the Word was with God, and the Word was God. John 1:1

Say ye of him, whom the Father hath sanctified, and sent into the world, Thou blasphemest; because I said, I am the Son of God? John 10:36

All things were made by him; and without him was not any thing made that was made. John 1:3

And the Word was made flesh, and dwelt among us, and we beheld his glory as of the only begotten of the Father, full of grace and truth.
John 1:14

Your father Abraham rejoiced to see my day: and he saw it, and was glad. John 8:56

Then said the Jews unto him, Thou art not yet fifty years old, and hast thou seen Abraham? Jesus said unto them, Verily, verily, I say unto you, Before Abraham was, I am. John 8:57-58

Father, I will that they also, whom thou hast given me, be with me where I am; that they may behold my glory, which thou hast given me: for thou lovedst me before the foundation of the world. John 17:24

Who is the image of the invisible God, the firstborn of every creature: For by him were all things created, that are in heaven, and that are in earth, visible and invisible, whether they be thrones, or dominions, or principalities, or powers: all things were created by him, and for him: And he is before all things, and by him all things consist.
Colossians 1:15-17

Who being the brightness of his glory, and the express image of his person, and upholding all things by the word of his power, when he had by himself purged our sins, sat down on the right hand of the Majesty on high; Hebrews 1:3

But unto the Son he saith, Thy throne, O God, is for ever and ever: a sceptre of righteousness is the sceptre of thy kingdom. Thou hast loved righteousness, and hated iniquity; therefore God, even thy God, hath anointed thee with the oil of gladness above thy fellows. And, Thou, Lord, in the beginning hast laid the foundation of the earth; and the heavens are the works of thine hands: They shall perish; but thou remainest; and they all shall wax old as doth a garment; And as a vesture shalt thou fold them up, and they shall be changed: but thou art the same, and thy years shall not fail. Hebrews 1:8-12

Jesus Christ the same yesterday, and today, and forever. Hebrews 13:8

I am Alpha and Omega, the beginning and the end, the first and the last. Revelation 22:13

5. Jesus is the Word of God

In the beginning was the Word, and the Word was with God, and the Word was God. John 1:1

And the Word was made flesh, and dwelt among us, and we beheld his glory, the glory as of the only begotten of the Father, full of grace and truth. John 1:14

For there are three that bear record in heaven, the Father, the Word, and the Holy Ghost: and these three are one. 1 John 5:7

And he was clothed with a vesture dipped in blood: and his name is called The Word of God. Revelation 19:13

6. Jesus is Wisdom

But unto them which are called, both Jews and Greeks, Christ the power of God, and the wisdom of God. 1 Corinthians 1:24

But of him are ye in Christ Jesus, who of God is made unto us wisdom, and righteousness, and sanctification, and redemption: 1 Corinthians 1:30

In whom are hid all the treasures of wisdom and knowledge. Colossians 2:3

The Trinity (The Father, The Son, and The Holy Ghost)

And God said, Let us make man in our image, after our likeness: and let them have dominion over the fish of the sea, and over the fowl of the air, and over the cattle, and over all the earth, and over every creeping thing that creepeth upon the earth. Genesis 1:26

And the Lord God said, Behold, the man is become as one of us, to know good and evil: and now, lest he put forth his hand, and take also of the tree of life, and eat, and live for ever: Genesis 3:22

Come ye near unto me, hear ye this; I have not spoken in secret from the beginning; from the time that it was, there am I: and now the Lord God, and his Spirit, hath sent me. Isaiah 48:16

Go ye therefore, and teach all nations, baptizing them in the name of the Father, and of the Son, and of the Holy Ghost: Matthew 28:19

> *The sun, in my opinion, is the best example of the Trinity. God is the sun; Jesus is the light of the sun; and the Holy Ghost is the heat of the sun. - Benny Hinn*

And the Holy Ghost descended in a bodily shape like a dove upon him, and a voice came from heaven, which said, Thou art my beloved Son; in thee I am well pleased. John 3:22

For he whom God hath sent speaketh the words of God: for God giveth not the Spirit by measure unto him. The Father loveth the Son, and hath given all things into his hand. John 3:34-35

I and my Father are one. John 10:30

And I will pray the Father, and he shall give you another Comforter, that he may abide with you for ever; Even the Spirit of truth; whom the world cannot receive, because it seeth him not, neither knoweth him: but ye know him; for he dwelleth with you, and shall be in you. John 14:16-17

But the Comforter, which is the Holy Ghost, whom the Father will send in my name, he shall teach you all things, and bring all things to your remembrance, whatsoever I have said unto you. John 14:26

But when the Comforter is come, whom I will send unto you from the Father, even the Spirit of truth, which proceedeth from the Father, he shall testify of me: John 15:26

What? know ye not that your body is the temple of the Holy Ghost which is in you, which ye have of God, and ye are not your own?
1 Corinthians 6:19

But to us there is but one God, the Father, of whom are all things, and we in him; and one Lord Jesus Christ, by whom are all things, and we by him. 1 Corinthians 8:6

Now he which stablisheth us with you in Christ, and hath anointed us, is God; Who hath also sealed us, and given the earnest of the Spirit in our hearts. 2 Corinthians 1:21-22

The grace of the Lord Jesus Christ, and the love of God, and the communion of the Holy Ghost, be with you all. Amen. 2 Corinthians 13:14

But when the fulness of the time was come, God sent forth his Son, made of a woman, made under the law, And because ye are sons, God hath sent forth the Spirit of his Son into your hearts, crying, Abba, Father. Galatians 4:4,6

That their hearts might be comforted, being knit together in love, and unto all riches of the full assurance of understanding, to the acknowledgment of the mystery of God, and of the Father, and of Christ;
Colossians 2:2

But we are bound to give thanks alway to God for you, brethren beloved of the Lord, because God hath from the beginning chosen you to salvation through sanctification of the Spirit and belief of the truth: Whereunto he called you by our gospel, to the obtaining of the glory of our Lord Jesus Christ. 2 Thessalonians 2:13-14

But after that the kindness and love of God our Saviour toward man appeared, Not by works of righteousness which we have done, but according to his mercy he saved us, by the washing of regeneration, and renewing of the Holy Ghost; Which he shed on us abundantly through Jesus Christ our Saviour; Titus 3:4-6

Elect according to the foreknowledge of God the Father, through sanctification of the Spirit, unto obedience and sprinkling of the blood of Jesus Christ: Grace unto you, and peace, be multiplied. 1 Peter 1:2

For Christ also hath once suffered for sins, the just for the unjust, that he might bring us to God, being put to death in the flesh, but quickened by the Spirit: 1 Peter 3:18

This is he that came by water and blood, even Jesus Christ; not by water only, but by water and blood. And it is the Spirit that beareth witness, because the Spirit is truth. For there are three that bear record in heaven, the Father, the Word, and the Holy Ghost: and these three are one.
1 John 5:6-7

How to Reach God

Jesus saith unto him, I am the way, the truth, and the life: no man cometh unto the Father, but by me. John 14:6

For there is one God, and one mediator between God and men, the man Christ Jesus. 1 Timothy 2:5

Then said Jesus unto them again, Verily, verily, I say unto you, I am the door of the sheep. All that ever came before me are thieves and robbers:

but the sheep did not hear them. I am the door: by me if any man enter in, he shall be saved, and shall go in and out, and find pasture.
John 10:7-9

Whosoever denieth the Son, the same hath not the Father: (but) he that acknowledgeth the Son hath the Father also. 1 John 2:23

He that hath the Son hath life; and he that hath not the Son of God hath not life. 1 John 5:12

How to Love and Please God

If ye love me, keep my commandments. John 14:15

He that hath my commandments, and keepeth them, he it is that loveth me: and he that loveth me shall be loved of my Father, and I will love him, and will manifest myself to him. John 14:21

Jesus answered and said unto him, If a man love me, he will keep my words: and my Father will love him, and we will come unto him, and make our abode with him. He that loveth me not keepeth not my sayings: and the word which ye hear is not mine, but the Father's which sent me. John 14:23-24

If ye keep my commandments, ye shall abide in my love; even as I have kept my Father's commandments, and abide in his love. John 15:10

Ye are my friends, if ye do whatsoever I command you. John 15:14

By this we know that we love the children of God, when we love God, and keep his commandments. 1 John 5:2

For this is the love of God, that we keep his commandments: and his commandments are not grievous. 1 John 5:3

Communicating With God

But the hour cometh, and now is, when the true worshippers shall worship the Father in spirit and in truth: for the Father seeketh such to worship him. God is a Spirit: and they that worship him must worship him in spirit and in truth. John 4:23-24

Let us come before his presence with thanksgiving, and make a joyful noise unto him with psalms. Psalms 95:2

Enter into his gates with thanksgiving, and into his courts with praise: be thankful unto him, and bless his name. Psalms 100:4

For through him we both have access by one Spirit unto the Father.
Ephesians 2:18

In whom we have boldness and access with confidence by the faith of him. Ephesians 3:12

Life for the Christian is a dialogue with God. - J. H. Oldham

Let us therefore come boldly unto the throne of grace, that we may ob-tain mercy, and find grace to help in time of need. Hebrews 4:16

Having therefore, brethren, boldness to enter into the holiest by the blood of Jesus. Hebrews 10:19

Behold, I stand at the door, and knock: if any man hear my voice, and open the door, I will come in to him, and will sup with him, and he with me. Revelation 3:20

Praising God

I will praise the Lord according to his righteousness: and will sing praise to the name of the Lord most high. Psalms 7:17

The Lord is my strength and my shield; my heart trusted in him, and I am helped: therefore my heart greatly rejoiceth; and with my song will I praise him. Psalms 28:7

I will bless the Lord at all times: his praise shall continually be in my mouth. Psalms 34:1

And my tongue shall speak of thy righteousness and of thy praise all the day long. Psalms 35:28

In God we boast all the day long, and praise thy name for ever. Selah.
Psalms 44:8

Great is the Lord, and greatly to be praised in the city of our God, in the mountain of his holiness. Psalms 48:1

O Lord, open thou my lips; and my mouth shall shew forth thy praise.
Psalms 51:15

In God I will praise his word, in God I have put my trust; I will not fear what flesh can do unto me. Psalms 56:4

In God will I praise his word: in the Lord will I praise his word.
Psalms 56:10

My heart is fixed, O God, my heart is fixed: I will sing and give praise.
Psalms 57:7

So will I sing praise unto thy name for ever, that I may daily perform my vows. Psalms 61:8

Because thy lovingkindness is better than life, my lips shall praise thee.
Psalms 63:3

Make a joyful noise unto God, all ye lands: Sing forth the honour of his name: make his praise glorious. Psalms 66:1-2

Let the people praise thee, O God; let all the people praise thee.
Psalms 67:3

Sing unto God, ye kingdoms of the earth; O sing praises unto the Lord; Selah. Psalms 68:32

I will praise the name of God with a song, and will magnify him with thanksgiving. Psalms 69:30

Let the heaven and earth praise him, the seas, and everything that moveth therein. Psalms 69:34

Let my mouth be filled with thy praise and with thy honour all the day.
Psalms 71:8

But I will hope continually, and will yet praise thee more and more.
Psalms 71:14

I will praise thee, O Lord my God, with all my heart: and I will glorify thy name for evermore. Psalms 86:12

And the heavens shall praise thy wonders, O Lord: thy faithfulness also in the congregation of the saints. Psalms 89:5

It is a good thing to give thanks unto the Lord, and to sing praises unto thy name, O most High: To shew forth thy lovingkindness in the morning, and thy faithfulness every night, Upon an instrument of ten strings, and upon the psaltery; upon the harp with a solemn sound. For the Lord is great, and greatly to be praised: he is to be feared above all gods.
Psalms 92:1-4

Make a joyful noise unto the Lord, all the earth: make a loud noise, and rejoice, and sing praise. Psalms 98:4

Make a joyful noise unto the Lord, all ye lands. Serve the Lord with gladness: come before his presence with singing. Psalms 100:1-2

Enter into his gates with thanksgiving, and into his courts with praise: be thankful unto him, and bless his name. For the Lord is good; his mercy is everlasting; and his truth endureth to all generations. Psalms 100:4-5

O God, my heart is fixed; I will sing and give praise, even with my glory. Awake, psaltery and harp: I myself will awake early. I will praise thee, O Lord, among the people: and I will sing praises unto thee among the nations. Psalms 108:1-3

Praise ye the Lord. I will praise the Lord with my whole heart, in the assembly of the upright, and in the congregation. Psalms 111:1

Praise ye the Lord. Praise, O ye servants of the Lord, praise the name of the Lord. Blessed be the name of the Lord from this time forth and for evermore. From the rising of the sun unto the going down of the same the Lord's name is to be praised. Psalms 113:1-3

O praise the Lord, all ye nations: praise him, all ye people. For his merciful kindness is great toward us: and the truth of the Lord endureth for ever. Praise ye the Lord. Psalms 117:1-2

Thou art my God, and I will praise thee: thou art my God, I will exalt thee. O give thanks unto the Lord; for he is good: for his mercy endureth for ever. Psalms 118:28-29

I will praise thee with uprightness of heart, when I shall have learned thy righteous judgments. Psalms 119:7

Seven times a day do I praise thee because of thy righteous judgments. Psalms 119:164

Praise the Lord; for the Lord is good: sing praises unto his name; for it is pleasant. Psalms 135:3

I will praise thee with my whole heart: before the gods will I sing praise unto thee. I will worship toward thy holy temple, and praise thy name for thy lovingkindness and for thy truth: for thou hast magnified thy word above all thy name. Psalms 138:1-2

All the kings of the earth shall praise thee, O Lord, when they hear the words of thy mouth. Psalms 138:4

Great is the Lord, and greatly to be praised; and his greatness is unsearchable. Psalms 145:3

Praise ye the Lord: for it is good to sing praises unto our God; for it is pleasant; and praise is comely. Psalms 147:1

Praise ye the Lord. Praise ye the Lord from the heavens: praise him in the heights. Praise ye him, all his angels: praise ye him, all his hosts. Praise ye him, sun and moon: praise him, all ye stars of light. Praise him, ye heavens of heavens, and ye waters that be above the heavens. Let them praise the name of the Lord: for he commanded, and they were created. He hath also stablished them for ever and ever: he hath made a decree which shall not pass. Praise the Lord from the earth, ye dragons, and all deeps: Fire, and hail; snow, and vapour; stormy wind fulfilling his word: Mountains, and all hills; fruitful trees, and all cedars: Beasts, and all cattle; creeping things, and flying fowl: Kings of the earth, and all people; princes, and all judges of the earth: Both young men, and maidens; old men, and children: Let them praise the name of the Lord: for his name alone is excellent; his glory is above the earth and heaven.
Psalms 148:1-13

Praise ye the Lord. Praise God in his sanctuary: praise him in the firmament of his power. Praise him for his mighty acts: praise him according to his excellent greatness. Praise him with the sound of the trumpet: praise him with the psaltery and harp. Praise him with the timbrel and dance: praise him with stringed instruments and organs. Praise him upon the loud cymbals: praise him upon the high sounding cymbals. Let every thing that hath breath praise the Lord. Praise ye the Lord.
Psalms 150:1-6

O Lord, thou art my God; I will exalt thee, I will praise thy name; for thou hast done wonderful things; thy counsels of old are faithfulness and truth. Isaiah 25:1

To appoint unto them that mourn in Zion, to give unto them beauty for ashes, the oil of joy for mourning, the garment of praise for the spirit of heaviness; that they might be called trees of righteousness, the planting of the Lord, that he might be glorified. Isaiah 61:3

And said unto him, Hearest thou what these say? And Jesus saith unto them, Yea; have ye never read, Out of the mouth of babes and sucklings thou hast perfected praise? Matthew 21:16

By him therefore let us offer the sacrifice of praise to God continually, that is, the fruit of our lips giving thanks to his name. Hebrews 13:15

And a voice came out of the throne, saying, Praise our God, all ye his servants, and ye that fear him, both small and great. Revelation 19:5

Worshipping God

For thou shalt worship no other god: for the Lord, whose name is Jealous, is a jealous God. Exodus 34:14

Thou, even thou, art Lord alone; thou hast made heaven, the heaven of heavens, with all their host, the earth, and all things that are therein, the seas, and all that is therein, and thou preservest them all; and the host of heaven worshippeth thee. Nehemiah 9:6

All the ends of the world shall remember and turn unto the Lord: and all the kindreds of the nations shall worship before thee. Psalms 22:27

Give unto the Lord the glory due unto his name; worship the Lord in the beauty of holiness. Psalms 29:2

So shall the king greatly desire thy beauty: for he is thy Lord; and worship thou him. Psalms 45:11

All the earth shall worship thee, and shall sing unto thee; they shall sing to thy name. Selah. Psalms 66:4

All nations whom thou hast made shall come and worship before thee, O Lord; and shall glorify thy name. Psalms 86:9

O come, let us worship and bow down: let us kneel before the Lord our maker. Psalms 95:6

Exalt ye the Lord our God, and worship at his footstool; for he is holy.
Psalms 99:5

Exalt the Lord our God, and worship at his holy hill; for the Lord our God is holy. Psalms 99:9

We will go into his tabernacles: we will worship at his footstool.
Psalms 132:7

I will worship toward thy holy temple, and praise thy name for thy lovingkindness and for thy truth: for thou hast magnified thy word above all thy name. Psalms 138:2

Saying, Where is he that is born King of the Jews? for we have seen his star in the east, and are come to worship him. Matthew 2:2

Then saith Jesus unto him, Get thee hence, Satan: for it is written, Thou shalt worship the Lord thy God, and him only shalt thou serve.
Matthew 4:10

And as they went to tell his disciples, behold, Jesus met them, saying, All hail. And they came and held him by the feet, and worshipped him.
Matthew 28:9

And when they saw him, they worshipped him: but some doubted.
Matthew 28:17

But when he saw Jesus afar off, he ran and worshipped him. Mark 5:6

But the hour cometh, and now is, when the true worshippers shall worship the Father in spirit and in truth: for the Father seeketh such to worship him. God is a Spirit: and they that worship him must worship him in spirit and in truth. John 4:23-24

Now we know that God heareth not sinners: but if any man be a worshipper of God, and doeth his will, him he heareth. John 9:31

For we are the circumcision, which worship God in the spirit, and rejoice in Christ Jesus, and have no confidence in the flesh. Philippians 3:3

The four and twenty elders fall down before him that sat on the throne, and worship him that liveth for ever and ever, and cast their crowns before the throne, saying, Thou art worthy, O Lord, to receive glory and honour and power: for thou hast created all things, and for thy pleasure they are and were created. Revelation 4:10-11

And the four beasts said, Amen. And the four and twenty elders fell down and worshipped him that liveth for ever and ever. Revelation 5:14

Our Lord approved neither idol worship or idle worship but ideal worship in Spirit and truth. - Vance Havner

And all the angels stood round about the throne, and about the elders and the four beasts, and fell before the throne on their faces, and worshipped God, Saying, Amen: Blessing, and glory, and wisdom, and thanksgiving, and honour, and power, and might, be unto our God for ever and ever. Amen. Revelation 7:11-12

And the four and twenty elders, which sat before God on their seats, fell upon their faces, and worshipped God. Revelation 11:16

Saying with a loud voice, Fear God, and give glory to him; for the hour of his judgment is come: and worship him that made heaven, and earth, and the sea, and the fountains of waters. Revelation 14:7

Fear of the Lord

The fear of the Lord is clean, enduring for ever: the judgments of the Lord are true and righteous altogether. Psalms 19:9

The fear of the Lord is the beginning of wisdom: a good understanding have all they that do his commandments: his praise endureth for ever. Psalms 111:10

Then shalt thou understand the fear of the Lord, and find the knowledge of God. Proverbs 2:5

The fear of the Lord is the beginning of wisdom: and the knowledge of the holy is understanding. Proverbs 9:10

The fear of the Lord prolongeth days: but the years of the wicked shall be shortened. Proverbs 10:27

I fear God, yet I am not afraid of him. - Thomas Browne

In the fear of the Lord is strong confidence: and his children shall have a place of refuge. The fear of the Lord is a fountain of life, to depart from the snares of death. Proverbs 14:26-27

The fear of the Lord is the instruction of wisdom; and before honour is humility. Proverbs 15:33

The fear of the Lord is to hate evil: pride, and arrogancy, and the evil way, and the froward mouth, do I hate. Proverbs 8:13

Better is little with the fear of the Lord than great treasure and trouble therewith. Proverbs 15:16

By mercy and truth iniquity is purged: and by the fear of the Lord men depart from evil. Proverbs 16:6

The fear of the Lord tendeth to life: and he that hath it shall abide satisfied; he shall not be visited with evil. Proverbs 19:23

By humility and the fear of the Lord are riches, and honour, and life. Proverbs 22:4

Having therefore these promises, dearly beloved, let us cleanse ourselves from all filthiness of the flesh and spirit, perfecting holiness in the fear of God. 2 Corinthians 7:1

To fear God is to stand in awe of him; to be afraid of God is to run away from him. - Carroll E. Simcox

Let not thine heart envy sinners: but be thou in the fear of the Lord all the day long. Proverbs 23:17

Trusting God

The God of my rock; in him will I trust: he is my shield, and the horn of my salvation, my high tower, and my refuge, my saviour; thou savest me from violence. 2 Samuel 22:3

As for God, his way is perfect; the word of the Lord is tried: he is a buckler to all them that trust in him. 2 Samuel 22:31

Wilt thou trust him, because his strength is great? or wilt thou leave thy labour to him? Job 39:11

Offer the sacrifices of righteousness, and put your trust in the Lord. Psalms 4:5

But let all those that put their trust in thee rejoice: let them ever shout for joy, because thou defendest them: let them also that love thy name be joyful in thee. Psalms 5:11

O Lord my God, in thee do I put my trust: save me from all them that persecute me, and deliver me. Psalms 7:1

And they that know thy name will put their trust in thee: for thou, Lord, hast not forsaken them that seek thee. Psalms 9:10

But I have trusted in thy mercy; my heart shall rejoice in thy salvation. Psalms 13:5

Preserve me, O God: for in thee do I put my trust. Psalms 16:1

We do not usually learn that Christ is all we need until we reach that place where He is all we have! - Vance Havner

The Lord is my rock, and my fortress, and my deliverer; my God, my strength, in whom I will trust; my buckler, and the horn of my salvation, and my high tower. Psalms 18:2

As for God, his way is perfect: the word of the Lord is tried: he is a buckler to all those that trust in him. Psalms 18:30

Judge me, O Lord; for I have walked in mine integrity: I have trusted also in the Lord; therefore I shall not slide. Psalms 26:1

The Lord is my strength and my shield; my heart trusted in him, and I am helped: therefore my heart greatly rejoiceth; and with my song will I praise him. Psalms 28:7

In thee, O Lord, do I put my trust; let me never be ashamed: deliver me in thy righteousness. Psalms 31:1

Many sorrows shall be to the wicked: but he that trusteth in the Lord, mercy shall compass him about. Psalms 32:10

O taste and see that the Lord is good: blessed is the man that trusteth in him. Psalms 34:8

Trust in the Lord, and do good; so shalt thou dwell in the land, and verily thou shalt be fed. Psalms 37:3

Commit thy way unto the Lord; trust also in him; and he shall bring it to pass. Psalms 37:5

> *Jesus does not say, "There is no storm." He says, "I am here, do not toss but trust." - Vance Havner*

Blessed is that man that maketh the Lord his trust, and respecteth not the proud, nor such as turn aside to lies. Psalms 40:4

But I am like a green olive tree in the house of God: I trust in the mercy of God for ever and ever. Psalms 52:8

What time I am afraid, I will trust in thee. Psalms 56:3

Trust in him at all times; ye people, pour out your heart before him: God is a refuge for us. Selah. Psalms 62:8

In thee, O Lord, do I put my trust: let me never be put to confusion.
Psalms 71:1

I will say of the Lord, He is my refuge and my fortress: my God; in him will I trust. Psalms 91:2

They that trust in the Lord shall be as mount Zion, which cannot be removed, but abideth for ever. Psalms 125:1

Trust in the Lord with all thine heart; and lean not unto thine own understanding. Proverbs 3:5

Behold, God is my salvation; I will trust, and not be afraid: for the Lord Jehovah is my strength and my song; he also is become my salvation.
Isaiah 12:2

Faith in God and His Word

1. Great Faith

But Jesus turned him about, and when he saw her, he said, Daughter, be of good comfort; thy faith hath made thee whole. And the woman was made whole from that hour. Matthew 9:22

Then Jesus answered and said unto her, O woman, great is thy faith: be it unto thee even as thou wilt. And her daughter was made whole from that very hour. Matthew 15:28

And he said unto her, Daughter, thy faith hath made thee whole; go in peace, and be whole of thy plague. Mark 5:34

When Jesus heard these things, he marvelled at him, and turned him about, and said unto the people that followed him, I say unto you, I have not found so great faith, no, not in Israel. Luke 7:9

And he said unto them, Where is your faith? And they being afraid wondered, saying one to another, What manner of man is this! for he commandeth even the winds and water, and they obey him. Luke 8:25

As it is written, I have made thee a father of many nations, before him whom he believed, even God, who quickeneth the dead, and calleth those things which be not as though they were. Who against hope believed in hope, that he might become the father of many nations; according to that which was spoken, So shall thy seed be. And being not weak in faith, he considered not his own body now dead, when he was about an hundred years old, neither yet the deadness of Sara's womb: He staggered not at the promise of God through unbelief; but was strong in faith, giving glory to God; And being fully persuaded that, what he had promised, he was able also to perform. Romans 4:17-21

Through faith also Sara herself received strength to conceive seed, and was delivered of a child when she was past age, because she judged him faithful who had promised. Therefore sprang there even of one, and him as good as dead, so many as the stars of the sky in multitude, and as the sand which is by the sea shore innumerable. These all died in faith, not having received the promises, but having seen them afar off, and were persuaded of them, and embraced them, and confessed that they were strangers and pilgrims on the earth. Hebrews 11:11-13

2. Principles of Faith

For verily I say unto you, If ye have faith as a grain of mustard seed, ye shall say unto this mountain, Remove hence to yonder place; and it shall remove; and nothing shall be impossible unto you. Matthew 17:20

And Jesus answering saith unto them, Have faith in God. For verily I say unto you, That whosoever shall say unto this mountain, Be thou removed, and be thou cast into the sea; and shall not doubt in his heart, but shall believe that those things which he saith shall come to pass; he shall have whatsoever he saith. Therefore I say unto you, What things soever ye desire, when ye pray, believe that ye receive them, and ye shall have them. Mark 11:22-24

Then saith he to Thomas, reach hither thy finger, and behold my hands; and reach hither thy hand, and thrust it into my side: and be not faithless, but believing. John 20:27

Jesus saith unto him, Thomas, because thou hast seen me, thou hast believed: blessed are they that have not seen, and yet have believed. John 20:29

And he that doubteth is damned if he eat, because he eateth not of faith: for whatsoever is not of faith is sin. Romans 14:23

While we look not at the things which are seen, but at the things which are not seen: for the things which are seen are temporal; but the things which are not seen are eternal. 2 Corinthians 4:18

> *Nothing is more disastrous than to study faith, analyze faith, make noble resolves of faith, but never actually make the leap of faith. - Vance Havner*

For we walk by faith, not by sight. 2 Corinthians 5:7

Let us hold fast the profession of our faith without wavering; for he is faithful that promised. Hebrews 10:23

Now faith is the substance of things hoped for, the evidence of things not seen. Hebrews 11:1

Through faith we understand that the worlds were framed by the word of God, so that things which are seen were not made of things which do appear. Hebrews 11:3

Knowing this, that the trying of your faith worketh patience. James 1:3

Whom having not seen, ye love; in whom, though now ye see him not, yet believing, ye rejoice with joy unspeakable and full of glory. Receiving the end of your faith, even the salvation of your souls. 1 Peter 1:8-9

3. Faith in Action

But let him ask in faith, nothing wavering. For he that wavereth is like a wave of the sea driven with the wind and tossed. For let not that man think that he shall receive any thing of the Lord. A double minded man is unstable in all his ways. James 1:6-8

What doth it profit, my brethren, though a man say he hath faith, and have not works? can faith save him? If a brother or sister be naked, and destitute of daily food, And one of you say unto them, Depart in peace, be ye warmed and filled; notwithstanding ye give them not those things which are needful to the body; what doth it profit? Even so faith, if it hath not works, is dead, being alone. Yea, a man may say, Thou hast faith, and I have works: shew me thy faith without thy works, and I will shew thee my faith by my works. Thou believest that there is one God; thou doest well: the devils also believe, and tremble. But wilt thou know, O vain man, that faith without works is dead? Was not Abraham our father justified by works, when he had offered Isaac his son upon the altar? Seest thou how faith wrought with his works, and by works was faith made perfect? And the scripture was fulfilled which saith, Abraham believed God, and it was imputed unto him for righteousness: and he was called the Friend of God. Ye see then how that by works a man is justified, and not by faith only. Likewise also was not Rahab the harlot justified by works, when she had received the messengers, and had sent them out another way? For as the body without the spirit is dead, so faith without works is dead also. James 2:14-26

> *It's not how much you know, but it is what you do with what you know. - Ramiro Angulo*

Now in the morning as he returned into the city, he hungered. And when he saw a fig tree in the way, he came to it, and found nothing thereon, but leaves only, and said unto it, Let no fruit grow on thee henceforward for ever. And presently the fig tree withered away. And when the disciples saw it, they marvelled, saying, How soon is the fig tree withered away!
Matthew 21:18-20

And seeing a fig tree afar off having leaves, he came, if haply he might find any thing thereon: and when he came to it, he found nothing but leaves; for the time of figs was not yet. And Jesus answered and said unto it, No man eat fruit of thee hereafter for ever. And his disciples heard it. Mark 11:13-14

And in the morning, as they passed by, they saw the fig tree dried up from the roots. And Peter calling to remembrance saith unto him, Master, behold, the fig tree which thou cursedst is withered away.
Mark 11:20-21

Above all, taking the shield of faith, wherewith ye shall be able to quench all the fiery darts of the wicked. Ephesians 6:16

Fight the good fight of faith, lay hold on eternal life, whereunto thou art also called, and hast professed a good profession before many witnesses.
1 Timothy 6:12

But whoso hath this world's good, and seeth his brother have need, and shutteth up his bowels of compassion from him, how dwelleth the love of God in him? My little children, let us not love in word, neither in tongue; but in deed and in truth. 1 John 3:17-18

4. A Lifestyle of Faith

For therein is the righteousness of God revealed from faith to faith: as it is written, The just shall live by faith. Romans 1:17

But that no man is justified by the law in the sight of God, it is evident: for, The just shall live by faith. Galatians 3:11

Now the just shall live by faith: but if any man draw back, my soul shall have no pleasure in him. Hebrews 10:38

5. Through Faith

By whom also we have access by faith into this grace wherein we stand, and rejoice in hope of the glory of God. Romans 5:2

For by grace are ye saved through faith; and that not of yourselves: it is the gift of God. Ephesians 2:8

That the blessing of Abraham might come on the Gentiles through Jesus Christ; that we might receive the promise of the Spirit through faith.
Galatians 3:14

6. Obtaining Faith

Looking unto Jesus the author and finisher of our faith; who for the joy that was set before him endured the cross, despising the shame, and is set down at the right hand of the throne of God. Hebrews 12:2

So then faith cometh by hearing, and hearing by the word of God.
Romans 10:17

For I say, through the grace given unto me, to every man that is among you, not to think of himself more highly than he ought to think; but to think soberly, according as God hath dealt to every man the measure of faith. Romans 12:3

We having the same spirit of faith, according as it is written, I believed, and therefore have I spoken; we also believe, and therefore speak.
2 Corinthians 4:13

7. According to Your Faith

Then touched he their eyes, saying, According to your faith be it unto you. Matthew 9:29

Then Jesus answered and said unto her, O woman, great is thy faith: be it unto thee even as thou wilt. And her daughter was made whole from that very hour. Matthew 15:28

And he said unto her, Daughter, thy faith hath made thee whole; go in peace, and be whole of thy plague. Mark 5:34

And Jesus said unto him, Go thy way; thy faith hath made thee whole. And immediately he received his sight, and followed Jesus in the way.
Mark 10:52

8. Hindrances to Your Faith

a. Doubt and Unbelief

And he could there do no mighty work, save that he laid his hands upon a few sick fold, and healed them. And he marvelled because of their unbelief. And he went round about the villages, teaching.
Mark 6:5-6

He staggered not at the promise of God through unbelief; but was strong in faith, giving glory to God; Romans 4:20

Well; because of unbelief they were broken off, and thou standest by faith. Be not highminded, but fear: Romans 11:20

Negative, uncertain, doubtful living poisons the body, mind, and spirit; fills insane asylums, penitentiaries, graves, and hell itself. - Vance Havner

That is true. But they were broken (pruned) off because of their unbelief—their lack of real faith, and you are established through faith—because you do believe. So do not become proud and conceited, but rather stand in awe and be reverently afraid. Romans 11:20 AMP

Take heed, brethren, lest there be in any of you an evil heart of unbelief, in departing from the living God. Hebrews 3:12

[Therefore beware,] brethren; take care lest there be in any one of you a wicked, unbelieving heart—which refuses to cleave to, trust in and rely on Him—leading you to turn away and desert or stand aloof from the living God. Hebrews 3:12 AMP

The only limit to our realization of tomorrow will be our doubts of today. Let us move forward with strong and active faith.
- Franklin D. Roosevelt

b. Doubt and Unbelief Stop the Power of God in Your Life

And he did not many mighty works there because of their unbelief.
Matthew 13:58

And Jesus rebuked the devil; and he departed out of him: and the child was cured from that very hour. Then came the disciples to Jesus apart, and said, Why could not we cast him out? And Jesus said unto them, Because of your unbelief: for verily I say unto you, If ye have faith as a grain of mustard seed, ye shall say unto this mountain, Remove hence to yonder place; and it shall remove; and nothing shall be impossible unto you. Matthew 17:18-20

So we see that they could not enter in because of unbelief.
Hebrews 3:19

So we see that they were not able to enter [into His rest] because of their unwillingness to adhere to and trust and rely on God— unbelief had shut them out. Hebrews 3:19 AMP

Doubt's number one tactic is to invade your mind with thoughts and imaginations that are contrary to the Word of God or to your prayer of faith. Resist doubt every time it comes to you and audibly confess God's Word.

c. Doubt and Unbelief Frustrate God

Afterward he appeared unto the eleven as they sat at meat, and upbraided them with their unbelief and hardness of heart, because they believed not them which had seen him after he was risen. Mark 16:14

If then God so clothe the grass, which is to day in the field, and to morrow is cast into the oven; how much more will he clothe you, O ye of little faith? And seek not ye what ye shall eat, or what ye shall drink, neither be ye of doubtful mind. Luke 12:28-29

But let him ask in faith, nothing wavering. For he that wavereth is like a wave of the sea driven with the wind and tossed. For let not that man think that he shall receive any thing of the Lord. A double minded man is unstable in all his ways. James 1:6-8

Only it must be in faith that he asks, with no wavering—no hesitating, no doubting. For the one who wavers (hesitates, doubts) is like the billowing surge out at sea, that is blown hither and thither and tossed by the wind. For truly, let not such a person imagine that he will receive anything [he asks for] from the Lord, [For being as he is] a man of two minds—hesitating, dubious, irresolute—[he is] unstable and unreliable and uncertain about everything (he thinks, feels, decides). James 1:6-8 AMP

And immediately Jesus stretched forth his hand, and caught him, and said unto him, O thou of little faith, wherefore didst thou doubt?
Matthew 14:31

The Will of God

1. Obedience to God's Will (God's Word)

For whosoever shall do the will of God, the same is my brother, and my sister, and mother. Mark 3:35

For whosoever shall do the will of my Father which is in heaven, the same is my brother, and sister, and mother. Matthew 12:50

And that servant, which knew his lord's will, and prepared not himself, neither did according to his will, shall be beaten with many stripes.
Luke 12:47

If any man will do his will, he shall know of the doctrine, whether it be of God, or whether I speak of myself. John 7:17

Now we know that God heareth not sinners: but if any man be a worshipper of God, and doeth his will, him he heareth. John 9:31

Not with eyeservice, as menpleasers; but as the servants of Christ, doing the will of God from the heart; Ephesians 6:6

For ye have need of patience, that, after ye have done the will of God, ye might receive the promise. Hebrews 10:36

And the world passeth away, and the lust thereof: but he that doeth the will of God abideth for ever. 1 John 2:17

2. Praying in Agreement With His Will

And this is the confidence that we have in him, that, if we ask any thing according to his will, he heareth us: And if we know that he hear us, whatsoever we ask, we know that we have the petitions that we desired of him. 1 John 5:14-15

> *Prayer is not overcoming God's reluctance: it is laying hold of His highest willingness. - Richard Chenevix*

And he that searcheth the hearts knoweth what is the mind of the Spirit, because he maketh intercession for the saints according to the will of God. Romans 8:27

But I know, that even now, whatsoever thou wilt ask of God, God will give it thee. John 11:22

3. Submitting to God's Will

And he went a little further, and fell on his face, and prayed, saying, O my Father, if it be possible, let this cup pass from me: nevertheless not as I will, but as thou wilt. Matthew 26:39

Thy kingdom come. Thy will be done in earth, as it is in heaven.
Matthew 6:10

And he said to them all, If any man will come after me, let him deny himself, and take up his cross daily, and follow me. Luke 9:23

And be not conformed to this world: but be ye transformed by the renewing of your mind, that ye may prove what is that good, and acceptable, and perfect, will of God. Romans 12:2

And this they did, not as we hoped, but first gave their own selves to the Lord, and unto us by the will of God. 2 Corinthians 8:5

Who gave himself for our sins, that he might deliver us from this present evil world, according to the will of God and our Father: Galatians 1:4

For it is God which worketh in you both to will and to do of his good pleasure. Philippians 2:13

Epaphras, who is one of you, a servant of Christ, saluteth you, always labouring fervently for you in prayers, that ye may stand perfect and complete in all the will of God. Colossians 4:12

For this is the will of God, even your sanctification, that ye should abstain from fornication: 1 Thessalonians 4:3

Rejoice evermore. Pray without ceasing. In every thing give thanks: for this is the will of God in Christ Jesus concerning you.
1 Thessalonians 5:16-18

For so is the will of God, that with well doing ye may put to silence the ignorance of foolish men: 1 Peter 2:15

In His will is our peace. - Dante Alighieri

That he no longer should live the rest of his time in the flesh to the lusts of men, but to the will of God. 1 Peter 4:2

Wherefore let them that suffer according to the will of God commit the keeping of their souls to him in well doing, as unto a faithful Creator.
1 Peter 4:19

The Lord is not slack concerning his promise, as some men count slackness; but is longsuffering to us-ward, not willing that any should perish, but that all should come to repentance. 2 Peter 3:9

4. God is Willing to Bless, Heal and Save You

But I know, that even now, whatsoever thou wilt ask of God, God will give it thee. John 11:22

And Jesus answered and said unto him, What wilt thou that I should do unto thee? The blind man said unto him, Lord, that I might receive my sight. And Jesus said unto him, Go thy way; thy faith hath made thee whole. And immediately he received his sight, and followed Jesus in the way. Mark 10:51-52

And it came to pass, when he was in a certain city, behold a man full of leprosy: who seeing Jesus fell on his face, and besought him, saying, Lord, if thou wilt, thou canst make me clean. And he put forth his hand, and touched him, saying, I will; be thou clean. And immediately the leprosy departed him. Luke 5:12-13

Wherein God, willing more abundantly to shew unto the heirs of promise the immutability of his counsel, confirmed it by an oath:
Hebrews 6:17

The Lord is not slack concerning his promise, as some men count slackness; but is longsuffering to us-ward, not willing that any should perish, but that all should come to repentance. 2 Peter 3:9

God's Word

The Integrity of God's Word

God is not a man, that he should lie; neither the son of man, that he should repent: hath he said, and shall he not do it? or hath he spoken, and shall he not make it good? Numbers 23:19

Know therefore that the Lord thy God, he is God, the faithful God, which keepeth covenant and mercy with them that love him and keep his commandments to a thousand generations. Deuteronomy 7:9

And, behold, this day I am going the way of all the earth: and ye know in all your hearts and in all your souls, that not one thing hath failed of all the good things which the Lord your God spake concerning you; all are come to pass unto you, and not one thing hath failed thereof.
Joshua 23:14

The Lord of hosts hath sworn, saying, Surely as I have thought, so shall it come to pass; and as I have purposed, so shall it stand: Isaiah 14:24

And also the Strength of Israel will not lie nor repent: for he is not a man, that he should repent. 1 Samuel 15:29

The grass withereth, the flower fadeth: but the word of our God shall stand for ever. Isaiah 40:8

Blessed be the Lord, that hath given rest unto his people Israel, according to all that he promised: there hath not failed one word of all his good promise, which he promised by the hand of Moses his servant.
1 Kings 8:56

By the word of the Lord were the heavens made; and all the host of them by the breath of his mouth. Psalms 33:6

For he spake, and it was done; he commanded, and it stood fast.
Psalms 33:9

My covenant will I not break, nor alter the thing that is gone out of my lips. Psalms 89:34

He hath remembered his covenant for ever, the word which he commanded to a thousand generations. Psalms 105:8

He hath given meat unto them that fear him: he will ever be mindful of his covenant. Psalms 111:5

All thy commandments are faithful. Psalms 119:86

For ever, O Lord, thy word is settled in heaven. Psalms 119:89

Thy word is true from the beginning: and every one of thy righteous judgments endureth for ever. Psalms 119:160

I will worship toward thy holy temple, and praise thy name for thy lovingkindness and for thy truth: for thou hast magnified thy word above all thy name. Psalms 138:2

Every word of God is pure: he is a shield unto them that put their trust in him. Proverbs 30:5

I have spoken it, I will also bring it to pass; I have purposed it, I will also do it. Isaiah 46:11

For as the rain cometh down, and the snow from heaven, and returneth not thither, but watereth the earth, and maketh it bring forth and bud, that it may give seed to the sower, and bread to the eater: So shall my word be that goeth forth out of my mouth: it shall not return unto me void, but it shall accomplish that which I please, and it shall prosper in the thing whereto I sent it. Isaiah 55:10-11

I the Lord have spoken it: it shall come to pass, and I will do it; I will not go back, neither will I spare, neither will I repent; according to thy ways, and according to thy doings, shall they judge thee, saith the Lord God.
                                                                                  Ezekiel 24:14

Heaven and earth shall pass away: but my words shall not pass away.
                                                                                    Mark 13:31

Sanctify them through thy truth: thy word is truth. John 17:17

And being fully persuaded that, what he had promised, he was able also to perform. Romans 4:21

For all the promises of God in him are yea, and in him Amen, unto the glory of God by us. 2 Corinthians 1:20

In hope of eternal life, which God, that cannot lie, promised before the world began. Titus 1:2

Hath in these last days spoken unto us by his Son, whom he hath appointed heir of all things, by whom also he made the worlds; Who being the brightness of his glory, and the express image of his person, and upholding all things by the word of his power, when he had by himself purged our sins, sat down on the right hand of the Majesty on high.
Hebrews 1:2-3

And being fully persuaded that, what he had promised, he was able also to perform. Romans 4:21

That by two immutable things, in which it was impossible for God to lie, we might have a strong consolation, who have fled for refuge to lay hold upon the hope set before us. Hebrews 6:18

Through faith we understand that the worlds were framed by the word of God, so that things which are seen were not made of things which do appear. Hebrews 11:3

Jesus Christ the same yesterday, and today, and forever. Hebrews 13:8

Being born again, not of corruptible seed, but of incorruptible, by the word of God, which liveth and abideth for ever. 1 Peter 1:23

But the word of the Lord endureth for ever. And this is the word which by the gospel is preached unto you. 1 Peter 1:25

The Lord is not slack concerning his promise, as some men count slackness; but is longsuffering to us-ward, not willing that any should perish, but that all should come to repentance. 2 Peter 3:9

> *His promises are checks to be cashed, not mere mottoes to hang on the wall! - Vance Havner*

God's Word is Spiritual Food

But he answered and said, It is written, Man shall not live by bread alone, but by every word that proceedeth out of the mouth of God. Matthew 4:4

And Jesus answered him, saying, It is written, That man shall not live by bread alone, but by every word of God. Luke 4:4

But he said unto them, I have meat to eat that ye know not of. John 4:32

Labour not for the meat which perisheth, but for that meat which endureth unto everlasting life, which the Son of man shall give unto you: for him hath God the Father sealed. John 6:27

Then Jesus said unto them, Verily, verily, I say unto you, Moses gave you not that bread from heaven; but my Father giveth you the true bread from heaven. For the bread of God is he which cometh down from heaven, and giveth life unto the world. Then said they unto him, Lord, evermore give us this bread. And Jesus said unto them, I am the bread of life: he that cometh to me shall never hunger; and he that believeth on me shall never thirst. John 6:32-35

Hunger for God's Word is not a natural appetite. We are not born with it. It comes with the new birth when we begin with milk and should go on to meat. - Vance Havner

I am the living bread which came down from heaven: if any man eat of this bread, he shall live for ever: and the bread that I will give is my flesh, which I will give for the life of the world. John 6:51

This is that bread which came down from heaven: not as your fathers did eat manna, and are dead: he that eateth of this bread shall live for ever.
John 6:58

So when they had dined, Jesus saith to Simon Peter, Simon, son of Jonas, lovest thou me more than these? He saith unto him, Yea, Lord; thou knowest that I love thee. He saith unto him, Feed my lambs. He saith to him again the second time, Simon, son of Jonas, lovest thou me? He saith unto him, Yea, Lord; thou knowest that I love thee. He saith unto him, Feed my sheep. John 21:15-16

And I, brethren, could not speak unto you as unto spiritual, but as unto carnal, even as unto babes in Christ. I have fed you with milk, and not with meat: for hitherto ye were not able to bear it, neither yet now are ye able. For ye are yet carnal: for whereas there is among you envying, and strife, and divisions, are ye not carnal, and walk as men?
1 Corinthians 3:1-3

And did all eat the same spiritual meat; And did all drink the same spiritual drink: for they drank of that spiritual Rock that followed them: and that Rock was Christ. 1 Corinthians 10:3-4

For when for the time ye ought to be teachers, ye have need that one teach you again which be the first principles of the oracles of God; and are become such as have need of milk, and not of strong meat. For every one that useth milk is unskilful in the word of righteousness: for he is a babe. **But** strong meat belongeth to them that are of full age, even those who by reason of use have their senses exercised to discern both good and evil. Hebrews 5:12-14

As newborn babes, desire the sincere milk of the word, that ye may grow thereby. 1 Peter 2:2

The Word of God in the Heart

I delight to do thy will, O my God: yea, thy law is within my heart.
Psalms 40:8

I have not hid thy righteousness within my heart; I have declared thy faithfulness and thy salvation. Psalms 40:10

Thy word have I hid in mine heart, that I might not sin against thee.
Psalms 119:11

Incline my heart unto thy testimonies, and not to covetousness.
Psalms 119:36

Let my heart be sound in thy statutes; that I be not ashamed.
Psalms 119:80

My son, forget not my law; but let thine heart keep my commandments.
Proverbs 3:1

He taught me also, and said unto me, Let thine heart retain my words: keep my commandments, and live. Proverbs 4:4

> *It is not the Word hidden in the head but in the heart that keeps us from sin. - Vance Havner*

My son, attend to my words; incline thine ear unto my sayings. Let them not depart from thine eyes; keep them in the midst of thine heart. **For** they are life unto those that find them, and health to all their flesh. **Keep** thy heart with all diligence; for out of it are the issues of life.
Proverbs 4:20-23

My son, keep thy father's commandment, and forsake not the law of thy mother: **Bind** them continually upon thine heart, and tie them about thy neck. Proverbs 6:20-21

My son, keep my words, and lay up my commandments with thee. **Keep** my commandments, and live; and my law as the apple of thine eye. **Bind** them upon thy fingers, write them upon the table of thine heart.
Proverbs 7:1-3

He that soweth iniquity shall reap vanity: and the rod of his anger shall fail. Proverbs 22:8

Bow down thine ear, and hear the words of the wise, and apply thine heart unto my knowledge. Proverbs 22:17

But this shall be the covenant that I will make with the house of Israel; After those days, saith the Lord, I will put my law in their inward parts, and write it in their hearts; and will be their God, and they shall be my people. Jeremiah 31:33

But what saith it? The word is nigh thee, even in thy mouth, and in thy heart: that is, the word of faith, which we preach. Romans 10:8

This is the covenant that I will make with them after those days, saith the Lord, I will put my laws into their hearts, and in their minds will I write them. Hebrews 10:16

Ye are our epistle written in our hearts, known and read of all men: Forasmuch as ye are manifestly declared to be the epistle of Christ ministered by us, written not with ink, but with the Spirit of the living God; not in tables of stone, but in fleshy tables of the heart.
2 Corinthians 3:2-3

1. Different Ways the Word of God is Taken Out of the Heart of Man

a. Not Understanding the Word of God

When any one heareth the word of the kingdom, and understandeth it not, then cometh the wicked one, and catcheth away that which was sown in his heart. This is he which received seed by the way side. Matthew 13:19

While any one is hearing the Word of the kingdom and does not grasp and comprehend it, the evil one comes and snatches away what is sown in his heart. This is what was sown along the roadside.
Matthew 13:19 AMP

b. Tribulation and Persecution

But he that received the seed into stony places, the same is he that heareth the word, and anon with joy receiveth it; Yet hath he not root in himself, but dureth for a while: for when tribulation or persecution ariseth because of the word, by and by he is offended.
Matthew 13:20-21

As for what was sown on thin (rocky) soil, this is he who hears the Word and at once welcomes and accepts it with joy. Yet it has no real root in himself, but is temporary–inconstant, lasts but a little while and when affliction or trouble or persecution comes on account of the Word, at once he is caused to stumble–he is repelled and begins to distrust and desert Him Whom he ought to trust and obey, and he falls away. Matthew 13:20-21 AMP

c. The Cares of This World and Deceitfulness of Riches

He also that received seed among the thorns is he that heareth the word; and the care of this world, and the deceitfulness of riches, choke the word, and he becometh unfruitful. Matthew 13:22

As for what was sown among thorns, this is he who hears the Word, but the cares of the world and the pleasure and delight and glamour and deceitfulness of riches choke and suffocate the Word and it yields no fruit. Matthew 13:22 AMP

d. satan Will Try to Steal the Word of God

And these are they by the way side, where the word is sown; but when they have heard, Satan cometh immediately, and taketh away the word that was sown in their hearts. Mark 4:15

The ones along the path are those who have the Word sown [in their hearts], but when they hear, satan comes at once and (by force) takes away the message which is sown in them. Mark 4:15 AMP

2. A Good Heart for the Word of God

But he that received seed into the good ground is he that heareth the word, and understandeth it; which also beareth fruit, and bringeth forth, some an hundredfold, some sixty, some thirty. Matthew 13:23

And these are they which are sown on good ground; such as hear the word, and receive it, and bring forth fruit, some thirtyfold, some sixty, and some an hundred. Mark 4:20

And those that were sown on the good (well-adapted) soil are the ones who hear the Word, and receive and accept and welcome it and bear fruit, some thirty times as much as was sown, some sixty times as much, and some [even] a hundred times as much. Mark 4:20 AMP

Meditating on God's Word

DEFINITIONS FOR MEDITATING
1. To care for, to attend to, practice, to ponder, or imagine
2. To pass some time thinking in a quiet way; reflect
3. To plan or consider

This book of the law shall not depart out of thy mouth; but thou shalt meditate therein day and night, that thou mayest observe to do according to all that is written therein: for then thou shalt make thy way prosperous, and then thou shalt have good success. Joshua 1:8

But his delight is in the law of the Lord; and in his law doth he meditate day and night. Psalms 1:2

Give ear to my words, O Lord, consider my meditation. Psalms 5:1

Let the words of my mouth, and the meditation of my heart, be acceptable in thy sight, O Lord, my strength, and my redeemer. Psalms 19:14

My mouth shall speak of wisdom; and the meditation of my heart shall be of understanding. Psalms 49:3

When I remember thee upon my bed, and meditate on thee in the night watches. Psalms 63:6

I will meditate also of all thy work, and talk of thy doings. Psalms 77:12

My meditation of him shall be sweet: I will be glad in the Lord. Psalms 104:34

I will meditate in thy precepts, and have respect unto thy ways. Psalms 119:15

Princes also did sit and speak against me: but thy servant did meditate in thy statutes. Psalms 119:23

My hands also will I lift up unto thy commandments, which I have loved; and I will meditate in thy statutes. Psalms 119:48

God does not give the soul a vacation, He gives it a vocation.
- Vance Havner

Let the proud be ashamed; for they dealt perversely with me without a cause: but I will meditate in thy precepts. Psalms 119:78

O how love I thy law! it is my meditation all the day. Psalms 119:97

I have more understanding than all my teachers: for thy testimonies are my meditation. Psalms 119:99

Mine eyes prevent the night watches, that I might meditate in thy word.
Psalms 119:148

I remember the days of old; I meditate on all thy works; I muse on the work of thy hands. Psalms 143:5

Till I come, give attendance to reading, to exhortation, to doctrine. Meditate upon these things; give thyself wholly to them; that thy profiting may appear to all. 1 Timothy 4:13,15

How to Obtain Promises From God's Word

1. Confess the Word of God

And take not the word of truth utterly out of my mouth; for I have hoped in thy judgments. Psalms 119:43

My tongue shall speak of thy word: for all thy commandments are righteousness. Psalms 119:172

We having the same spirit of faith, according as it is written, I believed, and therefore have I spoken; we also believe, and therefore speak.
2 Corinthians 4:13

Fight the good fight of faith, lay hold on eternal life, whereunto thou art also called, and hast professed a good profession before many witnesses.
1 Timothy 6:12

Seeing then that we have a great high priest, that is passed into the heavens, Jesus the Son of God, let us hold fast our profession. Hebrews 4:14

Let us hold fast the profession of our faith without wavering; for he is faithful that promised. Hebrews 10:23

But what saith it? The word is nigh thee, even in thy mouth, and in thy heart: that is, the word of faith, which we preach. Romans 10:8

Say unto them, As truly as I live, saith the Lord, as ye have spoken in mine ears, so will I do to you. Numbers 14:28

2. Remain Patient

But that on the good ground are they, which in an honest and good heart, having heard the word, keep it, and bring forth fruit with patience.
Luke 8:15

For whatsoever things were written aforetime were written for our learning, that we through patience and comfort of the scriptures might have hope. Romans 15:4

And let us not be weary in well doing: for in due season we shall reap, if we faint not. Galatians 6:9

For all the promises of God in him are yea, and in him Amen, unto the glory of God by us. 2 Corinthians 1:20

That ye be not slothful, but followers of them who through faith and patience inherit the promises. Hebrews 6:12

Just as faith without works is dead, so is faith without patience.

Cast not away therefore your confidence, which hath great recompence of reward. For ye have need of patience, that, after ye have done the will of God, ye might receive the promise. For yet a little while, and he that shall come will come, and will not tarry. Hebrews 10:35-37

Who through faith subdued kingdoms, wrought righteousness, obtained promises, stopped the mouths of lions. Hebrews 11:33

3. Do Not Doubt the Ability of God and His Word

But let him ask in faith, nothing wavering. For he that wavereth is like a wave of the sea driven with the wind and tossed. For let not that man think that he shall receive any thing of the Lord. A double minded man is unstable in all his ways. James 1:6-8

Only it must be in faith that he asks, with no wavering–no hesitating, no doubting. For the one who wavers (hesitates, doubts) is like the billowing surge out at sea, that is blown hither and thither and tossed by the wind. For truly, let not such a person imagine that he will receive anything [he asks for] from the Lord, [For being as he is] a man of two minds–hesitating, dubious, irresolute–[he is] unstable and unreliable and uncertain about everything (he thinks, feels, decides). James 1:6-8 AMP

And Jesus answering saith unto them, Have faith in God. For verily I say unto you, That whosoever shall say unto this mountain, Be thou removed, and be thou cast into the sea; and shall not doubt in his heart, but shall believe that those things which he saith shall come to pass; he shall have whatsoever he saith. Therefore I say unto you, What things soever ye desire, when ye pray, believe that ye receive them, and ye shall have them. Mark 11:22-24

He staggered not at the promise of God through unbelief; but was strong in faith, giving glory to God; Romans 4:20

Well; because of unbelief they were broken off, and thou standest by faith. Be not highminded, but fear: Romans 11:20

That is true. But they were broken (pruned) off because of their unbelief–their lack of real faith, and you are established through faith–because you do believe. So do not become proud and conceited, but rather stand in awe and be reverently afraid. Romans 11:20 AMP

And he did not many mighty works there because of their unbelief.
Matthew 13:58

The Cleansing of the Word of God

Wherewithal shall a young man cleanse his way? by taking heed thereto according to thy word. Psalms 119:9

Seeing ye have purified your souls in obeying the truth through the Spirit unto unfeigned love of the brethren, see that ye love one another with a pure heart fervently. 1 Peter 1:22

Having therefore these promises, dearly beloved, let us cleanse ourselves from all filthiness of the flesh and spirit, perfecting holiness in the fear of God. 2 Corinthians 7:1

That he might sanctify and cleanse it with the washing of water by the word. Ephesians 5:26

The words of the Lord are pure words: as silver tried in a furnace of earth, purified seven times. Psalms 12:6

The statutes of the Lord are right, rejoicing the heart: the commandment of the Lord is pure, enlightening the eyes. Psalms 19:8

And now, brethren, I commend you to God, and to the word of his grace, which is able to build you up, and to give you an inheritance among all them which are sanctified. Acts 20:32

Memorizing the Word of God

And ye shall know the truth, and the truth shall make you free. John 8:32

That ye may remember, and do all my commandments, and be holy unto your God. Numbers 15:40

Beware that thou forget not the Lord thy God, in not keeping his commandments, and his judgments, and his statutes, which I command thee this day. Deuteronomy 8:11

But the mercy of the Lord is from everlasting to everlasting upon them that fear him, and his righteousness unto children's children. To such as keep his covenant, and to those that remember his commandments to do them. Psalms 103:17-18

I will delight myself in thy statutes: I will not forget thy word.
Psalms 119:16

For I am become like a bottle in the smoke; yet do I not forget thy statutes. Psalms 119:83

I will never forget thy precepts: for with them thou hast quickened me.
Psalms 119:93

I am small and despised: yet do not I forget thy precepts. Psalms 119:141

My son, forget not my law; but let thine heart keep my commandments.
Proverbs 3:1

By which also ye are saved, if ye keep in memory what I preached unto you, unless ye have believed in vain. 1 Corinthians 15:2

But whoso looketh into the perfect law of liberty, and continueth therein, he being not a forgetful hearer, but a doer of the work, this man shall be blessed in his deed. James 1:25

But, beloved, remember ye the words which were spoken before of the apostles of our Lord Jesus Christ. Jude 1:17

Guidance from God's Word

Thou shalt guide me with thy counsel, and afterward receive me to glory.
Psalms 73:24

Thy word is a lamp unto my feet, and a light unto my path. Psalms 119:105

Order my steps in thy word: and let not any iniquity have dominion over me. Psalms 119:133

I thought on my ways, and turned my feet unto thy testimonies.
Psalms 119:59

The entrance of thy words giveth light; it giveth understanding unto the simple. Psalms 119:130

God's Word

All scripture is given by inspiration of God, and is profitable for doctrine, for reproof, for correction, for instruction in righteousness. That the man of God may be perfect, thoroughly furnished unto all good works.
2 Timothy 3:16-17

For whatsoever things were written aforetime were written for our learning, that we through patience and comfort of the scriptures might have hope. Romans 15:4

The Spoken Word of God

1. Is the Sword of the Spirit

Yea, a sword shall pierce through thy own soul also, that the thoughts of many hearts may be revealed. Luke 2:35

And take the helmet of salvation, and the sword of the Spirit, which is the word of God. Ephesians 6:17

For the word of God is quick, and powerful, and sharper than any twoedged sword, piercing even to the dividing asunder of soul and spirit, and of the joints and marrow, and is a discerner of the thoughts and intents of the heart. Hebrews 4:12

And then shall that Wicked be revealed, whom the Lord shall consume with the spirit of his mouth, and shall destroy with the brightness of his coming. 2 Thessalonians 2:8

And he had in his right hand seven stars: and out of his mouth went a sharp twoedged sword: and his countenance was as the sun shineth in his strength. Revelation 1:16

And to the angel of the church in Pergamos write; These things saith he which hath the sharp sword with two edges. Revelation 2:12

Repent; or else I will come unto thee quickly, and will fight against them with the sword of my mouth. Revelation 2:16

And out of his mouth goeth a sharp sword, that with it he should smite the nations: and he shall rule them with a rod of iron: and he treadeth the winepress of the fierceness and wrath of Almighty God. Revelation 19:15

2. Gives Faith to the Believer

So then faith cometh by hearing, and hearing by the word of God.
Romans 10:17

3. Convicts and Converts the Unbeliever

For whosoever shall call upon the name of the Lord shall be saved. How then shall they call on him in whom they have not believed? and how shall they believe in him of whom they have not heard? and how shall they hear without a preacher? Romans 10:13-14

Now when they heard this, they were pricked in their heart, and said unto Peter and to the rest of the apostles, Men and brethren, what shall we do? Acts 2:37

4. Angers the Sinner

When they heard that, they were cut to the heart, and took counsel to slay them. Acts 5:33

When they heard these things, they were cut to the heart, and they gnashed on him with their teeth. Acts 7:54

5. Will Cast Out demon spirits

When the even was come, they brought unto him many that were possessed with devils: and he cast out the spirits with his word, and healed all that were sick: Matthew 8:16

> *Jesus met the devil not in His own name, not in His own power, but with the Scriptures: "It is written... It is written..." If he could defeat the devil with three verses out of Deuteronomy, we ought to be able to do it with the whole Bible. - Vance Havner*

6. Puts satan to Flight

And when the tempter came to him, he said, If thou be the Son of God, command that these stones be made bread. But he answered and said, it is written, man shall not live by bread alone, but by every word that proceedeth out of the mouth of God. Then the devil taketh him up into the holy city, and setteth him on a pinnacle of the temple, And saith unto him, If thou be the Son of God, cast thyself down: for it is written, He shall give his angels charge concerning thee: and in their hands they shall bear thee up, lest at any time thou dash thy foot against a stone. Jesus said unto him, it is written again, thou shalt not tempt the Lord thy God. Again, the devil taketh him up into an exceeding high mountain, and sheweth him all the kingdoms of the world, and the glory of them; And saith unto him, All these things will I give thee, if thou wilt fall down and worship me. Then saith Jesus unto him, get thee hence, satan: for it is written, Thou shalt worship the Lord thy God, and him only shalt thou serve. Then the devil leaveth him, and, behold, angels came and ministered unto him. Matthew 4:3-11

The Holy Spirit

Respecting the Holy Spirit

Wherefore I say unto you, All manner of sin and blasphemy shall be forgiven unto men: but the blasphemy against the Holy Ghost shall not be forgiven unto men. And whosoever speaketh a word against the Son of man, it shall be forgiven him: but whosoever speaketh against the Holy Ghost, it shall not be forgiven him, neither in this world, neither in the world to come. Matthew 12:31-32

And grieve not the holy Spirit of God, whereby ye are sealed unto the day of redemption. Ephesians 4:30

Quench not the Spirit. 1 Thessalonians 5:19

Of how much sorer punishment, suppose ye, shall he be thought worthy, who hath trodden under foot the Son of God, and hath counted the blood of the covenant, wherewith he was sanctified, an unholy thing, and hath done despite unto the Spirit of grace? Hebrews 10:29

The first step toward establishing a relationship with the Holy Spirit is to respect and acknowledge Him as God and not as an "it."

Receiving the Baptism of the Holy Spirit

If ye then, being evil, know how to give good gifts unto your children: how much more shall your heavenly Father give the Holy Spirit to them that ask him? Luke 11:13

And when he had said this, he breathed on them, and saith unto them, Receive ye the Holy Ghost. John 20:22

And be not drunk with wine, wherein is excess; but be filled with the Spirit. Ephesians 5:18

But ye, beloved, building up yourselves on your most holy faith, praying in the Holy Ghost. Jude 1:20

Wherefore, brethren, covet to prophesy, and forbid not to speak with tongues. 1 Corinthians 14:39

The Benefits of Praying in the Holy Spirit

Likewise the Spirit also helpeth our infirmities: for we know not what we should pray for as we ought: but the Spirit itself maketh intercession for us with groanings which cannot be uttered. And he that searcheth the hearts knoweth what is the mind of the Spirit, because he maketh intercession for the saints according to the will of God. Romans 8:26-27

For he that speaketh in an unknown tongue speaketh not unto men, but unto God: for no man understandeth him; howbeit in the spirit he speaketh mysteries. 1 Corinthians 14:2

For if I pray in an unknown tongue, my spirit prayeth, but my understanding is unfruitful. What is it then? I will pray with the spirit, and I will pray with the understanding also: I will sing with the spirit, and I will sing with the understanding also. 1 Corinthians 14:14-15

> *Praying in the Spirit guarantees perfect prayer that is directed by the Holy Spirit; untouched by doubt and fear of the mind; and impossible for the devil to understand or hinder.*

Praying always with all prayer and supplication in the Spirit, and watching thereunto with all perseverance and supplication for all saints.
Ephesians 6:18

Examples of Believers Being Filled With the Holy Spirit

And they were all filled with the Holy Ghost, and began to speak with other tongues, as the Spirit gave them utterance. Acts 2:4

Now when the apostles which were at Jerusalem heard that Samaria had received the word of God, they sent unto them Peter and John: Who, when they were come down, prayed for them, that they might receive the Holy Ghost: For as yet he was fallen upon none of them: only they were baptized in the name of the Lord Jesus. Then laid they their hands on them, and they received the Holy Ghost. Acts 8:14-17

And Ananias went his way, and entered into the house; and putting his hands on him said, Brother Saul, the Lord, even Jesus, that appeared unto thee in the way as thou camest, hath sent me, that thou mightest receive thy sight, and be filled with the Holy Ghost. Acts 9:17

While Peter yet spake these words, the Holy Ghost fell on all them which heard the word. And they of the circumcision which believed were astonished, as many as came with Peter, because that on the Gentiles also was poured out the gift of the Holy Ghost. For they heard them speak with tongues, and magnify God. Then answered Peter, Can any man forbid water, that these should not be baptized, which have received the Holy Ghost as well as we? Acts 10:44-47

And God, which knoweth the hearts, bare them witness, giving them the Holy Ghost, even as he did unto us; And put no difference between us and them, purifying their hearts by faith. Acts 15:8-9

He said unto them, Have ye received the Holy Ghost since ye believed? And they said unto him, We have not so much as heard whether there be any Holy Ghost. And he said unto them, Unto what then were ye baptized? And they said, Unto John's baptism. Then said Paul, John verily baptized with the baptism of repentance, saying unto the people, that they should believe on him which should come after him, that is, on Christ Jesus. When they heard this, they were baptized in the name of the Lord Jesus. And when Paul had laid his hands upon them, the Holy Ghost came on them; and they spake with tongues, and prophesied.
Acts 19:2-6

The Holy Spirit is the Teacher, Leader, Guide and Counselor

For the Holy Ghost shall teach you in the same hour what ye ought to say. Luke 12:12

But this spake he of the Spirit, which they that believe on him should receive: for the Holy Ghost was not yet given; because that Jesus was not yet glorified. John 7:39

But the Comforter, which is the Holy Ghost, whom the Father will send in my name, he shall teach you all things, and bring all things to your remembrance, whatsoever I have said unto you. John 14:26

Howbeit when he, the Spirit of truth, is come, he will guide you into all truth: for he shall not speak of himself; but whatsoever he shall hear, that shall he speak: and he will shew you things to come. John 16:13

For as many as are led by the Spirit of God, they are the sons of God.
Romans 8:14

The Spirit itself beareth witness with our spirit, that we are the children of God. Romans 8:16

But God hath revealed them unto us by his Spirit: for the Spirit searcheth all things, yea, the deep things of God. For what man knoweth the things of a man, save the spirit of man which is in him? even so the things of God knoweth no man, but the Spirit of God. 1 Corinthians 2:10-11

Which things also we speak, not in the words which man's wisdom teacheth, but which the Holy Ghost teacheth; comparing spiritual things with spiritual. 1 Corinthians 2:13

But if ye be led of the Spirit, ye are not under the law. Galatians 5:18

The Holy Spirit Living Inside the Believer

And I will put my spirit within you, and cause you to walk in my statutes, and ye shall keep my judgments, and do them. Ezekiel 36:27

Even the Spirit of truth; whom the world cannot receive, because it seeth him not, neither knoweth him: but ye know him; for he dwelleth with you, and shall be in you. John 14:17

Know ye not that ye are the temple of God, and that the Spirit of God dwelleth in you? 1 Corinthians 3:16

What? know ye not that your body is the temple of the Holy Ghost which is in you, which ye have of God, and ye are not your own?
1 Corinthians 6:19

And because ye are sons, God hath sent forth the Spirit of his Son into your hearts, crying, Abba, Father. Galatians 4:6

That he would grant you, according to the riches of his glory, to be strengthened with might by his Spirit in the inner man. Ephesians 3:16

That good thing which was committed unto thee keep by the Holy Ghost which dwelleth in us. 2 Timothy 1:14

> *If you have been born of the Holy Spirit, you will not have to serve God ...it will become the natural thing to do. - D. L. Moody*

And he that keepeth his commandments dwelleth in him, and he in him. And hereby we know that he abideth in us, by the Spirit which he hath given us. 1 John 3:24

Hereby know we that we dwell in him, and he in us, because he hath given us of his Spirit. 1 John 4:13

Sealed by the Holy Spirit

Who hath also sealed us, and given the earnest of the Spirit in our hearts.
2 Corinthians 1:22

In whom ye also trusted, after that ye heard the word of truth, the gospel of your salvation: in whom also after that ye believed, ye were sealed with that holy Spirit of promise, Ephesians 1:13

And grieve not the holy Spirit of God, whereby ye are sealed unto the day of redemption. Ephesians 4:30

The Power of the Holy Spirit

But ye shall receive power, after that the Holy Ghost is come upon you: and ye shall be witnesses unto me both in Jerusalem, and in all Judaea, and in Samaria, and unto the uttermost part of the earth. Acts 1:8

And it shall come to pass in the last days, saith God, I will pour out of my Spirit upon all flesh: and your sons and your daughters shall prophesy, and your young men shall see visions, and your old men shall dream dreams: And on my servants and on my handmaidens I will pour out in those days of my Spirit; and they shall prophesy. Acts 2:17-18

And when they were come up out of the water, the Spirit of the Lord caught away Philip, that the eunuch saw him no more: and he went on his way rejoicing. Acts 8:39

But if the Spirit of him that raised up Jesus from the dead dwell in you, he that raised up Christ from the dead shall also quicken your mortal bodies by his Spirit that dwelleth in you. Romans 8:11

To be "fervent in spirit" is to be "boiling in spirit," and to boil we must be near the Fire. - Vance Havner

And my speech and my preaching was not with enticing words of man's wisdom, but in demonstration of the Spirit and of power.
1 Corinthians 2:4

And such were some of you: but ye are washed, but ye are sanctified, but ye are justified in the name of the Lord Jesus, and by the Spirit of our God. 1 Corinthians 6:11

For our gospel came not unto you in word only, but also in power, and in the Holy Ghost, and in much assurance; as ye know what manner of men we were among you for your sake. 1 Thessalonians 1:5

> *Never let a person or man-made doctrine talk you out of the power of God. The gods of the pagans are dead and powerless but the God of Israel heals, delivers and manifests His glory in Sovereign miracles through His Son Jesus Christ.*

God also bearing them witness, both with signs and wonders, and with divers miracles, and gifts of the Holy Ghost, according to his own will? Hebrews 2:4

Jesus Christ is the same yesterday, and today, and forever. Hebrews 13:8

The Gifts of the Holy Spirit

Now there are diversities of gifts, but the same Spirit. And there are differences of administrations, but the same Lord. And there are diversities of operations, but it is the same God which worketh all in all. But the manifestation of the Spirit is given to every man to profit withal. For to one is given by the Spirit the word of wisdom; to another the word of knowledge by the same Spirit; To another faith by the same Spirit; to another the gifts of healing by the same Spirit; To another the working of miracles; to another prophecy; to another discerning of spirits; to another divers kinds of tongues; to another the interpretation of tongues: But all these worketh that one and the selfsame Spirit, dividing to every man severally as he will. 1 Corinthians 12:4-11

The Name of Jesus

The Different Names of Jesus

Advocate with the Father	1 John 2:1
Alpha and Omega	Revelation 22:13
Almighty, The	Revelation 1:8
Amen, The	Revelation 3:14
Apostle, The	Hebrews 3:1
Author and Finisher of Our Faith	Hebrews 12:2
Beginning, The	Colossians 1:18
Beginning and the End	Revelation 21:6, 22:13
Beginning of the Creation of God	Revelation 3:14
Begotten of God	1 John 5:18
Beloved, The	Ephesians 1:6
Blessed Hope	Titus 2:13
Bishop of Your Souls	1 Peter 2:25
Branch, The	Isaiah 11:1, Matthew 2:23
Branch of Righteousness	Jeremiah 33:15
Bridegroom	Matthew 9:15
Bright and Morning Star	Revelation 22:16
Bread of Life	John 6:35
Captain of the Lord's Host	Joshua 5:15
Chief Corner Stone	1 Peter 2:6
Chiefest Among Ten Thousand	Song of Solomon 5:10
Christ, The	John 1:41
Consolation	Luke 2:25
Cornerstone	Ephesians 2:20
Counsellor	Isaiah 9:6
Day Spring, The	Luke 1:78
Day Star, The	2 Peter 1:19
Deliverer, The	Romans 11:26
Door, The	John 10:9
Elect, The	1 Peter 2:6

Emmanuel	Matthew 1:23
Eternal Life	1 John 5:20
Everlasting Father	Isaiah 9:6
Faithful, The	Revelation 3:14
Faithful Witness	Revelation 1:5
Faithful and True	Revelation 19:11
First Begotten	Hebrews 1:6
First Begotten of the Dead	Revelation 1:5
First and the Last	Revelation 22:13
Firstborn	Psalms 89:27
Firstborn Among Many Brethren	Romans 8:29
Firstborn From the Dead	Colossians 1:18
Firstborn of Every Creature	Colossians 1:15
Firstfruit, The	1 Corinthians 15:23
Glorious Lord	Isaiah 33:21
God	John 1:1, Isaiah 9:6
God with Us	Matthew 1:23
Good Shepherd	John 10:11
Governor	Matthew 2:6
Great High Priest	Hebrews 4:14
Head of the Body	Colossians 1:18
Head of the Church	Ephesians 5:23
Head Over All Things	Ephesians 1:22
Head Stone of the Corner	Psalms 118:22
Heir of All Things	Hebrews 1:2
High Priest	Hebrews 3:1
Holy One of Israel	Isaiah 41:14
Hope of Glory	Colossians 1:27
I Am	John 8:58
Image of the Invisible God	Colossians 1:15
Immanuel	Isaiah 7:14
King	Zechariah 9:9
King Eternal	1 Timothy 1:17
King of Glory	Psalms 24:7
King of Kings	1 Timothy 6:15
King Over All the Earth	Zechariah 14:9
Lamb of God	John 1:29
Last Adam	1 Corinthians 15:45
Life, The	John 14:6
Light of the Gentiles	Isaiah 42:6
Light of the World	John 8:12

Lily of the Valleys	Song of Solomon 2:1
Living Bread	John 6:51
Lord and Saviour	2 Peter 2:20
Lord of All	Acts 10:36
Lord of Lords	1 Timothy 6:15
Lord Our Righteousness	Jeremiah 23:6
Lord God Almighty	Revelation 4:8
Love	1 John 4:8
Made Perfect	Hebrews 5:9
Man	1 Timothy 2:5
Master	Matthew 23:10
Messiah	Daniel 9:25-26, John 1:41
Mighty God	Isaiah 9:6
Most Mighty	Psalms 45:3
Nazarene	Matthew 2:23
Offspring of David	Revelation 22:16
Only Begotten of the Father	John 1:14
Only Wise God, The	1 Timothy 1:17
Our Lord	Romans 8:39
Our Passover	1 Corinthians 5:7
Our Profession	Hebrews 3:1
Precious	1 Peter 2:6
Precious Corner Stone	Isaiah 28:16
Prince of Peace	Isaiah 9:6
Prince of the Kings of the Earth	Revelation 1:5
Propitiation, The	Romans 3:25
Rabbi	John 1:49
Redeemer	Isaiah 41:14
Root, The	Revelation 22:16
Root of Jesse	Isaiah 11:10
Rose of Sharon	Song of Solomon 2:1
Resurrection, The	John 11:25
Righteous, The	1 John 2:1
Saviour	Titus 2:13
Saviour of the World	1 John 4:14
Second Man, The	1 Corinthians 15:47
Seed of David	Romans 1:3
Shepherd	1 Peter 2:25
Son of God	Romans 1:4
Son of Man	Acts 7:56, John 7:42
Son of Mary	Mark 6:3

Son of the Highest .... Luke 1:32
Spiritual Rock .... 1 Corinthians 10:4
Star Out of Jacob .... Numbers 24:17
Stone, The .... Matthew 21:42, Psalms 118:22
Sun of Righteousness .... Malachi 4:2
True .... 1 John 5:20
True Vine .... John 15:1
True Witness .... Revelation 3:14
Truth, The .... John 14:6
Unspeakable Gift .... 2 Corinthians 9:15
Way, The .... John 14:6
Which Is .... Revelation 1:8
Which Was .... Revelation 1:8
Which is to Come .... Revelation 1:8
Wisdom of God .... 1 Corinthians 1:24
Wonderful .... Isaiah 9:6
Word, The .... John 1:14
Word of God, The .... Revelation 19:13

The Name Above All Names

Wherefore God also hath highly exalted him, and given him a name which is above every name: That at the name of Jesus every knee should bow, of things in heaven, and things in earth, and things under the earth; And that every tongue should confess that Jesus Christ is Lord, to the glory of God the Father. Philippians 2:9-11

Being made so much better than the angels, as he hath by inheritance obtained a more excellent name than they. Hebrews 1:4

Praying in the Name of Jesus

Again I say unto you, That if two of you shall agree on earth as touching any thing that they shall ask, it shall be done for them of my Father which is in heaven. For where two or three are gathered together in my name, there am I in the midst of them. Matthew 18:19-20

And whatsoever ye shall ask in my name, that will I do, that the Father may be glorified in the Son. If ye shall ask any thing in my name, I will do it. John 14:13-14

Ye have not chosen me, but I have chosen you, and ordained you, that ye should go and bring forth fruit, and that your fruit should remain: that

whatsoever ye shall ask of the Father in my name, he may give it you.
John 15:16

And in that day ye shall ask me nothing. Verily, verily, I say unto you, Whatsoever ye shall ask the Father in my name, he will give it you. Hitherto have ye asked nothing in my name: ask, and ye shall receive, that your joy may be full. John 16:23-24

At that day ye shall ask in my name: and I say not unto you, that I will pray the Father for you. John 16:26

Is any sick among you? let him call for the elders of the church; and let them pray over him, anointing him with oil in the name of the Lord.
James 5:14

Power in the Name of Jesus

And these signs shall follow them that believe; In my name shall they cast out devils; they shall speak with new tongues; They shall take up serpents; and if they drink any deadly thing, it shall not hurt them; they shall lay hands on the sick, and they shall recover. Mark 16:17-18

And the seventy returned again with joy, saying, Lord, even the devils are subject unto us through thy name. Luke 10:17

But as many as received him, to them gave he power to become the sons of God, even to them that believe on his name. John 1:12

Then Peter said, Silver and gold have I none; but such as I have give I thee: In the name of Jesus Christ of Nazareth rise up and walk. Acts 3:6

And his name through faith in his name hath made this man strong, whom ye see and know: yea, the faith which is by him hath given him this perfect soundness in the presence of you all. Acts 3:16

And when they had set them in the midst, they asked, By what power, or by what name, have ye done this? Then Peter, filled with the Holy Ghost, said unto them, Ye rulers of the people, and elders of Israel, **Be** it known unto you all, and to all the people of Israel, that by the name of Jesus Christ of Nazareth, whom ye crucified, whom God raised from the dead, even by him doth this man stand here before you whole. Acts 4:7-8,10

And this did she many days. But Paul, being grieved, turned and said to the spirit, I command thee in the name of Jesus Christ to come out of her. And he came out the same hour. Acts 16:18

The name of the Lord is a strong tower: the righteous runneth into it, and is safe. Proverbs 18:10

Believing in the Name of Jesus

He that believeth on him is not condemned: but he that believeth not is condemned already, because he hath not believed in the name of the only begotten Son of God. John 3:18

But these are written, that ye might believe that Jesus is the Christ, the Son of God; and that believing ye might have life through his name.
John 20:31

And it shall come to pass, that whosoever shall call on the name of the Lord shall be saved. Acts 2:21

Then Peter said unto them, Repent, and be baptized every one of you in the name of Jesus Christ for the remission of sins, and ye shall receive the gift of the Holy Ghost. Acts 2:38

Neither is there salvation in any other: for there is none other name under heaven given among men, whereby we must be saved. Acts 4:12

To him give all the prophets witness, that through his name whosoever believeth in him shall receive remission of sins. Acts 10:43

For whosoever shall call upon the name of the Lord shall be saved.
Romans 10:13

And in his name shall the Gentiles trust. Matthew 12:21

And this is his commandment, That we should believe on the name of his Son Jesus Christ, and love one another, as he gave us commandment.
1 John 3:23

These things have I written unto you that believe on the name of the Son of God; that ye may know that ye have eternal life, and that ye may believe on the name of the Son of God. 1 John 5:13

Now when he was in Jerusalem at the passover, in the feast day, many believed in his name, when they saw the miracles which he did.
John 2:23

Serving in the Name of Jesus

For whosoever shall give you a cup of water to drink in my name, because ye belong to Christ, verily I say unto you, he shall not lose his reward. Mark 9:41

And whatsoever ye do in word or deed, do all in the name of the Lord Jesus, giving thanks to God and the Father by him. Colossians 3:17

For God is not unrighteous to forget your work and labour of love, which ye have shewed toward his name, in that ye have ministered to the saints, and do minister. Hebrews 6:10

Suffering for the Name of Jesus

And every one that hath forsaken houses, or brethren, or sisters, or father, or mother, or wife, or children, or lands, for my name's sake, shall receive an hundredfold, and shall inherit everlasting life. Matthew 19:29

Remember the word that I said unto you, The servant is not greater than his lord. If they have persecuted me, they will also persecute you; if they have kept my saying, they will keep yours also. **But all these things will they do unto you for my name's sake, because they know not him that sent me.** John 15:20-21

And Jesus answered and said, Verily I say unto you, There is no man that hath left house, or brethren, or sisters, of father, or mother, or wife, or children, of lands, for my sake, and the gospel's. **But he shall receive an hundredfold now in this time, houses, and brethren, and sisters, and mothers, and children, and lands, with persecutions; and in the world to come eternal life.** Mark 10:29-30

And to him they agreed: and when they had called the apostles, and beaten them, they commanded that they should not speak in the name of Jesus, and let them go. And they departed from the presence of the council, rejoicing that they were counted worthy to suffer shame for his name. And daily in the temple, and in every house, they ceased not to teach and preach Jesus Christ. Acts 5:40-42

If ye be reproached for the name of Christ, happy are ye; for the spirit of glory and of God resteth upon you: on their part he is evil spoken of, but on your part he is glorified. 1 Peter 4:14

Consecration

Seeking God

If my people, which are called by my name, shall humble themselves, and pray, and seek my face, and turn from their wicked ways; then will I hear from heaven, and will forgive their sin, and will heal their land.
2 Chronicles 7:14

I would seek unto God, and unto God would I commit my cause. Job 5:8

And they that know thy name will put their trust in thee: for thou, Lord, hast not forsaken them that seek thee. Psalms 9:10

When thou saidst, Seek ye my face; my heart said unto thee, Thy face, Lord, will I seek. Psalms 27:8

God looked down from heaven upon the children of men, to see if there were any that did understand, that did seek God. Psalms 53:2

The humble shall see this, and be glad: and your heart shall live that seek God. Psalms 69:32

> *Jesus Christ is the first and last, author and finisher, beginning and end, alpha and omega, and by Him all other things hold together. He must be first or nothing. God never comes next!*
> *- Vance Havner*

But it is good for me to draw near to God: I have put my trust in the Lord God, that I may declare all thy works. Psalms 73:28

And I set my face unto the Lord God, to seek by prayer and supplication, with fasting, and sackcloth, and ashes. Daniel 9:3

For thus saith the Lord unto the house of Israel, Seek ye me, and ye shall live. Amos 5:4

Seek him that maketh the seven stars and Orion, and turneth the shadow of death into the morning, and maketh the day dark with night: that calleth for the waters of the sea, and poureth them out upon the face of the earth: The Lord is his name. Amos 5:8

Seek ye the Lord, all ye meek of the earth, which have wrought his judgment; seek righteousness, seek meekness: it may be ye shall be hid in the day of the Lord's anger. Zephaniah 2:3

Yea, many people and strong nations shall come to seek the Lord of hosts in Jerusalem, and to pray before the Lord. Zechariah 8:22

But seek ye first the kingdom of God, and his righteousness; and all these things shall be added unto you. Matthew 6:33

Ask, and it shall be given you; seek, and ye shall find; knock, and it shall be opened unto you: For every one that asketh receiveth; and he that seeketh findeth; and to him that knocketh it shall be opened.
Matthew 7:7-8

And I say unto you, Ask, and it shall be given you; seek, and ye shall find; knock, and it shall be opened unto you. For every one that asketh receiveth; and he that seeketh findeth; and to him that knocketh it shall be opened. Luke 11:9-10

And seek not ye what ye shall eat, or what ye shall drink, neither be ye of doubtful mind. For all these things do the nations of the world seek after: and your Father knoweth that ye have need of these things. But rather seek ye the kingdom of God; and all these things shall be added unto you. Luke 12:29-31

But the hour cometh, and now is, when the true worshippers shall worship the Father in spirit and in truth: for the Father seeketh such to worship him. John 4:23

That they should seek the Lord, if haply they might feel after him, and find him, though he be not far from every one of us. Acts 17:27

If ye then be risen with Christ, seek those things which are above, where Christ sitteth on the right hand of God. Colossians 3:1

For the law made nothing perfect, but the bringing in of a better hope did; by the which we draw nigh unto God. Hebrews 7:19

Draw nigh to God, and he will draw nigh to you. Cleanse your hands, ye sinners; and purify your hearts, ye double minded. James 4:8

1. Seek After God With Your Whole Being (Spirit, Soul and Body)

But if from thence thou shalt seek the Lord thy God, thou shalt find him, if thou seek him with all thy heart and with all thy soul.
Deuteronomy 4:29

Now set your heart and your soul to seek the Lord your God.
1 Chronicles 22:19

And they entered into a covenant to seek the Lord God of their fathers with all their heart and with all their soul. 2 Chronicles 15:12

Blessed are they that keep his testimonies, and that seek him with the whole heart. Psalms 119:2

And ye shall seek me, and find me, when ye shall search for me with all your heart. Jeremiah 29:13

2. Seek God Early in the Morning

O God, thou art my God; early will I seek thee: my soul thirsteth for thee, my flesh longeth for thee in a dry and thirsty land, where no water is. Psalms 63:1

With my soul have I desired thee in the night; yea, with my spirit within me will I seek thee early: for when thy judgments are in the earth, the inhabitants of the world will learn righteousness. Isaiah 26:9

I will go and return to my place, till they acknowledge their offence, and seek my face: in their affliction they will seek me early. Hosea 5:15

> *Whatever is your best time in the day, give that to communion with God. - Hudson Taylor*

I love them that love me; and those that seek me early shall find me.
Proverbs 8:17

3. Seek God Continuously

Therefore came I forth to meet thee, diligently to seek thy face, and I have found thee. Proverbs 7:15

Glory ye in his holy name: let the heart of them rejoice that seek the Lord. Seek the Lord and his strength, seek his face continually.
1 Chronicles 16:10-11

Seek the Lord, and his strength: seek his face evermore. Psalms 105:4

Seek ye the Lord while he may be found, call ye upon him while he is near. Isaiah 55:6

Yet they seek me daily, and delight to know my ways, as a nation that did righteousness, and forsook not the ordinance of their God: they ask of me the ordinances of justice; they take delight in approaching to God.
Isaiah 58:2

But without faith it is impossible to please him: for he that cometh to God must believe that he is, and that he is a rewarder of them that diligently seek him. Hebrews 11:6

4. The Results of Continuously Seeking God

The meek shall eat and be satisfied: they shall praise the Lord that seek him: your heart shall live for ever. Psalms 22:26

The young lions do lack, and suffer hunger: but they that seek the Lord shall not want any good thing. Psalms 34:10

Evil men understand not judgment: but they that seek the Lord understand all things. Proverbs 28:5

The Lord is good unto them that wait for him, to the soul that seeketh him. Lamentations 3:25

5. The Consequences of Not Seeking God

And he did evil, because he prepared not his heart to seek the Lord.
2 Chronicles 12:14

Obeying the Word of God

O that there were such an heart in them, that they would fear me, and keep all my commandments always, that it might be well with them, and with their children for ever! Deuteronomy 5:29

And thou shalt do that which is right and good in the sight of the Lord: that it may be well with thee, and that thou mayest go in and possess the good land which the Lord sware unto thy fathers. Deuteronomy 6:18

Wherefore it shall come to pass, if ye hearken to these judgments, and keep, and do them, that the Lord thy God shall keep unto thee the covenant and the mercy which he sware unto thy fathers. Deuteronomy 7:12

Keep therefore the words of this covenant, and do them, that ye may prosper in all that ye do. Deuteronomy 29:9

See, I have set before thee this day life and good, and death and evil; In that I command thee this day to love the Lord thy God, to walk in his ways, and to keep his commandments and his statutes and his judgments, that thou mayest live and multiply: and the Lord thy God shall bless thee in the land whither thou goest to possess it. Deuteronomy 30:15-16

If they obey and serve him, they shall spend their days in prosperity, and their years in pleasures. Job 36:11

Blessed are they that keep judgment, and he that doeth righteousness at all times. Psalms 106:3

So shall I keep thy law continually for ever and ever. Psalms 119:44

I made haste, and delayed not to keep thy commandments. Psalms 119:60

I have refrained my feet from every evil way, that I might keep thy word.
Psalms 119:101

Thy testimonies are wonderful: therefore doth my soul keep them.
Psalms 119:129

Wherewithal shall a young man cleanse his way? by taking heed thereto according to thy word. Psalms 119:9

My son, keep thy father's commandment, and forsake not the law of thy mother: **Bind** them continually upon thine heart, and tie them about thy neck. **When** thou goest, it shall lead thee; when thou sleepest, it shall keep thee; and when thou awakest, it shall talk with thee.
Proverbs 6:20-22

Whoso despiseth the word shall be destroyed: but he that feareth the commandment shall be rewarded. Proverbs 13:13

Whosoever therefore shall break one of these least commandments, and shall teach men so, he shall be called the least in the kingdom of heaven: but whosoever shall do and teach them, the same shall be called great in the kingdom of heaven. Matthew 5:19

Not every one that saith unto me, Lord, Lord, shall enter into the kingdom of heaven; but he that doeth the will of my Father which is in heaven.
Matthew 7:21

For whosoever shall do the will of my Father which is in heaven, the same is my brother, and sister, and mother. Matthew 12:50

But Jesus said, Suffer little children, and forbid them not, to come unto me: for of such is the kingdom of heaven. Matthew 19:14

Verily, verily, I say unto you, He that heareth my word, and believeth on him that sent me, hath everlasting life, and shall not come into condemnation; but is passed from death unto life. John 5:24

Verily, verily, I say unto you, If a man keep my saying, he shall never see death. John 8:51

If ye know these things, happy are ye if ye do them. John 13:17

If ye love me, keep my commandments. John 14:15

He that hath my commandments, and keepeth them, he it is that loveth me: and he that loveth me shall be loved of my Father, and I will love him, and will manifest myself to him. John 14:21

Jesus answered and said unto him, If a man love me, he will keep my words: and my Father will love him, and we will come unto him, and make our abode with him. He that loveth me not keepeth not my sayings: and the word which ye hear is not mine, but the Father's which sent me. John 14:23-24

If ye keep my commandments, ye shall abide in my love; even as I have kept my Father's commandments, and abide in his love. John 15:10

Ye are my friends, if ye do whatsoever I command you. John 15:14

Let every soul be subject unto the higher powers. For there is no power but of God: the powers that be are ordained of God. Romans 13:1

Those things, which ye have both learned, and received, and heard, and seen in me, do: and the God of peace shall be with you. Philippians 4:9

> *Believing and confessing Jesus Christ as Lord and Savior is the prerequisite for salvation, but obedience to God's Word and a loving heart is the proof of salvation.*

And being made perfect, he became the author of eternal salvation unto all them that obey him. Hebrews 5:9

And hereby we do know that we know him, if we keep his commandments. He that saith, I know him, and keepeth not his commandments, is a liar, and the truth is not in him. But whoso keepeth his word, in him verily is the love of God perfected: hereby know we that we are in him. He that saith he abideth in him ought himself also so to walk, even as he walked. 1 John 2:3-6

And the world passeth away, and the lust thereof: but he that doeth the will of God abideth for ever. 1 John 2:17

And whatsoever we ask, we receive of him, because we keep his commandments and do those things that are pleasing in his sight. 1 John 3:22

1. True Obedience

But he said, Yea rather, blessed are they that hear the word of God, and keep it. Luke 11:28

For not the hearers of the law are just before God, but the doers of the law shall be justified. Romans 2:13

Therefore whosoever heareth these sayings of mine, and doeth them, I will liken him unto a wise man, which built his house upon a rock: And the rain descended, and the floods came, and the winds blew, and beat upon that house; and it fell not: for it was founded upon a rock.
Matthew 7:24-25

But whoso looketh into the perfect law of liberty, and continueth therein, he being not a forgetful hearer, but a doer of the work, this man shall be blessed in his deed. James 1:25

> We have not learned the commandments until we have learned to do them. - Vance Havner

Submitting to the Correction of God

Behold, happy is the man whom God correcteth: therefore despise not thou the chastening of the Almighty: For he maketh sore, and bindeth up: he woundeth, and his hands make whole. Job 5:17-18

Blessed is the man whom thou chastenest, O Lord, and teachest him out of thy law; That thou mayest give him rest from the days of adversity, until the pit be digged for the wicked. Psalms 94:12-13

My son, despise not the chastening of the Lord; neither be weary of his correction. For whom the Lord loveth he correcteth; even as a father the son in whom he delighteth. Proverbs 3:11-12

But when we are judged, we are chastened of the Lord, that we should not be condemned with the world. 1 Corinthians 11:32

And ye have forgotten the exhortation which speaketh unto you as unto children, My son, despise not thou the chastening of the Lord, nor faint when thou art rebuked of him: For whom the Lord loveth he chasteneth, and scourgeth every son whom he receiveth. If ye endure chastening, God dealeth with you as with sons; for what son is he whom the father chasteneth not? But if ye be without chastisement, whereof all are partakers, then are ye bastards, and not sons. Furthermore we have had fathers of our flesh which corrected us, and we gave them reverence: shall we not much rather be in subjection unto the Father of spirits, and live? For they verily for a few days chastened us after their own pleasure; but he for our profit, that we might be partakers of his holiness. Now no chastening for the present seemeth to be joyous, but grievous: nevertheless afterward it yieldeth the peaceable fruit of righteousness unto them which are exercised thereby. Hebrews 12:5-11

As many as I love, I rebuke and chasten: be zealous therefore, and repent. Revelation 3:19

Dying to Self

He that findeth his life shall lose it: and he that loseth his life for my sake shall find it. Matthew 10:39

For whosoever will save his life shall lose it; but whosoever shall lose his life for my sake and the gospel's, the same shall save it. Mark 8:35

And he said to them all, If any man will come after me, let him deny himself, and take up his cross daily, and follow me. For whosoever will save his life shall lose it: but whosoever will lose his life for my sake, the same shall save it. For what is a man advantaged, if he gain the whole world, and lose himself, or be cast away? Luke 9:23-25

Whosoever shall seek to save his life shall lose it; and whosoever shall lose his life shall preserve it. Luke 17:33

The man who is prepared to die is prepared to live.
- Vance Havner

He that loveth his life shall lose it; and he that hateth his life in this world shall keep it unto life eternal. John 12:25

Likewise reckon ye also yourselves to be dead indeed unto sin, but alive unto God through Jesus Christ our Lord. Let not sin therefore reign in your mortal body, that ye should obey it in the lusts thereof.
Romans 6:11-12

All things are lawful for me, but all things are not expedient: all things are lawful for me, but all things edify not. 1 Corinthians 10:23

For the love of Christ constraineth us; because we thus judge, that if one died for all, then were all dead: And that he died for all, that they which live should not henceforth live unto themselves, but unto him which died for them, and rose again. Wherefore henceforth know we no man after the flesh: yea, though we have known Christ after the flesh, yet now henceforth know we him no more. Therefore if any man be in Christ, he is a new creature: old things are passed away; behold, all things are become new. 2 Corinthians 5:14-17

> *In this day of self-exaltation the Bible teaches self-execution. Not that we execute ourselves but that we submit to the death of self by the hand of God. Paul witnessed his own execution, but there came forth a new Paul: "I live, yet not I, but Christ liveth in me." - Vance Havner*

For though he was crucified through weakness, yet he liveth by the power of God. For we also are weak in him, but we shall live with him by the power of God toward you. 2 Corinthians 13:4

I am crucified with Christ: nevertheless I live; yet not I, but Christ liveth in me: and the life which I now live in the flesh I live by the faith of the Son of God, who loved me, and gave himself for me. Galatians 2:20

That ye put off concerning the former conversation the old man, which is corrupt according to the deceitful lusts; And be renewed in the spirit of your mind; And that ye put on the new man, which after God is created in righteousness and true holiness. Ephesians 4:22-24

> *We are always trying to "find ourselves" when that is exactly what we need to lose. - Vance Havner*

But what things were gain to me, those I counted loss for Christ.
Philippians 3:7

Following Christ and Carrying Your Cross

And he that taketh not his cross, and followeth after me, is not worthy of me. Matthew 10:38

Then said Jesus unto his disciples, If any man will come after me, let him deny himself, and take up his cross, and follow me. Matthew 16:24

And when he had called the people unto him with his disciples also, he said unto them, Whosoever will come after me, let him deny himself, and take up his cross, and follow me. Mark 8:34

Then Jesus beholding him loved him, and said unto him, One thing thou lackest: go thy way, sell whatsoever thou hast, and give to the poor, and thou shalt have treasure in heaven: and come, take up the cross, and follow me. Mark 10:21

But God forbid that I should glory, save in the cross of our Lord Jesus Christ, by whom the world is crucified unto me, and I unto the world.
Galatians 6:14

And he said to them all, If any man will come after me, let him deny himself, and take up his cross daily, and follow me. Luke 9:23

And whosoever doth not bear his cross, and come after me, cannot be my disciple. Luke 14:27

> Salvation is free. The gift of God is eternal life. It is not cheap for it cost God his Son and the Son His life, but it is free. However, when we become believers we become disciples and that will cost everything we have. - Vance Havner

Being a True Representative of God

1. Living the Life of Christ Before God and Man

The just man walketh in his integrity: his children are blessed after him.
Proverbs 20:7

Let your light so shine before men, that they may see your good works, and glorify your Father which is in heaven. Matthew 5:16

Thou therefore which teachest another, teachest thou not thyself? thou that preachest a man should not steal, dost thou steal? Thou that sayest a man should not commit adultery, dost thou commit adultery? thou that abhorrest idols, dost thou commit sacrilege? Thou that makest thy boast of the law, through breaking the law dishonourest thou God? For the name of God is blasphemed among the Gentiles through you, as it is written. Romans 2:21-24

But I keep under my body, and bring it into subjection: lest that by any means, when I have preached to others, I myself should be a castaway.
1 Corinthians 9:27

> Where one reads the Bible, a hundred read you and me. - D. L. Moody

Teaching us that, denying ungodliness and worldly lusts, we should live soberly, righteously, and godly, in this present world. Titus 2:12

They profess that they know God; but in works they deny him, being abominable, and disobedient, and unto every good work reprobate.
Titus 1:16

A righteous man falling down before the wicked is as a troubled fountain, and a corrupt spring. Proverbs 25:26

Like a muddied fountain and a polluted spring is a righteous man who yields, falls down and compromises his integrity before the wicked.
Proverbs 25:26 AMP

He that saith, I know him, and keepeth not his commandments, is a liar, and the truth is not in him. 1 John 2:4

Giving no offence in any thing, that the ministry be not blamed: **But** in all things approving ourselves as the ministers of God, in much patience, in afflictions, in necessities, in distresses, **In** stripes, in imprisonments, in tumults, in labours, in watchings, in fastings; **By** pureness, by knowledge, by longsuffering, by kindness, by the Holy Ghost, by love unfeigned, **By** the word of truth, by the power of God, by the armour of righteousness on the right hand and on the left, **By** honour and dishonour, by evil report and good report: as deceivers, and yet true; **As** unknown, and yet well known; as dying, and, behold, we live; as chastened, and not killed; **As** sorrowful, yet alway rejoicing; as poor, yet making many rich; as having nothing, and yet possessing all things.
2 Corinthians 6:3-10

Avoiding this, that no man should blame us in this abundance which is administered by us: **Providing** for honest things, not only in the sight of the Lord, but also in the sight of men. 2 Corinthians 8:20-21

2. Being a True Representative of God is

a. Knowing the Word of God When Sharing with Unbelievers

Then will I teach transgressors thy ways; and sinners shall be converted unto thee. Psalms 51:13

The heart of the righteous studieth to answer. Proverbs 15:28

The fruit of the righteous is a tree of life; and he that winneth souls is wise. Proverbs 11:30

That I might make thee know the certainty of the words of truth; that thou mightest answer the words of truth to them that send unto thee?
Proverbs 22:21

You and I are human post offices. We are daily giving out messages of some sort to the world. They do not come from us, but through us we do not create, we convey. And they come either from hell or from heaven. - Vance Havner

Study to shew thyself approved unto God, a workman that needeth not to be ashamed, rightly dividing the word of truth. 2 Timothy 2:15

That the communication of thy faith may become effectual by the acknowledging of every good thing which is in you in Christ Jesus.
Philemon 1:6

But sanctify the Lord God in your hearts: and be ready always to give an answer to every man that asketh you a reason of the hope that is in you with meekness and fear: **H**aving a good conscience; that, whereas they speak evil of you, as of evildoers, they may be ashamed that falsely accuse your good conversation in Christ. 1 Peter 3:15-16

Holding fast the faithful word as he hath been taught, that he may be able by sound doctrine both to exhort and to convince the gainsayers. Titus 1:9

And moreover, because the preacher was wise, he still taught the people knowledge; yea, he gave good heed, and sought out, and set in order many proverbs. The preacher sought to find out acceptable words: and that which was written was upright, even words of truth. The words of the wise are as goads, and as nails fastened by the masters of assemblies, which are given from one shepherd.
Ecclesiastes 12:9-11

b. Loving Everyone From Your Heart

We know that we have passed from death unto life, because we love the brethren. He that loveth not his brother abideth in death.
1 John 3:14

By this shall all men know that ye are my disciples, if ye have love one to another. John 13:35

c. Never Denying Jesus Christ

Whosoever therefore shall confess me before men, him will I confess also before my Father which is in heaven. **B**ut whosoever shall deny me before men, him will I also deny before my Father which is in heaven. Matthew 10:32-33

Also I say unto you, Whosoever shall confess me before men, him shall the Son of man also confess before the angels of God: **B**ut he that denieth me before men shall be denied before the angels of God.
Luke 12:8-9

If we suffer, we shall also reign with him: if we deny him, he also will deny us. 2 Timothy 2:12

I know thy works: behold, I have set before thee an open door, and no man can shut it: for thou hast a little strength, and hast kept my word, and hast not denied my name. Revelation 3:8

d. Being a Vessel for God's Power to Flow Through

But ye shall receive power, after that the Holy Ghost is come upon you: and ye shall be witnesses unto me both in Jerusalem, and in all Judaea, and in Samaria, and unto the uttermost part of the earth.
Acts 1:8

And such as do wickedly against the covenant shall he corrupt by flatteries: but the people that do know their God shall be strong, and do exploits. Daniel 11:32

Verily, verily, I say unto you, He that believeth on me, the works that I do shall he do also; and greater works than these shall he do; because I go unto my Father. John 14:12

And he said unto them, Go ye into all the world, and preach the gospel to every creature. He that believeth and is baptized shall be saved; but he that believeth not shall be damned. And these signs shall follow them that believe; In my name shall they cast out devils; they shall speak with new tongues; They shall take up serpents; and if they drink any deadly thing, it shall not hurt them; they shall lay hands on the sick, and they shall recover. Mark 16:15-18

Fasting

Is it such a fast that I have chosen? a day for a man to afflict his soul? is it to bow down his head as a bulrush, and to spread sackcloth and ashes under him? wilt thou call this a fast, and an acceptable day to the Lord? Is not this the fast that I have chosen? to loose the bands of wickedness, to undo the heavy burdens, and to let the oppressed go free, and that ye break every yoke? Isaiah 58:5-6

But as for me, when they were sick, my clothing was sackcloth: I humbled my soul with fasting; and my prayer returned into mine own bosom.
Psalms 35:13

And I set my face unto the Lord God, to seek by prayer and supplication, with fasting, and sackcloth, and ashes: Daniel 9:3

And when he had fasted forty days and forty nights, he was afterward an hungered. Matthew 4:2

Fasting is the attitude of, "Lord, empty me of self." Prayer is the insistent cry of one's soul, "Lord, fill me with thyself." - H. H. Leavitt

1. Fasting Gives You Power Over satan

When Jesus saw that the people came running together, he rebuked the foul spirit, saying unto him, Thou dumb and deaf spirit, I charge thee, come out of him, and enter no more into him. And the spirit cried, and rent him sore, and came out of him: and he was as one dead; insomuch that many said, He is dead. But Jesus took him by the hand, and lifted him up; and he arose. And when he was come into the house, his disciples asked him privately, Why could not we cast him out? And he said unto them, This kind can come forth by nothing, but by prayer and fasting. Mark 9:25-29

2. Fasting with Pure Motives

Moreover when ye fast, be not, as the hypocrites, of a sad countenance: for they disfigure their faces, that they may appear unto men to fast. Verily I say unto you, They have their reward. But thou, when thou fastest, anoint thine head, and wash thy face; That thou appear not unto men to fast, but unto thy Father which is in secret: and thy Father, which seeth in secret, shall reward thee openly. Matthew 6:16-18

The Pharisee stood and prayed thus with himself, God, I thank thee, that I am not as other men are, extortioners, unjust, adulterers, or even as this publican. I fast twice in the week, I give tithes of all that I possess. And the publican, standing afar off, would not lift up so much as his eyes unto heaven, but smote upon his breast, saying, God be merciful to me a sinner. Luke 18:11-13

LEARNING TO LOVE

God is love; and he that dwelleth in love dwelleth in God, and God in him. 1 John 4:16

There is no fear in love; but perfect love casteth out fear: because fear hath torment. He that feareth is not made perfect in love. 1 John 4:18

Characteristics of Love

Charity suffereth long, and is kind; charity envieth not; charity vaunteth not itself, is not puffed up, **D**oth not behave itself unseemly, seekteh not her own, is not easily provoked, thinketh no evil; **R**ejoiceth not in iniquity, but rejoiceth in the truth; **B**eareth all things, believeth all things, hopeth all things, endureth all things. Charity never faileth.
1 Corinthians 13:4-8a

1. **Love is patient.**
2. **Love is kind.**
3. **Love does not envy.**
4. **Love does not boast.**
5. **Love is not proud.**
6. **Love is not rude.**
7. **Love is not self-seeking.**
8. **Love is not easily angered.**
9. **Love keeps no record of wrongs.**
10. **Love does not delight in evil but rejoices with the truth.**
11. **Love always protects.**
12. **Love always trusts.**
13. **Love always hopes.**
14. **Love always perseveres.**
15. **Love never fails.**

Though I speak with the tongues of men and of angels, and have not charity (love), I am become as sounding brass, or a tinkling cymbal. And though I have the gift of prophecy, and understand all mysteries, and all knowledge; and though I have all faith, so that I could remove mountains, and have not charity (love), I am nothing. And though I bestow all my goods to feed the poor, and though I give my body to be burned, and have not charity (love), it profiteth me nothing.

1 Corinthians 13:1-3

And now abideth faith, hope, charity, these three; but the greatest of these is charity. 1 Corinthians 13:13

God's Love

The Lord openeth the eyes of the blind: the Lord raiseth them that are bowed down: the Lord loveth the righteous. Psalms 146:8

For as a young man marrieth a virgin, so shall thy sons marry thee: and as the bridegroom rejoiceth over the bride, so shall thy God rejoice over thee. Isaiah 62:5

The Lord hath appeared of old unto me, saying, Yea, I have loved thee with an everlasting love: therefore with lovingkindness have I drawn thee. Jeremiah 31:3

I will heal their backsliding, I will love them freely: for mine anger is turned away from him. Hosea 14:4

For God so loved the world, that he gave his only begotten Son, that whosoever believeth in him should not perish, but have everlasting life.

John 3:16

For the Father himself loveth you, because ye have loved me, and have believed that I came out from God. John 16:27

And the glory which thou gavest me I have given them; that they may be one, even as we are one: I in them, and thou in me, that they may be made perfect in one; and that the world may know that thou hast sent me, and hast loved them, as thou hast loved me. John 17:22-23

And I have declared unto them thy name, and will declare it: that the love wherewith thou hast loved me may be in them, and I in them.

John 17:26

But God commendeth his love toward us, in that, while we were yet sinners, Christ died for us. Romans 5:8

But God, who is rich in mercy, for his great love wherewith he loved us, Even when we were dead in sins, hath quickened us together with Christ, by grace ye are saved. And hath raised us up together, and made us sit together in heavenly places in Christ Jesus: That in the ages to come he might shew the exceeding riches of his grace in his kindness toward us through Christ Jesus. Ephesians 2:4-7

And to know the love of Christ, which passeth knowledge, that ye might be filled with all the fulness of God. Ephesians 3:19

Now our Lord Jesus Christ himself, and God, even our Father, which hath loved us, and hath given us everlasting consolation and good hope through grace, Comfort your hearts, and stablish you in every good word and work 2 Thessalonians 2:16-17

Behold, what manner of love the Father hath bestowed upon us, that we should be called the sons of God: therefore the world knoweth us not, because it knew him not. 1 John 3:1

Beloved, let us love one another: for love is of God; and every one that loveth is born of God, and knoweth God. He that loveth not knoweth not God; for God is love. In this was manifested the love of God toward us, because that God sent his only begotten Son into the world, that we might live through him. Herein is love, not that we loved God, but that he loved us, and sent his Son to be the propitiation for our sins. Beloved, if God so loved us, we ought also to love one another. 1 John 4:7-11

And we have known and believed the love that God hath to us. God is love; and he that dwelleth in love dwelleth in God, and God in him.
1 John 4:16

We love him, because he first loved us. 1 John 4:19

Loving God

But as it is written, Eye hath not seen, nor ear heard, neither have entered into the heart of man, the things which God hath prepared for them that love him. 1 Corinthians 2:9

Know therefore that the Lord thy God, he is God, the faithful God, which keepeth covenant and mercy with them that love him and keep his commandments to a thousand generations. Deuteronomy 7:9

Delight thyself also in the Lord; and he shall give thee the desires of thine heart. Psalms 37:4

Whom have I in heaven but thee? and there is none upon earth that I desire beside thee. Psalms 73:25

Because he hath set his love upon me, therefore will I deliver him: I will set him on high, because he hath known my name. Psalms 91:14

The Lord preserveth all them that love him: but all the wicked will he destroy. Psalms 145:20

I love them that love me; and those that seek me early shall find me. Proverbs 8:17

That I may cause those that love me to inherit substance; and I will fill their treasures. Proverbs 8:21

He that hath my commandments, and keepeth them, he it is that loveth me: and he that loveth me shall be loved of my Father, and I will love him, and will manifest myself to him. John 14:21

Grace be with all them that love our Lord Jesus Christ in sincerity. Amen. Ephesians 6:24

Loving Others

Behold, how good and how pleasant it is for brethren to dwell together in unity! Psalms 133:1

But I say unto you, Love your enemies, bless them that curse you, do good to them that hate you, and pray for them which despitefully use you, and persecute you. Matthew 5:44

Therefore all things whatsoever ye would that men should do to you, do ye even so to them: for this is the law and the prophets. Matthew 7:12

And thou shalt love the Lord thy God with all thy heart, and with all thy soul, and with all thy mind, and with all thy strength: this is the first commandment. And the second is like, namely this, Thou shalt love thy neighbour as thyself. There is none other commandment greater than these. Mark 12:30-31

This is my commandment, That ye love one another, as I have loved you. Greater love hath no man than this, that a man lay down his life for his friends. John 15:12-13

Be kindly affectioned one to another with brotherly love; in honour preferring one another. Romans 12:10

Love worketh no ill to his neighbour: therefore love is the fulfilling of the law. Romans 13:10

Finally, brethren, farewell. Be perfect, be of good comfort, be of one mind, live in peace; and the God of love and peace shall be with you.
2 Corinthians 13:11

Seeing ye have purified your souls in obeying the truth through the Spirit unto unfeigned love of the brethren, see that ye love one another with a pure heart fervently. 1 Peter 1:22

Finally, be ye all of one mind, having compassion one of another, love as brethren, be pitiful, be courteous: Not rendering evil for evil, or railing for railing: but contrariwise blessing; knowing that ye are thereunto called, that ye should inherit a blessing. 1 Peter 3:8-9

He that loveth his brother abideth in the light, and there is none occasion of stumbling in him. 1 John 2:10

We know that we have passed from death unto life, because we love the brethren. He that loveth not his brother abideth in death. 1 John 3:14

My little children, let us not love in word, neither in tongue; but in deed and in truth. And hereby we know that we are of the truth, and shall assure our hearts before him. 1 John 3:18-19

Beloved, let us love one another: for love is of God; and every one that loveth is born of God, and knoweth God. He that loveth not knoweth not God; for God is love. 1 John 4:7-8

Beloved, if God so loved us, we ought also to love one another. No man hath seen God at any time. If we love one another, God dwelleth in us, and his love is perfected in us. 1 John 4:11-12

If a man say, I love God, and hateth his brother, he is a liar: for he that loveth not his brother whom he hath seen, how can he love God whom he hath not seen? And this commandment have we from him, That he who loveth God love his brother also. 1 John 4:20-21

And now I beseech thee, lady, not as though I wrote a new commandment unto thee, but that which we had from the beginning, that we love one another. 2 John 1:5

Overcoming Sin

Sin

All unrighteousness is sin: and there is a sin not unto death. 1 John 5:17

Jesus answered them, Verily, verily, I say unto you, Whosoever committeth sin is the servant of sin. John 8:34

These six things doth the Lord hate: yea, seven are an abomination unto him. A proud look, a lying tongue, and hands that shed innocent blood. An heart that deviseth wicked imaginations, feet that be swift in running to mischief, A false witness that speaketh lies, and he that soweth discord among brethren. Proverbs 6:16-19

Now the works of the flesh are manifest, which are these; Adultery, fornication, uncleanness, lasciviousness, Idolatry, witchcraft, hatred, variance, emulations, wrath, strife, seditions, heresies, envyings, murders, drunkenness, revellings, and such like: of the which I tell you before, as I have also told you in time past, that they which do such things shall not inherit the kingdom of God. Galatians 5:19-21

He that committeth sin is of the devil; for the devil sinneth from the beginning. For this purpose the Son of God was manifested, that he might destroy the works of the devil. Whosoever is born of God doth not commit sin; for his seed remaineth in him: and he cannot sin, because he is born of God. In this the children of God are manifest, and the children of the devil: whosoever doeth not righteousness is not of God, neither he that loveth not his brother. 1 John 3:8-10

Whosoever abideth in him sinneth not: whosoever sinneth hath not seen him, neither known him. 1 John 3:6

Whosoever is born of God doth not commit sin; for his seed remaineth in him: and he cannot sin, because he is born of God. 1 John 3:9

We know that whosoever is born of God sinneth not; but he that is begotten of God keepeth himself, and that wicked one toucheth him not.
1 John 5:18

There is a way that seemeth right unto a man, but the end thereof are the ways of death. Proverbs 16:25

> *The Bible will keep you from sin, or sin will keep you from the Bible - D. L. Moody*

And he that doubteth is damned if he eat, because he eateth not of faith: for whatsoever is not of faith is sin. Romans 14:23

But the man who has doubts—misgivings, an uneasy conscience—about eating, and then eats [perhaps because of you], stands condemned [before God], because he is not true to his convictions and he does not act from faith. For whatever does not originate and proceed from faith is sin—that is, whatever is done without a conviction of its approval by God is sinful. Romans 14:23 AMP

Secret Sins

But if ye will not do so, behold, ye have sinned against the Lord: and be sure your sin will find you out. Numbers 32:23

He that covereth his sins shall not prosper: but whoso confesseth and forsaketh them shall have mercy. Proverbs 28:13

For God shall bring every work into judgment, with every secret thing, whether it be good, or whether it be evil. Ecclesiastes 12:14

For there is nothing hid, which shall not be manifested; neither was any thing kept secret, but that it should come abroad. Mark 4:22

For nothing is secret, that shall not be made manifest; neither any thing hid, that shall not be known and come abroad. Luke 8:17

For there is nothing covered, that shall not be revealed; neither hid, that shall not be known. Therefore whatsoever ye have spoken in darkness shall be heard in the light; and that which ye have spoken in the ear in closets shall be proclaimed upon the housetops. Luke 12:2-3

In the day when God shall judge the secrets of men by Jesus Christ according to my gospel. Romans 2:16

1. The Pleasure of Sin is Only Temporary

Choosing rather to suffer affliction with the people of God, than to enjoy the pleasures of sin for a season. Hebrews 11:25

Deliberate and Willful Sin

What shall we say then? Shall we continue in sin, that grace may abound?
Romans 6:1

For if we sin wilfully after that we have received the knowledge of the truth, there remaineth no more sacrifice for sins, But a certain fearful looking for of judgment and fiery indignation, which shall devour the adversaries. He that despised Moses' law died without mercy under two or three witnesses: Of how much sorer punishment, suppose ye, shall he be thought worthy, who hath trodden under foot the Son of God, and hath counted the blood of the covenant, wherewith he was sanctified, an unholy thing, and hath done despite unto the Spirit of grace? For we know him that hath said, Vengeance belongeth unto me, I will recompense, saith the Lord. And again, The Lord shall judge his people. It is a fearful thing to fall into the hands of the living God. Hebrews 10:26-31

> *We are not to tolerate evil but abhor it. The mood of the age is to put up with evil, allow it, and then move easily to play with it and finally practice it. - Vance Havner*

For if we go on deliberately and willingly sinning after once acquiring the knowledge of the Truth, there is no longer any sacrifice left to atone for [our] sins–no further offering to which to look forward. There is nothing left for us then but a kind of awful and fearful prospect and expectation of divine judgment and the fury of burning wrath and indignation which will consume those who put themselves in opposition to God. Any person who has violated and [thus] rejected and set at naught the Law of Moses is put to death without pity or mercy on the evidence of two or three witnesses. How much worse (sterner and heavier) punishment do you suppose he will be judged to deserve who has spurned and [thus] trampled under foot the Son of God, and who has considered the covenant blood by which he was consecrated common and unhallowed, thus profaning it and insulting and outraging the (Holy) Spirit [Who imparts] grace–he unmerited favor and blessing of God? For we know Him Who said, Vengeance is Mine–retribution and the meting out of full justice rest with Me; I will repay–I will exact the compensation, says the Lord. And again, The Lord will judge and determine and solve and settle the cause and the cases of His people. Is a fearful (formidable and terrible) thing to incur the divine penalties and be cast into the hands of the living God! Hebrews 10:26-31 AMP

Sowing Sin and Reaping the Consequences of Sin

But he that doeth wrong shall receive for the wrong which he hath done: and there is no respect of persons. Colossians 3:25

Even as I have seen, they that plow iniquity, and sow wickedness, reap the same. Job 4:8

Evil pursueth sinners: but to the righteous good shall be repayed.
Proverbs 13:21

Whoso rewardeth evil for good, evil shall not depart from his house.
Proverbs 17:13

He that soweth iniquity shall reap vanity: and the rod of his anger shall fail. Proverbs 22:8

Whoso diggeth a pit shall fall therein: and he that rolleth a stone, it will return upon him. Proverbs 26:27

Whoso causeth the righteous to go astray in an evil way, he shall fall himself into his own pit: but the upright shall have good things in possession. Proverbs 28:10

He that diggeth a pit shall fall into it; and whoso breaketh an hedge, a serpent shall bite him. Ecclesiastes 10:8

For they have sown the wind, and they shall reap the whirlwind: it hath no stalk: the bud shall yield no meal: if so be it yield, the strangers shall swallow it up. Hosea 8:7

Ye have plowed wickedness, ye have reaped iniquity; ye have eaten the fruit of lies: because thou didst trust in thy way, in the multitude of thy mighty men. Hosea 10:13

For the wages of sin is death; but the gift of God is eternal life through Jesus Christ our Lord. Romans 6:23

Be not deceived; God is not mocked: for whatsoever a man soweth, that shall he also reap. For he that soweth to his flesh shall of the flesh reap corruption; but he that soweth to the Spirit shall of the Spirit reap life everlasting. Galatians 6:7-8

A sinful lifestyle is spiritual insanity.

Sin Gives satan Entrance into Your Life

Be ye angry, and sin not: let not the sun go down upon your wrath: Neither give place to the devil. Ephesians 4:26-27

Overcoming Sin

Hereafter I will not talk much with you: for the prince of this world cometh, and hath nothing in me. John 14:30

Afterward Jesus findeth him in the temple, and said unto him, Behold, thou art made whole: sin no more, lest a worse thing come unto thee.
John 5:14

To whom ye forgive any thing, I forgive also: for if I forgave any thing, to whom I forgave it, for your sakes forgave I it in the person of Christ; Lest satan should get an advantage of us: for we are not ignorant of his devices. 2 Corinthians 2:10-11

Not a novice, lest being lifted up with pride he fall into the condemnation of the devil. Moreover he must have a good report of them which are without; lest he fall into reproach and the snare of the devil.
1 Timothy 3:6-7

And that they may recover themselves out of the snare of the devil, who are taken captive by him at his will. 2 Timothy 2:26

But I have a few things against thee, because thou hast there them that hold the doctrine of Balaam, who taught Balac to cast a stumblingblock before the children of Israel, to eat things sacrificed unto idols, and to commit fornication. Revelation 2:14

Then came Peter to him, and said, Lord, how oft shall my brother sin against me, and I forgive him? till seven times? Jesus saith unto him, I say not unto thee, Until seven times: but, Until seventy times seven. Therefore is the kingdom of heaven likened unto a certain king, which would take account of his servants. Then his lord, after that he had called him, said unto him, O thou wicked servant, I forgave thee all that debt, because thou desiredst me: Shouldest not thou also have had compassion on thy fellowservant, even as I had pity on thee? And his lord was wroth, and delivered him to the tormentors, till he should pay all that was due unto him. So likewise shall my heavenly Father do also unto you, if ye from your hearts forgive not every one his brother their trespasses. Matthew 18:21-23,32-35

A Life of Sin is Hard

Correction is grievous unto him that forsaketh the way: and he that hateth reproof shall die. Proverbs 15:10

For the wages of sin is death; but the gift of God is eternal life through Jesus Christ our Lord. Romans 6:23

The wicked man travaileth with pain all his days, and the number of years is hidden to the oppressor. Job 15:20

But the transgressors shall be destroyed together: the end of the wicked shall be cut off. Psalms 37:38

Fools because of their transgression, and because of their iniquities, are afflicted. Psalms 107:17

Thorns and snares are in the way of the froward: he that doth keep his soul shall be far from them. Proverbs 22:5

But the wicked shall be cut off from the earth, and the transgressors shall be rooted out of it. Proverbs 2:22

Good understanding giveth favour: but the way of transgressors is hard. Proverbs 13:15

In the transgression of an evil man there is a snare: but the righteous doth sing and rejoice. Proverbs 29:6

What Should I Do When I Sin?

1. Repent

Definition: Repent means to change one's mind or purpose with regard to sin, a sorrow for sin.

Or despisest thou the riches of his goodness and forbearance and longsuffering; not knowing that the goodness of God leadeth thee to repentance? Romans 2:4

The Lord is not slack concerning his promise, as some men count slackness; but is longsuffering to us-ward, not willing that any should perish, but that all should come to repentance. 2 Peter 3:9

I tell you, Nay: but, except ye repent, ye shall all likewise perish. Luke 13:3

Therefore I will judge you, O house of Israel, every one according to his ways, saith the Lord God. Repent, and turn yourselves from all your transgressions; so iniquity shall not be your ruin. Ezekiel 18:30

For godly sorrow worketh repentance to salvation not to be repented of: but the sorrow of the world worketh death. 2 Corinthians 7:10

Say unto them, As I live, saith the Lord God, I have no pleasure in the death of the wicked; but that the wicked turn from his way and live: turn

ye, turn ye from your evil ways; for why will ye die, O house of Israel?
Ezekiel 33:11

And saying, The time is fulfilled, and the kingdom of God is at hand: repent ye, and believe the gospel. Mark 1:15

And saying, Repent ye: for the kingdom of heaven is at hand.
Matthew 3:2

Repent ye therefore, and be converted, that your sins may be blotted out, when the times of refreshing shall come from the presence of the Lord.
Acts 3:19

From that time Jesus began to preach, and to say, Repent: for the kingdom of heaven is at hand. Matthew 4:17

I say unto you, that likewise joy shall be in heaven over one sinner that repenteth, more than over ninety and nine just persons, which need no repentance. Luke 15:7

> *True repentance has a double aspect; it looks upon things past with a weeping eye, and upon the future with a watchful eye. - Robert Smith*

When Jesus heard it, he saith unto them, They that are whole have no need of the physician, but they that are sick: I came not to call the righteous, but sinners to repentance. Mark 2:17

And the times of this ignorance God winked at; but now commandeth all men every where to repent. Acts 17:30

I came not to call the righteous, but sinners to repentance. Luke 5:32

Likewise, I say unto you, there is joy in the presence of the angels of God over one sinner that repenteth. Luke 15:10

Him hath God exalted with his right hand to be a Prince and a Saviour, for to give repentance to Israel, and forgiveness of sins. Acts 5:31

a. Proof of Repentance

I thought on my ways, and turned my feet unto thy testimonies.
Psalms 119:59

> *True repentance is proceeded by a passionate commitment to obey God's Word.*

But shewed first unto them of Damascus, and at Jerusalem, and throughout all the coasts of Judaea, and then to the Gentiles, that they should repent and turn to God, and do works meet for repentance. Acts 26:20

They profess that they know God; but in works they deny him, being abominable, and disobedient, and unto every good work reprobate.
Titus 1:16

Bring forth therefore fruits meet for repentance. Matthew 3:8

2. Confess the Sin

He that covereth his sins shall not prosper: but whoso confesseth and forsaketh them shall have mercy. Proverbs 28:13

And it shall be, when he shall be guilty in one of these things, that he shall confess that he hath sinned in that thing. Leviticus 5:5

If we confess our sins, he is faithful and just to forgive us our sins, and to cleanse us from all unrighteousness. 1 John 1:9

And the seed of Israel separated themselves from all strangers, and stood and confessed their sins, and the iniquities of their fathers. Nehemiah 9:2

Before you were even born God knew every sin that you would commit throughout your lifetime, therefore it is useless to run and hide from God. When you sin, run to God, repent, confess the sin, and humbly receive God's merciful forgiveness through the shed blood of his son Jesus Christ.

I acknowledged my sin unto thee, and mine iniquity have I not hid. I said, I will confess my transgressions unto the Lord; and thou forgavest the iniquity of my sin. Selah. Psalms 32:5

And were baptized of him in Jordan, confessing their sins. Matthew 3:6

And many that believed came, and confessed, and shewed their deeds.
Acts 19:18

Confess your faults one to another, and pray one for another, that ye may be healed. The effectual fervent prayer of a righteous man availeth much.
James 5:16

3. Stop Sinning

Ye have not yet resisted unto blood, striving against sin. Hebrews 12:4

You have not yet struggled and fought agonizingly against sin, nor have you yet resisted and withstood to the point of pouring out your [own] blood. Hebrews 12:4 AMP

If iniquity be in thine hand, put it far away, and let not wickedness dwell in thy tabernacles. Job 11:14

The night is far spent, the day is at hand: let us therefore cast off the works of darkness, and let us put on the armour of light. Romans 13:12

Wherefore, O king, let my counsel be acceptable unto thee, and break off thy sins by righteousness, and thine iniquities by shewing mercy to the poor; if it may be a lengthening of thy tranquillity. Daniel 4:27

She said, No man, Lord. And Jesus said unto her, Neither do I condemn thee: go, and sin no more. John 8:11

Mortify therefore your members which are upon the earth; fornication, uncleanness, inordinate affection, evil concupiscence, and covetousness, which is idolatry. Colossians 3:5

Lie not one to another, seeing that ye have put off the old man with his deeds. Colossians 3:9

Let all bitterness, and wrath, and anger, and clamour, and evil speaking, be put away from you, with all malice. Ephesians 4:31

> *Blunders we shall make and failures will shame our faces and dampen our eyes. But if we can manage not to remember what we ought to forget and not to forget what we ought to remember, then forgetting the things behind and stirring up our minds by way of remembrance, we shall press on for the prize. - Vance Havner*

Neither filthiness, nor foolish talking, nor jesting, which are not convenient: but rather giving of thanks. For this ye know, that no whoremonger, nor unclean person, nor covetous man, who is an idolater, hath any inheritance in the kingdom of Christ and of God. Ephesians 5:4-5

Nevertheless the foundation of God standeth sure, having this seal, The Lord knoweth them that are his. And, Let every one that nameth the name of Christ depart from iniquity. 2 Timothy 2:19

Wherefore lay apart all filthiness and superfluity of naughtiness, and receive with meekness the engrafted word, which is able to save your souls. James 1:21

Deliverance from Sin

And she shall bring forth a son, and thou shalt call his name Jesus: for he shall save his people from their sins. Matthew 1:21

The next day John seeth Jesus coming unto him, and saith, Behold the Lamb of God, which taketh away the sin of the world. John 1:29

For he hath made him to be sin for us, who knew no sin; that we might be made the righteousness of God in him. 2 Corinthians 5:21

For when we were yet without strength, in due time Christ died for the ungodly. Romans 5:6

But God commendeth his love toward us, in that, while we were yet sinners, Christ died for us. Romans 5:8

For the law of the Spirit of life in Christ Jesus hath made me free from the law of sin and death. Romans 8:2

> *Prayer will make a man cease from sin, or sin will entice a man to cease from prayer. - John Bunyan*

To wit, that God was in Christ, reconciling the world unto himself, not imputing their trespasses unto them; and hath committed unto us the word of reconciliation. 2 Corinthians 5:19

Who gave himself for our sins, that he might deliver us from this present evil world, according to the will of God and our Father. Galatians 1:4

And, having made peace through the blood of his cross, by him to reconcile all things unto himself; by him, I say, whether they be things in earth, or things in heaven. Colossians 1:20

Curses

DEFINITION OF CURSE: A curse (from God) is righteous judgement against disobedience. To curse is to pray against, or wish evil against a person or thing.

And I will bless them that bless thee, and curse him that curseth thee: and in thee shall all families of the earth be blessed. Genesis 12:3

How shall I curse, whom God hath not cursed? or how shall I defy, whom the Lord hath not defied? Numbers 23:8

Whoso curseth his father or his mother, his lamp shall be put out in obscure darkness. Proverbs 20:20

He that giveth unto the poor shall not lack: but he that hideth his eyes shall have many a curse. Proverbs 28:27

Thus saith the Lord; Cursed be the man that trusteth in man, and maketh flesh his arm, and whose heart departeth from the Lord. Jeremiah 17:5

And Peter calling to remembrance saith unto him, Master, behold, the fig tree which thou cursedst is withered away. Mark 11:21

1. Curses Activated by Disobedience to God's Word

And a curse, if ye will not obey the commandments of the Lord your God, but turn aside out of the way which I command you this day, to go after other gods, which ye have not known. Deuteronomy 11:28

The curse of the Lord is in the house of the wicked: but he blesseth the habitation of the just. Proverbs 3:33

And say thou unto them, Thus saith the Lord God of Israel; Cursed be the man that obeyeth not the words of this covenant. Jeremiah 11:3

2. Curses Activated by Words

Therewith bless we God, even the Father; and therewith curse we men, which are made after the similitude of God. Out of the same mouth proceedeth blessing and cursing. My brethren, these things ought not so to be. James 3:9-10

Death and life are in the power of the tongue: and they that love it shall eat the fruit thereof. Proverbs 18:21

3. How to Break Curses

Christ hath redeemed us from the curse of the law, being made a curse for us: for it is written, Cursed is every one that hangeth on a tree:
Galatians 3:13

a. Obey God's Word

Behold, I set before you this day a blessing and a curse; A blessing, if ye obey the commandments of the Lord your God, which I command you this day. Deuteronomy 11:26-27

I call heaven and earth to record this day against you, that I have set before you life and death, blessing and cursing: therefore choose life, that both thou and thy seed may live. Deuteronomy 30:19

The curse of the Lord is in the house of the wicked: but he blesseth the habitation of the just. Proverbs 3:33

b. Pray blessings on your enemies

But I say unto you, Love your enemies, bless them that curse you, do good to them that hate you, and pray for them which despitefully use you, and persecute you. Matthew 5:44

Bless them that curse you, and pray for them which despitefully use you. Luke 6:28

Bless them which persecute you: bless, and curse not. Romans 12:14

God's Forgiveness

Sins Cleansed by the Blood of Jesus

But now in Christ Jesus ye who sometimes were far off are made nigh by the blood of Christ. Ephesians 2:13

In whom we have redemption through his blood, even the forgiveness of sins. Colossians 1:14

For this is my blood of the new testament, which is shed for many for the remission of sins. Matthew 26:28

Neither by the blood of goats and calves, but by his own blood he entered in once into the holy place, having obtained eternal redemption for us. Hebrews 9:12

And almost all things are by the law purged with blood; and without shedding of blood is no remission. Hebrews 9:22

And from Jesus Christ, who is the faithful witness, and the first begotten of the dead, and the prince of the kings of the earth. Unto him that loved us, and washed us from our sins in his own blood. Revelation 1:5

God Will Forgive Your Sins

For if ye turn again unto the Lord, your brethren and your children shall find compassion before them that lead them captive, so that they shall come again into this land: for the Lord your God is gracious and merciful, and will not turn away his face from you, if ye return unto him.
2 Chronicles 30:9

Blessed is he whose transgression is forgiven, whose sin is covered. Blessed is the man unto whom the Lord imputeth not iniquity, and in whose spirit there is no guile. Psalms 32:1-2

I acknowledged my sin unto thee, and mine iniquity have I not hid. I said, I will confess my transgressions unto the Lord; and thou forgavest the iniquity of my sin. Selah. Psalms 32:5

For thou, Lord, art good, and ready to forgive; and plenteous in mercy unto all them that call upon thee. Psalms 86:5

And the inhabitant shall not say, I am sick: the people that dwell therein shall be forgiven their iniquity. Isaiah 33:24

I have blotted out, as a thick cloud, thy transgressions, and, as a cloud, thy sins: return unto me; for I have redeemed thee. Isaiah 44:22

> *The forgiveness of God is the foundation of every bridge from a hopeless past to a courageous present. - George Adam Smith*

Who is a God like unto thee, that pardoneth iniquity, and passeth by the transgression of the remnant of his heritage? he retaineth not his anger for ever, because he delighteth in mercy. He will turn again, he will have compassion upon us; he will subdue our iniquities; and thou wilt cast all their sins into the depths of the sea. Micah 7:18-19

And forgive us our debts, as we forgive our debtors. Matthew 6:12

For if ye forgive men their trespasses, your heavenly Father will also forgive you: But if ye forgive not men their trespasses, neither will your Father forgive your trespasses. Matthew 6:14-15

In whom we have redemption through his blood, the forgiveness of sins, according to the riches of his grace. Ephesians 1:7

For I will be merciful to their unrighteousness, and their sins and their iniquities will I remember no more. Hebrews 8:12

But this man, after he had offered one sacrifice for sins for ever, sat down on the right hand of God. Hebrews 10:12

And their sins and iniquities will I remember no more. Now where remission of these is, there is no more offering for sin. Hebrews 10:17-18

If we confess our sins, he is faithful and just to forgive us our sins, and to cleanse us from all unrighteousness. 1 John 1:9

My little children, these things write I unto you, that ye sin not. And if any man sin, we have an advocate with the Father, Jesus Christ the righteous: And he is the propitiation for our sins: and not for ours only, but also for the sins of the whole world. 1 John 2:1-2

God Will Not Remember Your Sins

Remember not the sins of my youth, nor my transgressions: according to thy mercy remember thou me for thy goodness' sake, O Lord. Psalms 25:7

O remember not against us former iniquities: let thy tender mercies speedily prevent us: for we are brought very low. Psalms 79:8

And they shall teach no more every man his neighbour, and every man his brother, saying, Know the Lord: for they shall all know me, from the least of them unto the greatest of them, saith the Lord; for I will forgive their iniquity, and I will remember their sin no more. Jeremiah 31:34

He will turn again, he will have compassion upon us; he will subdue our iniquities; and thou wilt cast all their sins into the depths of the sea.
Micah 7:19

This is the covenant that I will make with them after those days, saith the Lord, I will put my laws into their hearts, and in their minds will I write them; And their sins and iniquities will I remember no more.
Hebrews 10:16-17

God Will Blot Out Your Sins

Have mercy upon me, O God, according to thy lovingkindness: according unto the multitude of thy tender mercies blot out my transgressions.
Psalms 51:1

Hide thy face from my sins, and blot out all mine iniquities. Psalms 51:9

I, even I, am he that blotteth out thy transgressions for mine own sake, and will not remember thy sins. Isaiah 43:25

I have blotted out, as a thick cloud, thy transgressions, and, as a cloud, thy sins: return unto me; for I have redeemed thee. Isaiah 44:22

Repent ye therefore, and be converted, that your sins may be blotted out, when the times of refreshing shall come from the presence of the Lord.
Acts 3:19

Overcoming Guilt

Brethren, I count not myself to have apprehended: but this one thing I do, forgetting those things which are behind, and reaching forth unto those things which are before, Philippians 3:13

For if ye turn again unto the Lord, your brethren and your children shall find compassion before them that lead them captive, so that they shall come again into this land: for the Lord your God is gracious and merciful, and will not turn away his face from you, if ye return unto him.
2 Chronicles 30:9

As far as the east is from the west, so far hath he removed our transgressions from us. Psalms 103:12

> Memory can become a tyrant instead of a treasure chest. From the mistakes of the past, let us learn whatever lessons they teach, then forget them, even as God remembers our sins no more. Let precious memories be benedictions but not bonds. - Vance Havner

Let the wicked forsake his way, and the unrighteous man his thoughts: and let him return unto the Lord, and he will have mercy upon him; and to our God, for he will abundantly pardon. Isaiah 55:7

And they shall teach no more every man his neighbour, and every man his brother, saying, Know the Lord: for they shall all know me, from the least of them unto the greatest of them, saith the Lord; for I will forgive their iniquity, and I will remember their sin no more. Jeremiah 31:34

And I will cleanse them from all their iniquity, whereby they have sinned against me; and I will pardon all their iniquities, whereby they have sinned, and whereby they have transgressed against me. Jeremiah 33:8

For God sent not his Son into the world to condemn the world; but that the world through him might be saved. He that believeth on him is not condemned: but he that believeth not is condemned already, because he hath not believed in the name of the only begotten Son of God.
John 3:17-18

Therefore if any man be in Christ, he is a new creature: old things are passed away; behold, all things are become new. 2 Corinthians 5:17

For I will be merciful to their unrighteousness, and their sins and their iniquities will I remember no more. Hebrews 8:12

Let us draw near with a true heart in full assurance of faith, having our hearts sprinkled from an evil conscience, and our bodies washed with pure water. Hebrews 10:22

But if we walk in the light, as he is in the light, we have fellowship one with another, and the blood of Jesus Christ his Son cleanseth us from all sin. 1 John 1:7

If we confess our sins, he is faithful and just to forgive us our sins, and to cleanse us from all unrighteousness. 1 John 1:9

I write unto you, little children, because your sins are forgiven you for his name's sake. 1 John 2:12

For if our heart condemn us, God is greater than our heart, and knoweth all things. 1 John 3:20

> Sometimes, we want to fly before we walk; we want to be perfect before we start toward perfection. It is not a mark of godliness to be forever condemning oneself in morbid self-accusation. - Vance Havner

Overcoming Condemnation

For God sent not his Son into the world to condemn the world; but that the world through him might be saved. John 3:17

Verily, verily, I say unto you, He that heareth my word, and believeth on him that sent me, hath everlasting life, and shall not come into condemnation; but is passed from death unto life. John 5:24

There is therefore now no condemnation to them which are in Christ Jesus, who walk not after the flesh, but after the Spirit. Romans 8:1

For if our heart condemn us, God is greater than our heart, and knoweth all things. Beloved, if our heart condemn us not, then have we confidence toward God. 1 John 3:20-21

> The voice of sin may be loud, but the voice of forgiveness is louder. - D. L. Moody

You Are Condemned When You

1. Reject Christ

He that believeth on him is not condemned: but he that believeth not is condemned already, because he hath not believed in the name of the only begotten Son of God. And this is the condemnation, that light is come into the world, and men loved darkness rather than light, because their deeds were evil. John 3:18-19

2. Willfully Sin

Hast thou faith? have it to thyself before God. Happy is he that condemneth not himself in that thing which he alloweth. Romans 14:22

Knowing that he that is such is subverted, and sinneth, being condemned of himself. Titus 3:11

Salvation

Believing in Jesus Christ

Verily, verily, I say unto you, He that believeth on me hath everlasting life. John 6:47

But as many as received him, to them gave he power to become the sons of God, even to them that believe on his name. John 1:12

That whosoever believeth in him should not perish, but have eternal life. John 3:15

For God so loved the world, that he gave his only begotten Son, that whosoever believeth in him should not perish, but have everlasting life. John 3:16

For God sent not his Son into the world to condemn the world; but that the world through him might be saved. He that believeth on him is not condemned: but he that believeth not is condemned already, because he hath not believed in the name of the only begotten Son of God. John 3:17-18

He that believeth on the Son hath everlasting life: and he that believeth not the Son shall not see life; but the wrath of God abideth on him. John 3:36

Verily, verily, I say unto you, He that heareth my word, and believeth on him that sent me, hath everlasting life, and shall not come into condemnation; but is passed from death unto life. John 5:24

Then Jesus said unto them, Verily, verily, I say unto you, Moses gave you not that bread from heaven; but my Father giveth you the true bread from heaven. For the bread of God is he which cometh down from heaven, and giveth life unto the world. Then said they unto him, Lord, evermore give us this bread. And Jesus said unto them, I am the bread of life: he that cometh to me shall never hunger; and he that believeth on me shall never thirst. John 6:32-35

Verily, verily, I say unto you, He that believeth on me hath everlasting life. John 6:47

And we believe and are sure that thou art that Christ, the Son of the living God. John 6:69

He that believeth on me, as the scripture hath said, out of his belly shall flow rivers of living water. John 7:38

I said therefore unto you, that ye shall die in your sins: for if ye believe not that I am he, ye shall die in your sins. John 8:24

But if I do, though ye believe not me, believe the works: that ye may know, and believe, that the Father is in me, and I in him. John 10:38

But these are written, that ye might believe that Jesus is the Christ, the Son of God; and that believing ye might have life through his name.
John 20:31

For he saith, I have heard thee in a time accepted, and in the day of salvation have I succoured thee: behold, now is the accepted time; behold, now is the day of salvation. 2 Corinthians 6:2

Plan of Salvation

1. How to Obtain Eternal Life Through Jesus Christ

That if thou shalt confess with thy mouth the Lord Jesus, and shalt believe in thine heart that God hath raised him from the dead, thou shalt be saved. Romans 10:9

2. How to be Saved

a. Admit that you have sinned and confess (to God) and repent.

b. Confess (speak aloud) that Jesus Christ is Lord – the Son of God.

c. Believe in your heart (inner most being, spirit, the real you) that God raised Jesus Christ from the dead.

d. After completing the above three steps (according to the Word of God), you are now saved and have eternal life through Jesus Christ.

For with the heart man believeth unto righteousness; and with the mouth confession is made unto salvation. Romans 10:10

Salvation

3. How to Know You are Really Saved

a. Read what God's Word says about your salvation

For whosoever shall call upon the name of the Lord shall be saved. Romans 10:1

Verily, verily, I say unto you, He that heareth my word, and believeth on him that sent me, hath everlasting life, and shall not come into condemnation; but is passed from death unto life. John 5:24

And I give unto them eternal life; and they shall never perish, neither shall any man pluck them out of my hand. John 10:28

These things have I written unto you that believe on the name of the Son of God; that ye may know that ye have eternal life, and that ye may believe on the name of the Son of God. 1 John 5:13

And we know that the Son of God is come, and hath given us an understanding, that we may know him that is true, and we are in him that is true, even in his Son Jesus Christ. This is the true God, and eternal life. 1 John 5:20

For with the heart man believeth unto righteousness; and with the mouth confession is made unto salvation. Romans 10:10

b. The devil might lie and try to play with your mind and tell you that "you are not saved"

He was a murderer from the beginning, and abode not in the truth, because there is no truth in him. When he speaketh a lie, he speaketh of his own: for he is a liar, and the father of it. John 8:44

c. You will obey God's Word

If ye know that he is righteous, ye know that every one that doeth righteousness is born of him. 1 John 2:29

Whosoever abideth in him sinneth not: whosoever sinneth hath not seen him, neither known him. 1 John 3:6

Whosoever is born of God doth not commit sin; for his seed remaineth in him: and he cannot sin, because he is born of God. 1 John 3:9

We know that whosoever is born of God sinneth not; but he that is begotten of God keepeth himself, and that wicked one toucheth him not. 1 John 5:18

4. Now That You are Saved

   a. Receive the baptism of the Holy Spirit.

   b. Find a Bible believing church that is on fire and alive (Read the book of Acts).

   c. Pray and read God's Word everyday of your life.

   d. Obtain a Bible that you can understand (Living Bible, NIV Bible, or the Amplified Bible).

   e. Learn and know your inheritance in Jesus Christ.

   f. Obey the Word of God.

   g. Don't be deceived.

   h. Know and use your authority in Jesus Christ over satan.

   i. Tell others what God has done for you.

Saved by Grace

Even when we were dead in sins, hath quickened us together with Christ, by grace ye are saved. Ephesians 2:5

For by grace are ye saved through faith; and that not of yourselves: it is the gift of God. Ephesians 2:8

For the grace of God that bringeth salvation hath appeared to all men.
Titus 2:11

That being justified by his grace, we should be made heirs according to the hope of eternal life. Titus 3:7

Who hath saved us, and called us with an holy calling, not according to our works, but according to his own purpose and grace, which was given us in Christ Jesus before the world began. 2 Timothy 1:9

1. Respecting the Grace of God

We then, as workers together with him, beseech you also that ye receive not the grace of God in vain. 2 Corinthians 6:1

I do not frustrate the grace of God: for if righteousness come by the law, then Christ is dead in vain. Galatians 2:21

Salvation

What shall we say then? Shall we continue in sin, that grace may abound?
Romans 6:1

Sanctification

And ye shall keep my statutes, and do them: I am the Lord which sanctify you. Leviticus 20:8

That I should be the minister of Jesus Christ to the Gentiles, ministering the gospel of God, that the offering up of the Gentiles might be acceptable, being sanctified by the Holy Ghost. Romans 15:16

And the very God of peace sanctify you wholly; and I pray God your whole spirit and soul and body be preserved blameless unto the coming of our Lord Jesus Christ. 1 Thessalonians 5:23

But we are bound to give thanks alway to God for you, brethren beloved of the Lord, because God hath from the beginning chosen you to salvation through sanctification of the Spirit and belief of the truth:
2 Thessalonians 2:13

For both he that sanctifieth and they who are sanctified are all of one: for which cause he is not ashamed to call them brethren. Hebrews 2:11

For both He Who sanctifies–making men holy–and those who are sanctified all have one [Father]. For this reason He is not ashamed to call them brethren. Hebrews 2:11 AMP

Elect according to the foreknowledge of God the Father, through sanctification of the Spirit, unto obedience and sprinkling of the blood of Jesus Christ: Grace unto you, and peace, be multiplied. 1 Peter 1:2

Jude, the servant of Jesus Christ, and brother of James, to them that are sanctified by God the Father, and preserved in Jesus Christ, and called:
Jude 1:1

1. Sanctified by the Word of God

Sanctify them through thy truth: thy word is truth. John 17:17

That he might sanctify and cleanse it with the washing of water by the word. Ephesians 5:26

2. Sanctified Through Jesus Christ

Unto the church of God which is at Corinth, to them that are sanctified in Christ Jesus, called to be saints, with all that in every place call upon the name of Jesus Christ our Lord, both theirs and ours: 1 Corinthians 1:2

But of him are ye in Christ Jesus, who of God is made unto us wisdom, and righteousness, and sanctification, and redemption: 1 Corinthians 1:30

And such were some of you: but ye are washed, but ye are sanctified, but ye are justified in the name of the Lord Jesus, and by the Spirit of our God. 1 Corinthians 6:11

By the which will we are sanctified through the offering of the body of Jesus Christ once for all. Hebrews 10:10

Wherefore Jesus also, that he might sanctify the people with his own blood, suffered without the gate. Hebrews 13:12

To open their eyes, and to turn them from darkness to light, and from the power of Satan unto God, that they may receive forgiveness of sins, and inheritance among them which are sanctified by faith that is in me.

Acts 26:18

3. Set Apart From the Sins of the World

For this is the will of God, even your sanctification, that ye should abstain from fornication: 1 Thessalonians 4:3

That every one of you should know how to possess his vessel in sancti-fication and honour; 1 Thessalonians 4:4

If a man therefore purge himself from these, he shall be a vessel unto honour, sanctified, and meet for the master's use, and prepared unto ev-ery good work. 2 Timothy 2:21

And now, brethren, I commend you to God, and to the word of his grace, which is able to build you up, and to give you an inheritance among all them which are sanctified. Acts 20:32

Righteousness

1. Righteous Through Jesus Christ

Even the righteousness of God which is by faith of Jesus Christ unto all and upon all them that believe: for there is no difference: For all have sinned, and come short of the glory of God; Romans 3:22-23

For if by one man's offence death reigned by one; much more they which receive abundance of grace and of the gift of righteousness shall reign in

life by one, Jesus Christ. Therefore as by the offence of one judgment came upon all men to condemnation; even so by the righteousness of one the free gift came upon all men unto justification of life.
Romans 5:17-18

> *This is the mystery of the riches of divine grace for sinners; for by a wonderful exchange our sins are now not ours but Christ's, and Christ's righteousness is not Christ's but ours. - Martin Luther*

Moreover the law entered, that the offence might abound. But where sin abounded, grace did much more abound: That as sin hath reigned unto death, even so might grace reign through righteousness unto eternal life by Jesus Christ our Lord. Romans 5:20-21

And if Christ be in you, the body is dead because of sin; but the Spirit is life because of righteousness. Romans 8:10

But of him are ye in Christ Jesus, who of God is made unto us wisdom, and righteousness, and sanctification, and redemption: 1 Corinthians 1:30

For he hath made him to be sin for us, who knew no sin; that we might be made the righteousness of God in him. 2 Corinthians 5:21

And that ye put on the new man, which after God is created in righteousness and true holiness. Ephesians 4:24

Being filled with the fruits of righteousness, which are by Jesus Christ, unto the glory and praise of God. Philippians 1:11

Who his own self bare our sins in his own body on the tree, that we, being dead to sins, should live unto righteousness: by whose stripes ye were healed. 1 Peter 2:24

2. Believing Unto Righteousness

For what saith the scripture? Abraham believed God, and it was counted unto him for righteousness. Romans 4:3

For with the heart man believeth unto righteousness; and with the mouth confession is made unto salvation. Romans 10:10

3. The Word of God is Our Instruction for Righteous Living

All scripture is given by inspiration of God, and is profitable for doctrine, for reproof, for correction, for instruction in righteousness:
2 Timothy 3:16

For every one that useth milk is unskillful in the word of righteousness: for he is a babe. Hebrews 5:13

4. Man-Made Righteousness

For I bear them record that they have a zeal of God, but not according to knowledge. For they being ignorant of God's righteousness, and going about to establish their own righteousness, have not submitted themselves unto the righteousness of God. Romans 10:2-3

And be found in him, not having mine own righteousness, which is of the law, but that which is through the faith of Christ, the righteousness which is of God by faith: Philippians 3:9

Justification

And by him all that believe are justified from all things, from which ye could not be justified by the law of Moses. Acts 13:39

Being justified freely by his grace through the redemption that is in Christ Jesus: Romans 3:24

To declare, I say, at this time his righteousness: that he might be just, and the justifier of him which believeth in Jesus. Romans 3:26

But to him that worketh not, but believeth on him that justifieth the ungodly, his faith is counted for righteousness. Romans 4:5

Therefore being justified by faith, we have peace with God through our Lord Jesus Christ: Romans 5:1

Who was delivered for our offences, and was raised again for our justification. Romans 4:25

Much more then, being now justified by his blood, we shall be saved from wrath through him. Romans 5:9

Therefore as by the offence of one judgment came upon all men to con-demnation; even so by the righteousness of one the free gift came upon all men unto justification of life. Romans 5:18

And such were some of you: but ye are washed, but ye are sanctified, but ye are justified in the name of the Lord Jesus, and by the Spirit of our God. 1 Corinthians 6:11

And without controversy great is the mystery of godliness: God was manifest in the flesh, justified in the Spirit, seen of angels, preached unto the Gentiles, believed on in the world, received up into glory.
1 Timothy 3:16

That being justified by his grace, we should be made heirs according to the hope of eternal life. Titus 3:7

For not the hearers of the law are just before God, but the doers of the law shall be justified. Romans 2:13

Remaining in the Kingdom of God

Blessed are the pure in heart: for they shall see God. Matthew 5:8

And ye shall be hated of all men for my name's sake: but he that endureth to the end shall be saved. Matthew 10:22

But he that shall endure unto the end, the same shall be saved.
Matthew 24:13

He that hath an ear, let him hear what the Spirit saith unto the churches; To him that overcometh will I give to eat of the tree of life, which is in the midst of the paradise of God. Revelation 2:7

He that hath an ear, let him hear what the Spirit saith unto the churches; He that overcometh shall not be hurt of the second death.
Revelation 2:11

He that hath an ear, let him hear what the Spirit saith unto the churches; To him that overcometh will I give to eat of the hidden manna, and will give him a white stone, and in the stone a new name written, which no man knoweth saving he that receiveth it. Revelation 2:17

And he that overcometh, and keepeth my works unto the end, to him will I give power over the nations. Revelation 2:26

He that overcometh, the same shall be clothed in white raiment; and I will not blot out his name out of the book of life, but I will confess his name before my Father, and before his angels. Revelation 3:5

Him that overcometh will I make a pillar in the temple of my God, and he shall go no more out: and I will write upon him the name of my God, and the name of the city of my God, which is new Jerusalem, which cometh down out of heaven from my God: and I will write upon him my new name. Revelation 3:12

To him that overcometh will I grant to sit with me in my throne, even as I also overcame, and am set down with my Father in his throne.
Revelation 3:21

He that overcometh shall inherit all things; and I will be his God, and he shall be my son. Revelation 21:7

The Return of Christ (The Rapture)

For the Son of man shall come in the glory of his Father with his angels; and then he shall reward every man according to his works.
Matthew 16:27

For as the lightning cometh out of the east, and shineth even unto the west; so shall also the coming of the Son of man be. Matthew 24:27

And then shall appear the sign of the Son of man in heaven: and then shall all the tribes of the earth mourn, and they shall see the Son of man coming in the clouds of heaven with power and great glory.
Matthew 24:30

And Jesus said, I am: and ye shall see the Son of man sitting on the right hand of power, and coming in the clouds of heaven. Mark 14:62

Verily, verily, I say unto you, The hour is coming, and now is, when the dead shall hear the voice of the Son of God: and they that hear shall live.
John 5:25

Marvel not at this: for the hour is coming, in the which all that are in the graves shall hear his voice. John 5:28

And if I go and prepare a place for you, I will come again, and receive you unto myself; that where I am, there ye may be also. John 14:3

Ye have heard how I said unto you, I go away, and come again unto you. If ye loved me, ye would rejoice, because I said, I go unto the Father: for my Father is greater than I. John 14:28

Which also said, Ye men of Galilee, why stand ye gazing up into heaven? this same Jesus, which is taken up from you into heaven, shall so come in like manner as ye have seen him go into heaven. Acts 1:11

Therefore judge nothing before the time, until the Lord come, who both will bring to light the hidden things of darkness, and will make manifest the counsels of the hearts: and then shall every man have praise of God.
1 Corinthians 4:5

When Christ, who is our life, shall appear, then shall ye also appear with him in glory. Colossians 3:4

For the Lord himself shall descend from heaven with a shout, with the voice of the archangel, and with the trump of God: and the dead in Christ shall rise first: Then we which are alive and remain shall be caught up together with them in the clouds, to meet the Lord in the air: and so shall we ever be with the Lord. 1 Thessalonians 4:16-17

Looking for that blessed hope, and the glorious appearing of the great God and our Saviour Jesus Christ. Titus 2:13

So Christ was once offered to bear the sins of many; and unto them that look for him shall he appear the second time without sin unto salvation.
Hebrews 9:28

And when the chief Shepherd shall appear, ye shall receive a crown of glory that fadeth not away. 1 Peter 5:4

Beloved, now are we the sons of God, and it doth not yet appear what we shall be: but we know that, when he shall appear, we shall be like him; for we shall see him as he is. 1 John 3:2

Behold, he cometh with clouds; and every eye shall see him, and they also which pierced him: and all kindreds of the earth shall wail because of him. Even so, Amen. Revelation 1:7

And, behold, I come quickly; and my reward is with me, to give every man according as his work shall be. Revelation 22:12

He which testifieth these things saith, Surely I come quickly. Amen. Even so, come, Lord Jesus. Revelation 22:20

1. Are You Ready for the Rapture

Watch therefore: for ye know not what hour your Lord doth come.
Matthew 24:42

Watch ye therefore, and pray always, that ye may be accounted worthy to escape all these things that shall come to pass, and to stand before the Son of man. Luke 21:36

Behold, I show you a mystery; We shall not all sleep, but we shall all be changed, 1 Corinthians 15:51

In a moment, in the twinkling of an eye, at the last trump: for the trumpet shall sound, and the dead shall be raised incorruptible, and we shall be changed. 1 Corinthians 15:52

When You Need Eternal Life

For God so loved the world, that he gave his only begotten Son, that whosoever believeth in him should not perish, but have everlasting life. John 3:16

But whosoever drinketh of the water that I shall give him shall never thirst; but the water that I shall give him shall be in him a well of water springing up into everlasting life. John 4:14

Verily, verily, I say unto you, He that heareth my word, and believeth on him that sent me, hath everlasting life, and shall not come into condemnation; but is passed from death unto life. John 5:24

Labour not for the meat which perisheth, but for that meat which endureth unto everlasting life, which the Son of man shall give unto you: for him hath God the Father sealed. John 6:27

Verily, verily, I say unto you, He that believeth on me hath everlasting life. John 6:47

I am the living bread which came down from heaven: if any man eat of this bread, he shall live for ever: and the bread that I will give is my flesh, which I will give for the life of the world. John 6:51

Whoso eateth my flesh, and drinketh my blood, hath eternal life; and I will raise him up at the last day. John 6:54

My sheep hear my voice, and I know them, and they follow me: And I give unto them eternal life; and they shall never perish, neither shall any man pluck them out of my hand. John 10:27-28

Jesus said unto her, I am the resurrection, and the life: he that believeth in me, though he were dead, yet shall he live: And whosoever liveth and believeth in me shall never die. Believest thou this? John 11:25-26

As thou hast given him power over all flesh, that he should give eternal life to as many as thou hast given him. John 17:2

And these shall go away into everlasting punishment: but the righteous into life eternal. Matthew 25:46

To them who by patient continuance in well doing seek for glory and honour and immortality, eternal life. Romans 2:7

But now being made free from sin, and become servants to God, ye have your fruit unto holiness, and the end everlasting life. For the wages of sin is death; but the gift of God is eternal life through Jesus Christ our Lord. Romans 6:22-23

For our light affliction, which is but for a moment, worketh for us a far more exceeding and eternal weight of glory; While we look not at the things which are seen, but at the things which are not seen: for the things which are seen are temporal; but the things which are not seen are eternal. 2 Corinthians 4:17-18

For he that soweth to his flesh shall of the flesh reap corruption; but he that soweth to the Spirit shall of the Spirit reap life everlasting.
Galatians 6:8

In hope of eternal life, which God, that cannot lie, promised before the world began. Titus 1:2

That being justified by his grace, we should be made heirs according to the hope of eternal life. Titus 3:7

And this is the promise that he hath promised us, even eternal life.
1 John 2:25

And this is the record, that God hath given to us eternal life, and this life is in his Son. 1 John 5:11

These things have I written unto you that believe on the name of the Son of God; that ye may know that ye have eternal life, and that ye may believe on the name of the Son of God. 1 John 5:13

And we know that the Son of God is come, and hath given us an understanding, that we may know him that is true, and we are in him that is true, even in his Son Jesus Christ. This is the true God, and eternal life.
1 John 5:20

Backslider

DEFINITION: A Christian that no longer walks in fellowship with GOD nor obeys His Word

As a dog returneth to his vomit, so a fool returneth to his folly.
Proverbs 26:11

The backslider in heart shall be filled with his own ways: and a good man shall be satisfied from himself. Proverbs 14:14

Thine own wickedness shall correct thee, and thy backslidings shall reprove thee: know therefore and see that it is an evil thing and bitter, that thou hast forsaken the Lord thy God, and that my fear is not in thee, saith the Lord God of hosts. Jeremiah 2:19

Go and proclaim these words toward the north, and say, Return, thou backsliding Israel, saith the Lord; and I will not cause mine anger to fall upon you: for I am merciful, saith the Lord, and I will not keep anger for ever. Jeremiah 3:12

Turn, O backsliding children, saith the Lord; for I am married unto you: and I will take you one of a city, and two of a family, and I will bring you to Zion. Jeremiah 3:14

Return, ye backsliding children, and I will heal your backslidings. Behold, we come unto thee; for thou art the Lord our God. Jeremiah 3:22

O Israel, return unto the Lord thy God; for thou hast fallen by thine iniquity. Hosea 14:1

But now, after that ye have known God, or rather are known of God, how turn ye again to the weak and beggarly elements, whereunto ye desire again to be in bondage? Galatians 4:9

Having damnation, because they have cast off their first faith.
1 Timothy 5:12

Compromising Christian

DEFINITION: Luke warm, Uncommitted

They profess that they know God; but in works they deny him, being abominable, and disobedient, and unto every good work reprobate.
Titus 1:16

What shall we say then? Shall we continue in sin, that grace may abound?
Romans 6:1

Salt is good: but if the salt have lost his saltness, wherewith will ye season it? Have salt in yourselves, and have peace one with another.
Mark 9:50

And that, knowing the time, that now it is high time to awake out of sleep: for now is our salvation nearer than when we believed. The night is far spent, the day is at hand: let us therefore cast off the works of darkness, and let us put on the armour of light. Let us walk honestly, as in the day; not in rioting and drunkenness, not in chambering and wantonness, not in strife and envying. But put ye on the Lord Jesus Christ, and make not provision for the flesh, to fulfil the lusts thereof.
Romans 13:11-14

But I keep under my body, and bring it into subjection: lest that by any means, when I have preached to others, I myself should be a castaway.
1 Corinthians 9:27

Now this I say, brethren, that flesh and blood cannot inherit the kingdom of God; neither doth corruption inherit incorruption. 1 Corinthians 15:50

We then, as workers together with him, beseech you also that ye receive not the grace of God in vain. For he saith, I have heard thee in a time accepted, and in the day of salvation have I succoured thee: behold, now is the accepted time; behold, now is the day of salvation.
2 Corinthians 6:1-2

A whole new generation of Christians has come up believing that it is possible to "accept" Christ without forsaking the world.
- A. W. Tozer

I do not frustrate the grace of God: for if righteousness come by the law, then Christ is dead in vain. Galatians 2:21

Set your affection on things above, not on things on the earth.
Colossians 3:2

Now the Spirit speaketh expressly, that in the latter times some shall depart from the faith, giving heed to seducing spirits, and doctrines of devils. 1 Timothy 4:1

We are not here to learn how to live in the dark but to walk in the light. We are not here to get along with evil but to overcome it with good. - Vance Havner

Teaching us that, denying ungodliness and worldly lusts, we should live soberly, righteously, and godly, in this present world; Looking for that blessed hope, and the glorious appearing of the great God and our Saviour Jesus Christ. Titus 2:12-13

Ye have not yet resisted unto blood, striving against sin. Hebrews 12:4

Christians are not just nice people. They're new creatures. If you are what you have always been you are not a Christian. A Christian is something new; old things have passed away and all things are become new. - Vance Havner

You have not yet struggled and fought agonizingly against sin, nor have you yet resisted and withstood to the point of pouring out your [own] blood. Hebrews 12:4 AMP

Pure religion and undefiled before God and the Father is this, To visit the fatherless and widows in their affliction, and to keep himself unspotted from the world. James 1:27

For if after they have escaped the pollutions of the world through the knowledge of the Lord and Saviour Jesus Christ, they are again entangled therein, and overcome, the latter end is worse with them than the beginning. For it had been better for them not to have known the way of righteousness, than, after they have known it, to turn from the holy commandment delivered unto them. But it is happened unto them according to the true proverb, The dog is turned to his own vomit again; and the sow that was washed to her wallowing in the mire. 2 Peter 2:20-22

Love not the world, neither the things that are in the world. If any man love the world, the love of the Father is not in him. For all that is in the world, the lust of the flesh, and the lust of the eyes, and the pride of life, is not of the Father, but is of the world. And the world passeth away, and the lust thereof: but he that doeth the will of God abideth for ever.
1 John 2:15-17

Is your lifestyle taking the people around you to heaven or hell?

Then shall the kingdom of heaven be likened unto ten virgins, which took their lamps, and went forth to meet the bridegroom. And five of them were wise, and five were foolish. They that were foolish took their lamps, and took no oil with them: But the wise took oil in their vessels with their lamps. While the bridegroom tarried, they all slumbered and slept. And at midnight there was a cry made, Behold, the bridegroom cometh; go ye out to meet him. Then all those virgins arose, and trimmed their lamps. And the foolish said unto the wise, Give us of your oil; for our lamps are gone out. But the wise answered, saying, Not so; lest there be not enough for us and you: but go ye rather to them that sell, and buy for yourselves. And while they went to buy, the bridegroom came; and they that were ready went in with him to the marriage: and the door was shut. Afterward came also the other virgins, saying, Lord, Lord, open to us. But he answered and said, Verily I say unto you, I know you not. Watch therefore, for ye know neither the day nor the hour wherein the Son of man cometh. Matthew 25:1-13

A Warning for the Backslider or Compromising Christian

I know thy works, that thou art neither cold nor hot: I would thou wert cold or hot. So then because thou art lukewarm, and neither cold nor hot, I will spue thee out of my mouth. Because thou sayest, I am rich, and

increased with goods, and have need of nothing; and knowest not that thou art wretched, and miserable, and poor, and blind, and naked.
Revelation 3:15-17

Enter ye in at the strait gate: for wide is the gate, and broad is the way, that leadeth to destruction, and many there be which go in thereat: **Because strait is the gate, and narrow is the way, which leadeth unto life, and few there be that find it.** Matthew 7:13-14

> *Life is too short and hell is too hot to play games with your eternal future.*

Not every one that saith unto me, Lord, Lord, shall enter into the kingdom of heaven; but he that doeth the will of my Father which is in heaven. Many will say to me in that day, Lord, Lord, have we not prophesied in thy name? and in thy name have cast out devils? and in thy name done many wonderful works? And then will I profess unto them, I never knew you: depart from me, ye that work iniquity. Matthew 7:21-23

Strive to enter in at the strait gate: for many, I say unto you, will seek to enter in, and shall not be able. **When once the master of the house is risen up, and hath shut to the door, and ye begin to stand without, and to knock at the door, saying, Lord, Lord, open unto us; and he shall answer and say unto you, I know you not whence ye are: Then shall ye begin to** say, We have eaten and drunk in thy presence, and thou hast taught in our streets. **But he shall say, I tell you, I know you not whence ye are; depart from me, all ye workers of iniquity. There shall be weeping and gnashing of teeth, when ye shall see Abraham, and Isaac, and Jacob, and all the prophets, in the kingdom of God, and you yourselves thrust out.**
Luke 13:24-28

For it is impossible for those who were once enlightened, and have tasted of the heavenly gift, and were made partakers of the Holy Ghost, And have tasted the good word of God, and the powers of the world to come, If they shall fall away, to renew them again unto repentance; seeing they crucify to themselves the Son of God afresh, and put him to an open shame. Hebrews 6:4-6

For it is impossible [to restore and bring again to repentance] those who have been once for all enlightened, who have consciously tasted the heavenly gift, and have become sharers of the Holy Spirit. And have felt how good the Word of God is and the mighty powers of the age and world to come. If they then deviate from the faith and turn away from their allegiance; [it is impossible] to bring them back to repentance, for (because, while, as long as) they nail up on the cross the Son of God afresh, as far as they are concerned, and are holding [him] up to contempt and shame and public disgrace. Hebrews 6:4-6 AMP

For if we sin wilfully after that we have received the knowledge of the truth, there remaineth no more sacrifice for sins, **But a certain fearful looking for of judgment and fiery indignation, which shall devour the adversaries. He that despised Moses' law died without mercy under two or three witnesses: Of how much sorer punishment, suppose ye, shall he be thought worthy, who hath trodden under foot the Son of God, and hath counted the blood of the covenant, wherewith he was sanctified, an unholy thing, and hath done despite unto the Spirit of grace? For we know him that hath said, Vengeance belongeth unto me, I will recompense, saith the Lord. And again, The Lord shall judge his people. It is a fearful thing to fall into the hands of the living God. Hebrews 10:26-31

For if we go on deliberately and willingly sinning after once acquiring the knowledge of the Truth, there is no longer any sacrifice left to atone for [our] sins–no further offering to which to look forward. There is nothing left for us then but a kind of awful and fearful prospect and expectation of divine judgment and the fury of burning wrath and indignation which will consume those who put themselves in opposition to God. Any person who has violated and [thus] rejected and set at naught the Law of Moses is put to death without pity or mercy on the evidence of two or three witnesses. How much worse (sterner and heavier) punishment do you suppose he will be judged to deserve who has spurned and [thus] trampled under foot the Son of God, and who has considered the covenant blood by which he was consecrated common and unhallowed, thus profaning it and insulting and outraging the (Holy) Spirit [Who imparts] grace–the unmerited favor and blessing of God? For we know Him Who said, Vengeance is Mine–retribution and the meting out of full justice rest with Me; I will repay–I will exact the compensation, says the Lord. And again, The Lord will judge and determine and solve and settle the cause and the cases of His people. Is a fearful (formidable and terrible) thing to incur the divine penalties and be cast into the hands of the living God! Hebrews 10:26-31 AMP

Nevertheless I have somewhat against thee, because thou hast left thy first love. **R**emember therefore from whence thou art fallen, and repent, and do the first works; or else I will come unto thee quickly, and will remove thy candlestick out of his place, except thou repent.

Revelation 2:4-5

ETERNITY

Heaven

1. Who's Going to Heaven and Why?

Blessed are they that do his commandments, that they may have right to the tree of life, and may enter in through the gates into the city.
Revelation 22:14

And these shall go away into everlasting punishment: but the righteous into life eternal. Matthew 25:46

Jesus answered and said unto his, Verily, verily, I say unto thee, Except a man be born again, he cannot see the kingdom of God. Nicodemus saith unto him, How can a man be born when he is old? can he enter the second time into his mother's womb, and be born? Jesus answered, Verily, verily, I say unto thee, Except a man be born of water and of the Spirit, he cannot enter into the kingdom of God. That which is born of the flesh is flesh; and that which is born of the Spirit is spirit. Marvel not that I said unto thee, Ye must be born again. John 3:3-7

> *Our Savior has gone to prepare a place, but there are places only for those who make reservations. The dying thief made a reservation: "Remember me." - Vance Havner*

But whosoever drinketh of the water that I shall give him shall never thirst; but the water that I shall give him shall be in him a well of water springing up into everlasting life. John 4:14

Verily, verily, I say unto you, He that heareth my word, and believeth on him that sent me, hath everlasting life, and shall not come into condemnation; but is passed from death unto life. John 5:24

Verily, verily, I say unto you, If a man keep my saying, he shall never see death. John 8:51

Jesus said unto her, I am the resurrection, and the life: he that believeth in me, though he were dead, yet shall he live: And whosoever liveth and believeth in me shall never die. Believest thou this? John 11:25-26

2. What is Heaven Like?

But as it is written, Eye hath not seen, nor ear heard, neither have entered into the heart of man, the things which God hath prepared for them that love him. 1 Corinthians 2:9

The Lord hath prepared his throne in the heavens; and his kingdom ruleth over all. Psalms 103:19

Thy sun shall no more go down; neither shall thy moon withdraw itself: for the Lord shall be thine everlasting light, and the days of thy mourning shall be ended. Thy people also shall be all righteous: they shall inherit the land for ever, the branch of my planting, the work of my hands, that I may be glorified. Isaiah 60:20-21

In my Father's house are many mansions: if it were not so, I would have told you. I go to prepare a place for you. And if I go and prepare a place for you, I will come again, and receive you unto myself; that where I am, there ye may be also. John 14:2-3

But now they desire a better country, that is, an heavenly: wherefore God is not ashamed to be called their God: for he hath prepared for them a city. Hebrews 11:16

> *There is only one thing better than going to heaven and that is to take someone with you. - Anonymous*

Nevertheless we, according to his promise, look for new heavens and a new earth, wherein dwelleth righteousness. 2 Peter 3:13

Therefore are they before the throne of God, and serve him day and night in his temple: and he that sitteth on the throne shall dwell among them. They shall hunger no more, neither thirst any more; neither shall the sun light on them, nor any heat. For the Lamb which is in the midst of the throne shall feed them, and shall lead them unto living fountains of waters: and God shall wipe away all tears from their eyes.
Revelation 7:15-17

He that hath an ear, let him hear what the Spirit saith unto the churches; To him that overcometh will I give to eat of the tree of life, which is in the midst of the paradise of God. Revelation 2:7

And the city had no need of the sun, neither of the moon, to shine in it: for the glory of God did lighten it, and the Lamb is the light thereof. And the nations of them which are saved shall walk in the light of it: and the kings of the earth do bring their glory and honour into it. And the gates of it shall not be shut at all by day: for there shall be no night there. And they shall bring the glory and honour of the nations into it.
Revelation 21:23-26

And he shewed me a pure river of water of life, clear as crystal, proceeding out of the throne of God and of the Lamb. In the midst of the street of it, and on either side of the river, was there the tree of life, which bare twelve manner of fruits, and yielded her fruit every month: and the leaves of the tree were for the healing of the nations. And there shall be no more curse: but the throne of God and of the Lamb shall be in it; and his servants shall serve him: And they shall see his face; and his name shall be in their foreheads. And there shall be no night there; and they need no candle, neither light of the sun; for the Lord God giveth them light: and they shall reign for ever and ever. Revelation 22:1-5

> *Christians are not citizens of earth trying to get to heaven but citizens of heaven making their way through this world. - Vance Havner*

3. Buildings in Heaven

For we know that if our earthly house of this tabernacle were dissolved, we have a building of God, an house not made with hands, eternal in the heavens. 2 Corinthians 5:1

For he looked for a city which hath foundations, whose builder and maker is God. Hebrews 11:10

Blessed and holy is he that hath part in the first resurrection: on such the second death hath no power, but they shall be priests of God and of Christ, and shall reign with him a thousand years. Revelation 20:6

And I saw a new heaven and a new earth: for the first heaven and the first earth were passed away; and there was no more sea. And I John saw the holy city, new Jerusalem, coming down from God out of heaven, prepared as a bride adorned for her husband. Revelation 21:1-2

Having the glory of God: and her light was like unto a stone most precious, even like a jasper stone, clear as crystal; And had a wall great and high, and had twelve gates, and at the gates twelve angels, and names written thereon, which are the names of the twelve tribes of the children of Israel: On the east three gates; on the north three gates; on the south three gates; and on the west three gates. And the wall of the city had twelve foundations, and in them the names of the twelve apostles of the Lamb. And he that talked with me had a golden reed to measure the city, and the gates thereof, and the wall thereof. And the city lieth foursquare, and the length is as large as the breadth: and he measured the city with the reed, twelve thousand furlongs. The length and the breadth and the height of it are equal. And he measured the wall thereof, an hundred and forty and four cubits, according to the measure of a man, that is, of the angel. And the building of the wall of it was of jasper: and the city was pure gold, like unto clear glass. And the foundations of the wall of the city were garnished with all manner of precious stones. The first foundation was jasper; the second, sapphire; the third, a chalcedony; the fourth, an emerald; The fifth, sardonyx; the sixth, sardius; the seventh, chrysolite; the eighth, beryl; the ninth, a topaz; the tenth, a chrysoprasus; the eleventh, a jacinth; the twelfth, an amethyst. And the twelve gates were twelve pearls; every several gate was of one pearl: and the street of the city was pure gold, as it were transparent glass. And I saw no temple therein: for the Lord God Almighty and the Lamb are the temple of it.

Revelation 21:11-22

4. Fellowship in Heaven

And I appoint unto you a kingdom, as my Father hath appointed unto me; That ye may eat and drink at my table in my kingdom, and sit on thrones judging the twelve tribes of Israel. Luke 22:29-30

And I say unto you, That many shall come from the east and west, and shall sit down with Abraham, and Isaac, and Jacob, in the kingdom of heaven. Matthew 8:11

To him that overcometh will I grant to sit with me in my throne, even as I also overcame, and am set down with my Father in his throne.

Revelation 3:21

Hell

For we must all appear before the judgment seat of Christ; that every one may receive the things done in his body, according to that he hath done, whether it be good or bad. 2 Corinthians 5:10

I am he that liveth, and was dead; and, behold, I am alive for evermore, Amen; and have the keys of hell and of death. Revelation 1:18

And fear not them which kill the body, but are not able to kill the soul: but rather fear him which is able to destroy both soul and body in hell.

Matthew 10:28

Hell is naked before him, and destruction hath no covering. Job 26:6

But I say unto you, That whosoever is angry with his brother without a cause shall be in danger of the judgment: and whosoever shall say to his brother, Raca, shall be in danger of the council: but whosoever shall say, Thou fool, shall be in danger of hell fire. Matthew 5:22

Hell is truth seen too late - duty neglected in its season. - Tryon Edwards

Ye serpents, ye generation of vipers, how can ye escape the damnation of hell? Matthew 23:33

But he that shall blaspheme against the Holy Ghost hath never forgiveness, but is in danger of eternal damnation. Mark 3:29

1. Who is Hell For?

Then shall he say also unto them on the left hand, Depart from me, ye cursed, into everlasting fire, prepared for the devil and his angels.
Matthew 25:41

And through covetousness shall they with feigned words make merchandise of you: whose judgment now of a long time lingereth not, and their damnation slumbereth not. For if God spared not the angels that sinned, but cast them down to hell, and delivered them into chains of darkness, to be reserved unto judgment. 2 Peter 2:3-4

And the beast was taken, and with him the false prophet that wrought miracles before him, with which he deceived them that had received the mark of the beast, and them that worshipped his image. These both were cast alive into a lake of fire burning with brimstone. Revelation 19:20

And I saw an angel come down from heaven, having the key of the bottomless pit and a great chain in his hand. And he laid hold on the dragon, that old serpent, which is the Devil, and Satan, and bound him a thousand years, And cast him into the bottomless pit, and shut him up, and set a seal upon him, that he should deceive the nations no more, till the thousand years should be fulfilled: and after that he must be loosed a little season. Revelation 20:1-3

There are no humanists, agnostics or atheists in hell, because every soul in hell believes in Jesus, bows to Jesus, and confess that Jesus is Lord. Only after damnation awakes does reality break.

And the devil that deceived them was cast into the lake of fire and brimstone, where the beast and the false prophet are, and shall be tormented day and night for ever and ever. Revelation 20:10

And death and hell were cast into the lake of fire. This is the second death. And whosoever was not found written in the book of life was cast into the lake of fire. Revelation 20:14-15

2. Who's Going to Hell and Why?

The wicked shall be turned into hell, and all the nations that forget God.
Psalms 9:17

He that believeth and is baptized shall be saved; but he that believeth not shall be damned. Mark 16:16

Whosoever therefore resisteth the power, resisteth the ordinance of God: and they that resist shall receive to themselves damnation. Romans 13:2

For the Lord knoweth the way of the righteous: but the way of the ungodly shall perish. Psalms 1:6

That they all might be damned who believed not the truth, but had pleasure in unrighteousness. 2 Thessalonians 2:12

That thou mayest give him rest from the days of adversity, until the pit be digged for the wicked. Psalms 94:13

> *Life is too short and hell is too hot to play games with your eternal future.*

Nay, ye do wrong, and defraud, and that your brethren. Know ye not that the unrighteous shall not inherit the kingdom of God? Be not deceived: neither fornicators, nor idolaters, nor adulterers, nor effeminate, nor abusers of themselves with mankind, Nor thieves, nor covetous, nor drunkards, nor revilers, nor extortioners, shall inherit the kingdom of God.
1 Corinthians 6:8-10

Envyings, murders, drunkenness, revellings, and such like: of the which I tell you before, as I have also told you in time past, that they which do such things shall not inherit the kingdom of God. Galatians 5:21

Having damnation, because they have cast off their first faith.
1 Timothy 5:12

3. How Serious is Hell?

And if thine eye offend thee, pluck it out, and cast it from thee: it is better for thee to enter into life with one eye, rather than having two eyes to be cast into hell fire. Matthew 18:9

And if thy right eye offend thee, pluck it out, and cast it from thee: for it is profitable for thee that one of thy members should perish, and not that thy whole body should be cast into hell. And if thy right hand offend thee, cut if off, and cast it from thee: for it is profitable for thee that one of thy members should perish, and not that thy whole body should be cast into hell. Matthew 5:29-30

And if thy hand offend thee, cut it off: it is better for thee to enter into life maimed, than having two hands to go into hell, into the fire that never shall be quenched: Where their worm dieth not, and the fire is not quenched. And if thy foot offend thee, cut it off: it is better for thee to enter halt into life, than having two feet to be cast into hell, into the fire that never shall be quenched: Where their worm dieth not, and the fire is not quenched. And if thine eye offend thee, pluck it out: it is better for thee to enter into the kingdom of God with one eye, than having two eyes to be cast into hell fire: Where their worm dieth not, and the fire is not quenched. Mark 9:43-48

4. Example of Hell

And there was a certain beggar named Lazarus, which was laid at his gate, full of sores, And desiring to be fed with the crumbs which fell from the rich man's table: moreover the dogs came and licked his sores. And it came to pass, that the beggar died, and was carried by the angels into Abraham's bosom: the rich man also died, and was buried; And in hell he lift up his eyes, being in torments, and seeth Abraham afar off, and Lazarus in his bosom. And he cried and said, Father Abraham, have mercy on me, and send Lazarus, that he may dip the tip of his finger in water, and cool my tongue; for I am tormented in this flame. But Abraham said, Son, remember that thou in thy lifetime receivedst thy good things, and likewise Lazarus evil things: but now he is comforted, and thou art tormented. And beside all this, between us and you there is a great gulf fixed: so that they which would pass from hence to you cannot; neither can they pass to us, that would come from thence. Then he said, I pray thee therefore, father, that thou wouldest send him to my father's house: For I have five brethren; that he may testify unto them, lest they also come into this place of torment. Abraham saith unto him, They have Moses and the prophets; let them hear them. And he said, Nay, father Abraham: but if one went unto them from the dead, they will repent. And he said unto him, If they hear not Moses and the prophets, neither will they be persuaded, though one rose from the dead. Luke 16:20-31

5. What is Hell Like?

And he opened the bottomless pit; and there arose a smoke out of the pit, as the smoke of a great furnace; and the sun and the air were darkened by reason of the smoke of the pit. Revelation 9:2

And the devil that deceived them was cast into the lake of fire and brimstone, where the beast and the false prophet are, and shall be tormented day and night for ever and ever. Revelation 20:10

As for thee also, by the blood of thy covenant I have sent forth thy prisoners out of the pit wherein is no water. Zechariah 9:11

The sinners in Zion are afraid; fearfulness hath surprised the hypocrites. Who among us shall dwell with the devouring fire: who among us shall dwell with everlasting burnings? Isaiah 33:14

Where their worm dieth not, and the fire is not quenched. Mark 9:48

6. Different Levels of Punishment in Hell

Woe unto you, scribes and Pharisees, hypocrites! for ye devour widows' houses, and for a pretence make long prayer: therefore ye shall receive the greater damnation. Matthew 23:14

But and if that servant say in his heart, My lord delayeth his coming; and shall begin to beat the menservants and maidens, and to eat and drink, and to be drunken; The lord of that servant will come in a day when he looketh not for him, and at an hour when he is not aware, and will cut him in sunder, and will appoint him his portion with the unbelievers. And that servant, which knew his lord's will, and prepared not himself, neither did according to his will, shall be beaten with many stripes. But he that knew not, and did commit things worthy of stripes, shall be beaten with few stripes. For unto whomsoever much is given, of him shall be much required: and to whom men have committed much, of him they will ask the more. Luke 12:45-48

7. Location of Hell

When I shall bring thee down with them that descend into the pit, with the people of old time, and shall set thee in the low parts of the earth, in places desolate of old, with them that go down to the pit, that thou be not inhabited; and I shall set glory in the land of the living; I will make thee a terror, and thou shalt be no more: though thou be sought for, yet shalt thou never be found again, saith the Lord God. Ezekiel 26:20-21

I made the nations to shake at the sound of his fall, when I cast him down to hell with them that descend into the pit: and all the trees of Eden, the choice and best of Lebanon, all that drink water, shall be comforted in the nether parts of the earth. Ezekiel 31:16

But he knoweth not that the dead are there; and that her guests are in the depths of hell. Proverbs 9:18

The way of life is above to the wise, that he may depart from hell beneath. Proverbs 15:24

Therefore hell hath enlarged herself, and opened her mouth without measure: and their glory, and their multitude, and their pomp, and he that rejoiceth, shall descend into it. Isaiah 5:14

Wherefore he saith, When he ascended up on high, he led captivity captive, and gave gifts unto men. Now that he ascended, what is it but that he also descended first into the lower parts of the earth? He that descended is the same also that ascended up far above all heavens, that he might fill all things. Ephesians 4:8-10

8. Hell is a Bottomless Pit

And the fifth angel sounded, and I saw a star fall from heaven unto the earth: and to him was given the key of the bottomless pit. And he opened the bottomless pit; and there arose a smoke out of the pit, as the smoke of a great furnace; and the sun and the air were darkened by reason of the smoke of the pit. Revelation 9:1-2

And they had a king over them, which is the angel of the bottomless pit, whose name in the Hebrew tongue is Abaddon, but in the Greek tongue hath his name Apollyon. Revelation 9:11

And when they shall have finished their testimony, the beast that ascendeth out of the bottomless pit shall make war against them, and shall overcome them, and kill them. Revelation 11:7

And I saw an angel come down from heaven, having the key of the bottomless pit and a great chain in his hand. And he laid hold on the dragon, that old serpent, which is the Devil, and Satan, and bound him a thousand years, And cast him into the bottomless pit, and shut him up, and set a seal upon him, that he should deceive the nations no more, till the thousand years should be fulfilled: and after that he must be loosed a little season. Revelation 20:1-3

PRAYER

Let us therefore come boldly unto the throne of grace, that we may obtain mercy, and find grace to help in time of need. Hebrews 4:16

Having therefore, brethren, boldness to enter into the holiest by the blood of Jesus. Hebrews 10:19

If ye then, being evil, know how to give good gifts unto your children, how much more shall your Father which is in heaven give good things to them that ask him? Matthew 7:11

Ask, and it shall be given you; seek, and ye shall find; knock, and it shall be opened unto you: For every one that asketh receiveth; and he that seeketh findeth; and to him that knocketh it shall be opened. Or what man is there of you, whom if his son ask bread, will he give him a stone? Or if he ask a fish, will he give him a serpent? If ye then, being evil, know how to give good gifts unto your children, how much more shall your Father which is in heaven give good things to them that ask him?
Matthew 7:7-11

Prayer moves the hand which moves the world. - John A. Wallace

Praying in the Name of Jesus

Again I say unto you, That if two of you shall agree on earth as touching any thing that they shall ask, it shall be done for them of my Father which is in heaven. For where two or three are gathered together in my name, there am I in the midst of them. Matthew 18:19-20

And whatsoever ye shall ask in my name, that will I do, that the Father may be glorified in the Son. If ye shall ask any thing in my name, I will do it. John 14:13-14

Ye have not chosen me, but I have chosen you, and ordained you, that ye should go and bring forth fruit, and that your fruit should remain: that

whatsoever ye shall ask of the Father in my name, he may give it you.
John 15:16

And in that day ye shall ask me nothing. Verily, verily, I say unto you, Whatsoever ye shall ask the Father in my name, he will give it you. Hitherto have ye asked nothing in my name: ask, and ye shall receive, that your joy may be full. John 16:23-24

At that day ye shall ask in my name: and I say not unto you, that I will pray the Father for you. John 16:26

Is any sick among you? let him call for the elders of the church; and let them pray over him, anointing him with oil in the name of the Lord.
James 5:14

The Lord's Prayer

After this manner therefore pray ye: Our Father which art in heaven, Hallowed be thy name. Thy kingdom come. Thy will be done in earth, as it is in heaven. Give us this day our daily bread. And forgive us our debts, as we forgive our debtors. And lead us not into temptation, but deliver us from evil: For thine is the kingdom, and the power, and the glory, for ever. Amen. Matthew 6:9-13

God Hears Your Prayers

Am I a God at hand, saith the Lord, and not a God afar off?
Jeremiah 23:23

But know that the Lord hath set apart him that is godly for himself: the Lord will hear when I call unto him. Psalms 4:3

My voice shalt thou hear in the morning, O Lord; in the morning will I direct my prayer unto thee, and will look up. Psalms 5:3

I waited patiently for the Lord; and he inclined unto me, and heard my cry. Psalms 40:1

Evening, and morning, and at noon, will I pray, and cry aloud: and he shall hear my voice. Psalms 55:17

The Lord is far from the wicked: but he heareth the prayer of the righteous. Proverbs 15:29

The eyes of the Lord are upon the righteous, and his ears are open unto their cry. Psalms 34:15

Therefore I will look unto the Lord; I will wait for the God of my salvation: my God will hear me. Micah 7:7

And this is the confidence that we have in him, that, if we ask any thing according to his will, he heareth us: And if we know that he hear us, whatsoever we ask, we know that we have the petitions that we desired of him. 1 John 5:14-15

Hindrances to Prayer

If I regard iniquity in my heart, the Lord will not hear me. Psalms 66:18

Whoso stoppeth his ears at the cry of the poor, he also shall cry himself, but shall not be heard. Proverbs 21:13

He that turneth away his ear from hearing the law, even his prayer shall be abomination. Proverbs 28:9

Behold, the Lord's hand is not shortened, that it cannot save; neither his ear heavy, that it cannot hear: But your iniquities have separated between you and your God, and your sins have hid his face from you, that he will not hear. Isaiah 59:1-2

Then shall they cry unto the Lord, but he will not hear them: he will even hide his face from them at that time, as they have behaved themselves ill in their doings. Micah 3:4

Ye lust, and have not: ye kill, and desire to have, and cannot obtain: ye fight and war, yet ye have not, because ye ask not. Ye ask, and receive not, because ye ask amiss, that ye may consume it upon your lusts.
James 4:2-3

Likewise, ye husbands, dwell with them according to knowledge, giving honour unto the wife, as unto the weaker vessel, and as being heirs together of the grace of life; that your prayers be not hindered. 1 Peter 3:7

For the eyes of the Lord are over the righteous, and his ears are open unto their prayers: but the face of the Lord is against them that do evil. 1 Peter 3:12

Praying With the Right Attitude and Motives

And when thou prayest, thou shalt not be as the hypocrites are: for they love to pray standing in the synagogues and in the corners of the streets, that they may be seen of men. Verily I say unto you, They have their reward. But thou, when thou prayest, enter into thy closet, and when thou hast shut thy door, pray to thy Father which is in secret; and thy

Father which seeth in secret shall reward thee openly. But when ye pray, use not vain repetitions, as the heathen do: for they think that they shall be heard for their much speaking. Be not ye therefore like unto them: for your Father knoweth what things ye have need of, before ye ask him.
Matthew 6:5-8

Praying only when you are in trouble or when you need something; being thankful only when you get your way; and ignoring God when things are going great, is a terrible way to treat God!

For if ye forgive men their trespasses, your heavenly Father will also forgive you: But if ye forgive not men their trespasses, neither will your Father forgive your trespasses. Moreover when ye fast, be not, as the hypocrites, of a sad countenance: for they disfigure their faces, that they may appear unto men to fast. Verily I say unto you, They have their reward. But thou, when thou fastest, anoint thine head, and wash thy face; That thou appear not unto men to fast, but unto thy Father which is in secret: and thy Father, which seeth in secret, shall reward thee openly.
Matthew 6:14-18

And when ye stand praying, forgive, if ye have ought against any: that your Father also which is in heaven may forgive you your trespasses.
Mark 11:25

Different Kinds of Prayer

I cried to thee, O Lord; and unto the Lord I made supplication.
Psalms 30:8

I will offer to thee the sacrifice of thanksgiving, and will call upon the name of the Lord. Psalms 116:17

And I set my face unto the Lord God, to seek by prayer and supplication, with fasting, and sackcloth, and ashes. Daniel 9:3

Praying always with all prayer and supplication in the Spirit, and watching thereunto with all perseverance and supplication for all saints.
Ephesians 6:18

I exhort therefore, that, first of all, supplications, prayers, intercessions, and giving of thanks, be made for all men. 1 Timothy 2:1

The measure of any Christian is his prayer life. - Vance Havner

Prayer of Agreement

How should one chase a thousand, and two put ten thousand to flight.
Deuteronomy 32:30

This is the third time I am coming to you. In the mouth of two or three witnesses shall every word be established. 2 Corinthians 13:1

Verily I say unto you, Whatsoever ye shall bind on earth shall be bound in heaven: and whatsoever ye shall loose on earth shall be loosed in heaven. Again I say unto you, That if two of you shall agree on earth as touching any thing that they shall ask, it shall be done for them of my Father which is in heaven. Matthew 18:18-19

Praying in Faith

Jesus answered and said unto them, Verily I say unto you, If ye have faith, and doubt not, ye shall not only do this which is done to the fig tree, but also if ye shall say unto this mountain, Be thou removed, and be thou cast into the sea; it shall be done. And all things, whatsoever ye shall ask in prayer, believing, ye shall receive. Matthew 21:21-22

Jesus said unto him, If thou canst believe, all things are possible to him that believeth. And straightway the father of the child cried out, and said with tears, Lord, I believe; help thou mine unbelief. Mark 9:23-24

Therefore I say unto you, What things soever ye desire, when ye pray, believe that ye receive them, and ye shall have them. Mark 11:24

And the prayer of faith shall save the sick, and the Lord shall raise him up; and if he have committed sins, they shall be forgiven him James 5:15

Waiting on God in Prayer

But they that wait upon the Lord shall renew their strength; they shall mount up with wings as eagles; they shall run, and not be weary; and they shall walk, and not faint. Isaiah 40:31

Call unto me, and I will answer thee, and shew thee great and mighty things, which thou knowest not. Jeremiah 33:3

Praying in the Holy Spirit

Likewise the Spirit also helpeth our infirmities: for we know not what we should pray for as we ought: but the Spirit itself maketh intercession for us with groanings which cannot be uttered. And he that searcheth the hearts knoweth what is the mind of the Spirit, because he maketh intercession for the saints according to the will of God. Romans 8:26-27

Praying in the Spirit guarantees perfect prayer that is directed by the Holy Spirit; untouched by doubt and fear of the mind; and impossible for the devil to understand or hinder.

For if I pray in an unknown tongue, my spirit prayeth, but my understanding is unfruitful. What is it then? I will pray with the spirit, and I will pray with the understanding also: I will sing with the spirit, and I will sing with the understanding also. 1 Corinthians 14:14-15

But ye, beloved, building up yourselves on your most holy faith, praying in the Holy Ghost. Jude 1:20

Intercessory Prayer

And he saw that there was no man, and wondered that there was no intercessor: therefore his arm brought salvation unto him; and his righteousness, it sustained him. Isaiah 59:16

And I sought for a man among them, that should make up the hedge, and stand in the gap before me for the land, that I should not destroy it: but I found none. Ezekiel 22:30

But I have prayed for thee, that thy faith fail not: and when thou art converted, strengthen thy brethren. Luke 22:32

At that day ye shall ask in my name: and I say not unto you, that I will pray the Father for you. John 16:26

I pray for them: I pray not for the world, but for them which thou hast given me; for they are thine. John 17:9

Neither pray I for these alone, but for them also which shall believe on me through their word. John 17:20

Brethren, my heart's desire and prayer to God for Israel is, that they might be saved. Romans 10:1

Now I beseech you, brethren, for the Lord Jesus Christ's sake, and for the love of the Spirit, that ye strive together with me in your prayers to God for me. Romans 15:30

For this cause we also, since the day we heard it, do not cease to pray for you, and to desire that ye might be filled with the knowledge of his will in all wisdom and spiritual understanding. Colossians 1:9

Withal praying also for us, that God would open unto us a door of utterance, to speak the mystery of Christ, for which I am also in bonds.
Colossians 4:3

Wherefore also we pray always for you, that our God would count you worthy of this calling, and fulfil all the good pleasure of his goodness, and the work of faith with power. 2 Thessalonians 1:11

Finally, brethren, pray for us, that the word of the Lord may have free course, and be glorified, even as it is with you: And that we may be delivered from unreasonable and wicked men: for all men have not faith.
2 Thessalonians 3:1-2

Confess your faults one to another, and pray one for another, that ye may be healed. The effectual fervent prayer of a righteous man availeth much.
James 5:16

Examples of Prayer Warriors

And she was a widow of about fourscore and four years, which departed not from the temple, but served God with fastings and prayers night and day. Luke 2:37

And it came to pass in those days, that he went out into a mountain to pray, and continued all night in prayer to God. Luke 6:12

And suddenly there came a sound from heaven as of a rushing mighty wind, and it filled all the house where they were sitting. And there appeared unto them cloven tongues like as of fire, and it sat upon each of them. And they were all filled with the Holy Ghost, and began to speak with other tongues, as the Spirit gave them utterance. Acts 2:2-4

Praying Continuously

Watch and pray, that ye enter not into temptation: the spirit indeed is willing, but the flesh is weak. Matthew 26:41

And he spake a parable unto them to this end, that men ought always to pray, and not to faint. Luke 18:1

Watch ye therefore, and pray always, that ye may be accounted worthy to escape all these things that shall come to pass, and to stand before the Son of man. Luke 21:36

And said unto them, Why sleep ye? rise and pray, lest ye enter into temptation. Luke 22:46

Continue in prayer, and watch in the same with thanksgiving;
Colossians 4:2

Pray without ceasing. 1 Thessalonians 5:17

But the end of all things is at hand: be ye therefore sober, and watch unto prayer. 1 Peter 4:7

> *To be a Christian without prayer is no more possible than to be alive without breathing. - Martin Luther*

Life's Challenges

Fear

Fear not, little flock; for it is your Father's good pleasure to give you the kingdom. Luke 12:32

Peace I leave with you, my peace I give unto you: not as the world giveth, give I unto you. Let not your heart be troubled, neither let it be afraid.
John 14:27

1. Fear is an evil spirit from satan

For ye have not received the spirit of bondage again to fear; but ye have received the Spirit of adoption, whereby we cry, Abba, Father.
Romans 8:15

For God hath not given us the spirit of fear; but of power, and of love, and of a sound mind. 2 Timothy 1:7

There is no fear in love; but perfect love casteth out fear: because fear hath torment. He that feareth is not made perfect in love. 1 John 4:18

2. Fear Brings the Problem to You

The fear of the wicked, it shall come upon him: but the desire of the righteous shall be granted. Proverbs 10:24

The fear of man bringeth a snare: but whoso putteth his trust in the Lord shall be safe. Proverbs 29:25

For the thing which I greatly feared is come upon me, and that which I was afraid of is come unto me. Job 3:25

3. Don't Fear! God is with You

And he answered, Fear not: for they that be with us are more than they that be with them. 2 Kings 6:16

For I the Lord thy God will hold thy right hand, saying unto thee, Fear not; I will help thee. Isaiah 41:13

Yea, though I walk through the valley of the shadow of death, I will fear no evil: for thou art with me; thy rod and thy staff they comfort me.
Psalms 23:4

The Lord is my light and my salvation; whom shall I fear? the Lord is the strength of my life; of whom shall I be afraid? Psalms 27:1

Though an host should encamp against me, my heart shall not fear: though war should rise against me, in this will I be confident. Psalms 27:3

God is our refuge and strength, a very present help in trouble.
Psalms 46:1

But whoso hearkeneth unto me shall dwell safely, and shall be quiet from fear of evil. Proverbs 1:33

When thou liest down, thou shalt not be afraid: yea, thou shalt lie down, and thy sleep shall be sweet. Be not afraid of sudden fear, neither of the desolation of the wicked, when it cometh. For the Lord shall be thy confidence, and shall keep thy foot from being taken. Proverbs 3:24-26

And it shall come to pass in the day that the Lord shall give thee rest from thy sorrow, and from thy fear, and from the hard bondage wherein thou wast made to serve. Isaiah 14:3

When thou passest through the waters, I will be with thee; and through the rivers, they shall not overflow thee: when thou walkest through the fire, thou shalt not be burned; neither shall the flame kindle upon thee.
Isaiah 43:2

Enemies

For the Lord your God is he that goeth with you, to fight for you against your enemies, to save you. Deuteronomy 20:4

The Lord shall cause thine enemies that rise up against thee to be smitten before thy face: they shall come out against thee one way, and flee before thee seven ways. Deuteronomy 28:7

And he answered, Fear not: for they that be with us are more than they that be with them. 2 Kings 6:16

But the Lord your God ye shall fear; and he shall deliver you out of the hand of all your enemies. 2 Kings 17:39

In famine he shall redeem thee from death: and in war from the power of the sword. Job 5:20

They that hate thee shall be clothed with shame; and the dwelling place of the wicked shall come to nought. Job 8:22

For in the time of trouble he shall hide me in his pavilion: in the secret of his tabernacle shall he hide me; he shall set me up upon a rock. And now shall mine head be lifted up above mine enemies round about me: therefore will I offer in his tabernacle sacrifices of joy; I will sing, yea, I will sing praises unto the Lord. Psalms 27:5-6

And the Lord shall help them and deliver them: he shall deliver them from the wicked, and save them, because they trust in him. Psalms 37:40

Through God we shall do valiantly: for he it is that shall tread down our enemies. Psalms 60:12

Ye that love the Lord, hate evil: he preserveth the souls of his saints; he delivereth them out of the hand of the wicked. Psalms 97:10

His heart is established, he shall not be afraid, until he see his desire upon his enemies. Psalms 112:8

The Lord taketh my part with them that help me: therefore shall I see my desire upon them that hate me. Psalms 118:7

For the rod of the wicked shall not rest upon the lot of the righteous; lest the righteous put forth their hands unto iniquity. Psalms 125:3

Be not afraid of sudden fear, neither of the desolation of the wicked, when it cometh. For the Lord shall be thy confidence, and shall keep thy foot from being taken. Proverbs 3:25-26

When a man's ways please the Lord, he maketh even his enemies to be at peace with him. Proverbs 16:7

Behold, all they that were incensed against thee shall be ashamed and confounded: they shall be as nothing; and they that strive with thee shall perish. Thou shalt seek them, and shalt not find them, even them that contended with thee: they that war against thee shall be as nothing, and as a thing of nought. Isaiah 41:11-12

Behold, they shall surely gather together, but not by me: whosoever shall gather together against thee shall fall for thy sake. Isaiah 54:15

But I will deliver thee in that day, saith the Lord: and thou shalt not be given into the hand of the men of whom thou art afraid. For I will surely

deliver thee, and thou shalt not fall by the sword, but thy life shall be for a prey unto thee: because thou hast put thy trust in me, saith the Lord.
Jeremiah 39:17-18

That we should be saved from our enemies, and from the hand of all that hate us. Luke 1:71

That he would grant unto us, that we being delivered out of the hand of our enemies might serve him without fear. Luke 1:74

And shall not God avenge his own elect, which cry day and night unto him, though he bear long with them? Luke 18:7

For I am with thee, and no man shall set on thee to hurt thee: for I have much people in this city. Acts 18:10

1. How to Treat Your Enemies

If thine enemy be hungry, give him bread to eat; and if he be thirsty, give him water to drink. Proverbs 25:21

But I say unto you, Love your enemies, bless them that curse you, do good to them that hate you, and pray for them which despitefully use you, and persecute you. Matthew 5:44

But I say unto you which hear, Love your enemies, do good to them which hate you, **Bless** them that curse you, and pray for them which despitefully use you. Luke 6:27-28

But love ye your enemies, and do good, and lend, hoping for nothing again; and your reward shall be great, and ye shall be the children of the Highest: for he is kind unto the unthankful and to the evil. **Be** ye therefore merciful, as your Father also is merciful. Luke 6:35-36

Bless them which persecute you: bless, and curse not. Romans 12:14

Love worketh no ill to his neighbour: therefore love is the fulfilling of the law. Romans 13:10

Therefore if thine enemy hunger, feed him; if he thirst, give him drink: for in so doing thou shalt heap coals of fire on his head. Romans 12:20

And labour, working with our own hands: being reviled, we bless; being persecuted, we suffer it. 1 Corinthians 4:12

2. Do Not Rejoice When Your Enemies Suffer

Whoso mocketh the poor reproacheth his Maker: and he that is glad at calamities shall not be unpunished. Proverbs 17:5

Say not thou, I will recompense evil; but wait on the Lord, and he shall save thee. Proverbs 20:22

Rejoice not when thine enemy falleth, and let not thine heart be glad when he stumbleth: Proverbs 24:17

Revenge

1. Revenge is God's Job

For we know him that hath said, Vengeance belongeth unto me, I will recompense, saith the Lord. And again, The Lord shall judge his people. Hebrews 10:30

To me belongeth vengeance, and recompence; their foot shall slide in due time: for the day of their calamity is at hand, and the things that shall come upon them make haste. Deuteronomy 32:35

O Lord God, to whom vengeance belongeth; O God, to whom vengeance belongeth, shew thyself. Psalms 94:1

Therefore thus saith the Lord; Behold, I will plead thy cause, and take vengeance for thee; and I will dry up her sea, and make her springs dry. Jeremiah 51:36

That no man go beyond and defraud his brother in any matter: because that the Lord is the avenger of all such, as we also have forewarned you and testified. 1 Thessalonians 4:6

2. Do Not Seek Revenge

Whoso rewardeth evil for good, evil shall not depart from his house. Proverbs 17:13

And having in a readiness to revenge all disobedience, when your obedience is fulfilled. 2 Corinthians 10:6

Whoso rewardeth evil for good, evil shall not depart from his house. Proverbs 17:13

The Lord judge between me and thee, and the Lord avenge me of thee: but mine hand shall not be upon thee. 1 Samuel 24:12

Say not, I will do so to him as he hath done to me: I will render to the man according to his work. Proverbs 24:29

Recompense to no man evil for evil. Provide things honest in the sight of all men. Romans 12:17

Dearly beloved, avenge not yourselves, but rather give place unto wrath: for it is written, Vengeance is mine; I will repay, saith the Lord.
Romans 12:19

Revenge is often like biting a dog because the dog bit you.- Austin O'Malley

Thou shalt not avenge, nor bear any grudge against the children of thy people, but thou shalt love thy neighbour as thyself: I am the Lord.
Leviticus 19:18

See that none render evil for evil unto any man; but ever follow that which is good, both among yourselves, and to all men.
1 Thessalonians 5:15

Persecution

He that hideth hatred with lying lips, and he that uttereth a slander, is a fool. Proverbs 10:18

Blessed are they which are persecuted for righteousness' sake: for theirs is the kingdom of heaven. **B**lessed are ye, when men shall revile you, and persecute you, and shall say all manner of evil against you falsely, for my sake. **R**ejoice, and be exceeding glad: for great is your reward in heaven: for so persecuted they the prophets which were before you.
Matthew 5:10-12

But I say unto you, Love your enemies, bless them that curse you, do good to them that hate you, and pray for them which despitefully use you, and persecute you; Matthew 5:44

But he shall receive an hundredfold now in this time, houses, and brethren, and sisters, and mothers, and children, and lands, with persecutions; and in the world to come eternal life. Mark 10:30

When you are living right and doing something for God, you will be criticized by three types of people: those who are jealous, those who are ill-informed, and those who are influenced by or filled with the devil.

But before all these, they shall lay their hands on you, and persecute you, delivering you up to the synagogues, and into prisons, being brought before kings and rulers for my name's sake. Luke 21:12

Remember the word that I said unto you, The servant is not greater than his lord. If they have persecuted me, they will also persecute you; if they have kept my saying, they will keep yours also. John 15:20

Who shall separate us from the love of Christ? shall tribulation, or distress, or persecution, or famine, or nakedness, or peril, or sword?
Romans 8:35

Bless them which persecute you: bless, and curse not. Romans 12:14

And labour, working with our own hands: being reviled, we bless; being persecuted, we suffer it: 1 Corinthians 4:12

Persecuted, but not forsaken; cast down, but not destroyed;
2 Corinthians 4:9

Therefore I take pleasure in infirmities, in reproaches, in necessities, in persecutions, in distresses for Christ's sake: for when I am weak, then am I strong. 2 Corinthians 12:10

But as then he that was born after the flesh persecuted him that was born after the Spirit, even so it is now. Galatians 4:29

So that we ourselves glory in you in the churches of God for your patience and faith in all your persecutions and tribulations that ye endure:
2 Thessalonians 1:4

> *We Christians are not called to respond to criticism; we are called to respond to God. - John Mason*

Persecutions, afflictions, which came unto me at Antioch, at Iconium, at Lystra; what persecutions I endured: but out of them all the Lord delivered me. 2 Timothy 3:11

Yea, and all that will live godly in Christ Jesus shall suffer persecution.
2 Timothy 3:12

Loneliness

And, behold, I am with thee, and will keep thee in all places whither thou goest, and will bring thee again into this land; for I will not leave thee, until I have done that which I have spoken to thee of. Genesis 28:15

Be strong and of a good courage, fear not, nor be afraid of them: for the Lord thy God, he it is that doth go with thee; he will not fail thee, nor forsake thee. Deuteronomy 31:6

The Lord also will be a refuge for the oppressed, a refuge in times of trouble. And they that know thy name will put their trust in thee: for thou, Lord, hast not forsaken them that seek thee. Psalms 9:9-10

I will be glad and rejoice in thy mercy: for thou hast considered my trouble; thou hast known my soul in adversities. Psalms 31:7

But I am poor and needy; yet the Lord thinketh upon me: thou art my help and my deliverer; make no tarrying, O my God. Psalms 40:17

God is our refuge and strength, a very present help in trouble.
Psalms 46:1

Cast thy burden upon the Lord, and he shall sustain thee: he shall never suffer the righteous to be moved. Psalms 55:22

For the people shall dwell in Zion at Jerusalem: thou shalt weep no more: he will be very gracious unto thee at the voice of thy cry; when he shall hear it, he will answer thee. Isaiah 30:19

Fear thou not; for I am with thee: be not dismayed; for I am thy God: I will strengthen thee; yea, I will help thee; yea, I will uphold thee with the right hand of my righteousness. Isaiah 41:10

Then shalt thou call, and the Lord shall answer; thou shalt cry, and he shall say, Here I am. If thou take away from the midst of thee the yoke, the putting forth of the finger, and speaking vanity. Isaiah 58:9

In all their affliction he was afflicted, and the angel of his presence saved them: in his love and in his pity he redeemed them; and he bare them, and carried them all the days of old. Isaiah 63:9

Am I a God at hand, saith the Lord, and not a God afar off?
Jeremiah 23:23

The Lord is good, a strong hold in the day of trouble; and he knoweth them that trust in him. Nahum 1:7

Teaching them to observe all things whatsoever I have commanded you: and, lo, I am with you alway, even unto the end of the world. Amen.
Matthew 28:20

Let not your heart be troubled: ye believe in God, believe also in me.
John 14:1

I will not leave you comfortless: I will come to you. John 14:18

Who shall separate us from the love of Christ? shall tribulation, or distress, or persecution, or famine, or nakedness, or peril, or sword? As it is written, For thy sake we are killed all the day long; we are accounted as sheep for the slaughter. Nay, in all these things we are more than conquerors through him that loved us. For I am persuaded, that neither death, nor life, nor angels, nor principalities, nor powers, nor things present, nor things to come, Nor height, nor depth, nor any other creature, shall be able to separate us from the love of God, which is in Christ Jesus our Lord. Romans 8:35-39

Let your conversation be without covetousness; and be content with such things as ye have: for he hath said, I will never leave thee, nor forsake thee. Hebrews 13:5

Casting all your care upon him; for he careth for you. 1 Peter 5:7

Ye are of God, little children, and have overcome them: because greater is he that is in you, than he that is in the world. 1 John 4:4

Temptation

And lead us not into temptation, but deliver us from evil: For thine is the kingdom, and the power, and the glory, for ever. Amen. Matthew 6:13

Watch and pray, that ye enter not into temptation: the spirit indeed is willing, but the flesh is weak. Matthew 26:41

Watch ye and pray, lest ye enter into temptation. The spirit truly is ready, but the flesh is weak. Mark 14:38

And Jesus answering said unto him, It is said, Thou shalt not tempt the Lord thy God. And when the devil had ended all the temptation, he departed from him for a season. Luke 4:12-13

And when he was at the place, he said unto them, Pray that ye enter not into temptation. Luke 22:40

And said unto them, Why sleep ye? rise and pray, lest ye enter into temptation. Luke 22:46

> *Temptations either tests your ability to say no, or it tests your conscience to promptly repent.*

Neither let us tempt Christ, as some of them also tempted, and were destroyed of serpents. 1 Corinthians 10:9

There hath no temptation taken you but such as is common to man: but God is faithful, who will not suffer you to be tempted above that ye are able; but will with the temptation also make a way to escape, that ye may be able to bear it. 1 Corinthians 10:13

And my temptation which was in my flesh ye despised not, nor rejected; but received me as an angel of God, even as Christ Jesus. Galatians 4:14

Brethren, if a man be overtaken in a fault, ye which are spiritual, restore such an one in the spirit of meekness; considering thyself, lest thou also be tempted. Galatians 6:1

For this cause, when I could no longer forbear, I sent to know your faith, lest by some means the tempter have tempted you, and our labour be in vain. 1 Thessalonians 3:5

But they that will be rich fall into temptation and a snare, and into many foolish and hurtful lusts, which drown men in destruction and perdition.
1 Timothy 6:9

For in that he himself hath suffered being tempted, he is able to succour them that are tempted. Hebrews 2:18

For we have not an high priest which cannot be touched with the feeling of our infirmities; but was in all points tempted like as we are, yet without sin. Hebrews 4:15

My brethren, count it all joy when ye fall into divers temptations.
James 1:2

Blessed is the man that endureth temptation: for when he is tried, he shall receive the crown of life, which the Lord hath promised to them that love him. Let no man say when he is tempted, I am tempted of God: for God cannot be tempted with evil, neither tempteth he any man: But every man is tempted, when he is drawn away of his own lust, and enticed. James 1:12-14

Wherein ye greatly rejoice, though now for a season, if need be, ye are in heaviness through manifold temptations. 1 Peter 1:6

The Lord knoweth how to deliver the godly out of temptations, and to reserve the unjust unto the day of judgment to be punished. 2 Peter 2:9

Because thou hast kept the word of my patience, I also will keep thee from the hour of temptation, which shall come upon all the world, to try them that dwell upon the earth. Revelation 3:10

If you would master temptation, you must first let Christ master you. - Anonymous

Stress and Depression

He shall deliver thee in six troubles: yea, in seven there shall no evil touch thee. Job 5:19

Life's Challenges

The Lord also will be a refuge for the oppressed, a refuge in times of trouble. Psalms 9:9

For his anger endureth but a moment; in his favour is life: weeping may endure for a night, but joy cometh in the morning. Psalms 30:5

Be of good courage, and he shall strengthen your heart, all ye that hope in the Lord. Psalms 31:24

Many are the afflictions of the righteous: but the Lord delivereth him out of them all. Psalms 34:19

That ye be not soon shaken in mind, or be troubled, neither by spirit, nor by word, nor by letter as from us, as that the day of Christ is at hand.
2 Thessalonians 2:2

For this shall every one that is godly pray unto thee in a time when thou mayest be found: surely in the floods of great waters they shall not come nigh unto him. Thou art my hiding place; thou shalt preserve me from trouble; thou shalt compass me about with songs of deliverance. Selah.
Psalms 32:6-7

Though he fall, he shall not be utterly cast down: for the Lord upholdeth him with his hand. Psalms 37:24

But the salvation of the righteous is of the Lord: he is their strength in the time of trouble. Psalms 37:39

Though I walk in the midst of trouble, thou wilt revive me: thou shalt stretch forth thine hand against the wrath of mine enemies, and thy right hand shall save me. Psalms 138:7

He healeth the broken in heart, and bindeth up their wounds.
Psalms 147:3

The wicked is snared by the transgression of his lips: but the just shall come out of trouble. Proverbs 12:13

There shall no evil happen to the just: but the wicked shall be filled with mischief. Proverbs 12:21

We should glory in our infirmities but not glorify them. - Vance Havner

Therefore the redeemed of the Lord shall return, and come with singing unto Zion; and everlasting joy shall be upon their head: they shall obtain gladness and joy; and sorrow and mourning shall flee away. Isaiah 51:11

The Lord is good, a strong hold in the day of trouble; and he knoweth them that trust in him. Nahum 1:7

And he spake a parable unto them to this end, that men ought always to pray, and not to faint. Luke 18:1

Let not your heart be troubled: ye believe in God, believe also in me.
John 14:1

I will not leave you comfortless: I will come to you. John 14:18

And we know that all things work together for good to them that love God, to them who are the called according to his purpose. Romans 8:28

For I reckon that the sufferings of this present time are not worthy to be compared with the glory which shall be revealed in us. Romans 8:18

For I am persuaded, that neither death, nor life, nor angels, nor principalities, nor powers, nor things present, nor things to come, Nor height, nor depth, nor any other creature, shall be able to separate us from the love of God, which is in Christ Jesus our Lord. Romans 8:38-39

There hath no temptation taken you but such as is common to man: but God is faithful, who will not suffer you to be tempted above that ye are able; but will with the temptation also make a way to escape, that ye may be able to bear it. 1 Corinthians 10:13

A Christian is like a teabag-he's not worth much until he's been through some hot water. - Anonymous

Blessed be God, even the Father of our Lord Jesus Christ, the Father of mercies, and the God of all comfort; Who comforteth us in all our tribulation, that we may be able to comfort them which are in any trouble, by the comfort wherewith we ourselves are comforted of God.
2 Corinthians 1:3-4

We are troubled on every side, yet not distressed; we are perplexed, but not in despair; Persecuted, but not forsaken; cast down, but not destroyed.
2 Corinthians 4:8-9

Wherefore seeing we also are compassed about with so great a cloud of witnesses, let us lay aside every weight, and the sin which doth so easily beset us, and let us run with patience the race that is set before us.
Hebrews 12:1

My brethren, count it all joy when ye fall into divers temptations; Knowing this, that the trying of your faith worketh patience. But let patience have her perfect work, that ye may be perfect and entire, wanting nothing. James 1:2-4

Wherefore also it is contained in the scripture, Behold, I lay in Sion a chief corner stone, elect, precious: and he that believeth on him shall not be confounded. 1 Peter 2:6

Beloved, think it not strange concerning the fiery trial which is to try you, as though some strange thing happened unto you: But rejoice, inasmuch as ye are partakers of Christ's sufferings; that, when his glory shall be revealed, ye may be glad also with exceeding joy. 1 Peter 4:12-13

> *All the tribulations of this life are but incidents on the road from Groans to Glory. - Vance Havner*

Casting all your care upon him; for he careth for you. 1 Peter 5:7

And God shall wipe away all tears from their eyes; and there shall be no more death, neither sorrow, nor crying, neither shall there be any more pain: for the former things are passed away. Revelation 21:4

Anxiety and Worry

Therefore I say unto you, Take no thought for your life, what ye shall eat, or what ye shall drink; nor yet for your body, what ye shall put on. Is not the life more than meat, and the body than raiment? Behold the fowls of the air: for they sow not, neither do they reap, nor gather into barns; yet your heavenly Father feedeth them. Are ye not much better than they? Which of you by taking thought can add one cubit unto his stature? And why take ye thought for raiment? Consider the lilies of the field, how they grow; they toil not, neither do they spin: And yet I say unto you, That even Solomon in all his glory was not arrayed like one of these. Wherefore, if God so clothe the grass of the field, which to day is, and to morrow is cast into the oven, shall he not much more clothe you, O ye of little faith? Therefore take no thought, saying, What shall we eat? or, What shall we drink? or, Wherewithal shall we be clothed? For after all these things do the Gentiles seek: for your heavenly Father knoweth that ye have need of all these things. But seek ye first the kingdom of God, and his righteousness; and all these things shall be added unto you. Take therefore no thought for the morrow: for the morrow shall take thought for the things of itself. Sufficient unto the day is the evil thereof.
Matthew 6:25-34

Be careful for nothing; but in every thing by prayer and supplication with thanksgiving let your requests be made known unto God.
Philippians 4:6

My brethren, count it all joy when ye fall into divers temptations; **Knowing** this, that the trying of your faith worketh patience. James 1:2-3

Casting all your care upon him; for he careth for you. 1 Peter 5:7

> *Worry is like a rocking chair. It keeps you going but you don't get anywhere. - Anonymous*

Your Mind

Renewing Your Mind

That ye be not soon shaken in mind, or be troubled, neither by spirit, nor by word, nor by letter as from us, as that the day of Christ is at hand.
2 Thessalonians 2:2

For God hath not given us the spirit of fear; but of power, and of love, and of a sound mind. 2 Timothy 1:7

Young men likewise exhort to be sober minded. Titus 2:6

Wherefore gird up the loins of your mind, be sober, and hope to the end for the grace that is to be brought unto you at the revelation of Jesus Christ. 1 Peter 1:13

He hath delivered my soul in peace from the battle that was against me: for there were many with me. Psalms 55:18

Focusing Your Mind on the Word of God

The law of the Lord is perfect, converting the soul: the testimony of the Lord is sure, making wise the simple. Psalms 19:7

When wisdom entereth into thine heart, and knowledge is pleasant unto thy soul. Proverbs 2:10

My son, let not them depart from thine eyes: keep sound wisdom and discretion: So shall they be life unto thy soul, and grace to thy neck.
Proverbs 3:21-22

Thus saith the Lord, Stand ye in the ways, and see, and ask for the old paths, where is the good way, and walk therein, and ye shall find rest for your souls. But they said, We will not walk therein. Jeremiah 6:16

And be not conformed to this world: but be ye transformed by the renewing of your mind, that ye may prove what is that good, and acceptable, and perfect, will of God. Romans 12:2

And be renewed in the spirit of your mind. Ephesians 4:23

This is the covenant that I will make with them after those days, saith the Lord, I will put my laws into their hearts, and in their minds will I write them. Hebrews 10:16

Wherefore lay apart all filthiness and superfluity of naughtiness, and receive with meekness the engrafted word, which is able to save your souls. James 1:21

This second epistle, beloved, I now write unto you; in both which I stir up your pure minds by way of remembrance: That ye may be mindful of the words which were spoken before by the holy prophets, and of the commandment of us the apostles of the Lord and Saviour. 2 Peter 3:1-2

For the word of God is quick, and powerful, and sharper than any twoedged sword, piercing even to the dividing asunder of soul and spirit, and of the joints and marrow, and is a discerner of the thoughts and intents of the heart. Hebrews 4:12

Focusing Your Mind on Jesus

Thou wilt keep him in perfect peace, whose mind is stayed on thee: because he trusteth in thee. Isaiah 26:3

Jesus said unto him, Thou shalt love the Lord thy God with all thy heart, and with all thy soul, and with all thy mind. Matthew 22:37

For who hath known the mind of the Lord, that he may instruct him? But we have the mind of Christ. 1 Corinthians 2:16

And the peace of God, which passeth all understanding, shall keep your hearts and minds through Christ Jesus. Philippians 4:7

Controlling Imaginations and Thoughts

I hate vain thoughts: but thy law do I love. Psalms 119:113

The thoughts of the righteous are right: but the counsels of the wicked are deceit. Proverbs 12:5

Commit thy works unto the Lord, and thy thoughts shall be established. Proverbs 16:3

The thought of foolishness is sin: and the scorner is an abomination to men. Proverbs 24:9

Your Mind

For the weapons of our warfare are not carnal, but mighty through God to the pulling down of strong holds; Casting down imaginations, and every high thing that exalteth itself against the knowledge of God, and bringing into captivity every thought to the obedience of Christ.
2 Corinthians 10:4-5

For to be carnally minded is death; but to be spiritually minded is life and peace. Because the carnal mind is enmity against God: for it is not subject to the law of God, neither indeed can be. Romans 8:6-7

Finally, brethren, whatsoever things are true, whatsoever things are honest, whatsoever things are just, whatsoever things are pure, whatsoever things are lovely, whatsoever things are of good report; if there be any virtue, and if there be any praise, think on these things. Philippians 4:8

Controlling Lust

Lust not after her beauty in thine heart; neither let her take thee with her eyelids. Proverbs 6:25

But I say unto you, That whosoever looketh on a woman to lust after her hath committed adultery with her already in his heart. Matthew 5:28

And the cares of this world, and the deceitfulness of riches, and the lusts of other things entering in, choke the word, and it becometh unfruitful.
Mark 4:19

Ye are of your father the devil, and the lusts of your father ye will do. He was a murderer from the beginning, and abode not in the truth, because there is no truth in him. When he speaketh a lie, he speaketh of his own: for he is a liar, and the father of it. John 8:44

Wherefore God also gave them up to uncleanness through the lusts of their own hearts, to dishonour their own bodies between themselves.
Romans 1:24

Let not sin therefore reign in your mortal body, that ye should obey it in the lusts thereof. Romans 6:12

But put ye on the Lord Jesus Christ, and make not provision for the flesh, to fulfil the lusts thereof. Romans 13:14

Now these things were our examples, to the intent we should not lust after evil things, as they also lusted. 1 Corinthians 10:6

This I say then, Walk in the Spirit, and ye shall not fulfill the lust of the flesh. For the flesh lusteth against the Spirit, and the Spirit against the flesh: and these are contrary the one to the other: so that ye cannot do the things that ye would. Galatians 5:16-17

And they that are Christ's have crucified the flesh with the affections and lusts. Galatians 5:24

Wherein in time past ye walked according to the course of this world, according to the prince of the power of the air, the spirit that now worketh in the children of disobedience: Among whom also we all had our conversation in times past in the lusts of our flesh, fulfilling the desires of the flesh and of the mind; and were by nature the children of wrath, even as others. But God, who is rich in mercy, for his great love wherewith he loved us, Even when we were dead in sins, hath quickened us together with Christ, (by grace ye are saved;) And hath raised us up together, and made us sit together in heavenly places in Christ Jesus. Ephesians 2:2-6

That ye put off concerning the former conversation the old man, which is corrupt according to the deceitful lusts. Ephesians 4:22

Flee also youthful lusts: but follow righteousness, faith, charity, peace, with them that call on the Lord out of a pure heart. 2 Timothy 2:22

Teaching us that, denying ungodliness and worldly lusts, we should live soberly, righteously, and godly, in this present world. Titus 2:12

Let no man say when he is tempted, I am tempted of God: for God cannot be tempted with evil, neither tempteth he any man: But every man is tempted, when he is drawn away of his own lust, and enticed. Then when lust hath conceived, it bringeth forth sin: and sin, when it is finished, bringeth forth death. James 1:13-15

From whence come wars and fightings among you? come they not hence, even of your lusts that war in your members? Ye lust, and have not: ye kill, and desire to have, and cannot obtain: ye fight and war, yet ye have not, because ye ask not. Ye ask, and receive not, because ye ask amiss, that ye may consume it upon your lusts. James 4:1-3

As obedient children, not fashioning yourselves according to the former lusts in your ignorance. 1 Peter 1:14

Dearly beloved, I beseech you as strangers and pilgrims, abstain from fleshly lusts, which war against the soul. 1 Peter 2:11

That he no longer should live the rest of his time in the flesh to the lusts of men, but to the will of God. 1 Peter 4:2

Whereby are given unto us exceeding great and precious promises: that by these ye might be partakers of the divine nature, having escaped the corruption that is in the world through lust. 2 Peter 1:4

For all that is in the world, the lust of the flesh, and the lust of the eyes, and the pride of life, is not of the Father, but is of the world. And the world passeth away, and the lust thereof: but he that doeth the will of God abideth for ever. 1 John 2:16-17

Television, Movies and Music

1. Would Jesus listen to this music, or watch this TV program or movie?

Then spake Jesus again unto them, saying, I am the light of the world: he that followeth me shall not walk in darkness, but shall have the light of life. John 8:12

I am come a light into the world, that whosoever believeth on me should not abide in darkness. John 12:46

2. Through your TV and music what kind of people or evil spirits are you inviting into your home?

I wrote unto you in an epistle not to company with fornicators: Yet not altogether with the fornicators of this world, or with the covetous, or extortioners, or with idolaters; for then must ye needs go out of the world. But now I have written unto you not to keep company, if any man that is called a brother be a fornicator, or covetous, or an idolater, or a railer, or a drunkard, or an extortioner; with such an one no not to eat.
1 Corinthians 5:9-11

Be ye not unequally yoked together with unbelievers: for what fellowship hath righteousness with unrighteousness? and what communion hath light with darkness? And what concord hath Christ with Belial? or what part hath he that believeth with an infidel? 2 Corinthians 6:14-15

And have no fellowship with the unfruitful works of darkness, but rather reprove them. Ephesians 5:11

3. Is this TV program, movie or music contrary to God's Word?

The thought of foolishness is sin: and the scorner is an abomination to men. Proverbs 24:9

Cease, my son, to hear the instruction that causeth to err from the words of knowledge. Proverbs 19:27

Casting down imaginations, and every high thing that exalteth itself against the knowledge of God, and bringing into captivity every thought to the obedience of Christ. 2 Corinthians 10:5

4. Is the TV program or music bringing you closer to Christ?

Ye adulterers and adulteresses, know ye not that the friendship of the world is enmity with God? whosoever therefore will be a friend of the world is the enemy of God. James 4:4

All things are lawful unto me, but all things are not expedient: all things are lawful for me, but I will not be brought under the power of any.
1 Corinthians 6:12

All things are lawful for me, but all things are not expedient: all things are lawful for me, but all things edify not. 1 Corinthians 10:23

Wherefore seeing we also are compassed about with so great a cloud of witnesses, let us lay aside every weight, and the sin which doth so easily beset us, and let us run with patience the race that is set before us.
Hebrews 12:1

5. Is it causing you to compromise and sin?

Ye cannot drink the cup of the Lord, and the cup of devils: ye cannot be partakers of the Lord's table, and of the table of devils.
1 Corinthians 10:21

And if thine eye offend thee, pluck it out, and cast it from thee: it is better for thee to enter into life with one eye, rather than having two eyes to be cast into hell fire. Matthew 18:9

6. What are you putting in your heart (through your eyes and ears)?

I will set no wicked thing before mine eyes: I hate the work of them that turn aside; it shall not cleave to me. Psalms 101:3

Turn away mine eyes from beholding vanity; and quicken thou me in thy way. Psalms 119:37

Thine eyes shall behold strange women, and thine heart shall utter perverse things. Proverbs 23:33

A wicked doer giveth heed to false lips; and a liar giveth ear to a naughty tongue. Proverbs 17:4

And he said unto them, Take heed what ye hear. Mark 4:24

Be not deceived: evil communications corrupt good manners.
1 Corinthians 15:33

Abstain from all appearance of evil. 1 Thessalonians 5:22

Being filled with all unrighteousness, fornication, wickedness, covetousness, maliciousness; full of envy, murder, debate, deceit, malignity; whisperers, **B**ackbiters, haters of God, despiteful, proud, boasters, inventors of evil things, disobedient to parents, **W**ithout understanding, covenantbreakers, without natural affection, implacable, unmerciful: **W**ho knowing the judgment of God, that they which commit such things are worthy of death, not only do the same, but have pleasure in them that do them. Romans 1:29-32

Until they were filled–permeated and saturated–with every kind of unrighteousness, iniquity, grasping and covetous greed, [and] malice. [They were] full of envy and jealousy, murder, strife, deceit and treachery, ill will and cruel ways. [They were] secret backbiters and gossipers, Slanderers, hateful to and hating God, full of insolence, arrogance [and] boasting; inventors of new forms of evil, disobedient and undutiful to parents. [They were] without understanding, conscienceless and faithless, heartless and loveless [and] merciless. Though they are fully aware of God's righteous decree that those who do such things deserve to die, they not only do them themselves but approve and applaud others who practice them. Romans 1:29-32 AMP

7. Are you wasting time?

Redeeming the time, because the days are evil. Ephesians 5:16

Walk in wisdom toward them that are without, redeeming the time.
Colossians 4:5

And if ye call on the Father, who without respect of persons judgeth according to every man's work, pass the time of your sojourning here in fear. 1 Peter 1:17

8. How do you qualify good TV programs, movies, and music?

If ye then be risen with Christ, seek those things which are above, where Christ sitteth on the right hand of God. Colossians 3:1

Finally, brethren, whatsoever things are true, whatsoever things are honest, whatsoever things are just, whatsoever things are pure, whatsoever things are lovely, whatsoever things are of good report; if there be any virtue, and if there be any praise, think on these things. Philippians 4:8

Every good gift and every perfect gift is from above, and cometh down from the Father of lights, with whom is no variableness, neither shadow of turning. James 1:17

Your Body

The Temple of the Holy Spirit

Know ye not that ye are the temple of God, and that the Spirit of God dwelleth in you? If any man defile the temple of God, him shall God destroy; for the temple of God is holy, which temple ye are.
1 Corinthians 3:16-17

What? know ye not that your body is the temple of the Holy Ghost which is in you, which ye have of God, and ye are not your own? For ye are bought with a price: therefore glorify God in your body, and in your spirit, which are God's. 1 Corinthians 6:19-20

Whether therefore ye eat, or drink, or whatsoever ye do, do all to the glory of God. 1 Corinthians 10:31

For bodily exercise profiteth little: but godliness is profitable unto all things, having promise of the life that now is, and of that which is to come. 1 Timothy 4:8

Beloved, I wish above all things that thou mayest prosper and be in health, even as thy soul prospereth. 3 John 1:2

Sex Before Marriage

But that we write unto them, that they abstain from pollutions of idols, and from fornication, and from things strangled, and from blood.
Acts 15:20

That ye abstain from meats offered to idols, and from blood, and from things strangled, and from fornication: from which if ye keep yourselves, ye shall do well. Fare ye well. Acts 15:29

As touching the Gentiles which believe, we have written and concluded that they observe no such thing, save only that they keep themselves from things offered to idols, and from blood, and from strangled, and from fornication. Acts 21:25

But now I have written unto you not to keep company, if any man that is called a brother be a fornicator, or covetous, or an idolater, or a railer, or a drunkard, or an extortioner; with such an one no not to eat.
1 Corinthians 5:11

Know ye not that your bodies are the members of Christ? shall I then take the members of Christ, and make them the members of an harlot? God forbid. What? know ye not that he which is joined to an harlot is one body? for two, saith he, shall be one flesh. 1 Corinthians 6:15-16

Flee fornication. Every sin that a man doeth is without the body; but he that commiteth fornication sinneth against his own body. What? know ye not that your body is the temple of the Holy Ghost which is in you, which ye have of God, and ye are not your own? For ye are bought with a price: therefore glorify God in your body, and in your spirit, which are God's. 1 Corinthians 6:18-20

Now concerning the things whereof ye wrote unto me: It is good for a man not to touch a woman. Nevertheless, to avoid fornication, let every man have his own wife, and let every woman have her own husband.
1 Corinthians 7:1-2

Neither let us commit fornication, as some of them committed, and fell in one day three and twenty thousand. 1 Corinthians 10:8

But fornication, and all uncleanness, or covetousness, let it not be once named among you, as becometh saints. Ephesians 5:3

For this is the will of God, even your sanctification, that ye should abstain from fornication: 1 Thessalonians 4:3

1. Sex is Only for Married Couples

Let the husband render unto the wife due benevolence: and likewise also the wife unto the husband. The wife hath not power of her own body, but the husband: and likewise also the husband hath not power of his own body, but the wife. Defraud ye not one the other, except it be with consent for a time, that ye may give yourselves to fasting and prayer; and come together again, that Satan tempt you not for your incontinency.
1 Corinthians 7:3-5

The Consequences of Fornication

Now the works of the flesh are manifest, which are these; Adultery, fornication, uncleanness, lasciviousness, Envyings, murders, drunkenness, revellings, and such like: of the which I tell you before, as I have also told you in time past, that they which do such things shall not inherit the kingdom of God. Galatians 5:19,21

Marriage is honourable in all, and the bed undefiled: but whoremongers and adulterers God will judge. Hebrews 13:4

Even as Sodom and Gomorrha, and the cities about them in like manner, giving themselves over to fornication, and going after strange flesh, are set forth for an example, suffering the vengeance of eternal fire. Jude 1:7

Adultery

Thou shalt not commit adultery. Exodus 20:14

And the man that committeth adultery with another man's wife, even he that committeth adultery with his neighbour's wife, the adulterer and the adulteress shall surely be put to death. Leviticus 20:10

Neither shalt thou commit adultery. Deuteronomy 5:18

Such is the way of an adulterous woman; she eateth, and wipeth her mouth, and saith, I have done no wickedness. Proverbs 30:20

But I say unto you, That whosoever looketh on a woman to lust after her hath committed adultery with her already in his heart. Matthew 5:28

The Consequences of Adultery

For by means of a whorish woman a man is brought to a piece of bread: and the adulteress will hunt for the precious life. Proverbs 6:26

But whoso committeth adultery with a woman lacketh understanding: he that doeth it destroyeth his own soul. Proverbs 6:32

Know ye not that the unrighteous shall not inherit the kingdom of God? Be not deceived: neither fornicators, nor idolaters, nor adulterers, nor effeminate, nor abusers of themselves with mankind. 1 Corinthians 6:9

Marriage is honourable in all, and the bed undefiled: but whoremongers and adulterers God will judge. Hebrews 13:4

Homosexuality and Lesbianism

Thou shalt not lie with mankind, as with womankind: it is abomination.
Leviticus 18:22

If a man also lie with mankind, as he lieth with a woman, both of them have committed an abomination: they shall surely be put to death; their blood shall be upon them. Leviticus 20:13

Wherefore God also gave them up to uncleanness through the lusts of their own hearts, to dishonour their own bodies between themselves.
Romans 1:24

For this cause God gave them up unto vile affections: for even their women did change the natural use into that which is against nature: And likewise also the men, leaving the natural use of the woman, burned in their lust one toward another; men with men working that which is unseemly, and receiving in themselves that recompence of their error which was meet. And even as they did not like to retain God in their knowledge, God gave them over to a reprobate mind, to do those things which are not convenient. Romans 1:26-28

Without understanding, covenantbreakers, without natural affection, implacable, unmerciful. Romans 1:31

Mortify therefore your members which are upon the earth; fornication, uncleanness, inordinate affection, evil concupiscence, and covetousness, which is idolatry. Colossians 3:5

Without natural affection, trucebreakers, false accusers, incontinent, fierce, despisers of those that are good. 2 Timothy 3:3

> *God hates sin but loves the sinner. To enter Heaven, one must do but three things: accept Jesus Christ as your Lord and Savior, repent from sin, and obey His commandments.*

Gluttony

When thou sittest to eat with a ruler, consider diligently what is before thee: And put a knife to thy throat, if thou be a man given to appetite. Be not desirous of his dainties: for they are deceitful meat. Proverbs 23:1-3

Be not among winebibbers; among riotous eaters of flesh: For the drunkard and the glutton shall come to poverty: and drowsiness shall clothe a man with rags. Proverbs 23:20-21

Hast thou found honey? eat so much as is sufficient for thee, lest thou be filled therewith, and vomit it. Proverbs 25:16

He that hath no rule over his own spirit is like a city that is broken down, and without walls. Proverbs 25:28

Blessed art thou, O land, when thy king is the son of nobles, and thy princes eat in due season, for strength, and not for drunkenness! Ecclesiastes 10:17

Whose end is destruction, whose God is their belly, and whose glory is in their shame, who mind earthly things. Philippians 3:19

For the time past of our life may suffice us to have wrought the will of the Gentiles, when we walked in lasciviousness, lusts, excess of wine, revellings, banquetings, and abominable idolatries. 1 Peter 4:3

Biblical Diet

And God said, Behold, I have given you every herb bearing seed, which is upon the face of all the earth, and every tree, in the which is the fruit of a tree yielding seed; to you it shall be for meat. Genesis 1:29

Ye shall keep my statutes. Thou shalt not let thy cattle gender with a diverse kind: thou shalt not sow thy field with mingled seed: neither shall a garment mingled of linen and woollen come upon thee.
Leviticus 19:19

Take thou also unto thee wheat, and barley, and beans, and lentiles, and millet, and fitches, and put them in one vessel, and make thee bread thereof, according to the number of the days that thou shalt lie upon thy side, three hundred and ninety days shalt thou eat thereof. Ezekiel 4:9

And by the river upon the bank thereof, on this side and on that side, shall grow all trees for meat, whose leaf shall not fade, neither shall the fruit thereof be consumed: it shall bring forth new fruit according to his months, because their waters they issued out of the sanctuary: and the fruit thereof shall be for meat, and the leaf thereof for medicine.
Ezekiel 47:12

Prove thy servants, I beseech thee, ten days; and let them give us pulse to eat, and water to drink. Then let our countenances be looked upon before thee, and the countenance of the children that eat of the portion of the king's meat: and as thou seest, deal with thy servants. So he consented to them in this matter, and proved them ten days. And at the end of ten days their countenances appeared fairer and fatter in flesh than all the children which did eat the portion of the king's meat. Thus Melzar took away the portion of their meat, and the wine that they should drink; and gave them pulse. Daniel 1:12-16

Healing

1. Provisions for Healing

But he was wounded for our transgressions, he was bruised for our iniquities: the chastisement of our peace was upon him; and with his stripes we are healed. Isaiah 53:5

Who his own self bare our sins in his own body on the tree, that we, being dead to sins, should live unto righteousness: by whose stripes ye were healed. 1 Peter 2:24

2. Preventive Medicine

And said, If thou wilt diligently hearken to the voice of the Lord thy God, and wilt do that which is right in his sight, and wilt give ear to his commandments, and keep all his statutes, I will put none of these diseases upon thee, which I have brought upon the Egyptians: for I am the Lord that healeth thee. Exodus 15:26

Thou shalt therefore keep the commandments, and the statutes, and the judgments, which I command thee this day, to do them. Wherefore it shall come to pass, if ye hearken to these judgments, and keep, and do them, that the Lord thy God shall keep unto thee the covenant and the mercy which he sware unto thy fathers: And he will love thee, and bless thee, and multiply thee: he will also bless the fruit of thy womb, and the fruit of thy land, thy corn, and thy wine, and thine oil, the increase of thy kine, and the flocks of thy sheep, in the land which he sware unto thy fathers to give thee. Thou shalt be blessed above all people: there shall not be male or female barren among you, or among your cattle. And the Lord will take away from thee all sickness, and will put none of the evil diseases of Egypt, which thou knowest, upon thee; but will lay them upon all them that hate thee. Deuteronomy 7:11-15

Trust in the Lord with all thine heart; and lean not unto thine own understanding. In all thy ways acknowledge him, and he shall direct thy paths. Be not wise in thine own eyes: fear the Lord, and depart from evil. It shall be health to thy navel, and marrow to thy bones. Proverbs 3:5-8

3. God's Promises for Healing

And ye shall serve the Lord your God, and he shall bless thy bread, and thy water; and I will take sickness away from the midst of thee. Exodus 23:25

Behold, thou hast instructed many, and thou hast strengthened the weak hands. Thy words have upholden him that was falling, and thou hast strengthened the feeble knees. Job 4:3-4

O Lord my God, I cried unto thee, and thou hast healed me. Psalms 30:2

He keepeth all his bones: not one of them is broken. Psalms 34:20

The Lord will strengthen him upon the bed of languishing: thou wilt make all his bed in his sickness. Psalms 41:3

Why art thou cast down, O my soul? and why art thou disquieted within me? hope thou in God: for I shall yet praise him, who is the health of my countenance, and my God. Psalms 42:11

Surely he shall deliver thee from the snare of the fowler, and from the noisome pestilence. Psalms 91:3

There shall no evil befall thee, neither shall any plague come nigh thy dwelling. Psalms 91:10

Who forgiveth all thine iniquities; who healeth all thy diseases. Who redeemeth thy life from destruction; who crowneth thee with lovingkindness and tender mercies; Who satisfieth thy mouth with good things; so that thy youth is renewed like the eagle's. Psalms 103:3-5

He sent his word, and healed them, and delivered them from their destructions. Psalms 107:20

The Lord upholdeth all that fall, and raiseth up all those that be bowed down. Psalms 145:14

The Lord openeth the eyes of the blind: the Lord raiseth them that are bowed down: the Lord loveth the righteous. Psalms 146:8

He healeth the broken in heart, and bindeth up their wounds.
Psalms 147:3

My son, attend to my words; incline thine ear unto my sayings. Let them not depart from thine eyes; keep them in the midst of thine heart. For they are life unto those that find them, and health to all their flesh.
Proverbs 4:20-22

For by me thy days shall be multiplied, and the years of thy life shall be increased. Proverbs 9:11

A sound heart is the life of the flesh: but envy the rottenness of the bones.
Proverbs 14:30

Pleasant words are as an honeycomb, sweet to the soul, and health to the bones. Proverbs 16:24

Strengthen ye the weak hands, and confirm the feeble knees. Isaiah 35:3

He giveth power to the faint; and to them that have no might he increaseth strength. Isaiah 40:29

And the Lord shall guide thee continually, and satisfy thy soul in drought, and make fat thy bones: and thou shalt be like a watered garden, and like a spring of water, whose waters fail not. Isaiah 58:11

Heal me, O Lord, and I shall be healed; save me, and I shall be saved: for thou art my praise. Jeremiah 17:14

For I will restore health unto thee, and I will heal thee of thy wounds, saith the Lord; because they called thee an Outcast, saying, This is Zion, whom no man seeketh after. Jeremiah 30:17

Behold, I will bring it health and cure, and I will cure them, and will reveal unto them the abundance of peace and truth. Jeremiah 33:6

For I will cleanse their blood that I have not cleansed: for the Lord dwelleth in Zion. Joel 3:21

And they that were vexed with unclean spirits: and they were healed. And the whole multitude sought to touch him: for there went virtue out of him, and healed them all. Luke 6:18-19

Christ hath redeemed us from the curse of the law, being made a curse for us: for it is written, Cursed is every one that hangeth on a tree:
Galatians 3:13

Wherefore lift up the hands which hang down, and the feeble knees; And make straight paths for your feet, lest that which is lame be turned out of the way; but let it rather be healed. Hebrews 12:12-13

Beloved, I wish above all things that thou mayest prosper and be in health, even as thy soul prospereth. 3 John 1:2

4. Praying for Healing

Is any among you afflicted? let him pray. Is any merry? let him sing psalms. Is any sick among you? let him call for the elders of the church; and let them pray over him, anointing him with oil in the name of the Lord: And the prayer of faith shall save the sick, and the Lord shall raise him up; and if he have committed sins, they shall be forgiven him. Confess your faults one to another, and pray one for another, that ye may be healed. The effectual fervent prayer of a righteous man availeth much.
James 5:13-16

Maturing in Christ

Forgiveness

Thou shalt not avenge, nor bear any grudge against the children of thy people, but thou shalt love thy neighbour as thyself: I am the Lord.
Leviticus 19:18

Therefore if thou bring thy gift to the altar, and there rememberest that thy brother hath ought against thee; Leave there thy gift before the altar, and go thy way; first be reconciled to thy brother, and then come and offer thy gift. Matthew 5:23-24

But I say unto you, Love your enemies, bless them that curse you, do good to them that hate you, and pray for them which despitefully use you, and persecute you. Matthew 5:44

And forgive us our debts, as we forgive our debtors. Matthew 6:12

For if ye forgive men their trespasses, your heavenly Father will also forgive you: But if ye forgive not men their trespasses, neither will your Father forgive your trespasses. Matthew 6:14-15

> *"I can forgive, but I cannot forget," is only another way of saying, "I cannot forgive." - Henry Ward Beecher*

Then came Peter to him, and said, Lord, how oft shall my brother sin against me, and I forgive him? till seven times? Jesus saith unto him, I say not unto thee, Until seven times: but, Until seventy times seven.
Matthew 18:21-22

Judge not, and ye shall not be judged: condemn not, and ye shall not be condemned: forgive, and ye shall be forgiven. Luke 6:37

Whose soever sins ye remit, they are remitted unto them; and whose soever sins ye retain, they are retained. John 20:23

To whom ye forgive any thing, I forgive also: for if I forgave any thing, to whom I forgave it, for your sakes forgave I it in the person of Christ;

Lest satan should get an advantage of us: for we are not ignorant of his devices. 2 Corinthians 2:10-11

Let all bitterness, and wrath, and anger, and clamour, and evil speaking, be put away from you, with all malice: And be ye kind one to another, tenderhearted, forgiving one another, even as God for Christ's sake hath forgiven you. Ephesians 4:31-32

Grudge not one against another, brethren, lest ye be condemned: behold, the judge standeth before the door. James 5:9

Use hospitality one to another without grudging. 1 Peter 4:9

Forbearing one another, and forgiving one another, if any man have a quarrel against any: even as Christ forgave you, so also do ye.
Colossians 3:13

Forgiving your offenders sets you free more than it does anyone else.

Patience

Wait on the Lord: be of good courage, and he shall strengthen thine heart: wait, I say, on the Lord. Psalms 27:14

Rest in the Lord, and wait patiently for him: fret not thyself because of him who prospereth in his way, because of the man who bringeth wicked devices to pass. Cease from anger, and forsake wrath: fret not thyself in any wise to do evil. For evildoers shall be cut off: but those that wait upon the Lord, they shall inherit the earth. Psalms 37:7-9

Wait on the Lord, and keep his way, and he shall exalt thee to inherit the land: when the wicked are cut off, thou shalt see it. Psalms 37:34

I waited patiently for the Lord; and he inclined unto me, and heard my cry. Psalms 40:1

Better is the end of a thing than the beginning thereof: and the patient in spirit is better than the proud in spirit. Ecclesiastes 7:8

These wait all upon thee; that thou mayest give them their meat in due season. Psalms 104:27

Impatience and doubt are thieves of the perfect will of God and His greatest blessings.

Say not thou, I will recompense evil; but wait on the Lord, and he shall save thee. Proverbs 20:22

And it shall be said in that day, Lo, this is our God; we have waited for him, and he will save us: this is the Lord; we have waited for him, we will be glad and rejoice in his salvation. Isaiah 25:9

It is good that a man should both hope and quietly wait for the salvation of the Lord. Lamentations 3:26

In your patience possess ye your souls. Luke 21:19

To them who by patient continuance in well doing seek for glory and honour and immortality, eternal life. Romans 2:7

But if we hope for that we see not, then do we with patience wait for it.
Romans 8:25

Strengthened with all might, according to his glorious power, unto all patience and longsuffering with joyfulness. Colossians 1:11

Now we exhort you, brethren, warn them that are unruly, comfort the feebleminded, support the weak, be patient toward all men.
1 Thessalonians 5:14

Just as faith without works is dead, so is faith without patience.

And the Lord direct your hearts into the love of God, and into the patient waiting for Christ. 2 Thessalonians 3:5

Wherefore seeing we also are compassed about with so great a cloud of witnesses, let us lay aside every weight, and the sin which doth so easily beset us, and let us run with patience the race that is set before us,
Hebrews 12:1

Be patient therefore, brethren, unto the coming of the Lord. Behold, the husbandman waiteth for the precious fruit of the earth, and hath long patience for it, until he receive the early and latter rain. **Be** ye also patient; stablish your hearts: for the coming of the Lord draweth nigh.
James 5:7-8

Take, my brethren, the prophets, who have spoken in the name of the Lord, for an example of suffering affliction, and of patience. James 5:10

Whereby are given unto us exceeding great and precious promises: that by these ye might be partakers of the divine nature, having escaped the corruption that is in the world through lust. 2 Peter 1:4

And to knowledge temperance; and to temperance patience; and to patience godliness. 2 Peter 1:6

The Lord is not slack concerning his promise, as some men count slackness; but is longsuffering to us-ward, not willing that any should perish, but that all should come to repentance. 2 Peter 3:9

Because thou hast kept the word of my patience, I also will keep thee from the hour of temptation, which shall come upon all the world, to try them that dwell upon the earth. Revelation 3:10

Here is the patience of the saints: here are they that keep the commandments of God, and the faith of Jesus. Revelation 14:12

1. Remaining Patient in Tribulations

And not only so, but we glory in tribulations also: knowing that tribulation worketh patience; And patience, experience; and experience, hope. And hope maketh not ashamed; because the love of God is shed abroad in our hearts by the Holy Ghost which is given unto us. Romans 5:3-5

Rejoicing in hope; patient in tribulation; continuing instant in prayer. Romans 12:12

Some experiences may not contribute ot happiness, but all can be made to contribute to the development of patience.

Knowing this, that the trying of your faith worketh patience. But let patience have her perfect work, that ye may be perfect and entire, wanting nothing. James 1:3-4

Living in Holiness

For I am the Lord your God: ye shall therefore sanctify yourselves, and ye shall be holy; for I am holy: neither shall ye defile yourselves with any manner of creeping thing that creepeth upon the earth. For I am the Lord that bringeth you up out of the land of Egypt, to be your God: ye shall therefore be holy, for I am holy. Leviticus 11:44-45

There is none holy as the Lord: for there is none beside thee: neither is there any rock like our God. Isaiah 2:2

That he would grant unto us, that we being delivered out of the hand of our enemies might serve him without fear, In holiness and righteousness before him, all the days of our life. Luke 1:74-75

The essence of true holiness consists in conformity to the nature and will of God. - Samuel Lucas

I speak after the manner of men because of the infirmity of your flesh: for as ye have yielded your members servants to uncleanness and to iniquity unto iniquity; even so now yield your members servants to righteousness unto holiness. Romans 6:19

But now being made free from sin, and become servants to God, ye have your fruit unto holiness, and the end everlasting life. Romans 6:22

I beseech you therefore, brethren, by the mercies of God, that ye present your bodies a living sacrifice, holy, acceptable unto God, which is your reasonable service. Romans 12:1

Having therefore these promises, dearly beloved, let us cleanse ourselves from all filthiness of the flesh and spirit, perfecting holiness in the fear of God. 2 Corinthians 7:1

According as he hath chosen us in him before the foundation of the world, that we should be holy and without blame before him in love:
Ephesians 1:4

And that ye put on the new man, which after God is created in righteousness and true holiness. Ephesians 4:24

That he might present it to himself a glorious church, not having spot, or wrinkle, or any such thing; but that it should be holy and without blemish. Ephesians 5:27

To the end he may stablish your hearts unblameable in holiness before God, even our Father, at the coming of our Lord Jesus Christ with all his saints. 1 Thessalonians 3:13

For God hath not called us unto uncleanness, but unto holiness.
1 Thessalonians 4:7

The aged women likewise, that they be in behaviour as becometh holiness, not false accusers, not given to much wine, teachers of good things;
Titus 2:3

For they verily for a few days chastened us after their own pleasure; but he for our profit, that we might be partakers of his holiness.
Hebrews 12:10

Follow peace with all men, and holiness, without which no man shall see the Lord: Hebrews 12:14

> *A man ought to live so that everybody knows he is a Christian.... and most of all, his family ought to know. - D. L. Moody*

But as he which hath called you is holy, so be ye holy in all manner of conversation; Because it is written, Be ye holy; for I am holy.
1 Peter 1:15-16

Fruitful Living

Bring forth therefore fruits meet for repentance. Matthew 3:8

And now also the axe is laid unto the root of the trees: therefore every tree which bringeth not forth good fruit is hewn down, and cast into the fire. Matthew 3:10

Ye shall know them by their fruits. Do men gather grapes of thorns, or figs of thistles? Even so every good tree bringeth forth good fruit; but a corrupt tree bringeth forth evil fruit. A good tree cannot bring forth evil fruit, neither can a corrupt tree bring forth good fruit. Every tree that bringeth not forth good fruit is hewn down, and cast into the fire. Wherefore by their fruits ye shall know them. Matthew 7:16-20

And all the people were amazed, and said, Is not this the son of David?
Matthew 12:23

> *Faith makes a Christian.*
> *Life proves a Christian.*
> *Trials confirm a Christian.*
> *Death crowns a Christian.*
> *- Anonymous*

Either make the tree good, and his fruit good; or else make the tree corrupt, and his fruit corrupt: for the tree is known by his fruit.
Matthew 12:33

I am the true vine, and my Father is the husbandman. Every branch in me that beareth not fruit he taketh away: and every branch that beareth fruit, he purgeth it, that it may bring forth more fruit. Now ye are clean through the word which I have spoken unto you. Abide in me, and I in you. As the branch cannot bear fruit of itself, except it abide in the vine; no more can ye, except ye abide in me. I am the vine, ye are the branches: He that abideth in me, and I in him, the same bringeth forth much fruit: for without me ye can do nothing. John 15:1-5

Herein is my Father glorified, that ye bear much fruit; so shall ye be my disciples. John 15:8

Ye have not chosen me, but I have chosen you, and ordained you, that ye should go and bring forth fruit, and that your fruit should remain: that whatsoever ye shall ask of the Father in my name, he may give it you.
John 15:16

But now being made free from sin, and become servants to God, ye have your fruit unto holiness, and the end everlasting life. Romans 6:22

Therefore, as ye abound in every thing, in faith, and utterance, and knowledge, and in all diligence, and in your love to us, see that ye abound in this grace also. 2 Corinthians 8:7

But if I live in the flesh, this is the fruit of my labour: yet what I shall choose I wot not. Philippians 1:22

Which is come unto you, as it is in all the world; and bringeth forth fruit, as it doth also in you, since the day ye heard of it, and knew the grace of God in truth. Colossians 1:6

That ye might walk worthy of the Lord unto all pleasing, being fruitful in every good work, and increasing in the knowledge of God.
Colossians 1:10

Now no chastening for the present seemeth to be joyous, but grievous: nevertheless afterward it yieldeth the peaceable fruit of righteousness unto them which are exercised thereby. Hebrews 12:11

For if these things be in you, and abound, they make you that ye shall neither be barren nor unfruitful in the knowledge of our Lord Jesus Christ.
2 Peter 1:8

Peacemaker

Hatred stirreth up strifes: but love covereth all sins. Proverbs 10:12

A soft answer turneth away wrath: but grievous words stir up anger.
Proverbs 15:1

A wrathful man stirreth up strife: but he that is slow to anger appeaseth strife. Proverbs 15:18

He that covereth a transgression seeketh love; but he that repeateth a matter separateth very friends. Proverbs 17:9

A gift in secret pacifieth anger: and a reward in the bosom strong wrath.
Proverbs 21:14

By long forbearing is a prince persuaded, and a soft tongue breaketh the bone. Proverbs 25:15

By long forbearing and calmness of spirit a judge or ruler is persuaded, and soft speech breaks down the most bonelike resistance.
Proverbs 25:15 AMP

Scornful men bring a city into a snare: but wise men turn away wrath.
Proverbs 29:8

If the spirit of the ruler rise up against thee, leave not thy place; for yielding pacifieth great offences. Ecclesiastes 10:4

Blessed are the peacemakers: for they shall be called the children of God. Matthew 5:9

If it be possible, as much as lieth in you, live peaceably with all men.
Romans 12:18

And to esteem them very highly in love for their work's sake. And be at peace among yourselves. 1 Thessalonians 5:13

Follow peace with all men, and holiness, without which no man shall see the Lord. Hebrews 12:14

Let him eschew evil, and do good; let him seek peace, and ensue it.
1 Peter 3:11

And the fruit of righteousness is sown in peace of them that make peace.
James 3:18

Overcoming Covetousness

Thou shalt not covet thy neighbour's house, thou shalt not covet thy neighbour's wife, nor his manservant, nor his maidservant, nor his ox, nor his ass, nor any thing that is thy neighbour's. Exodus 20:17

Incline my heart unto thy testimonies, and not to covetousness.
Psalms 119:36

And he said unto them, Take heed, and beware of covetousness: for a man's life consisteth not in the abundance of the things which he possesseth. And he spake a parable unto them, saying, The ground of a certain rich man brought forth plentifully: And he thought within himself, saying, What shall I do, because I have no room where to bestow all my fruits and my goods. And I will say to my soul, Soul, thou hast much goods laid up for many years; take thine ease, eat, drink, and be merry. But God said unto him, Thou fool, this night thy soul shall be required of thee: then whose shall those things be, which thou hast provided? So is he that layeth up treasure for himself, and is not rich toward God.
Luke 12:15-21

Let your conversation be without covetousness; and be content with such things as ye have: for he hath said, I will never leave thee, nor forsake thee. Hebrews 13:5

The prince that wanteth understanding is also a great oppressor: but he that hateth covetousness shall prolong his days. Proverbs 28:16

1. The Consequences of Covetousness

Nor thieves, nor covetous, nor drunkards, nor revilers, nor extortioners, shall inherit the kingdom of God. 1 Corinthians 6:10

For this ye know, that no whoremonger, nor unclean person, nor covetous man, who is an idolater, hath any inheritance in the kingdom of Christ and of God. Ephesians 5:5

Overcoming the Fear of Man

In God I will praise his word, in God I have put my trust; I will not fear what flesh can do unto me. Psalms 56:4

The Lord is on my side; I will not fear: what can man do unto me?
Psalms 118:6

The fear of man bringeth a snare: but whoso putteth his trust in the Lord shall be safe. Proverbs 29:25

> *There is one guaranteed formula for failure, and that is to try to please everyone. - John Mason*

So that we may boldly say, The Lord is my helper, and I will not fear what man shall do unto me. Hebrews 13:6

And fear not them which kill the body, but are not able to kill the soul: but rather fear him which is able to destroy both soul and body in hell.
Matthew 10:28

And who is he that will harm you, if ye be followers of that which is good? **But and if ye suffer for righteousness' sake, happy are ye: and be not afraid of their terror, neither be troubled;** 1 Peter 3:13-14

Becoming Bold in Christ

I will speak of thy testimonies also before kings, and will not be ashamed.
Psalms 119:46

The wicked flee when no man pursueth: but the righteous are bold as a lion. Proverbs 28:1

Whosoever therefore shall be ashamed of me and of my words in this adulterous and sinful generation; of him also shall the Son of man be ashamed, when he cometh in the glory of his Father with the holy angels. Mark 8:38

In whom we have boldness and access with confidence by the faith of him. Ephesians 3:12

And for me, that utterance may be given unto me, that I may open my mouth boldly, to make known the mystery of the gospel, For which I am an ambassador in bonds: that therein I may speak boldly, as I ought to speak. Ephesians 6:19-20

> *A boldness in Christ should be accompanied by wisdom, divine timing, and a spirit of love.*

And many of the brethren in the Lord, waxing confident by my bonds, are much more bold to speak the word without fear. Philippians 1:14

Wherefore, though I might be much bold in Christ to enjoin thee that which is convenient. Philemon 1:8

Let us therefore come boldly unto the throne of grace, that we may obtain mercy, and find grace to help in time of need. Hebrews 4:16

Having therefore, brethren, boldness to enter into the holiest by the blood of Jesus. Hebrews 10:19

So that we may boldly say, The Lord is my helper, and I will not fear what man shall do unto me. Hebrews 13:6

Herein is our love made perfect, that we may have boldness in the day of judgment: because as he is, so are we in this world. 1 John 4:17

Character

Honesty

He that walketh uprightly, and worketh righteousness, and speaketh the truth in his heart. Psalms 15:2

These are the things that ye shall do; Speak ye every man the truth to his neighbour; execute the judgment of truth and peace in your gates.
Zechariah 8:16

He that speaketh truth sheweth forth righteousness: but a false witness deceit. Proverbs 12:17

But that on the good ground are they, which in an honest and good heart, having heard the word, keep it, and bring forth fruit with patience.
Luke 8:15

Wherefore, brethren, look ye out among you seven men of honest report, full of the Holy Ghost and wisdom, whom we may appoint over this business. Acts 6:3

> *Your lifestyle may be the only Christ that some people may ever see or read about.*

Providing for honest things, not only in the sight of the Lord, but also in the sight of men. 2 Corinthians 8:21

Not slothful in business; fervent in spirit; serving the Lord. Romans 12:11

Recompense to no man evil for evil. Provide things honest in the sight of all men. Romans 12:17

Let us walk honestly, as in the day; not in rioting and drunkenness, not in chambering and wantonness, not in strife and envying. Romans 13:13

Now I pray to God that ye do no evil; not that we should appear approved, but that ye should do that which is honest, though we be as reprobates. 2 Corinthians 13:7

If so be that ye have heard him, and have been taught by him, as the truth is in Jesus. Ephesians 4:21

That ye may walk honestly toward them that are without, and that ye may have lack of nothing. 1 Thessalonians 4:12

Honesty is doing what is right when no one else is around.

Pray for us: for we trust we have a good conscience, in all things willing to live honestly. Hebrews 13:18

Having your conversation honest among the Gentiles: that, whereas they speak against you as evildoers, they may by your good works, which they shall behold, glorify God in the day of visitation. 1 Peter 2:12

Being Honest With Yourself

Take heed to yourselves, that your heart be not deceived, and ye turn aside, and serve other gods, and worship them. Deuteronomy 11:16

Thus saith the Lord; Deceive not yourselves, saying, The Chaldeans shall surely depart from us: for they shall not depart. Jeremiah 37:9

Let no man deceive himself. If any man among you seemeth to be wise in this world, let him become a fool, that he may be wise.
1 Corinthians 3:18

For if a man think himself to be something, when he is nothing, he deceiveth himself. Galatians 6:3

But be ye doers of the word, and not hearers only, deceiving your own selves. James 1:22

If any man among you seem to be religious, and bridleth not his tongue, but deceiveth his own heart, this man's religion is vain. James 1:26

And shall receive the reward of unrighteousness, as they that count it pleasure to riot in the day time. Spots they are and blemishes, sporting themselves with their own deceivings while they feast with you.
2 Peter 2:13

If we say that we have fellowship with him, and walk in darkness, we lie, and do not the truth. 1 John 1:6

If we say that we have no sin, we deceive ourselves, and the truth is not in us. 1 John 1:8

He that committeth sin is of the devil; for the devil sinneth from the beginning. For this purpose the Son of God was manifested, that he might destroy the works of the devil. Whosoever is born of God doth not commit sin; for his seed remaineth in him: and he cannot sin, because he is born of God. In this the children of God are manifest, and the children of the devil: whosoever doeth not righteousness is not of God, neither he that loveth not his brother. 1 John 3:8-10

Be not deceived; God is not mocked: for whatsoever a man soweth, that shall he also reap. Galatians 6:7

Keeping Your Word (Promises, Vows and Commitments)

If a man vow a vow unto the Lord, or swear an oath to bind his soul with a bond; he shall not break his word, he shall do according to all that proceedeth out of his mouth. Numbers 30:2

When thou shalt vow a vow unto the Lord thy God, thou shalt not slack to pay it: for the Lord thy God will surely require it of thee; and it would be sin in thee. Deuteronomy 23:21

That which is gone out of thy lips thou shalt keep and perform; even a freewill offering, according as thou hast vowed unto the Lord thy God, which thou hast promised with thy mouth. Deuteronomy 23:23

Say not unto thy neighbour, Go, and come again, and to morrow I will give; when thou hast it by thee. Proverbs 3:28

It is a snare to the man who devoureth that which is holy, and after vows to make inquiry. Proverbs 20:25

It is a snare to a man to utter a vow [of consecration] rashly, and not until afterward inquire [whether he can fulfill it]. Proverbs 20:25 AMP

When thou vowest a vow unto God, defer not to pay it; for he hath no pleasure in fools: pay that which thou hast vowed. Better is it that thou shouldest not vow, than that thou shouldest vow and not pay.
Ecclesiastes 5:4-5

Accepting Advice and Positive Criticism

A wise man will hear, and will increase learning; and a man of understanding shall attain unto wise counsels. Proverbs 1:5

But whoso hearkeneth unto me shall dwell safely, and shall be quiet from fear of evil. Proverbs 1:33

Hear, O my son, and receive my sayings; and the years of thy life shall be many. Proverbs 4:10

Hear instruction, and be wise, and refuse it not. Proverbs 8:33

He is in the way of life that keepeth instruction: but he that refuseth reproof erreth. Proverbs 10:17

Whoso loveth instruction loveth knowledge: but he that hateth reproof is brutish. Proverbs 12:1

Poverty and shame shall be to him that refuseth instruction: but he that regardeth reproof shall be honoured. Proverbs 13:18

The ear that heareth the reproof of life abideth among the wise. He that refuseth instruction despiseth his own soul: but he that heareth reproof getteth understanding. Proverbs 15:31-32

A reproof entereth more into a wise man than an hundred stripes into a fool. Proverbs 17:10

Hear counsel, and receive instruction, that thou mayest be wise in thy latter end. Proverbs 19:20

Buy the truth, and sell it not; also wisdom, and instruction, and understanding. Proverbs 23:23

For the commandment is a lamp; and the law is light; and reproofs of instruction are the way of life. Proverbs 6:23

Learning to Control the Words that You Speak

Set a watch, O Lord, before my mouth; keep the door of my lips.
Psalms 141:3

I said, I will take heed to my ways, that I sin not with my tongue: I will keep my mouth with a bridle, while the wicked is before me.
Psalms 39:1

In the multitude of words there wanteth not sin: but he that refraineth his lips is wise. Proverbs 10:19

He that keepeth his mouth keepeth his life: but he that openeth wide his lips shall have destruction. Proverbs 13:3

Thou has proved mine heart; thou hast visited me in the night; thou has tried me, and shalt find nothing; I am purposed that my mouth shall not transgress. Psalms 17:3

> *The secret of a governable tongue is not self-control but Christ-control. - G. S.*

A soft answer turneth away wrath: but grievous words stir up anger.
Proverbs 15:1

1. Avoid Speaking Evil, Useless and Meaningless Words

All the while my breath is in me, and the spirit of God is in my nostrils; My lips shall not speak wickedness, nor my tongue utter deceit.
Job 27:3-4

Keep thy tongue from evil, and thy lips from speaking guile.
Psalms 34:13

For he that will love life, and see good days, let him refrain his tongue from evil, and his lips that they speak no guile. 1 Peter 3:10

That ye put off concerning the former conversation the old man, which is corrupt according to the deceitful lusts. Ephesians 4:22

Let all bitterness, and wrath, and anger, and clamour, and evil speaking, be put away from you, with all malice. Ephesians 4:31

Neither filthiness, nor foolish talking, nor jesting, which are not convenient: but rather giving of thanks. Ephesians 5:4

O Timothy, keep that which is committed to thy trust, avoiding profane and vain babblings, and oppositions of science falsely so called: Which some professing have erred concerning the faith. Grace be with thee. Amen. 1 Timothy 6:20-21

But shun profane and vain babblings: for they will increase unto more ungodliness. 2 Timothy 2:16

Speak not evil one of another, brethren. He that speaketh evil of his brother, and judgeth his brother, speaketh evil of the law, and judgeth the law: but if thou judge the law, thou art not a doer of the law, but a judge.
James 4:11

Be not deceived: evil communications corrupt good manners.
1 Corinthians 15:33

2. Evil Words are Destructive

An hypocrite with his mouth destroyeth his neighbour: but through knowledge shall the just be delivered. Proverbs 11:9

The wicked is snared by the transgression of his lips: but the just shall come out of trouble. Proverbs 12:13

There is that speaketh like the piercings of a sword; but the tongue of the wise is health. Proverbs 12:18

Real spiritual maturity is evident by a controlled tongue. But hypocrisy can be disguised by fluent scripture quotation, spiritual cliches, religious mannerism, and emotionalism.

3. Don't Talk too Much

He that hath knowledge spareth his words: and a man of understanding is of an excellent spirit. Even a fool, when he holdeth his peace, is counted wise: and he that shutteth his lips is esteemed a man of understanding.
Proverbs 17:27-28

Whoso keepeth his mouth and his tongue keepeth his soul from troubles.
Proverbs 21:23

Talk no more so exceeding proudly; let not arrogancy come out of your mouth: for the Lord is a God of knowledge, and by him actions are weighed. Isaiah 2:3

But let your communication be, Yea, yea; Nay, nay: for whatsoever is more than these cometh of evil. Matthew 5:37

The best time for you to hold your tongue is the time you feel you must say something or bust. - Josh Billings

4. A Fool Talks too Much

A fool uttereth all his mind: but a wise man keepeth it in till afterwards.
Proverbs 29:11

The heart of him that hath understanding seeketh knowledge: but the mouth of fools feedeth on foolishness. Proverbs 15:14

A fool's lips enter into contention, and his mouth calleth for strokes. A fool's mouth is his destruction, and his lips are the snare of his soul.
Proverbs 18:6-7

Better to remain silent and be thought a fool than to speak and to remove all doubt. - Abraham Lincoln

The words of a wise man's mouth are gracious; but the lips of a fool will swallow up himself. The beginning of the words of his mouth is foolishness: and the end of his talk is mischievous madness. A fool also is full of words: a man cannot tell what shall be; and what shall be after him, who can tell him? Ecclesiastes 10:12-14

5. You will be Judged by the Words that You Speak

But I say unto you, That every idle word that men shall speak, they shall give account thereof in the day of judgment. For by thy words thou shalt be justified, and by thy words thou shalt be condemned.
Matthew 12:36-37

> *In times like the present, men should utter nothing for which the would not willingly be responsible through time and eternity. - Abraham Lincoln*

6. Think Before You Speak

The heart of the righteous studieth to answer: but the mouth of the wicked poureth out evil things. Proverbs 15:28

The heart of the wise teacheth his mouth, and addeth learning to his lips.
Proverbs 16:23

He that answereth a matter before he heareth it, it is folly and shame unto him. Proverbs 18:13

Seest thou a man that is hasty in his words? there is more hope of a fool than of him. Proverbs 29:20

Be not rash with thy mouth, and let not thine heart be hasty to utter any thing before God: for God is in heaven, and thou upon earth: therefore let thy words be few. Ecclesiastes 5:2

But foolish and unlearned questions avoid, knowing that they do gender strifes. 2 Timothy 2:23

> *Besser stumm als dumm—Better silent than stupid.*
> *- German Proverb*

7. Speaking Positive Words

Hear; for I will speak of excellent things; and the opening of my lips shall be right things. For my mouth shall speak truth; and wickedness is an abomination to my lips. All the words of my mouth are in righteousness; there is nothing froward or perverse in them. Proverbs 8:6-8

The mouth of a righteous man is a well of life: but violence covereth the mouth of the wicked. Proverbs 10:11

The tongue of the just is as choice silver: the heart of the wicked is little worth. The lips of the righteous feed many: but fools die for want of wisdom. Proverbs 10:20-21

The mouth of the just bringeth forth wisdom: but the froward tongue shall be cut out. Proverbs 10:31

Heaviness in the heart of man maketh it stoop: but a good word maketh it glad. Proverbs 12:25

A wholesome tongue is a tree of life: but perverseness therein is a breach in the spirit. Proverbs 15:4

> *The angels of heaven and the demons of hell bring to past whatever you speak out of your mouth. The angels respond to the Word of God and demons respond to negative, vain, and destructive words.*

Pleasant words are as an honeycomb, sweet to the soul, and health to the bones. Proverbs 16:24

8. Speaking Words of Wisdom and Integrity

The words of wise men are heard in quiet more than the cry of him that ruleth among fools. Ecclesiastes 9:17

The words of a wise man's mouth are gracious; but the lips of a fool will swallow up himself. Ecclesiastes 10:12

For I will give you a mouth and wisdom, which all your adversaries shall not be able to gainsay nor resist. Luke 21:15

Sound speech, that cannot be condemned; that he that is of the contrary part may be ashamed, having no evil thing to say of you. Titus 2:8

> *Blessed is the man who, having nothing to say, abstains from giving wordy evidence of the fact. - George Eliot*

Who is a wise man and endued with knowledge among you? let him shew out of a good conversation his works with meekness of wisdom.
James 3:13

9. Speaking the Right Words at the Appropriate Time

The lips of the righteous know what is acceptable: but the mouth of the wicked speaketh frowardness. Proverbs 10:32

A man hath joy by the answer of his mouth: and a word spoken in due season, how good is it! Proverbs 15:23

My son, if thine heart be wise, my heart shall rejoice, even mine. Yea, my reins shall rejoice, when thy lips speak right things.
Proverbs 23:15-16

A word fitly spoken is like apples of gold in pictures of silver.
Proverbs 25:11

To every thing there is a season, and a time to every purpose under the heaven: A time to rend, and a time to sew; a time to keep silence, and a time to speak; Ecclesiastes 3:1-7

The Lord God hath given me the tongue of the learned, that I should know how to speak a word in season to him that is weary: he wakeneth morning by morning, he wakeneth mine ear to hear as the learned.
Isaiah 50:4

Let your speech be alway with grace, seasoned with salt, that ye may know how ye ought to answer every man. Colossians 4:6

10. Speaking Knowledgeable Words

The tongue of the wise useth knowledge aright: but the mouth of fools poureth out foolishness. Proverbs 15:2

The lips of the wise disperse knowledge: but the heart of the foolish doeth not so. Proverbs 15:7

There is gold, and a multitude of rubies: but the lips of knowledge are a precious jewel. Proverbs 20:15

Should a wise man utter vain knowledge, and fill his belly with the east wind? Job 15:2

My words shall be of the uprightness of my heart: and my lips shall utter knowledge clearly. Job 33:3

Job hath spoken without knowledge, and his words were without wisdom. Job 34:35

Therefore doth Job open his mouth in vain; he multiplieth words without knowledge. Job 35:16

For truly my words shall not be false: he that is perfect in knowledge is with thee. Job 36:4

That thou mayest regard discretion, and that thy lips may keep knowledge. Proverbs 5:2

For the priest's lips should keep knowledge, and they should seek the law at his mouth: for he is the messenger of the Lord of hosts.

Malachi 2:7

Who is a wise man and endued with knowledge among you? let him shew out of a good conversation his works with meekness of wisdom.

James 3:13

Positive Attitude

Humility

Lord, thou hast heard the desire of the humble: thou wilt prepare their heart, thou wilt cause thine ear to hear. Psalms 10:17

The humble shall see this, and be glad: and your heart shall live that seek God. Psalms 69:32

Lord, my heart is not haughty, nor mine eyes lofty: neither do I exercise myself in great matters, or in things too high for me. Surely I have behaved and quieted myself, as a child that is weaned of his mother: my soul is even as a weaned child. Psalms 131:1-2

Though the Lord be high, yet hath he respect unto the lowly: but the proud he knoweth afar off. Psalms 138:6

True humility is not an abject, groveling, self-despising spirit; it is but a right estimate of ourselves as God sees us. - Tryon Edwards

The Lord lifteth up the meek: he casteth the wicked down to the ground. Psalms 147:6

For the Lord taketh pleasure in his people: he will beautify the meek with salvation. Psalms 149:4

The fear of the Lord is the instruction of wisdom; and before honour is humility. Proverbs 15:33

For all those things hath mine hand made, and those things have been, saith the Lord: but to this man will I look, even to him that is poor and of a contrite spirit, and trembleth at my word. Isaiah 66:2

He hath shewed thee, O man, what is good; and what doth the Lord require of thee, but to do justly, and to love mercy, and to walk humbly with thy God? Micah 6:8

Blessed are the poor in spirit: for theirs is the kingdom of heaven.
Matthew 5:3

True and pure humility is believing and obeying God's Word.

But it shall not be so among you: but whosoever will be great among you, let him be your minister; And whosoever will be chief among you, let him be your servant. Matthew 20:26-27

And whosoever shall exalt himself shall be abased; and he that shall humble himself shall be exalted. Matthew 23:12

He hath put down the mighty from their seats, and exalted them of low degree. Luke 1:52

But when thou art bidden, go and sit down in the lowest room; that when he that bade thee cometh, he may say unto thee, Friend, go up higher: then shalt thou have worship in the presence of them that sit at meat with thee. Luke 14:10

And the publican, standing afar off, would not lift up so much as his eyes unto heaven, but smote upon his breast, saying, God be merciful to me a sinner. I tell you, this man went down to his house justified rather than the other: for every one that exalteth himself shall be abased; and he that humbleth himself shall be exalted. Luke 18:13-14

And there was also a strife among them, which of them should be accounted the greatest. And he said unto them, The kings of the Gentiles exercise lordship over them; and they that exercise authority upon them are called benefactors. But ye shall not be so: but he that is greatest among you, let him be as the younger; and he that is chief, as he that doth serve. For whether is greater, he that sitteth at meat, or he that serveth? is not he that sitteth at meat? but I am among you as he that serveth.
Luke 22:24-27

The man who is to take a high place before his fellows must take a low place before his God. - Anonymous

He must increase, but I must decrease. John 3:30

Be of the same mind one toward another. Mind not high things, but condescend to men of low estate. Be not wise in your own conceits.
Romans 12:16

But by the grace of God I am what I am: and his grace which was bestowed upon me was not in vain; but I laboured more abundantly than they all: yet not I, but the grace of God which was with me.
1 Corinthians 15:10

With all lowliness and meekness, with longsuffering, forbearing one another in love. Ephesians 4:2

I know both how to be abased, and I know how to abound: every where and in all things I am instructed both to be full and to be hungry, both to abound and to suffer need. Philippians 4:12

Let the brother of low degree rejoice in that he is exalted: But the rich, in that he is made low: because as the flower of the grass he shall pass away. James 1:9-10

Humble yourselves in the sight of the Lord, and he shall lift you up.
James 4:10

Likewise, ye younger, submit yourselves unto the elder. Yea, all of you be subject one to another, and be clothed with humility: for God resisteth the proud, and giveth grace to the humble. **H**umble yourselves therefore under the mighty hand of God, that he may exalt you in due time.
1 Peter 5:5-6

When that confidence comes, then strive for humility:
- Robert G. Lee

Meekness

Now the man Moses was very meek, above all the men which were upon the face of the earth. Numbers 12:3

The meek shall eat and be satisfied: they shall praise the Lord that seek him: your heart shall live for ever. Psalms 22:26

The meek will he guide in judgment: and the meek will he teach his way.
Psalms 25:9

But the meek shall inherit the earth; and shall delight themselves in the abundance of peace. Psalms 37:11

And in thy majesty ride prosperously because of truth and meekness and righteousness; and thy right hand shall teach thee terrible things.
Psalms 45:4

When God arose to judgment, to save all the meek of the earth. Selah.
Psalms 76:9

The Lord lifteth up the meek: he casteth the wicked down to the ground.
Psalms 147:6

For the Lord taketh pleasure in his people: he will beautify the meek with salvation. Psalms 149:4

But with righteousness shall he judge the poor, and reprove with equity for the meek of the earth: and he shall smite the earth with the rod of his mouth, and with the breath of his lips shall he slay the wicked.
Isaiah 11:4

The meek also shall increase their joy in the Lord, and the poor among men shall rejoice in the Holy One of Israel. Isaiah 29:19

The Spirit of the Lord God is upon me; because the Lord hath anointed me to preach good tidings unto the meek; he hath sent me to bind up the brokenhearted, to proclaim liberty to the captives, and the opening of the prison to them that are bound. Isaiah 61:1

Seek ye the Lord, all ye meek of the earth, which have wrought his judgment; seek righteousness, seek meekness: it may be ye shall be hid in the day of the Lord's anger. Zephaniah 2:3

Blessed are the meek: for they shall inherit the earth. Matthew 5:5

Take my yoke upon you, and learn of me; for I am meek and lowly in heart: and ye shall find rest unto your souls. Matthew 11:29

Tell ye the daughter of Sion, Behold, thy King cometh unto thee, meek, and sitting upon an ass, and a colt the foal of an ass. Matthew 21:5

What will ye? shall I come unto you with a rod, or in love, and in the spirit of meekness? 1 Corinthians 4:21

Now I Paul myself beseech you by the meekness and gentleness of Christ, who in presence am base among you, but being absent am bold toward you. 2 Corinthians 10:1

But the fruit of the Spirit is love, joy, peace, longsuffering, gentleness, goodness, faith, **M**eekness, temperance: against such there is no law.
Galatians 5:22-23

Brethren, if a man be overtaken in a fault, ye which are spiritual, restore such an one in the spirit of meekness; considering thyself, lest thou also be tempted. Galatians 6:1

With all lowliness and meekness, with longsuffering, forbearing one another in love. Ephesians 4:2

Put on therefore, as the elect of God, holy and beloved, bowels of mercies, kindness, humbleness of mind, meekness, longsuffering.
Colossians 3:12

But thou, O man of God, flee these things; and follow after righteousness, godliness, faith, love, patience, meekness. 1 Timothy 6:11

To speak evil of no man, to be no brawlers, but gentle, shewing all meekness unto all men. Titus 3:2

Wherefore lay apart all filthiness and superfluity of naughtiness, and receive with meekness the engrafted word, which is able to save your souls. James 1:21

Who is a wise man and endued with knowledge among you? let him shew out of a good conversation his works with meekness of wisdom.
James 3:13

But let it be the hidden man of the heart, in that which is not corruptible, even the ornament of a meek and quiet spirit, which is in the sight of God of great price. 1 Peter 3:4

But sanctify the Lord God in your hearts: and be ready always to give an answer to every man that asketh you a reason of the hope that is in you with meekness and fear. 1 Peter 3:15

Overcoming Pride

Hear ye, and give ear; be not proud: for the Lord hath spoken.
Jeremiah 13:15

Look on every one that is proud, and bring him low; and tread down the wicked in their place. Job 40:12

Thou hast rebuked the proud that are cursed, which do err from thy commandments. Psalms 119:21

An high look, and a proud heart, and the plowing of the wicked, is sin.
Proverbs 21:4

Seest thou a man wise in his own conceit? there is more hope of a fool than of him. Proverbs 26:12

> *The wonderful thing about cockiness is that it can be overcome by a little maturity. - Delton Trueblood*

Woe unto them that are wise in their own eyes, and prudent in their own sight! Isaiah 5:21

And Jesus called a little child unto him, and set him in the midst of them, And said, Verily I say unto you, Except ye be converted, and become as little children, ye shall not enter into the kingdom of heaven. Whosoever therefore shall humble himself as this little child, the same is greatest in the kingdom of heaven. Matthew 18:2-4

But he that is greatest among you shall be your servant. And whosoever shall exalt himself shall be abased; and he that shall humble himself shall be exalted. Matthew 23:11-12

And he sat down, and called the twelve, and saith unto them, If any man desire to be first, the same shall be last of all, and servant of all.
Mark 9:35

For I say, through the grace given unto me, to every man that is among you, not to think of himself more highly than he ought to think; but to think soberly, according as God hath dealt to every man the measure of faith. Romans 12:3

Be of the same mind one toward another. Mind not high things, but condescend to men of low estate. Be not wise in your own conceits.
Romans 12:16

That, according as it is written, He that glorieth, let him glory in the Lord. 1 Corinthians 1:31

Let no man deceive himself. If any man among you seemeth to be wise in this world, let him become a fool, that he may be wise.
1 Corinthians 3:18

Charity suffereth long, and is kind; charity envieth not; charity vaunteth not itself, is not puffed up. 1 Corinthians 13:4

Not that we are sufficient of ourselves to think any thing as of ourselves; but our sufficiency is of God. 2 Corinthians 3:5

But we have this treasure in earthen vessels, that the excellency of the power may be of God, and not of us. 2 Corinthians 4:7

God knows best; he hasn't arranged your anatomy so as to make it easy for you to pat yourself on the back. - Anonymous

But he that glorieth, let him glory in the Lord. 2 Corinthians 10:17

If I must needs glory, I will glory of the things which concern mine infirmities. 2 Corinthians 11:30

But God forbid that I should glory, save in the cross of our Lord Jesus Christ, by whom the world is crucified unto me, and I unto the world.
Galatians 6:14

Humble yourselves in the sight of the Lord, and he shall lift you up.
James 4:10

Let nothing be done through strife or vainglory; but in lowliness of mind let each esteem other better than themselves. Philippians 2:3

Don't talk about yourself; it will be done when you leave.
- Wilson Mizner

1. God Hates Pride

Though the Lord be high, yet hath he respect unto the lowly: but the proud he knoweth afar off. Psalms 138:6

The fear of the Lord is to hate evil: pride, and arrogancy, and the evil way, and the froward mouth, do I hate. Proverbs 8:13

And he said unto them, Ye are they which justify yourselves before men; but God knoweth your hearts: for that which is highly esteemed among men is abomination in the sight of God. Luke 16:15

But he giveth more grace. Wherefore he saith, God resisteth the proud, but giveth grace unto the humble. Submit yourselves therefore to God. Resist the devil, and he will flee from you. James 4:6-7

Likewise, ye younger, submit yourselves unto the elder. Yea, all of you be subject one to another, and be clothed with humility: for God resisteth the proud, and giveth grace to the humble. 1 Peter 5:5

God sends no one away empty except those who are full of themselves. - D. L. Moody

2. Pride Will Cause You to Fall

Pride goeth before destruction, and an haughty spirit before a fall. Better it is to be of an humble spirit with the lowly, than to divide the spoil with the proud. Proverbs 16:18-19

Before destruction the heart of man is haughty, and before honour is humility. Proverbs 18:12

A man's pride shall bring him low: but honour shall uphold the humble in spirit. Proverbs 29:23

Wherefore let him that thinketh he standeth take heed lest he fall.
1 Corinthians 10:12

3. Being Prideful Starts Trouble

Only by pride cometh contention: but with the well advised is wisdom. Proverbs 13:10

He that is of a proud heart stirreth up strife: but he that putteth his trust in the Lord shall be made fat. He that trusteth in his own heart is a fool: but whoso walketh wisely, he shall be delivered. Proverbs 28:25-26

Controlling Anger

Cease from anger, and forsake wrath: fret not thyself in any wise to do evil. Psalms 37:8

He that is void of wisdom despiseth his neighbour: but a man of understanding holdeth his peace. Proverbs 11:12

He that is slow to wrath is of great understanding: but he that is hasty of spirit exalteth folly. Proverbs 14:29

A wrathful man stirreth up strife: but he that is slow to anger appeaseth strife. Proverbs 15:18

He that is slow to anger is better than the mighty; and he that ruleth his spirit than he that taketh a city. Proverbs 16:32

Even a fool, when he holdeth his peace, is counted wise: and he that shutteth his lips is esteemed a man of understanding. Proverbs 17:28

The discretion of a man deferreth his anger; and it is his glory to pass over a transgression. Proverbs 19:11

Scornful men bring a city into a snare: but wise men turn away wrath. Proverbs 29:8

A fool uttereth all his mind: but a wise man keepeth it in till afterwards. Proverbs 29:11

Be not hasty in thy spirit to be angry: for anger resteth in the bosom of fools. Ecclesiastes 7:9

Dearly beloved, avenge not yourselves, but rather give place unto wrath: for it is written, Vengeance is mine; I will repay, saith the Lord. Therefore if thine enemy hunger, feed him; if he thirst, give him drink: for in so doing thou shalt heap coals of fire on his head. Be not overcome of evil, but overcome evil with good. Romans 12:19-21

Let all bitterness, and wrath, and anger, and clamour, and evil speaking, be put away from you, with all malice: And be ye kind one to another, tenderhearted, forgiving one another, even as God for Christ's sake hath forgiven you. Ephesians 4:31-32

It is better to avoid strife than to appear justified.

But now ye also put off all these; anger, wrath, malice, blasphemy, filthy communication out of your mouth. Colossians 3:8

Wherefore, my beloved brethren, let every man be swift to hear, slow to speak, slow to wrath: For the wrath of man worketh not the righteousness of God. James 1:19-20

He who forgives ends the quarrel. - Proverb

Overcoming an Envious Heart

Envious is the feeling of displeasure produced by witnessing or hearing of the advantage or prosperity of others. Envy thou not the oppressor, and choose none of his ways. Proverbs 3:31

Let not thine heart envy sinners: but be thou in the fear of the Lord all the day long. Proverbs 23:17

Be not thou envious against evil men, neither desire to be with them.
Proverbs 24:1

Fret not thyself because of evil men, neither be thou envious at the wicked;
Proverbs 24:19

Let us walk honestly, as in the day; not in rioting and drunkenness, not in chambering and wantonness, not in strife and envying. Romans 13:13

Let us not be desirous of vain glory, provoking one another, envying one another. Galatians 5:26

For where envying and strife is, there is confusion and every evil work.
James 3:16

Wherefore laying aside all malice, and all guile, and hypocrisies, and envies, and all evil speakings, 1 Peter 2:1

A sound heart is the life of the flesh: but envy the rottenness of the bones.
Proverbs 14:30

Wrath is cruel, and anger is outrageous; but who is able to stand before envy? Proverbs 27:4

Overcoming a Judgmental Attitude

1. Judging Others

Judge not, that ye be not judged. For with what judgment ye judge, ye shall be judged: and with what measure ye mete, it shall be measured to you again. And why beholdest thou the mote that is in thy brother's eye, but considerest not the beam that is in thine own eye? Or how wilt thou say to thy brother, Let me pull out the mote out of thine eye; and, behold, a beam is in thine own eye? Thou hypocrite, first cast out the beam out of thine own eye; and then shalt thou see clearly to cast out the mote out of thy brother's eye. Matthew 7:1-5

Judge not, and ye shall not be judged: condemn not, and ye shall not be condemned: forgive, and ye shall be forgiven. Luke 6:37

And thinkest thou this, O man, that judgest them which do such things, and doest the same, that thou shalt escape the judgment of God?
Romans 2:3

But why dost thou judge thy brother? or why dost thou set at nought thy brother? for we shall all stand before the judgment seat of Christ.
Romans 14:10

How rarely we weigh our neighbor in the same balance in which we weigh ourselves! - Thomas A Kempis

2. Judging Others by Money, Race or Background

Ye shall do no unrighteousness in judgment: thou shalt not respect the person of the poor, nor honour the person of the mighty: but in righteousness shalt thou judge thy neighbour. Leviticus 19:15

Wherefore now let the fear of the Lord be upon you; take heed and do it: for there is no iniquity with the Lord our God, nor respect of persons, nor taking of gifts. 2 Chronicles 19:7

How much less to him that accepteth not the persons of princes, nor regardeth the rich more than the poor? for they all are the work of his hands. Job 34:19

To have respect of persons is not good: for a piece of bread that man will transgress. Proverbs 28:21

These things also belong to the wise. It is not good to have respect of persons in judgment. Proverbs 24:23

I returned, and saw under the sun, that the race is not to the swift, nor the battle to the strong, neither yet bread to the wise, nor yet riches to men of understanding, nor yet favour to men of skill; but time and chance happeneth to them all. Ecclesiastes 9:11

And they shall teach no more every man his neighbour, and every man his brother, saying, Know the Lord: for they shall all know me, from the least of them unto the greatest of them, saith the Lord; for I will forgive their iniquity, and I will remember their sin no more. Jeremiah 31:34

Judge not, and ye shall not be judged: condemn not, and ye shall not be condemned: forgive, and ye shall be forgiven. Luke 6:37

And they shall come from the east, and from the west, and from the north, and from the south, and shall sit down in the kingdom of God. And, behold, there are last which shall be first, and there are first which shall be last. Luke 13:29-30

And the lord commended the unjust steward, because he had done wisely: for the children of this world are in their generation wiser than the children of light. Luke 16:8

Judge not according to the appearance, but judge righteous judgment.
John 7:24

Even the righteousness of God which is by faith of Jesus Christ unto all and upon all them that believe: for there is no difference. Romans 3:22

If then ye have judgments of things pertaining to this life, set them to judge who are least esteemed in the church. 1 Corinthians 6:4

But unto every one of us is given grace according to the measure of the gift of Christ. Ephesians 4:7

My brethren, have not the faith of our Lord Jesus Christ, the Lord of glory, with respect of persons. For if there come unto your assembly a man with a gold ring, in goodly apparel, and there come in also a poor man in vile raiment; And ye have respect to him that weareth the gay clothing, and say unto him, Sit thou here in a good place; and say to the poor, Stand thou there, or sit here under my footstool: Are ye not then partial in yourselves, and are become judges of evil thoughts? Hearken, my beloved brethren, Hath not God chosen the poor of this world rich in faith, and heirs of the kingdom which he hath promised to them that love him? But ye have despised the poor. Do not rich men oppress you, and draw you before the judgment seats? Do not they blaspheme that worthy name by the which ye are called? If ye fulfil the royal law according to the scripture, Thou shalt love thy neighbour as thyself, ye do well: But if ye have respect to persons, ye commit sin, and are convinced of the law as transgressors. James 2:1-9

Overcoming the Tendency to Gossip or Slander

1. Gossip

Thou shalt not go up and down as a talebearer among thy people: neither shalt thou stand against the blood of thy neighbour: I am the Lord.
Leviticus 19:16

He that backbiteth not with his tongue, nor doeth evil to his neighbour, nor taketh up a reproach against his neighbour. Psalms 15:3

Keep thy tongue from evil, and thy lips from speaking guile.
Psalms 34:13

Thy tongue deviseth mischiefs; like a sharp razor, working deceitfully.
Psalms 52:2

A talebearer revealeth secrets: but he that is of a faithful spirit concealeth the matter. Proverbs 11:13

A froward man soweth strife: and a whisperer separateth chief friends.
Proverbs 16:28

He that covereth a transgression seeketh love; but he that repeateth a matter separateth very friends. Proverbs 17:9

Whoever gossips to you will gossip of you. - Spanish proverb

The words of a talebearer are as wounds, and they go down into the innermost parts of the belly. Proverbs 26:22

The words of a whisperer or slanderer are as dainty morsels or words of sport [to some, but to others are as deadly wound], and they go down into the innermost parts of the body [or of the victim's nature].
Proverbs 26:22 AMP

He that goeth about as a talebearer revealeth secrets: therefore meddle not with him that flattereth with his lips. Proverbs 20:19

Debate thy cause with thy neighbour himself; and discover not a secret to another: Lest he that heareth it put thee to shame, and thine infamy turn not away. Proverbs 25:9-10

The north wind driveth away rain: so doth an angry countenance a backbiting tongue. Proverbs 25:23

Where no wood is, there the fire goeth out: so where there is no talebearer, the strife ceaseth. As coals are to burning coals, and wood to fire; so is a contentious man to kindle strife. The words of a talebearer are as wounds, and they go down into the innermost parts of the belly.
Proverbs 26:20-22

But I say unto you, That every idle word that men shall speak, they shall give account thereof in the day of judgment. Matthew 12:36

And withal they learn to be idle, wandering about from house to house; and not only idle, but tattlers also and busybodies, speaking things which they ought not. 1 Timothy 5:13

And that ye study to be quiet, and to do your own business, and to work with your own hands, as we commanded you. 1 Thessalonians 4:11

> *You will not become a saint through other people's sins.*
> *- Anton Chekhov*

2. Slander

Thou shalt be hid from the scourge of the tongue: neither shalt thou be afraid of destruction when it cometh. Job 5:21

Thou shalt hide them in the secret of thy presence from the pride of man: thou shalt keep them secretly in a pavilion from the strife of tongues.
Psalms 31:20

He shall send from heaven, and save from the reproach of him that would swallow me up. Selah. God shall send forth his mercy and his truth.
Psalms 57:3

He that hideth hatred with lying lips, and he that uttereth a slander, is a fool. Proverbs 10:18

A froward man soweth strife: and a whisperer separateth chief friends.
Proverbs 16:28

Hearken unto me, ye that know righteousness, the people in whose heart is my law; fear ye not the reproach of men, neither be ye afraid of their revilings. Isaiah 51:7

> *People who are criticized are usually doing something so great and significant that their criticizers wish they had the commitment and discipline to do themselves.*

Blessed are ye, when men shall revile you, and persecute you, and shall say all manner of evil against you falsely, for my sake. **R**ejoice, and be exceeding glad: for great is your reward in heaven: for so persecuted they the prophets which were before you. Matthew 5:11-12

But if ye bite and devour one another, take heed that ye be not consumed one of another. Galatians 5:15

If ye be reproached for the name of Christ, happy are ye; for the spirit of glory and of God resteth upon you: on their part he is evil spoken of, but on your part he is glorified. 1 Peter 4:14

Building Your Self-Confidence Through Christ

Blessed shalt thou be when thou comest in, and blessed shalt thou be when thou goest out. Deuteronomy 28:6

And the Lord shall make thee the head, and not the tail; and thou shalt be above only, and thou shalt not be beneath; if that thou hearken unto the commandments of the Lord thy God, which I command thee this day, to observe and to do them. Deuteronomy 28:13

But Jesus beheld them, and said unto them, With men this is impossible; but with God all things are possible. Matthew 19:26

For with God nothing shall be impossible. Luke 1:37

Moreover whom he did predestinate, them he also called: and whom he called, them he also justified: and whom he justified, them he also glorified. Romans 8:30

Now thanks be unto God, which always causeth us to triumph in Christ, and maketh manifest the savour of his knowledge by us in every place.
2 Corinthians 2:14

I can do all things through Christ which strengtheneth me.
Philippians 4:13

Ye also, as lively stones, are built up a spiritual house, an holy priesthood, to offer up spiritual sacrifices, acceptable to God by Jesus Christ.
1 Peter 2:5

Ye are of God, little children, and have overcome them: because greater is he that is in you, than he that is in the world. 1 John 4:4

Building Your Self-Image Through God's Word

And God said, Let us make man in our image, after our likeness: and let them have dominion over the fish of the sea, and over the fowl of the air, and over the cattle, and over all the earth, and over every creeping thing that creepeth upon the earth. So God created man in his own image, in the image of God created he him; male and female created he them.
Genesis 1:26-27

And they fell upon their faces, and said, O God, the God of the spirits of all flesh, shall one man sin, and wilt thou be wroth with all the congregation? Numbers 16:22

Let the Lord, the God of the spirits of all flesh, set a man over the congregation. Numbers 27:16

Out of the mouth of babes and sucklings hast thou ordained strength because of thine enemies, that thou mightest still the enemy and the avenger. When I consider thy heavens, the work of thy fingers, the moon and the stars, which thou hast ordained; What is man, that thou art mindful of him? and the son of man, that thou visitest him? For thou hast made him a little lower than the angels, and hast crowned him with glory and honour. Thou madest him to have dominion over the works of thy hands; thou hast put all things under his feet. Psalms 8:2-6

I have said, Ye are gods; and all of you are children of the most High.
Psalms 82:6

The burden of the word of the Lord for Israel, saith the Lord, which stretcheth forth the heavens, and layeth the foundation of the earth, and formeth the spirit of man within him. Zechariah 12:1

Therefore if any man be in Christ, he is a new creature: old things are passed away; behold, all things are become new. 2 Corinthians 5:17

Now then we are ambassadors for Christ, as though God did beseech you by us: we pray you in Christ's stead, be ye reconciled to God.
2 Corinthians 5:20

The eyes of your understanding being enlightened; that ye may know what is the hope of his calling, and what the riches of the glory of his inheritance in the saints. Ephesians 1:18

And you hath he quickened, who were dead in trespasses and sins.
Ephesians 2:1

Even when we were dead in sins, hath quickened us together with Christ, by grace ye are saved; And hath raised us up together, and made us sit together in heavenly places in Christ Jesus. Ephesians 2:5-6

For we are his workmanship, created in Christ Jesus unto good works, which God hath before ordained that we should walk in them.
Ephesians 2:10

Now therefore ye are no more strangers and foreigners, but fellow citizens with the saints, and of the household of God. Ephesians 2:19

I can do all things through Christ which strengtheneth me.
Philippians 4:13

Lie not one to another, seeing that ye have put off the old man with his deeds; And have put on the new man, which is renewed in knowledge after the image of him that created him. Colossians 3:9-10

Furthermore we have had fathers of our flesh which corrected us, and we gave them reverence: shall we not much rather be in subjection unto the Father of spirits, and live? Hebrews 12:9

But whoso looketh into the perfect law of liberty, and continueth therein, he being not a forgetful hearer, but a doer of the work, this man shall be blessed in his deed. James 1:25

Herein is our love made perfect, that we may have boldness in the day of judgment: because as he is, so are we in this world. 1 John 4:17

ATTRIBUTES OF A PROVERBS 31 WOMAN

Who can find a virtuous woman? for her price is far above rubies. The heart of her husband doth safely trust in her, so that he shall have no need of spoil. She will do him good and not evil all the days of her life. She seeketh wool, and flax, and worketh willingly with her hands. She is like the merchants' ships; she bringeth her food from afar. She riseth also while it is yet night, and giveth meat to her household, and a portion to her maidens. She considereth a field, and buyeth it: with the fruit of her hands she planteth a vineyard. She girdeth her loins with strength, and strengtheneth her arms. She perceiveth that her merchandise is good: her candle goeth not out by night. She layeth her hands to the spindle, and her hands hold the distaff. She stretcheth out her hand to the poor; yea, she reacheth forth her hands to the needy. She is not afraid of the snow for her household: for all her household are clothed with scarlet. She maketh herself coverings of tapestry; her clothing is silk and purple. Her husband is known in the gates, when he sitteth among the elders of the land. She maketh fine linen, and selleth it; and delivereth girdles unto the merchant. Strength and honour are her clothing; and she shall rejoice in time to come. She openeth her mouth with wisdom; and in her tongue is the law of kindness. She looketh well to the ways of her household, and eateth not the bread of idleness. Her children arise up, and call her blessed; her husband also, and he praiseth her. Many daughters have done virtuously, but thou excellest them all. Favour is deceitful, and beauty is vain: but a woman that feareth the Lord, she shall be praised. Give her of the fruit of her hands; and let her own works praise her in the gates.

Proverbs 31:10-31

If you can find a truly good wife, she is worth more than precious gems! Her husband can trust her, and she will richly satisfy his needs. She will not hinder him but help him all her life. She finds wool and flax and busily spins it. She buys imported foods brought by ship from distant ports. She gets up before dawn to prepare breakfast for her household and plans the day's work for her servant girls. She goes out to inspect a field and buys it; with her own hands she plants a vineyard. She is energetic, a hard worker, and watches for bargains. She works far into the night! She sews for the poor and generously helps those in need. She has no fear of winter for her household, for she has made warm clothes for all of them. She also upholsters with finest tapestry; her own clothing is beautifully made–a purple gown of pure linen. Her husband is well known, for he sits in the council chamber with the other civic leaders. She makes belted linen garments to sell to the merchants. She is a woman of strength and dignity and has no fear of old age. When she speaks, her words are wise, and kindness is the rule for everything she says. She watches carefully all that goes on throughout her household and is never lazy. Her children stand and bless her; so does her husband. He praises her with these words: "There are many fine women in the world, but you are the best of them all!" Charm can be deceptive and beauty doesn't last, but a woman who fears and reverences God shall be greatly praised. Praise her for the many fine things she does. These good deeds of hers shall bring her honor and recognition from people of importance.

Proverbs 31:10-31 Living Bible

Wisdom

The fear of the Lord is the beginning of wisdom: a good understanding have all they that do his commandments: his praise endureth for ever.

Psalms 111:10

Wisdom crieth without; she uttereth her voice in the streets.

Proverbs 1:20

1. How to Obtain Wisdom

If any of you lack wisdom, let him ask of God, that giveth to all men liberally, and upbraideth not; and it shall be given him. James 1:5

If you lack knowledge, go to school. If you lack wisdom, get on your knees! Knowledge is not wisdom. Wisdom is proper use of knowledge. - Vance Havner

2. Wisdom Comes From God

For the Lord giveth wisdom: out of his mouth cometh knowledge and understanding. He layeth up sound wisdom for the righteous: he is a buckler to them that walk uprightly. Proverbs 2:6-7

For God giveth to a man that is good in his sight wisdom, and knowledge, and joy: but to the sinner he giveth travail, to gather and to heap up, that he may give to him that is good before God. This also is vanity and vexation of spirit. Ecclesiastes 2:26

There is no wisdom nor understanding nor counsel against the Lord.
Proverbs 21:30

Wherein he hath abounded toward us in all wisdom and prudence.
Ephesians 1:8

That the God of our Lord Jesus Christ, the Father of glory, may give unto you the spirit of wisdom and revelation in the knowledge of him.
Ephesians 1:17

To the intent that now unto the principalities and powers in heavenly places might be known by the church the manifold wisdom of God.
Ephesians 3:10

In whom are hid all the treasures of wisdom and knowledge.
Colossians 2:3

But unto them which are called, both Jews and Greeks, Christ the power of God, and the wisdom of God. 1 Corinthians 1:24

But of him are ye in Christ Jesus, who of God is made unto us wisdom, and righteousness, and sanctification, and redemption. 1 Corinthians 1:30

3. True Wisdom

But the wisdom that is from above is first pure, then peaceable, gentle, and easy to be entreated, full of mercy and good fruits, without partiality, and without hypocrisy. James 3:17

4. Pursue Wisdom

So that thou incline thine ear unto wisdom, and apply thine heart to understanding. Proverbs 2:2

Happy is the man that findeth wisdom, and the man that getteth understanding. Proverbs 3:13

My son, let not them depart from thine eyes: keep sound wisdom and discretion. Proverbs 3:21

Get wisdom, get understanding: forget it not; neither decline from the words of my mouth. Proverbs 4:5

Wisdom is the principal thing; therefore get wisdom: and with all thy getting get understanding. Proverbs 4:7

So shall the knowledge of wisdom be unto thy soul: when thou hast found it, then there shall be a reward, and thy expectation shall not be cut off. Proverbs 24:14

5. Wisdom Enters the Heart

Who hath put wisdom in the inward parts? or who hath given understanding to the heart? Job 38:36

Behold, thou desirest truth in the inward parts: and in the hidden part thou shalt make me to know wisdom. Psalms 51:6

When wisdom entereth into thine heart, and knowledge is pleasant unto thy soul. Proverbs 2:10

Wisdom resteth in the heart of him that hath understanding: but that which is in the midst of fools is made known. Proverbs 14:33

How much better is it to get wisdom than gold! and to get understanding rather to be chosen than silver! Proverbs 16:16

I applied mine heart to know, and to search, and to seek out wisdom, and the reason of things, and to know the wickedness of folly, even of foolishness and madness. Ecclesiastes 7:25

Let the word of Christ dwell in you richly in all wisdom; teaching and admonishing one another in psalms and hymns and spiritual songs, singing with grace in your hearts to the Lord. Colossians 3:16

6. Wisdom is Valuable

For wisdom is better than rubies; and all the things that may be desired are not to be compared to it. I wisdom dwell with prudence, and find out knowledge of witty inventions. Proverbs 8:11-12

7. Wisdom is Found in Counsel

Counsel is mine, and sound wisdom: I am understanding; I have strength. Proverbs 8:14

Only by pride cometh contention: but with the well advised is wisdom. Proverbs 13:10

8. The Benefits of Wisdom

With the ancient is wisdom; and in length of days understanding. With him is wisdom and strength, he hath counsel and understanding. Job 12:12-13

Thou through thy commandments hast made me wiser than mine enemies: for they are ever with me. Psalms 119:98

Give instruction to a wise man, and he will be yet wiser: teach a just man, and he will increase in learning. Proverbs 9:9

Wisdom is good with an inheritance: and by it there is profit to them that see the sun. For wisdom is a defence, and money is a defence: but the excellency of knowledge is, that wisdom giveth life to them that have it. Ecclesiastes 7:11-12

Wisdom strengtheneth the wise more than ten mighty men which are in the city. Ecclesiastes 7:19

Then said I, Wisdom is better than strength: nevertheless the poor man's wisdom is despised, and his words are not heard. Ecclesiastes 9:16

Happy is the man that findeth wisdom, and the man that getteth understanding. Proverbs 3:13

If the iron be blunt, and he do not whet the edge, then must he put to more strength: but wisdom is profitable to direct. Ecclesiastes 10:10

O the depth of the riches both of the wisdom and knowledge of God! how unsearchable are his judgments, and his ways past finding out!
Romans 11:33

And that from a child thou hast known the holy scriptures, which are able to make thee wise unto salvation through faith which is in Christ Jesus. 2 Timothy 3:15

The fear of the Lord is the beginning of wisdom: and the knowledge of the holy is understanding. Proverbs 9:10

9. Wisdom in Action

Who is a wise man and endued with knowledge among you? let him shew out of a good conversation his works with meekness of wisdom.
James 3:13

Walk in wisdom toward them that are without, redeeming the time.
Colossians 4:5

The wisdom of the prudent is to understand his way: but the folly of fools is deceit. Proverbs 14:8

Knowledge

1. God is the Source of Knowledge

The eyes of the Lord preserve knowledge, and he overthroweth the words of the transgressor. Proverbs 22:12

For God giveth to a man that is good in his sight wisdom, and knowledge, and joy: but to the sinner he giveth travail, to gather and to heap up, that he may give to him that is good before God. This also is vanity and vexation of spirit. Ecclesiastes 2:26

And the Lord hath given me knowledge of it, and I know it: then thou shewedst me their doings. Jeremiah 11:18

That in every thing ye are enriched by him, in all utterance, and in all knowledge; 1 Corinthians 1:5

For to one is given by the Spirit the word of wisdom; to another the word of knowledge by the same Spirit; 1 Corinthians 12:8

For God, who commanded the light to shine out of darkness, hath shined in our hearts, to give the light of the knowledge of the glory of God in the face of Jesus Christ. 2 Corinthians 4:6

In whom are hid all the treasures of wisdom and knowledge.
Colossians 2:3

2. Pursue Knowledge

The fear of the Lord is the beginning of knowledge: but fools despise wisdom and instruction. Proverbs 1:7

Then shalt thou understand the fear of the Lord, and find the knowledge of God. For the Lord giveth wisdom: out of his mouth cometh knowledge and understanding. Proverbs 2:5-6

Wise men lay up knowledge: but the mouth of the foolish is near destruction. Proverbs 10:14

Also, that the soul be without knowledge, it is not good; and he that hasteth with his feet sinneth. Proverbs 19:2

And I myself also am persuaded of you, my brethren, that ye also are full of goodness, filled with all knowledge, able also to admonish one another. Romans 15:14

> *Head-knowledge is useful, but unless it is sanctified by the Holy Spirit it can be the most dangerous thing in the world. - Vance Havner*

And beside this, giving all diligence, add to your faith virtue; and to virtue knowledge; And to knowledge temperance; and to temperance patience; and to patience godliness. 2 Peter 1:5-6

3. The Benefits of Obtaining Knowledge

When wisdom entereth into thine heart, and knowledge is pleasant unto thy soul; Proverbs 2:10

And by knowledge shall the chambers be filled with all precious and pleasant riches. Proverbs 24:4

Fortune favors the prepared mind. - Louis Pasteur

A wise man is strong; yea, a man of knowledge increaseth strength.
Proverbs 24:5

So shall the knowledge of wisdom be unto thy soul: when thou hast found it, then there shall be a reward, and thy expectation shall not be cut off. Proverbs 24:14

For wisdom is a defence, and money is a defence: but the excellency of knowledge is, that wisdom giveth life to them that have it.
Ecclesiastes 7:12

And wisdom and knowledge shall be the stability of thy times, and strength of salvation: the fear of the Lord is his treasure. Isaiah 33:6

4. The Consequences of Lacking Knowledge

Therefore my people are gone into captivity, because they have no knowledge: and their honourable men are famished, and their multitude dried up with thirst. Isaiah 5:13

My people are destroyed for lack of knowledge: because thou hast rejected knowledge, I will also reject thee, that thou shalt be no priest to me: seeing thou hast forgotten the law of thy God, I will also forget thy children. Hosea 4:6

And even as they did not like to retain God in their knowledge, God gave them over to a reprobate mind, to do those things which are not convenient; Romans 1:28

Awake to righteousness, and sin not; for some have not the knowledge of God: I speak this to your shame. 1 Corinthians 15:34

5. Knowledge from God's Word

Teach me good judgment and knowledge: for I have believed thy commandments. Psalms 119:66

Receive my instruction, and not silver; and knowledge rather than choice gold. Proverbs 8:10

Cease, my son, to hear the instruction that causeth to err from the words of knowledge. Proverbs 19:27

Yea doubtless, and I count all things but loss for the excellency of the knowledge of Christ Jesus my Lord: for whom I have suffered the loss of all things, and do count them but dung, that I may win Christ.
Philippians 3:8

Bow down thine ear, and hear the words of the wise, and apply thine heart unto my knowledge. Proverbs 22:17

Have not I written to thee excellent things in counsels and knowledge.
Proverbs 22:20

Apply thine heart unto instruction, and thine ears to the words of knowledge. Proverbs 23:12

Whereby, when ye read, ye may understand my knowledge in the mystery of Christ. Ephesians 3:4

And this I pray, that your love may abound yet more and more in knowledge and in all judgment; Philippians 1:9

For if we sin wilfully after that we have received the knowledge of the truth, there remaineth no more sacrifice for sins. Hebrews 10:26

But grow in grace, and in the knowledge of our Lord and Saviour Jesus Christ. To him be glory both now and for ever. Amen. 2 Peter 3:18

Understanding

Discretion shall preserve thee, understanding shall keep thee.
Proverbs 2:11

Good understanding giveth favour: but the way of transgressors is hard.
Proverbs 13:15

Understanding is a wellspring of life unto him that hath it: but the instruction of fools is folly. Proverbs 16:22

Through wisdom is an house builded; and by understanding it is established. Proverbs 24:3

With thy wisdom and with thine understanding thou hast gotten thee riches, and hast gotten gold and silver into thy treasures. Ezekiel 28:4

1. Godly Understanding

But there is a spirit in man: and the inspiration of the Almighty giveth them understanding. Job 32:8

Who hath put wisdom in the inward parts? or who hath given understanding to the heart? Job 38:36

For the Lord giveth wisdom: out of his mouth cometh knowledge and understanding. Proverbs 2:6

The fear of the Lord is the beginning of wisdom: and the knowledge of the holy is understanding. Proverbs 9:10

There is no wisdom nor understanding nor counsel against the Lord.
Proverbs 21:30

Then opened he their understanding, that they might understand the scriptures. Luke 24:25

The eyes of your understanding being enlightened; that ye may know what is the hope of his calling, and what the riches of the glory of his inheritance in the saints. Ephesians 1:18

> *If a great man says something that seems illogical, don't laugh; try to understand it. - The Talmud*

Consider what I say; and the Lord give thee understanding in all things.
2 Timothy 2:7

And we know that the Son of God is come, and hath given us an understanding, that we may know him that is true, and we are in him that is true, even in his Son Jesus Christ. This is the true God, and eternal life.
1 John 5:20

2. Obtaining Understanding

The fear of the Lord is the beginning of wisdom: a good understanding

have all they that do his commandments: his praise endureth for ever.
Psalms 111:10

Through thy precepts I get understanding: therefore I hate every false way. Psalms 119:104

The entrance of thy words giveth light; it giveth understanding unto the simple. Psalms 119:130

So that thou incline thine ear unto wisdom, and apply thine heart to understanding. Proverbs 2:2

Let not mercy and truth forsake thee: bind them about thy neck; write them upon the table of thine heart: So shalt thou find favour and good understanding in the sight of God and man. Trust in the Lord with all thine heart; and lean not unto thine own understanding. Proverbs 3:3-5

Hear, ye children, the instruction of a father, and attend to know understanding. Proverbs 4:1

Get wisdom, get understanding: forget it not; neither decline from the words of my mouth. Proverbs 4:5

Happy is the man that findeth wisdom, and the man that getteth understanding. Proverbs 3:13

Wisdom is the principal thing; therefore get wisdom: and with all thy getting get understanding. Proverbs 4:7

My son, attend unto my wisdom, and bow thine ear to my understanding. Proverbs 5:1

Doth not wisdom cry? and understanding put forth her voice?
Proverbs 8:1

Counsel is mine, and sound wisdom: I am understanding; I have strength.
Proverbs 8:14

How much better is it to get wisdom than gold! and to get understanding rather to be chosen than silver! Proverbs 16:16

He that getteth wisdom loveth his own soul: he that keepeth understanding shall find good. Proverbs 19:8

Wherefore be ye not unwise, but understanding what the will of the Lord is. Ephesians 5:17

For this cause we also, since the day we heard it, do not cease to pray for you, and to desire that ye might be filled with the knowledge of his will in all wisdom and spiritual understanding. Colossians 1:9

Direction

Thou wilt shew me the path of life: in thy presence is fulness of joy; at thy right hand there are pleasures for evermore. Psalms 16:11

Shew me thy ways, O Lord; teach me thy paths. Lead me in thy truth, and teach me: for thou art the God of my salvation; on thee do I wait all the day. Psalms 25:4-5

The meek will he guide in judgment: and the meek will he teach his way. All the paths of the Lord are mercy and truth unto such as keep his covenant and his testimonies. Psalms 25:9-10

I will instruct thee and teach thee in the way which thou shalt go: I will guide thee with mine eye. Psalms 32:8

The steps of a good man are ordered by the Lord: and he delighteth in his way. Though he fall, he shall not be utterly cast down: for the Lord upholdeth him with his hand. Psalms 37:23-24

For this God is our God for ever and ever: he will be our guide even unto death. Psalms 48:14

> *Once God speaks to you, do not confer with flesh and blood any longer.*

Nevertheless I am continually with thee: thou hast holden me by my right hand. Thou shalt guide me with thy counsel, and afterward receive me to glory. Psalms 73:23-24

So he fed them according to the integrity of his heart; and guided them by the skilfulness of his hands. Psalms 78:72

For he shall give his angels charge over thee, to keep thee in all thy ways. Psalms 91:11

The Lord shall preserve thy going out and thy coming in from this time forth, and even for evermore. Psalms 121:8

The Lord will perfect that which concerneth me: thy mercy, O Lord, endureth for ever: forsake not the works of thine own hands.
Psalms 138:8

He keepeth the paths of judgment, and preserveth the way of his saints.
Proverbs 2:8

Trust in the Lord with all thine heart; and lean not unto thine own understanding. In all thy ways acknowledge him, and he shall direct thy paths.
Proverbs 3:5-6

The integrity of the upright shall guide them: but the perverseness of transgressors shall destroy them. Proverbs 11:3

Without counsel purposes are disappointed: but in the multitude of counsellers they are established. Proverbs 15:22

Commit thy works unto the Lord, and thy thoughts shall be established.
Proverbs 16:3

Blessed is the man who finds out which way God is moving and then gets going in the same direction. - Anonymous.

A man's heart deviseth his way: but the Lord directeth his steps.
Proverbs 16:9

Man's goings are of the Lord; how can a man then understand his own way? Proverbs 20:24

And many people shall go and say, Come ye, and let us go up to the mountain of the Lord, to the house of the God of Jacob; and he will teach us of his ways, and we will walk in his paths: for out of Zion shall go forth the law, and the word of the Lord from Jerusalem. Isaiah 2:3

For his God doth instruct him to discretion, and doth teach him.
Isaiah 28:26

And thine ears shall hear a word behind thee, saying, This is the way, walk ye in it, when ye turn to the right hand, and when ye turn to the left.
Isaiah 30:21

And I will bring the blind by a way that they knew not; I will lead them in paths that they have not known: I will make darkness light before them, and crooked things straight. These things will I do unto them, and not forsake them. Isaiah 42:16

I will go before thee, and make the crooked places straight: I will break in pieces the gates of brass, and cut in sunder the bars of iron. Isaiah 45:2

I have raised him up in righteousness, and I will direct all his ways: he shall build my city, and he shall let go my captives, not for price nor reward, saith the Lord of hosts. Isaiah 45:13

Thus saith the Lord, thy Redeemer, the Holy One of Israel; I am the Lord thy God which teacheth thee to profit, which leadeth thee by the way that thou shouldest go. Isaiah 48:17

I have seen his ways, and will heal him: I will lead him also, and restore comforts unto him and to his mourners. Isaiah 57:18

But seek ye first the kingdom of God, and his righteousness; and all these things shall be added unto you. Matthew 6:33

And when he putteth forth his own sheep, he goeth before them, and the sheep follow him: for they know his voice. And a stranger will they not follow, but will flee from him: for they know not the voice of strangers.
John 10:4-5

My sheep hear my voice, and I know them, and they follow me:
John 10:27

Howbeit when he, the Spirit of truth, is come, he will guide you into all truth: for he shall not speak of himself; but whatsoever he shall hear, that shall he speak: and he will shew you things to come. John 16:13

This I say then, Walk in the Spirit, and ye shall not fulfil the lust of the flesh. Galatians 5:16

For it is God which worketh in you both to will and to do of his good pleasure. Philippians 2:13

If any of you lack wisdom, let him ask of God, that giveth to all men liberally, and upbraideth not; and it shall be given him. James 1:15

But ye have an unction from the Holy One, and ye know all things.
1 John 2:20

I know thy works: behold, I have set before thee an open door, and no man can shut it: for thou hast a little strength, and hast kept my word, and hast not denied my name. Revelation 3:8

Favor from God

And the child Samuel grew on, and was in favour both with the Lord, and also with men. 1 Samuel 2:26

For thou, Lord, wilt bless the righteous; with favour wilt thou compass him as with a shield. Psalms 5:12

For his anger endureth but a moment; in his favour is life: weeping may endure for a night, but joy cometh in the morning. Psalms 30:5

Lord, by thy favour thou hast made my mountain to stand strong: thou didst hide thy face, and I was troubled. Psalms 30:7

By this I know that thou favourest me, because mine enemy doth not triumph over me. Psalms 41:11

A good man sheweth favour, and lendeth: he will guide his affairs with discretion. Psalms 112:5

I entreated thy favour with my whole heart: be merciful unto me according to thy word. Psalms 119:58

For whoso findeth me findeth life, and shall obtain favour of the Lord.
Proverbs 8:35

A good man obtaineth favour of the Lord: but a man of wicked devices will he condemn. Proverbs 12:2

So shalt thou find favour and good understanding in the sight of God and man. Proverbs 3:4

And Jesus increased in wisdom and stature, and in favour with God and man. Luke 2:52

Decisions

And let the peace of God rule in your hearts, to the which also ye thankful. Colossians 3:15

1. Say "No"
    a. When it's contrary to God's Word
    b. When you have prayed and God has said "no"
    c. When you feel manipulated
    d. When you feel intimidated
    e. When you feel uneasy
    f. When you feel hesitant
    g. When you feel pushed
    h. When you feel used
    i. When you feel rushed
    j. When you feel unsure
    k. When it's an unrealistic offer
    l. When you feel condemned
    m. When you feel guilty
    n. When you feel convicted
    o. When you haven't sought godly counsel

2. Say "Yes"
    a. When it's in agreement with God's Word
    b. When you have prayed and received a confirmation from God
    c. When you feel at peace in your spirit
    d. When you have thoroughly thought out the consequences
    e. When you have sought godly counsel

Diligence

Thou hast commanded us to keep thy precepts diligently. Psalms 119:4

Therefore came I forth to meet thee, diligently to seek thy face, and I have found thee. Proverbs 7:15

He that diligently seeketh good procureth favour: but he that seeketh mischief, it shall come unto him. Proverbs 11:27

When thou sittest to eat with a ruler, consider diligently what is before thee. Proverbs 23:1

Attributes of a Proverbs 31 Woman

And we have sent with them our brother, whom we have oftentimes proved diligent in many things, but now much more diligent, upon the great confidence which I have in you. 2 Corinthians 8:22

Wherefore the rather, brethren, give diligence to make your calling and election sure: for if ye do these things, ye shall never fall. 2 Peter 1:10

Wherefore, beloved, seeing that ye look for such things, be diligent that ye may be found of him in peace, without spot, and blameless.
2 Peter 3:14

Destiny is not a matter of chance, it is a matter of choice; it is not a thing to be waited for, it is a thing to be achieved. - William Jennings Bryan

1. Diligence in Work and Business

The hand of the diligent shall bear rule: but the slothful shall be under tribute. Proverbs 12:24

The slothful man roasteth not that which he took in hunting: but the substance of a diligent man is precious. Proverbs 12:27

The soul of the sluggard desireth, and hath nothing: but the soul of the diligent shall be made fat. Proverbs 13:4

The thoughts of the diligent tend only to plenteousness; but of every one that is hasty only to want. Proverbs 21:5

Seest thou a man diligent in his business? he shall stand before kings; he shall not stand before mean men. Proverbs 22:29

Be thou diligent to know the state of thy flocks, and look well to thy herds. For riches are not for ever: and doth the crown endure to every generation? Proverbs 27:23-24

People can be divided into three groups: Those who make things happen, those who watch things happen, and those who wonder what happenned. - John W. Newbern

Faithfulness

O love the Lord, all ye his saints: for the Lord preserveth the faithful, and plentifully rewardeth the proud doer. Psalms 31:23

Mine eyes shall be upon the faithful of the land, that they may dwell with me: he that walketh in a perfect way, he shall serve me. Psalms 101:6

A talebearer revealeth secrets: but he that is of a faithful spirit concealeth the matter. Proverbs 11:13

A wicked messenger falleth into mischief: but a faithful ambassador is health. Proverbs 13:17

Most men will proclaim every one his own goodness: but a faithful man who can find? Proverbs 20:6

Confidence in an unfaithful man in time of trouble is like a broken tooth, and a foot out of joint. Proverbs 25:19

> *The ability to accept responsibility is the measure of the man. - Roy L. Smith*

A faithful man shall abound with blessings: but he that maketh haste to be rich shall not be innocent. Proverbs 28:20

His lord said unto him, Well done, good and faithful servant; thou hast been faithful over a few things, I will make thee ruler over many things: enter thou into the joy of thy lord. Matthew 25:23

And the Lord said, Who then is that faithful and wise steward, whom his lord shall make ruler over his household, to give them their portion of meat in due season? Blessed is that servant, whom his lord when he cometh shall find so doing. Luke 12:42-43

If therefore ye have not been faithful in the unrighteous mammon, who will commit to your trust the true riches? And if ye have not been faithful in that which is another man's, who shall give you that which is your own? Luke 16:11-12

> *The greatest ability is dependability. - Vance Havner*

Rejoicing in hope; patient in tribulation; continuing instant in prayer.
Romans 12:12

God is faithful, by whom ye were called unto the fellowship of his Son Jesus Christ our Lord. 1 Corinthians 1:9

Moreover it is required in stewards, that a man be found faithful.
1 Corinthians 4:2

And I thank Christ Jesus our Lord, who hath enabled me, for what he counted me faithful, putting me into the ministry. 1 Timothy 1:12

Who was faithful to him that appointed him, as also Moses was faithful in all his house. Hebrews 3:2

And Moses verily was faithful in all his house, as a servant, for a testimony of those things which were to be spoken after; But Christ as a son over his own house; whose house are we, if we hold fast the confidence and the rejoicing of the hope firm unto the end. Hebrews 3:5-6

Beloved, thou doest faithfully whatsoever thou doest to the brethren, and to strangers. 3 John 1:5

Here is the patience of the saints: here are they that keep the commandments of God, and the faith of Jesus. Revelation 14:12

> *Few ever die from commitment, perseverance, faith, and achievement, but many die from neglected responsibilities, impatience, doubt and unfulfilled dreams.*

Work

Six days shalt thou labour, and do all thy work. Exodus 20:9

He that is despised, and hath a servant, is better than he that honoureth himself, and lacketh bread. Proverbs 12:9

Better is he who is lightly esteemed but works for his own support, than he who assumes honor for himself and lacks bread. Proverbs 12:9 AMP

He that laboureth laboureth for himself; for his mouth craveth it of him.
Proverbs 16:26

The appetite of the laborer works for him, for the need of his mouth urges him on. Proverbs 16:26 AMP

Whatsoever thy hand findeth to do, do it with thy might; for there is no work, nor device, nor knowledge, nor wisdom, in the grave, whither thou goest. Ecclesiastes 9:10

And whatsoever ye do, do it heartily, as to the Lord, and not unto men.
Colossians 3:23

For God is not unrighteous to forget your work and labour of love, which ye have shewed toward his name, in that ye have ministered to the saints, and do minister. Hebrews 6:10

And in the same house remain, eating and drinking such things as they give: for the labourer is worthy of his hire. Go not from house to house.
Luke 10:7

I must work the works of him that sent me, while it is day: the night cometh, when no man can work. John 9:4

For we are labourers together with God: ye are God's husbandry, ye are God's building. 1 Corinthians 3:9

Wherefore, my beloved, as ye have always obeyed, not as in my presence only, but now much more in my absence, work out your own salvation with fear and trembling. Philippians 2:12

He also that is slothful in his work is brother to him that is a great waster.
Proverbs 18:9

Inspiration without perspiration leads to frustration and stagnation. - Bill Bright

1. Benefits of Working

Every man also to whom God hath given riches and wealth, and hath given him power to eat thereof, and to take his portion, and to rejoice in his labour; this is the gift of God. Ecclesiastes 5:19

He that tilleth his land shall be satisfied with bread: but he that followeth vain persons is void of understanding. Proverbs 12:11

Every man's work shall be made manifest: for the day shall declare it, because it shall be revealed by fire; and the fire shall try every man's work of what sort it is. If any man's work abide which he hath built thereupon, he shall receive a reward. If any man's work shall be burned, he shall suffer loss: but he himself shall be saved; yet so as by fire.
1 Corinthians 3:13-15

2. We Are Commanded to Work

But let every man prove his own work, and then shall he have rejoicing in himself alone, and not in another. Galatians 6:4

That ye might walk worthy of the Lord unto all pleasing, being fruitful in every good work, and increasing in the knowledge of God.
Colossians 1:10

And that ye study to be quiet, and to do your own business, and to work with your own hands, as we commanded you; That ye may walk honestly toward them that are without, and that ye may have lack of nothing.
1 Thessalonians 4:11-12

For even when we were with you, this we commanded you, that if any would not work, neither should he eat. 2 Thessalonians 3:10

3. Consequences of Not Working

Slothfulness casteth into a deep sleep; and an idle soul shall suffer hunger. Proverbs 19:15

Good Works

Let your light so shine before men, that they may see your good works, and glorify your Father which is in heaven. Matthew 5:16

And God is able to make all grace abound toward you; that ye, always having all sufficiency in all things, may abound to every good work:
2 Corinthians 9:8

That ye might walk worthy of the Lord unto all pleasing, being fruitful in every good work, and increasing in the knowledge of God;
Colossians 1:10

And whatsoever ye do in word or deed, do all in the name of the Lord Jesus, giving thanks to God and the Father by him. Colossians 3:17

Servants, obey in all things your masters according to the flesh; not with eyeservice, as menpleasers; but in singleness of heart, fearing God: And whatsoever ye do, do it heartily, as to the Lord, and not unto men.
Colossians 3:22-23

For we are his workmanship, created in Christ Jesus unto good works, which God hath before ordained that we should walk in them.
> Ephesians 2:10

When people do not mean business with Christ in their hearts they will not do business for Christ with their hands. - Vance Havner

Likewise also the good works of some are manifest beforehand; and they that are otherwise cannot be hid. 1 Timothy 5:25

Attempt something so impossible that unless God is in it, it is doomed to failure. - John Haggai

That they do good, that they be rich in good works, ready to distribute, willing to communicate; 1 Timothy 6:18

If a man therefore purge himself from these, he shall be a vessel unto honour, sanctified, and meet for the master's use, and prepared unto every good work. 2 Timothy 2:21

That the man of God may be perfect, throughly furnished unto all good works. 2 Timothy 3:17

In all things shewing thyself a pattern of good works: in doctrine shewing uncorruptness, gravity, sincerity. Titus 2:7

Who gave himself for us, that he might redeem us from all iniquity, and purify unto himself a peculiar people, zealous of good works. Titus 2:14

O Lord, let us not live to be useless, for Christ's sake. - John Wesley

Put them in mind to be subject to principalities and powers, to obey magistrates, to be ready to every good work. Titus 3:1

This is a faithful saying, and these things I will that thou affirm constantly, that they which have believed in God might be careful to maintain good works. These things are good and profitable unto men.
> Titus 3:8

And let ours also learn to maintain good works for necessary uses, that they be not unfruitful. Titus 3:14

And let us consider one another to provoke unto love and to good works.
Hebrews 10:24

Make you perfect in every good work to do his will, working in you that which is wellpleasing in his sight, through Jesus Christ; to whom be glory for ever and ever. Amen. Hebrews 13:21

Having your conversation honest among the Gentiles: that, whereas they speak against you as evildoers, they may by your good works, which they shall behold, glorify God in the day of visitation. 1 Peter 2:12

For so is the will of God, that with well doing ye may put to silence the ignorance of foolish men; 1 Peter 2:15

For it is God's will and intention that by doing right [your] good and honest lives should silence (muzzle, gag) the ignorant charges and ill-informed criticisms of foolish persons. 1 Peter 2:15 AMP

1. Your Good Works Will Be Judged by Christ

For the Son of man shall come in the glory of his Father with his angels; and then he shall reward every man according to his works.
Matthew 16:27

Every man's work shall be made manifest: for the day shall declare it, because it shall be revealed by fire; and the fire shall try every man's work of what sort it is. If any man's work abide which he hath built thereupon, he shall receive a reward. If any man's work shall be burned, he shall suffer loss: but he himself shall be saved; yet so as by fire.
1 Corinthians 3:13-15

The work of each [one] will become (plainly, openly known-shown for what it is; for the day (of Christ) will disclose and declare it, because it will be revealed with fire, and the fire will test and critically appraise the character and worth of the work each person has done. If the work which any person has built on this Foundation-any product of his efforts whatever–survives (this test), he will get his reward. But if any person's work is burned up [under the test], he will get his reward. But if any person's work is burned up [under the test], he will suffer the loss (of it all, losing his reward), though he himself will be saved, but only as [one who has passed] through fire. 1 Corinthians 3:13-15 AMP

For the Son of man shall come in the glory of his Father with his angels; and then he shall reward every man according to his works.

> Matthew 16:27

And, behold, I come quickly; and my reward is with me, to give every man according as his work shall be. Revelation 22:12

When God crowns our merits, it is nothing other than his own gifts that he crowns. - Augustine of Hippo

Relationships

Marriage

Therefore shall a man leave his father and his mother, and shall cleave unto his wife: and they shall be one flesh. Genesis 2:24

> *Husband and wives who would live happily ever after learn early to give and take, to reach agreements by mutual consent. - Vance Havner*

But from the beginning of the creation God made them male and female. For this cause shall a man leave his father and mother, and cleave to his wife; And they twain shall be one flesh: so then they are no more twain, but one flesh. What therefore God hath joined together, let not man put asunder. Mark 10:6-9

1. Husbands

Let thy fountain be blessed: and rejoice with the wife of thy youth. Let her be as the loving hind and pleasant roe; let her breasts satisfy thee at all times; and be thou ravished always with her love. Proverbs 5:18-19

Whoso findeth a wife findeth a good thing, and obtaineth favour of the Lord. Proverbs 18:22

Houses and riches are the inheritance of fathers and a prudent wife is from the Lord. Proverbs 19:14

Who can find a virtuous woman? for her price is far above rubies.
Proverbs 31:10

Give her of the fruit of her hands; and let her own works praise her in the gates. Proverbs 31:31

Live joyfully with the wife whom thou lovest all the days of the life of thy vanity, which he hath given thee under the sun, all the days of thy vanity: for that is thy portion in this life, and in thy labour which thou takest under the sun. Ecclesiastes 9:9

Success in marriage consist not only in finding the right mate, but also in being the right mate. - Anonymous

Yet ye say, Wherefore? Because the Lord hath been witness between thee and the wife of thy youth, against whom thou hast dealt treacherously: yet is she thy companion, and the wife of thy covenant. And did not he make one? Yet had he the residue of the spirit. And wherefore one? That he might seek a godly seed. Therefore take heed to your spirit, and let none deal treacherously against the wife of his youth. For the Lord, the God of Israel, saith that he hateth putting away: for one covereth violence with his garment, saith the Lord of hosts: therefore take heed to your spirit, that ye deal not treacherously. Malachi 2:14-16

Let the husband render unto the wife due benevolence: and likewise also the wife unto the husband. The wife hath not power of her own body, but the husband: and likewise also the husband hath not power of his own body, but the wife. Defraud ye not one the other, except it be with consent for a time, that ye may give yourselves to fasting and prayer; and come together again, that Satan tempt you not for your incontinency. But I speak this by permission, and not of commandment. 1 Corinthians 7:3-6

But I would have you know, that the head of every man is Christ; and the head of the woman is the man; and the head of Christ is God.
1 Corinthians 11:3

Wives, submit yourselves unto your own husbands, as unto the Lord. For the husband is the head of the wife, even as Christ is the head of the church: and he is the saviour of the body. Ephesians 5:22-23

Wives, submit yourselves unto your own husbands, as it is fit in the Lord. Husbands, love your wives, and be not bitter against them.
Colossians 3:18-19

Fathers, provoke not your children to anger, lest they be discouraged.
Colossians 3:21

2. Wives

A virtuous woman is a crown to her husband: but she that maketh ashamed is as rottenness in his bones. Proverbs 12:4

Every wise woman buildeth her house: but the foolish plucketh it down with her hands. Proverbs 14:1

Whoso findeth a wife findeth a good thing, and obtaineth favour of the Lord. Proverbs 18:22

House and riches are the inheritance of fathers and a prudent wife is from the Lord. Proverbs 19:14

Who can find a virtuous woman? for her price is far above rubies.
Proverbs 31:10

Give her of the fruit of her hands; and let her own works praise her in the gates. Proverbs 31:31

Let the husband render unto the wife due benevolence: and likewise also the wife unto the husband. The wife hath not power of her own body, but the husband: and likewise also the husband hath not power of his own body, but the wife. Defraud ye not one the other, except it be with consent for a time, that ye may give yourselves to fasting and prayer; and come together again, that Satan tempt you not for your incontinency. But I speak this by permission, and not of commandment. 1 Corinthians 7:3-6

But I would have you know, that the head of every man is Christ; and the head of the woman is the man; and the head of Christ is God.
1 Corinthians 11:3

Wives, submit yourselves unto your own husbands, as unto the Lord. For the husband is the head of the wife, even as Christ is the head of the church: and he is the saviour of the body. Ephesians 5:22-23

Wives, submit yourselves unto your own husbands, as it is fit in the Lord. Husbands, love your wives, and be not bitter against them.
Colossians 3:18-19

Divorce

It hath been said, Whosoever shall put away his wife, let him give her a writing of divorcement: But I say unto you, That whosoever shall put away his wife, saving for the cause of fornication, causeth her to commit adultery: and whosoever shall marry her that is divorced committeth adultery. Matthew 5:31-32

> *Divorcing your mate may look like it's the answer to your problems and the way out of pain and misery. However, most of the time it only leads to more pain and misery, not only for you, but also for your children and relatives. God created the institution of marriage and God can heal and revive it.*

And he answered and said unto them, Have ye not read, that he which made them at the beginning made them male and female, And said, For this cause shall a man leave father and mother, and shall cleave to his wife: and they twain shall be one flesh? Wherefore they are no more twain, but one flesh. What therefore God hath joined together, let not man put asunder. Matthew 19:4-6

But from the beginning of the creation God made them male and female. For this cause shall a man leave his father and mother, and cleave to his wife; And they twain shall be one flesh: so then they are no more twain, but one flesh. What therefore God hath joined together, let not man put asunder. And in the house his disciples asked him again of the same matter. And he saith unto them, Whosoever shall put away his wife, and marry another, committeth adultery against her. And if a woman shall put away her husband, and be married to another, she committeth adultery. Mark 10:6-12

Whosoever putteth away his wife, and marrieth another, committeth adultery: and whosoever marrieth her that is put away from her husband committeth adultery. Luke 16:18

And unto the married I command, yet not I, but the Lord, Let not the wife depart from her husband: But and if she depart, let her remain unmarried, or be reconciled to her husband: and let not the husband put away his wife. 1 Corinthians 7:10-11

But if the unbelieving depart, let him depart. A brother or a sister is not under bondage in such cases: but God hath called us to peace.

1 Corinthians 7:15

Art thou bound unto a wife? seek not to be loosed. Art thou loosed from a wife? seek not a wife. 1 Corinthians 7:27
The wife is bound by the law as long as her husband liveth; but if her husband be dead, she is at liberty to be married to whom she will; only in the Lord. But she is happier if she so abide, after my judgment: and I think also that I have the Spirit of God. 1 Corinthians 7:39-40

Unsaved Marriage Partner

But to the rest speak I, not the Lord: If any brother hath a wife that believeth not, and she be pleased to dwell with him, let him not put her away. For the unbelieving husband is sanctified by the wife,

and the unbelieving wife is sancti-fied by the husband: else were your children unclean; but now are they holy. But if the unbelieving depart, let him depart. A brother or a sister is not under bondage in such cases: but God hath called us to peace. For what knowest thou, O wife, whether thou shalt save thy husband? or how knowest thou, O man, whether thou shalt save thy wife?
1 Corinthians 7:12-16

Likewise, ye wives, be in subjection to your own husbands; that, if any obey not the word, they also may without the word be won by the con-versation of the wives; While they behold your chaste conversation coupled with fear. Whose adorning let it not be that outward adorning of plaiting the hair, and of wearing of gold, or of putting on of apparel; But let it be the hidden man of the heart, in that which is not corruptible, even the ornament of a meek and quiet spirit, which is in the sight of God of great price. For after this manner in the old time the holy women also, who trusted in God, adorned themselves, being in subjection unto their own husbands: Even as Sara obeyed Abraham, calling him lord: whose daughters ye are, as long as ye do well, and are not afraid with any amaze-ment. Likewise, ye husbands, dwell with them according to knowledge, giving honour unto the wife, as unto the weaker vessel, and as being heirs together of the grace of life; that your prayers be not hindered.   1 Peter 3:1-7

Child-Parent Relationship

1. Raising Children

A good man leaveth an inheritance to his children's children: and the wealth of the sinner is laid up for the just. Proverbs 13:22

Children's children are the crown of old men; and the glory of children are their fathers. Proverbs 17:6

The father of the righteous shall greatly rejoice: and he that begetteth a wise child shall have joy of him. Proverbs 23:24

One that ruleth well his own house, having his children in subjection with all gravity; For if a man know not how to rule his own house, how shall he take care of the church of God? 1 Timothy 3:4-5

But if any provide not for his own, and specially for those of his own house, he hath denied the faith, and is worse than an infidel.
1 Timothy 5:8

2. Physically Correcting Your Children

He that spareth his rod hateth his son: but he that loveth him chasteneth him betimes. Proverbs 13:24

Foolishness is bound in the heart of a child; but the rod of correction shall drive it far from him. Proverbs 22:15

Withhold not correction from the child: for if thou beatest him with the rod, he shall not die. Thou shalt beat him with the rod, and shalt deliver his soul from hell. Proverbs 23:13-14

The rod and reproof give wisdom: but a child left to himself bringeth his mother to shame. Proverbs 29:15

Correct thy son, and he shall give thee rest; yea, he shall give delight unto thy soul. Proverbs 29:17

3. Being Fair to Your Children

And, ye fathers, provoke not your children to wrath: but bring them up in the nurture and admonition of the Lord. Ephesians 6:4

Fathers, provoke not your children to anger, lest they be discouraged.
Colossians 3:21

4. Teaching Your Children the Word of God

And these words, which I command thee this day, shall be in thine heart: And thou shalt teach them diligently unto thy children, and shalt talk of them when thou sittest in thine house, and when thou walkest by the way, and when thou liest down, and when thou risest up. And thou shalt bind them for a sign upon thine hand, and they shall be as frontlets between thine eyes. And thou shalt write them upon the posts of thy house, and on thy gates. Deuteronomy 6:6-9

For I know him, that he will command his children and his household after him, and they shall keep the way of the Lord, to do justice and judgment; that the Lord may bring upon Abraham that which he hath spoken of him. Genesis 18:19

And thou shalt shew thy son in that day, saying, This is done because of that which the Lord did unto me when I came forth out of Egypt.
Exodus 13:8

Only take heed to thyself, and keep thy soul diligently, lest thou forget the things which thine eyes have seen, and lest they depart from thy heart all the days of thy life: but teach them thy sons, and thy sons' sons; Specially the day that thou stoodest before the Lord thy God in Horeb, when the Lord said unto me, Gather me the people together, and I will make them hear my words, that they may learn to fear me all the days that they shall live upon the earth, and that they may teach their children. Deuteronomy 4:9-10

> *Train your child in the way in which you know you should have gone yourself. - Charles H. Spurgeon*

And ye shall teach them your children, speaking of them when thou sittest in thine house, and when thou walkest by the way, when thou liest down, and when thou risest up. Deuteronomy 11:19

And if it seem evil unto you to serve the Lord, choose you this day whom ye will serve; whether the gods which your fathers served that were on the other side of the flood, or the gods of the Amorites, in whose land ye dwell: but as for me and my house, we will serve the Lord. Joshua 24:15

We will not hide them from their children, shewing to the generation to come the praises of the Lord, and his strength, and his wonderful works that he hath done. For he established a testimony in Jacob, and appointed a law in Israel, which he commanded our fathers, that they should make them known to their children: That the generation to come might know them, even the children which should be born; who should arise and declare them to their children: That they might set their hope in God, and not forget the works of God, but keep his commandments: Psalms 78:4-7

Train up a child in the way he should go: and when he is old, he will not depart from it. Proverbs 22:6

And all thy children shall be taught of the Lord; and great shall be the peace of thy children. Isaiah 54:13

Children and Teenagers

Honour thy father and thy mother, as the Lord thy God hath commanded thee; that thy days may be prolonged, and that it may go well with thee, in the land which the Lord thy God giveth thee. Deuteronomy 5:16

Ye shall fear every man his mother, and his father, and keep my sabbaths: I am the Lord your God. Leviticus 19:3

Cursed be he that setteth light by his father or his mother. And all the people shall say, Amen. Deuteronomy 27:16

My son, keep thy father's commandment, and forsake not the law of thy mother. Proverbs 6:20

Now therefore hearken unto me, O ye children: for blessed are they that keep my ways. Proverbs 8:32

The proverbs of Solomon. A wise son maketh a glad father: but a foolish son is the heaviness of his mother. Proverbs 10:1

A wise son heareth his father's instruction: but a scorner heareth not rebuke. Proverbs 13:1

A fool despiseth his father's instruction: but he that regardeth reproof is prudent. Proverbs 15:5

Even a child is known by his doings, whether his work be pure, and whether it be right. Proverbs 20:11

Hearken unto thy father that begat thee, and despise not thy mother when she is old. Proverbs 23:22

The father of the righteous shall greatly rejoice: and he that begetteth a wise child shall have joy of him. Thy father and thy mother shall be glad, and she that bare thee shall rejoice. My son, give me thine heart, and let thine eyes observe my ways. Proverbs 23:24-26

Whoso keepeth the law is a wise son: but he that is a companion of riotous men shameth his father. Proverbs 28:7

Thou knowest the commandments, Do not commit adultery, Do not kill, Do not steal, Do not bear false witness, Honour thy father and thy mother.
Luke 18:20

Children, obey your parents in the Lord: for this is right. Honour thy father and mother; which is the first commandment with promise; That it may be well with thee, and thou mayest live long on the earth.
Ephesians 6:1-3

Children, obey your parents in all things: for this is well pleasing unto the Lord. Colossians 3:20

Dating and Engagements

Questions to Think About or Ask

1. **Are they really committed to a personal relationship with Jesus Christ?**

Be ye not unequally yoked together with unbelievers: for what fellowship hath righteousness with unrighteousness? and what communion hath light with darkness? And what concord hath Christ with Belial? or what part hath he that believeth with an infidel? 2 Corinthians 6:14-15

And what agreement hath the temple of God with idols? for ye are the temple of the living God; as God hath said, I will dwell in them, and walk in them; and I will be their God, and they shall be my people. Wherefore come out from among them, and be ye separate, saith the Lord, and touch not the unclean thing; and I will receive you, And will be a Father unto you, and ye shall be my sons and daughters, saith the Lord Almighty. 2 Corinthians 6:16-18

Blessed is the man that walketh not in the counsel of the ungodly, nor standeth in the way of sinners, nor sitteth in the seat of the scornful.
Psalms 1:1

Ye cannot drink the cup of the Lord, and the cup of devils: ye cannot be partakers of the Lord's table, and of the table of devils.
1 Corinthians 10:21

Be not deceived: evil communications corrupt good manners.
1 Corinthians 15:33

And have no fellowship with the unfruitful works of darkness, but rather reprove them. Ephesians 5:11

If ye then be risen with Christ, seek those things which are above, where Christ sitteth on the right hand of God. Colossians 3:1

> *Success in marriage consist not only in finding the right mate, but also in being the right mate. - Anonymous*

Ye adulterers and adulteresses, know ye not that the friendship of the world is enmity with God? whosoever therefore will be a friend of the world is the enemy of God. James 4:4

2. **Who created your relationship? Was it God or you?**
3. **Is your relationship a result of impatience or loneliness?**
4. **Do they have a contentious spirit?**
5. **Are they lazy or do they have a poverty-stricken mentality?**
6. **Do they have good common sense (understanding)?**
7. **Are they under generational sins or curses that could affect your relationship?**

8. Will this relationship hinder or distract you from your relationship with Jesus Christ?
9. Did you ask God before making your decision for marriage?

Friends

A friend loveth at all times, and a brother is born for adversity.
Proverbs 17:17

A man that hath friends must shew himself friendly: and there is a friend that sticketh closer than a brother. Proverbs 18:24

The man of many friends [a friend of all the world] will prove himself a bad friend, but there is a friend who sticks closer than a brother.
Proverbs 18:24 AMP

A man of many companions may come to ruin, but there is a friend who sticks closer than a brother. Proverbs 18:24 NIV

Wealth maketh many friends; but the poor is separated from his neighbour.
Proverbs 19:4

A friend is the one who comes in when the whole world has gone out. - Anonymous

Two are better than one; because they have a good reward for their labour. For if they fall, the one will lift up his fellow: but woe to him that is alone when he falleth; for he hath not another to help him up. Again, if two lie together, then they have heat: but how can one be warm alone? And if one prevail against him, two shall withstand him; and a threefold cord is not quickly broken. Ecclesiastes 4:9-12

Many will entreat the favour of the prince: and every man is a friend to him that giveth gifts. Proverbs 19:6

To him that is afflicted pity should be shewed from his friend; but he forsaketh the fear of the Almighty. Job 6:14

He that loveth pureness of heart, for the grace of his lips the king shall be his friend. Proverbs 22:11

Faithful are the wounds of a friend; but the kisses of an enemy are deceitful. Proverbs 27:6

Ointment and perfume rejoice the heart: so doth the sweetness of a man's friend by hearty counsel. Thine own friend, and thy father's friend, for-

sake not; neither go into thy brother's house in the day of thy calamity: for better is a neighbour that is near than a brother far off.
Proverbs 27:9-10

A real friend covers your sins and protects your reputation in public and rebukes and admonishes you in private.

Iron sharpeneth iron; so a man sharpeneth the countenance of his friend.
Proverbs 27:17

Greater love hath no man than this, that a man lay down his life for his friends. Ye are my friends, if ye do whatsoever I command you.
John 15:13-14

Henceforth I call you not servants; for the servant knoweth not what his lord doeth: but I have called you friends; for all things that I have heard of my Father I have made known unto you. John 15:15

And the scripture was fulfilled which saith, Abraham believed God, and it was imputed unto him for righteousness: and he was called the Friend of God. James 2:23

Insomuch as any one pushes you nearer to God, he or she is your friend. - Anonymous

Avoiding or Breaking Bad Relationships

Blessed is the man that walketh not in the counsel of the ungodly, nor standeth in the way of sinners, nor sitteth in the seat of the scornful.
Psalms 1:1

Depart from me, ye evildoers: for I will keep the commandments of my God. Psalms 119:115

Forsake the foolish, and live; and go in the way of understanding.
Proverbs 9:6

The thoughts of the righteous are right: but the counsels of the wicked are deceit. Proverbs 12:5

He that tilleth his land shall be satisfied with bread: but he that followeth vain persons is void of understanding. Proverbs 12:11

He that walketh with wise men shall be wise: but a companion of fools shall be destroyed. Proverbs 13:20

Go from the presence of a foolish man, when thou perceivest not in him the lips of knowledge. Proverbs 14:7

Better it is to be of an humble spirit with the lowly, than to divide the spoil with the proud. Proverbs 16:19

A violent man enticeth his neighbour, and leadeth him into the way that is not good. Proverbs 16:29

The man that wandereth out of the way of understanding shall remain in the congregation of the dead. Proverbs 21:16

Make no friendship with an angry man; and with a furious man thou shalt not go. Lest thou learn his ways, and get a snare to thy soul.
Proverbs 22:24-25

Be not thou envious against evil men, neither desire to be with them.
Proverbs 24:1

My son, fear thou the Lord and the king: and meddle not with them that are given to change. Proverbs 24:21

For their calamity shall rise suddenly; and who knoweth the ruin of them both? Proverbs 24:22

Whoso keepeth the law is a wise son: but he that is a companion of riotous men shameth his father. Proverbs 28:7

Whoso loveth wisdom rejoiceth his father: but he that keepeth company with harlots spendeth his substance. Proverbs 29:3

I sat not in the assembly of the mockers, nor rejoiced; I sat alone because of thy hand: for thou hast filled me with indignation. Jeremiah 15:17

Blessed are ye, when men shall hate you, and when they shall separate you from their company, and shall reproach you, and cast out your name as evil, for the Son of man's sake. Luke 6:22

Then spake Jesus again unto them, saying, I am the light of the world: he that followeth me shall not walk in darkness, but shall have the light of life. John 8:12

I am come a light into the world, that whosoever believeth on me should not abide in darkness. John 12:46

I wrote unto you in an epistle not to company with fornicators: Yet not altogether with the fornicators of this world, or with the covetous, or extortioners, or with idolaters; for then must ye needs go out of the world. But now I have written unto you not to keep company, if any man that is called a brother be a fornicator, or covetous, or an idolater, or a railer, or

a drunkard, or an extortioner; with such an one no not to eat.
1 Corinthians 5:9-11

Ye cannot drink the cup of the Lord, and the cup of devils: ye cannot be partakers of the Lord's table, and of the table of devils.
1 Corinthians 10:21

Be not deceived: evil communications corrupt good manners.
1 Corinthians 15:33

Be ye not unequally yoked together with unbelievers: for what fellowship hath righteousness with unrighteousness? and what communion hath light with darkness? And what concord hath Christ with Belial? or what part hath he that believeth with an infidel? 2 Corinthians 6:14-15

And what agreement hath the temple of God with idols? for ye are the temple of the living God; as God hath said, I will dwell in them, and walk in them; and I will be their God, and they shall be my people. Wherefore come out from among them, and be ye separate, saith the Lord, and touch not the unclean thing; and I will receive you, And will be a Father unto you, and ye shall be my sons and daughters, saith the Lord Almighty. 2 Corinthians 6:16-18

And have no fellowship with the unfruitful works of darkness, but rather reprove them. Ephesians 5:11

If ye then be risen with Christ, seek those things which are above, where Christ sitteth on the right hand of God. Colossians 3:1

Abstain from all appearance of evil. 1 Thessalonians 5:22

Ye adulterers and adulteresses, know ye not that the friendship of the world is enmity with God? whosoever therefore will be a friend of the world is the enemy of God. James 4:4

> *Salt seasons, purifies, preserves. But somebody ought to remind us that salt also irritates. Real living Christianity rubs this world the wrong way. - Vance Havner*

Spiritual Warfare

The Superior Power and Authority of Christ

For it is written, As I live, saith the Lord, every knee shall bow to me, and every tongue shall confess to God. Romans 14:11

And Jesus came and spake unto them, saying, All power is given unto me in heaven and in earth. Go ye therefore, and teach all nations, baptizing them in the name of the Father, and of the Son, and of the Holy Ghost: Matthew 28:18-19

And what is the exceeding greatness of his power to usward who believe, according to the working of his mighty power, Which he wrought in Christ, when he raised him from the dead, and set him at his own right hand in the heavenly places, Far above all principality, and power, and might, and dominion, and every name that is named, not only in this world, but also in that which is to come: And hath put all things under his feet, and gave him to be the head over all things to the church, Which is his body, the fulness of him that filleth all in all. Ephesians 1:19-23

Who is the image of the invisible God, the firstborn of every creature: For by him were all things created, that are in heaven, and that are in earth, visible and invisible, whether they be thrones, or dominions, or principalities, or powers: all things were created by him, and for him: And he is before all things, and by him all things consist. And he is the head of the body, the church: who is the beginning, the firstborn from the dead; that in all things he might have the preeminence.
Colossians 1:15-18

And ye are complete in him, which is the head of all principality and power: Colossians 2:10

And having spoiled principalities and powers, he made a shew of them openly, triumphing over them in it. Colossians 2:15

Let every soul be subject unto the higher powers. For there is no power but of God: the powers that be are ordained of God. Romans 13:1

I am he that liveth, and was dead; and, behold, I am alive for evermore, Amen; and have the keys of hell and of death. Revelation 1:18

But this man, after he had offered one sacrifice for sins for ever, sat down on the right hand of God; From henceforth expecting till his enemies be made his footstool. Hebrews 10:12-13

He that committeth sin is of the devil; for the devil sinneth from the beginning. For this purpose the Son of God was manifested, that he might destroy the works of the devil. 1 John 3:8

You Have Power Over the devil and his demons

And when he had called unto him his twelve disciples, he gave them power against unclean spirits, to cast them out, and to heal all manner of sickness and all manner of disease. Matthew 10:1

Behold, I give unto you power to tread on serpents and scorpions, and over all the power of the enemy: and nothing shall by any means hurt you. Notwithstanding in this rejoice not, that the spirits are subject unto you; but rather rejoice, because your names are written in heaven.
Luke 10:19-20

And when all things shall be subdued unto him, then shall the Son also himself be subject unto him that put all things under him, that God may be all in all. 1 Corinthians 15:28

For God hath not given us the spirit of fear; but of power, and of love, and of a sound mind. 2 Timothy 1:7

Forasmuch then as the children are partakers of flesh and blood, he also himself likewise took part of the same; that through death he might destroy him that had the power of death, that is, the devil; And deliver them who through fear of death were all their lifetime subject to bondage.
Hebrews 2:14-15

Submit yourselves therefore to God. Resist the devil, and he will flee from you. James 4:7

Who is gone into heaven, and is on the right hand of God; angels and authorities and powers being made subject unto him. 1 Peter 3:22

Thou shalt bring down the noise of strangers, as the heat in a dry place; even the heat with the shadow of a cloud: the branch of the terrible ones shall be brought low. And he will destroy in this mountain the face of the covering cast over all people, and the veil that is spread over all nations.
Isaiah 25:5,7

For the terrible one is brought to nought, and the scorner is consumed, and all that watch for iniquity are cut off: Isaiah 29:20

No weapon that is formed against thee shall prosper; and every tongue that shall rise against thee in judgment thou shalt condemn. This is the heritage of the servants of the Lord, and their righteousness is of me, saith the Lord. Isaiah 54:17

I am he that liveth, and was dead; and, behold, I am alive for evermore, Amen; and have the keys of hell and of death. Revelation 1:18

Spiritual Warfare

1. The Armor for the Spiritual Realm

    a. **Loins Girt About with Truth**

    b. **Breastplate of Righteousness**

    c. **Feet Shod with the Preparation of the Gospel of Peace**

    d. **Shield of Faith**

    e. **Helmet of Salvation**

    f. **Sword of the Spirit, which is the Word of God**

Finally, my brethren, be strong in the Lord, and in the power of his might. Put on the whole armour of God, that ye may be able to stand against the wiles of the devil. For we wrestle not against flesh and blood, but against principalities, against powers, against the rulers of the darkness of this world, against spiritual wickedness in high places. Wherefore take unto you the whole armour of God, that ye may be able to withstand in the evil day, and having done all, to stand. Stand therefore, having your loins girt about with truth, and having on the breastplate of righteousness; And your feet shod with the preparation of the gospel of peace; Above all, taking the shield of faith, wherewith ye shall be able to quench all the fiery darts of the wicked. And take the helmet of salvation, and the sword of the Spirit, which is the word of God. Ephesians 6:10-17

The Weapons of the Spiritual Realm

1. The Name of Jesus

And the seventy returned again with joy, saying, Lord, even the devils are subject unto us through thy name. Luke 10:17

Wherefore God also hath highly exalted him, and given him a name which is above every name: That at the name of Jesus every knee should bow, of things in heaven, and things in earth, and things under the earth;
Philippians 2:9-10

2. The Blood of Jesus

And they (Christians) overcame him (devil) by the blood of the Lamb, and by the word of their testimony; and they loved not their lives unto the death. Revelation 12:11

3. The Sword of the Spirit (The Word of God)

Yea, a sword shall pierce through thy own soul also, that the thoughts of many hearts may be revealed. Luke 2:35

And take the helmet of salvation, and the sword of the Spirit, which is the word of God. Ephesians 6:17

And then shall that Wicked be revealed, whom the Lord shall consume with the spirit of his mouth, and shall destroy with the brightness of his coming. 2 Thessalonians 2:8

For the word of God is quick, and powerful, and sharper than any twoedged sword, piercing even to the dividing asunder of soul and spirit, and of the joints and marrow, and is a discerner of the thoughts and intents of the heart. Hebrews 4:12

And he had in his right hand seven stars: and out of his mouth went a sharp twoedged sword: and his countenance was as the sun shineth in his strength. Revelation 1:16

> *The devil is a spiritual being and the spoken Word of God is the sword of the Spirit. Nothing else cuts, controls, binds, hinders, and defeats the devil and his demons more than a Christian confessing God's Word in faith.*

And to the angel of the church in Pergamos write; These things saith he which hath the sharp sword with two edges. Revelation 2:12

Repent; or else I will come unto thee quickly, and will fight against them with the sword of my mouth. Revelation 2:16

> *You have to say "yes" to God first before you can effectively say "no" to the devil. - Vance Havner*

And out of his mouth goeth a sharp sword, that with it he should smite the nations: and he shall rule them with a rod of iron: and he treadeth the winepress of the fierceness and wrath of Almighty God. Revelation 19:15

"Submit yourselves therefore to God. Resist the devil, and he will flee from you." James 4:7

Binding and Loosing

Verily I say unto you, Whatsoever ye shall bind on earth shall be bound in heaven: and whatsoever ye shall loose on earth shall be loosed in heaven. Matthew 18:18

Or else how can one enter into a strong man's house, and spoil his goods, except he first bind the strong man? and then he will spoil his house.
Matthew 12:29

God's End-Time Army

Ye are of God, little children, and have overcome them: because greater is he that is in you, than he that is in the world. 1 John 4:4

Neither shall one thrust another; they shall walk every one in his path: and when they fall upon the sword, they shall not be wounded. They shall run to and fro in the city; they shall run upon the wall, they shall climb up upon the houses; they shall enter in at the windows like a thief. The earth shall quake before them; the heavens shall tremble: the sun and the moon shall be dark, and the stars shall withdraw their shining: And the Lord shall utter his voice before his army: for his camp is very great: for he is strong that executeth his word: for the day of the Lord is great and very terrible; and who can abide it? Joel 2:7-11

Spiritual Enemies

For though we walk in the flesh, we do not war after the flesh: For the weapons of our warfare are not carnal, but mighty through God to the pulling down of strong holds; Casting down imaginations, and every high thing that exalteth itself against the knowledge of God, and bringing into captivity every thought to the obedience of Christ;
2 Corinthians 10:3-5

For we wrestle not against flesh and blood, but against principalities, against powers, against the rulers of the darkness of this world, against spiritual wickedness in high places. Ephesians 6:12

Attacking the Enemy

And they blessed Rebekah, and said unto her, Thou art our sister, be thou the mother of thousands of millions, and let thy seed possess the gate of those which hate them. Genesis 24:60

And I say also unto thee, That thou art Peter, and upon this rock I will build my church; and the gates of hell shall not prevail against it.
Matthew 16:18

And I tell you, you are Peter [petros, masculine, a large piece of rock], and on this rock [petr *a*, feminine, a huge rock like Gibraltar] I will build My church, and the gates of Hades (the powers of the infernal region shall not overpower it–or be strong to its detriment, or hold out against it. Matthew 16:18 AMP

And from the days of John the Baptist until now the kingdom of heaven suffereth violence, and the violent take it by force. Matthew 11:12

And from the days of John the Baptist until the present time the kingdom of heaven has endured violent assault, and violent men seize it by force [as a precious prize]–a share in the heavenly kingdom is sought for with most ardent zeal and intense exertion. Matthew 11:12 AMP

And ye shall chase your enemies, and they shall fall before you by the sword. And five of you shall chase an hundred, and an hundred of you shall put ten thousand to flight: and your enemies shall fall before you by the sword. For I will have respect unto you, and make you fruitful, and multiply you, and establish my covenant with you. Leviticus 26:7-9

How should one chase a thousand, and two put ten thousand to flight, except their Rock had sold them, and the Lord had shut them up?
Deuteronomy 32:30

Quenched the violence of fire, escaped the edge of the sword, out of weakness were made strong, waxed valiant in fight, turned to flight the armies of the aliens. Hebrews 11:34

One man of you shall chase a thousand: for the Lord your God, he it is that fighteth for you, as he hath promised you. Joshua 23:10

A thousand shall fall at thy side, and ten thousand at thy right hand; but it shall not come nigh thee. Psalms 91:7

Spiritual Discernment

But the natural man receiveth not the things of the Spirit of God: for they are foolishness unto him: neither can he know them, because they are spiritually discerned. 1 Corinthians 2:14

To another the working of miracles; to another prophecy; to another discerning of spirits; to another divers kinds of tongues; to another the interpretation of tongues: 1 Corinthians 12:10

Lest satan should get an advantage of us: for we are not ignorant of his devices. 2 Corinthians 2:11

Discerning Good and Evil

Give therefore thy servant an understanding heart to judge thy people, that I may discern between good and bad: for who is able to judge this thy so great a people? 1 Kings 3:9

And they shall teach my people the difference between the holy and profane, and cause them to discern between the unclean and the clean.
Ezekiel 44:23

Then shall ye return, and discern between the righteous and the wicked, between him that serveth God and him that serveth him not.
Malachi 3:18

But strong meat belongeth to them that are of full age, even those who by reason of use have their senses exercised to discern both good and evil. Hebrews 5:14

Discernment From God's Word

My son, let not them depart from thine eyes: keep sound wisdom and discretion: So shall they be life unto thy soul, and grace to thy neck. Then shalt thou walk in thy way safely, and thy foot shall not stumble.

When thou liest down, thou shalt not be afraid: yea, thou shalt lie down, and thy sleep shall be sweet. Proverbs 3:21-24

For the word of God is quick, and powerful, and sharper than any twoedged sword, piercing even to the dividing asunder of soul and spirit, and of the joints and marrow, and is a discerner of the thoughts and intents of the heart. Hebrews 4:12

Spiritual Eyes and Ears

Open thou mine eyes, that I may behold wondrous things out of thy law.
Psalms 119:18

Make me to understand the way of thy precepts: so shall I talk of thy wondrous works. Psalms 119:27

Give me understanding, and I shall keep thy law; yea, I shall observe it with my whole heart. Psalms 119:34

The earth, O Lord, is full of thy mercy: teach me thy statutes.
Psalms 119:64

Thy hands have made me and fashioned me: give me understanding, that I may learn thy commandments. Psalms 119:73

Turn you at my reproof: behold, I will pour out my spirit unto you, I will make known my words unto you. Proverbs 1:23

And in that day shall the deaf hear the words of the book, and the eyes of the blind shall see out of obscurity, and out of darkness. Isaiah 29:18

They also that erred in spirit shall come to understanding, and they that murmured shall learn doctrine. Isaiah 29:24

And I will bring the blind by a way that they knew not; I will lead them in paths that they have not known: I will make darkness light before them, and crooked things straight. These things will I do unto them, and not forsake them. Isaiah 42:16

He answered and said unto them, Because it is given unto you to know the mysteries of the kingdom of heaven, but to them it is not given.
Matthew 13:11

But blessed are your eyes, for they see: and your ears, for they hear. For verily I say unto you, That many prophets and righteous men have desired to see those things which ye see, and have not seen them; and to hear those things which ye hear, and have not heard them.
Matthew 13:16-17

That the God of our Lord Jesus Christ, the Father of glory, may give unto you the spirit of wisdom and revelation in the knowledge of him. The eyes of your understanding being enlightened; that ye may know what is the hope of his calling, and what the riches of the glory of his inheritance in the saints. Ephesians 1:17-18

He that hath an ear, let him hear what the Spirit saith unto the churches; To him that overcometh will I give to eat of the tree of life, which is in the midst of the paradise of God. Revelation 2:7

Deception

1. Being Deceived by Others

And Jesus answered and said unto them, Take heed that no man deceive you. For many shall come in my name, saying, I am Christ; and shall deceive many. Matthew 24:4-5

Frowardness is in his heart, he deviseth mischief continually; he soweth discord. Proverbs 6:14

The thoughts of the righteous are right: but the counsels of the wicked are deceit. Proverbs 12:5

Deceit is in the heart of them that imagine evil: but to the counsellors of peace is joy. Proverbs 12:20

Be not a witness against thy neighbour without cause; and deceive not with thy lips. Proverbs 24:28

So is the man that deceiveth his neighbour, and saith, Am not I in sport?
Proverbs 26:19

He that hateth dissembleth with his lips, and layeth up deceit within him;
Proverbs 26:24

And many false prophets shall rise, and shall deceive many.
Matthew 24:11

For there shall arise false Christs, and false prophets, and shall shew great signs and wonders; insomuch that, if it were possible, they shall deceive the very elect. Matthew 24:24

> *satan has a false gospel, a false repentance, a false dedication, a false faith, a false everything. Weak Christians, not well read in the scriptures, will easily fall prey to modern magicians.*
> *- Vance Havner*

And Jesus answering them began to say, Take heed lest any man deceive you: For many shall come in my name, saying, I am Christ; and shall deceive many. Mark 13:5-6

And he said, Take heed that ye be not deceived: for many shall come in my name, saying, I am Christ; and the time draweth near: go ye not therefore after them. Luke 21:8

For they that are such serve not our Lord Jesus Christ, but their own belly; and by good words and fair speeches deceive the hearts of the simple. Romans 16:18

Be not deceived: evil communications corrupt good manners.
1 Corinthians 15:33

Know ye not that the unrighteous shall not inherit the kingdom of God? Be not deceived: neither fornicators, nor idolaters, nor adulterers, nor effeminate, nor abusers of themselves with mankind. 1 Corinthians 6:9

That we henceforth be no more children, tossed to and fro, and carried about with every wind of doctrine, by the sleight of men, and cunning craftiness, whereby they lie in wait to deceive. Ephesians 4:14

Let no man deceive you with vain words: for because of these things cometh the wrath of God upon the children of disobedience.
Ephesians 5:6

Let no man deceive you by any means: for that day shall not come, except there come a falling away first, and that man of sin be revealed, the son of perdition. 2 Thessalonians 2:3

But evil men and seducers shall wax worse and worse, deceiving, and being deceived. 2 Timothy 3:13

For there are many unruly and vain talkers and deceivers, specially they of the circumcision. Titus 1:10

Little children, let no man deceive you: he that doeth righteousness is righteous, even as he is righteous. 1 John 3:7

For many deceivers are entered into the world, who confess not that Jesus Christ is come in the flesh. This is a deceiver and an antichrist.
2 John 1:7

Wine is a mocker, strong drink is raging: and whosoever is deceived thereby is not wise. Proverbs 20:1

Be not a witness against thy neighbour without cause; and deceive not with thy lips. Proverbs 24:28

2. Self-Deception

Take heed to yourselves, that your heart be not deceived, and ye turn aside, and serve other gods, and worship them. Deuteronomy 11:16

Thus saith the Lord; Deceive not yourselves, saying, The Chaldeans shall surely depart from us: for they shall not depart. Jeremiah 37:9

Let no man deceive himself. If any man among you seemeth to be wise in this world, let him become a fool, that he may be wise.
1 Corinthians 3:18

For if a man think himself to be something, when he is nothing, he deceiveth himself. Galatians 6:3

But be ye doers of the word, and not hearers only, deceiving your own selves. James 1:22

> *We are challenged these days, but not changed, convicted, but not converted. We hear, but do not and thereby we deceive ourselves. - Vance Havner*

If any man among you seem to be religious, and bridleth not his tongue, but deceiveth his own heart, this man's religion is vain. James 1:26

And shall receive the reward of unrighteousness, as they that count it pleasure to riot in the day time. Spots they are and blemishes, sporting themselves with their own deceivings while they feast with you.
2 Peter 2:13

If we say that we have fellowship with him, and walk in darkness, we lie, and do not the truth. 1 John 1:6

If we say that we have no sin, we deceive ourselves, and the truth is not in us. 1 John 1:8

> *There is one thing worse than not coming to church, and that is to come and do nothing about the message one hears. James tells us that hearing without doing means self-deception. - Vance Havner*

He that committeth sin is of the devil; for the devil sinneth from the beginning. For this purpose the Son of God was manifested, that he might destroy the works of the devil. Whosoever is born of God doth not commit sin; for his seed remaineth in him: and he cannot sin, because he is born of God. In this the children of God are manifest, and the children of the devil: whosoever doeth not righteousness is not of God, neither he that loveth not his brother. 1 John 3:8-10

Be not deceived; God is not mocked: for whatsoever a man soweth, that shall he also reap. Galatians 6:7

3. Deceived by Darkness

And the great dragon was cast out, that old serpent, called the Devil, and Satan, which deceiveth the whole world: he was cast out into the earth, and his angels were cast out with him. Revelation 12:9

And deceiveth them that dwell on the earth by the means of those miracles which he had power to do in the sight of the beast; saying to them that dwell on the earth, that they should make an image to the beast, which had the wound by a sword, and did live. Revelation 13:14

And the light of a candle shall shine no more at all in thee; and the voice of the bridegroom and of the bride shall be heard no more at all in thee: for thy merchants were the great men of the earth; for by thy sorceries were all nations deceived. Revelation 18:23

And the beast was taken, and with him the false prophet that wrought miracles before him, with which he deceived them that had received the mark of the beast, and them that worshipped his image. These both were cast alive into a lake of fire burning with brimstone. Revelation 19:20

And cast him into the bottomless pit, and shut him up, and set a seal upon him, that he should deceive the nations no more, till the thousand years should be fulfilled: and after that he must be loosed a little season.
Revelation 20:3

And shall go out to deceive the nations which are in the four quarters of the earth, Gog and Magog, to gather them together to battle: the number of whom is as the sand of the sea. Revelation 20:8

And the devil that deceived them was cast into the lake of fire and brimstone, where the beast and the false prophet are, and shall be tormented day and night for ever and ever. Revelation 20:10

The Strategies of satan (the devil)

1. satan's most infamous strategy is lying.

He was a murderer from the beginning, and abode not in the truth, because there is no truth in him. When he speaketh a lie, he speaketh of his own: for he is a liar, and the father of it. John 8:44

2. satan seeks to steal from, kill, and destroy anybody that will let him.

The thief cometh not, but for to steal, and to kill, and to destroy:
John 10:10

Be sober, be vigilant; because your adversary the devil, AS a roaring lion, walketh about, seeking whom he MAY devour. 1 Peter 5:8

3. satan is the inventor of sin, and he is constantly tempting mankind to sin against God.

He that committeth sin is of the devil; for the devil sinneth from the beginning. For this purpose the Son of God was manifested, that he might destroy the works of the devil. 1 John 3:8

4. satan tries to steal and choke the Word of God out of the heart of man.

He also that received seed among the thorns is he that heareth the word; and the care of this world, and the deceitfulness of riches, choke the word, and he becometh unfruitful. Matthew 13:22

For all that is in the world, the lust of the flesh, and the lust of the eyes, and the pride of life, is not of the Father, but is of the world.
1 John 2:16

Those by the way side are they that hear; then cometh the devil, and taketh away the word out of their hearts, lest they should believe and be saved. Luke 8:12

5. satan will try to put evil, vile, crazy, doubtful, and fearful thoughts into your mind.

Casting down imaginations, and every high thing that exalteth itself against the knowledge of God, and bringing into captivity every thought to the obedience of Christ. 2 Corinthians 10:5

6. satan tries to deceive believers and unbelievers into new and old doctrines of devils, false religions, cults, and the occult, by using false christs, false teachers, false prophets, gurus, and so on....

And Jesus answered and said unto them, Take heed that no man deceive you. For many shall come in my name, saying, I am Christ; and shall deceive many. Matthew 24:4-5

And many false prophets shall rise, and shall deceive many.
Matthew 24:11

For there shall arise false Christs, and false prophets, and shall shew great signs and wonders; insomuch that, if it were possible, they shall deceive the very elect. Matthew 24:24

And Jesus answering them began to say, Take heed lest any man deceive you: For many shall come in my name, saying, I am Christ; and shall deceive many. Mark 13:5-6

And he said, Take heed that ye be not deceived: for many shall come in my name, saying, I am Christ; and the time draweth near: go ye not therefore after them. Luke 21:8

For such are false apostles, deceitful workers, transforming themselves into the apostles of Christ. And no marvel; for Satan himself is transformed into an angel of light. Therefore it is no great thing if his ministers also be transformed as the ministers of righteousness; whose end shall be according to their works. 2 Corinthians 11:13-15

I marvel that ye are so soon removed from him that called you into the grace of Christ unto another gospel: **Which** is not another; but there be some that trouble you, and would pervert the gospel of Christ. But though we, or an angel from heaven, preach any other gospel unto you than that which we have preached unto you, let him be accursed. As we said before, so say I now again, If any man preach any other gospel unto you than that ye have received, let him be accursed. Galatians 1:6-9

That we henceforth be no more children, tossed to and fro, and carried about with every wind of doctrine, by the sleight of men, and cunning craftiness, whereby they lie in wait to deceive. Ephesians 4:14

Let no man deceive you with vain words: for because of these things cometh the wrath of God upon the children of disobedience.
Ephesians 5:6

And this I say, lest any man should beguile you with enticing words.
Colossians 2:4

Little children, let no man deceive you: he that doeth righteousness is righteous, even as he is righteous. 1 John 3:7

7. satan and his forces work overtime to lure, trick and trap mankind with various sinful temptations.

Put on the whole armour of God, that ye may be able to stand against the wiles of the devil. Ephesians 6:11

DEFINITION OF WILES: A craft, deceit, or cunning device, clever trick used to fool or lure someone.

8. satan tries to condemn believers for their past life-styles and present walk with Christ.

For the accuser of our brethren is cast down, which accused them before our God day and night. Revelation 12:10

9. satan tries to convince sinners and believers that God is angry with them and that He condemns them for their sins.

I am come that they might have life, and that they might have it more abundantly. John 10:10

For God sent not his Son into the world to condemn the world; but that the world through him might be saved. John 3:17

Verily, verily, I say unto you, He that heareth my word, and believeth on him that sent me, hath everlasting life, and shall not come into condemnation; but is passed from death unto life. John 5:24

There is therefore now no condemnation to them which are in Christ Jesus, who walk not after the flesh, but after the Spirit. Romans 8:1

She said, No man, Lord. And Jesus said unto her, Neither do I condemn thee: go, and sin no more. John 8:11

For if our heart condemn us, God is greater than our heart, and knoweth all things. 1 John 3:20

Beloved, if our heart condemn us not, then have we confidence toward God. 1 John 3:21

10. satan tries to control the minds of mankind and hinder them from hearing and accepting the Gospel of Christ.

But if our gospel be hid, it is hid to them that are lost: In whom the god of this world hath blinded the minds of them which believe not, lest the light of the glorious gospel of Christ, who is the image of God, should shine unto them. 2 Corinthians 4:3-4

11. satan tries to control the lifestyle of mankind on the earth.

Wherein in time past ye walked according to the course of this world, according to the prince of the power of the air, the spirit that now worketh in the children of disobedience. Ephesians 2:2

12. satan and his forces try to delay believers' prayers from being answered on time, and satan tries to control the governments of nations around the world.

But the prince of the kingdom of Persia withstood me one and twenty days: but, lo, Michael, one of the chief princes, came to help me; and I remained there with the kings of Persia. Daniel 10:13

Then said he, Knowest thou wherefore I come unto thee? and now will I return to fight with the prince of Persia: and when I am gone forth, lo, the prince of Grecia shall come. Daniel 10:20

13. satan and his evil forces and human servants try to prevent normal citizens and leaders (especially) from hearing and receiving the Gospel of Jesus Christ.

But Elymas the sorcerer (for so is his name by interpretation) withstood them, seeking to turn away the deputy from the faith. Then Saul, (who also is called Paul,) filled with the Holy Ghost, set his eyes on him, And said, O full of all subtlety and all mischief, thou child of the devil, thou enemy of all righteousness, wilt thou not cease to pervert the right ways of the Lord? And now, behold, the hand of the Lord is upon thee, and thou shalt be blind, not seeing the sun for a season. And immediately there fell on him a mist and a darkness; and he went about seeking some to lead him by the hand. Acts 13:8-11

14. satan and his forces are highly organized and they are in constant spiritual battle with God's army around the world.

And if Satan cast out Satan, he is divided against himself; how shall then his kingdom stand? Matthew 12:26

For we wrestle not against flesh and blood, but against principalities, against powers, against the rulers of the darkness of this world, against spiritual wickedness in high places. Ephesians 6:12

15. Any sickness, death, tragedy, temptation, natural disaster, calamity, problem, or situation contrary to the Word of God can always be in some way, shape, or form linked with or traced directly to satan and his evil forces.

satan is never happier than when he has convinced people that he is nonexistent. The very popular modern denial of the existence of a personal devil is one of satan's major triumphs. We have a real enemy on our hands and we shall greatly weaken our position by blissfully disregarding his presence and power. - Vance Havner

Laying On of Hands

1. Miracles of Jesus Through the Laying On of Hands

And Jesus put forth his hand, and touched him, saying, I will; be thou clean. And immediately his leprosy was cleansed. Matthew 8:3

And he touched her hand, and the fever left her: and she arose, and ministered unto them. Matthew 8:15

While he spake these things unto them, behold, there came a certain ruler, and worshipped him, saying, My daughter is even now dead: but come and lay thy hand upon her, and she shall live. Matthew 9:18

And besought him greatly, saying, My little daughter lieth at the point of death: I pray thee, come and lay thy hands on her, that she may be healed; and she shall live. Mark 5:23

2. Spiritual Gifts Given Through the Laying On of Hands

Then laid they their hands on them, and they received the Holy Ghost. And when Simon saw that through laying on of the apostles' hands the Holy Ghost was given, he offered them money, Acts 8:17-18

And Ananias went his way, and entered into the house; and putting his hands on him said, Brother Saul, the Lord, even Jesus, that appeared unto thee in the way as thou camest, hath sent me, that thou mightest receive thy sight, and be filled with the Holy Ghost. Acts 9:17

He said unto them, Have ye received the Holy Ghost since ye believed? And they said unto him, We have not so much as heard whether there be any Holy Ghost. And he said unto them, Unto what then were ye baptized? And they said, Unto John's baptism. Then said Paul, John verily baptized with the baptism of repentance, saying unto the people, that they should believe on him which should come after him, that is, on Christ Jesus. When they heard this, they were baptized in the name of the Lord Jesus. And when Paul had laid his hands upon them, the Holy Ghost came on them; and they spake with tongues, and prophesied.
Acts 19:2-6

For I long to see you, that I may impart unto you some spiritual gift, to the end ye may be established; Romans 1:11

Neglect not the gift that is in thee, which was given thee by prophecy, with the laying on of the hands of the presbytery. 1 Timothy 4:14

Wherefore I put thee in remembrance that thou stir up the gift of God, which is in thee by the putting on of my hands. 2 Timothy 1:6

Of the doctrine of baptisms, and of laying on of hands, and of resurrection of the dead, and of eternal judgment. Hebrews 6:2

3. Blessing Through the Laying On of Hands

And Joseph took them both, Ephraim in his right hand toward Israel's left hand, and Manasseh in his left hand toward Israel's right hand, and brought them near unto him. And Israel stretched out his right hand, and laid it upon Ephraim's head, who was the younger, and his left hand upon Manasseh's head, guiding his hands wittingly; for Manasseh was the firstborn. Genesis 48:13-14

And when Joseph saw that his father laid his right hand upon the head of Ephraim, it displeased him: and he held up his father's hand, to remove it from Ephraim's head unto Manasseh's head. And Joseph said unto his father, Not so, my father: for this is the firstborn; put thy right hand upon his head. And his father refused, and said, I know it, my son, I know it: he also shall become a people, and he also shall be great: but truly his younger brother shall be greater than he, and his seed shall become a multitude of nations. And he blessed them that day, saying, In thee shall Israel bless, saying, God make thee as Ephraim and as Manasseh: and he set Ephraim before Manasseh. Genesis 48:17-20

4. Miracles of the Disciples Through the Laying On of Hands

Long time therefore abode they speaking boldly in the Lord, which gave testimony unto the word of his grace, and granted signs and wonders to be done by their hands. Acts 14:3

They shall take up serpents; and if they drink any deadly thing, it shall not hurt them; they shall lay hands on the sick, and they shall recover.
                                                    Mark 16:18

And God wrought special miracles by the hands of Paul: Acts 19:11

5. Transference of Spirits

And the Lord said unto Moses, Gather unto me seventy men of the elders of Israel, whom thou knowest to be the elders of the people, and officers over them; and bring them unto the tabernacle of the congregation, that they may stand there with thee. And I will come down and talk with thee there: and I will take of the spirit which is upon thee, and will put it upon them; and they shall bear the burden of the people with thee, that thou bear it not thyself alone. Numbers 11:16-17

And the Lord came down in a cloud, and spake unto him, and took of the spirit that was upon him, and gave it unto the seventy elders: and it came to pass, that, when the spirit rested upon them, they prophesied, and did not cease. Numbers 11:25

And the Lord said unto Moses, Take thee Joshua the son of Nun, a man in whom is the spirit, and lay thine hand upon him; And set him before Eleazar the priest, and before all the congregation; and give him a charge in their sight. And thou shalt put some of thine honour upon him, that all the congregation of the children of Israel may be obedient.
Numbers 27:18-20

> *Warning! Be careful about who you lay your hands upon, also be cautious about letting any one at random lay their hand upon you.*

Lay hands suddenly on no man, neither be partaker of other men's sins: keep thyself pure. 1 Timothy 5:22

False Brothers

For such are false apostles, deceitful workers, transforming themselves into the apostles of Christ. And no marvel; for Satan himself is transformed into an angel of light. Therefore it is no great thing if his ministers also be transformed as the ministers of righteousness; whose end shall be according to their works. 2 Corinthians 11:13-15

Recognizing False Brothers

1. They Claim to Have Power but They are Powerless

Whoso boasteth himself of a false gift is like clouds and wind without rain. Proverbs 25:14

These are spots in your feasts of charity, when they feast with you, feeding themselves without fear: clouds they are without water, carried about of winds; trees whose fruit withereth, without fruit, twice dead, plucked up by the roots; Raging waves of the sea, foaming out their own shame; wandering stars, to whom is reserved the blackness of darkness for ever.
Jude 1:12-13

2. They Will Deny Christ

Who is a liar but he that denieth that Jesus is the Christ? He is antichrist, that denieth the Father and the Son. Whosoever denieth the Son, the same hath not the Father: (but) he hat acknowledgeth the Son hath the Father also. 1 John 2:22-23

For there are certain men crept in unawares, who were before of old ordained to this condemnation, ungodly men, turning the grace of our God into lasciviousness, and denying the only Lord God, and our Lord Jesus Christ. Jude 1:4

3. Check Out Their Lifestyles

Ye shall know them by their fruits. Do men gather grapes of thorns, or figs of thistles? Matthew 7:16

Wherefore by their fruits ye shall know them. Matthew 7:20

Whosoever transgresseth, and abideth not in the doctrine of Christ, hath not God. He that abideth in the doctrine of Christ, he hath both the Father and the Son. 2 John 1:9

4. Unsound Doctrine

But there were false prophets also among the people, even as there shall be false teachers among you, who privily shall bring in damnable heresies, even denying the Lord that bought them, and bring upon themselves swift destruction. 2 Peter 2:1

Now I beseech you, brethren, mark them which cause divisions and offences contrary to the doctrine which ye have learned; and avoid them. For they that are such serve not our Lord Jesus Christ, but their own belly; and by good words and fair speeches deceive the hearts of the simple. Romans 16:17-18

I marvel that ye are so soon removed from him that called you into the grace of Christ unto another gospel. Which is not another; but there be some that trouble you, and would pervert the gospel of Christ. But though we, or an angel from heaven, preach any other gospel unto you than that which we have preached unto you, let him be accursed. As we said before, so say I now again, If any man preach any other gospel unto you than that ye have received, let him be accursed. Galatians 1:6-9

For the time will come when they will not endure sound doctrine; but after their own lusts shall they heap to themselves teachers, having itching ears; And they shall turn away their ears from the truth, and shall be turned unto fables. 2 Timothy 4:3-4

Holding fast the faithful word as he hath been taught, that he may be able by sound doctrine both to exhort and to convince the gainsayers. For there are many unruly and vain talkers and deceivers, specially they of the circumcision. Whose mouths must be stopped, who subvert whole houses, teaching things which they ought not, for filthy lucre's sake.
Titus 1:9-11

If there come any unto you, and bring not this doctrine, receive him not into your house, neither bid him God speed: For he that biddeth him God speed is partaker of his evil deeds. 2 John 1:10-11

5. They Promote Religion, Traditions and Rituals Rather than Christ

But he answered and said unto them, Why do ye also transgress the commandment of God by your tradition? Matthew 15:3

And honour not his father or his mother, he shall be free. Thus have ye made the commandment of God of none effect by your tradition.
Matthew 15:6

For laying aside the commandment of God, ye hold the tradition of men, as the washing of pots and cups: and many other such like things ye do. And he said unto them, Full well ye reject the commandment of God, that ye may keep your own tradition. Mark 7:8-9

Making the word of God of none effect through your tradition, which ye have delivered: and many such like things do ye. Mark 7:13

Beware lest any man spoil you through philosophy and vain deceit, after the tradition of men, after the rudiments of the world, and not after Christ.
Colossians 2:8

Forasmuch as ye know that ye were not redeemed with corruptible things, as silver and gold, from your vain conversation received by tradition from your fathers; 1 Peter 1:18

6. They are Smooth Talkers that Speak Deceptive Words

Let no man deceive you with vain words: for because of these things cometh the wrath of God upon the children of disobedience.
Ephesians 5:6

And this I say, lest any man should beguile you with enticing words.
Colossians 2:4

Neither give heed to fables and endless genealogies, which minister questions, rather than godly edifying which is in faith: so do. 1 Timothy 1:3-4

7. They Need to be Tested and Confronted

Who is a liar but he that denieth that Jesus is the Christ? He is antichrist, that denieth the Father and the Son. Whosoever denieth the Son, the same hath not the Father: (but) he that acknowledgeth the Son hath the Father also. 1 John 2:22-23

Beloved, believe not every spirit, but try the spirits whether they are of God: because many false prophets are gone out into the world.
1 John 4:1

Hereby know ye the Spirit of God: Every spirit that confesseth that Jesus Christ is come in the flesh is of God: And every spirit that confesseth not that Jesus Christ is come in the flesh is not of God: and this is that spirit of antichrist, whereof ye have heard that it should come; and even now already is it in the world. 1 John 4:2-3

We are of God: he that knoweth God heareth us; he that is not of God heareth not us. Hereby know we the spirit of truth, and the spirit of error.
1 John 4:6

For many deceivers are entered into the world, who confess not that Jesus Christ is come in the flesh. This is a deceiver and an antichrist.
2 John 1:7

False Prophets

Then the Lord said unto me, The prophets prophesy lies in my name: I sent them not, neither have I commanded them, neither spake unto them: they prophesy unto you a false vision and divination, and a thing of nought, and the deceit of their heart. Therefore thus saith the Lord concerning the prophets that prophesy in my name, and I sent them not, yet they say, Sword and famine shall not be in this land; By sword and famine shall those prophets be consumed. Jeremiah 14:14-15

For both prophet and priest are profane; yea, in my house have I found their wickedness, saith the Lord. Wherefore their way shall be unto them as slippery ways in the darkness: they shall be driven on, and fall therein: for I will bring evil upon them, even the year of their visitation, saith the Lord. And I have seen folly in the prophets of Samaria; they prophesied in Baal, and caused my people Israel to err. I have seen also in the prophets of Jerusalem an horrible thing: they commit adultery, and walk in lies: they strengthen also the hands of evildoers, that none doth return from his wickedness: they are all of them unto me as Sodom, and the inhabitants thereof as Gomorrah. Therefore thus saith the Lord of hosts concerning the prophets; Behold, I will feed them with wormwood, and make them drink the water of gall: for from the prophets of Jerusalem is profaneness gone forth into all the land. Thus saith the Lord of hosts, Hearken not unto the words of the prophets that prophesy unto you: they make you vain: they speak a vision of their own heart, and not out of the mouth of the Lord. Jeremiah 23:11-16

I have not sent these prophets, yet they ran: I have not spoken to them, yet they prophesied. Jeremiah 23:21

I have heard what the prophets said, that prophesy lies in my name, saying, I have dreamed, I have dreamed. How long shall this be in the heart of the prophets that prophesy lies? yea, they are prophets of the deceit of their own heart; Which think to cause my people to forget my name by their dreams which they tell every man to his neighbour, as their fathers have forgotten my name for Baal. The prophet that hath a dream, let him tell a dream; and he that hath my word, let him speak my word faithfully. What is the chaff to the wheat? saith the Lord. Is not my word like as a fire? saith the Lord; and like a hammer that breaketh the rock in pieces?
Jeremiah 23:25-29

In the Old Testament, prophets were stoned if their prophecies were not true. In the New Testament prophecies are examined in light of the word of God, accepted if they are true, and ignored if they are false.

Behold, I am against the prophets, saith the Lord, that use their tongues, and say, He saith. Behold, I am against them that prophesy false dreams, saith the Lord, and do tell them, and cause my people to err by their lies, and by their lightness; yet I sent them not, nor commanded them: therefore they shall not profit this people at all, saith the Lord.
Jeremiah 23:31-32

A prophecy spoken to you and for you should always confirm what God has already been speaking to your spirit.

But if they be prophets, and if the word of the Lord be with them, let them now make intercession to the Lord of hosts, that the vessels which are left in the house of the Lord, and in the house of the king of Judah, and at Jerusalem, go not to Babylon. Jeremiah 27:18

The prophets that have been before me and before thee of old prophesied both against many countries, and against great kingdoms, of war, and of evil, and of pestilence. The prophet which prophesieth of peace, when the word of the prophet shall come to pass, then shall the prophet be known, that the Lord hath truly sent him. Jeremiah 28:8-9

For thus saith the Lord of hosts, the God of Israel; Let not your prophets and your diviners, that be in the midst of you, deceive you, neither hearken to your dreams which ye cause to be dreamed. For they prophesy falsely unto you in my name: I have not sent them, saith the Lord.
Jeremiah 29:8-9

Son of man, prophesy against the prophets of Israel that prophesy, and say thou unto them that prophesy out of their own hearts, Hear ye the word of the Lord; **Thus saith the Lord God;** Woe unto the foolish prophets, that follow their own spirit, and have seen nothing! **O** Israel, thy prophets are like the foxes in the deserts. Ye have not gone up into the gaps, neither made up the hedge for the house of Israel to stand in the battle in the day of the Lord. They have seen vanity and lying divination, saying, The Lord saith: and the Lord hath not sent them: and they have made others to hope that they would confirm the word. **H**ave ye not seen a vain vision, and have ye not spoken a lying divination, whereas ye say, The Lord saith it; albeit I have not spoken? **T**herefore thus saith the Lord God; Because ye have spoken vanity, and seen lies, therefore, behold, I am against you, saith the Lord God. And mine hand shall be upon the prophets that see vanity, and that divine lies: they shall not be in the assembly of my people, neither shall they be written in the writing of the house of Israel, neither shall they enter into the land of Israel; and ye shall know that I am the Lord God. Ezekiel 13:2-9

And if the prophet be deceived when he hath spoken a thing, I the Lord have deceived that prophet, and I will stretch out my hand upon him, and will destroy him from the midst of my people Israel. And they shall bear the punishment of their iniquity: the punishment of the prophet shall be even as the punishment of him that seeketh unto him; Ezekiel 14:9-10

> *When a person starts prophesying over you and you know that it is contrary to God's Word and that it is a false prophecy coming from their flesh or the devil, stop them immediately. Tell them, in the spirit of love and boldness, that their prophecy is false and you will not receive it. It's better for them to be confronted with truth and publicly embarrassed than for you to be cursed and deceived.*

And it shall come to pass, that when any shall yet prophesy, then his father and his mother that begat him shall say unto him, Thou shalt not live; for thou speakest lies in the name of the Lord: and his father and his mother that begat him shall thrust him through when he prophesieth. And it shall come to pass in that day, that the prophets shall be ashamed every one of his vision, when he hath prophesied; neither shall they wear a rough garment to deceive: But he shall say, I am no prophet, I am an

husbandman; for man taught me to keep cattle from my youth.
Zechariah 13:3-5

Beware of false prophets, which come to you in sheep's clothing, but inwardly they are ravening wolves. Matthew 7:15

1. Always Test and Compare Prophecies to the Word of God

Beloved, believe not every spirit, but try the spirits whether they are of God: because many false prophets are gone out into the world.
1 John 4:1

The simple believeth every word: but the prudent man looketh well to his going. Proverbs 14:15

> *The word of God is the measuring rod by which we judge every prophetic utterance. - Rick Godwin*

Casting Out devils

1. Examples of Jesus Casting Out devils

And his fame went throughout all Syria: and they brought unto him all sick people that were taken with divers diseases and torments, and those which were possessed with devils, and those which were lunatic, and those that had the palsy; and he healed them. Matthew 4:24

When the even was come, they brought unto him many that were possessed with devils: and he cast out the spirits with his word, and healed all that were sick. Matthew 8:16

As they went out, behold, they brought to him a dumb man possessed with a devil. And when the devil was cast out, the dumb spake: and the multitudes marvelled, saying, It was never so seen in Israel.
Matthew 9:32-33

Then was brought unto him one possessed with a devil, blind, and dumb: and he healed him, insomuch that the blind and dumb both spake and saw. Matthew 12:22

And, behold, a woman of Canaan came out of the same coasts, and cried unto him, saying, Have mercy on me, O Lord, thou Son of David; my daughter is grievously vexed with a devil. Matthew 15:22

Then Jesus answered and said unto her, O woman, great is thy faith: be it unto thee even as thou wilt. And her daughter was made whole from that very hour. Matthew 15:28

And Jesus rebuked the devil; and he departed out of him: and the child was cured from that very hour. Matthew 17:18

And when he was come out of the ship, immediately there met him out of the tombs a man with an unclean spirit, Who had his dwelling among the tombs; and no man could bind him, no, not with chains: Because that he had been often bound with fetters and chains, and the chains had been plucked asunder by him, and the fetters broken in pieces: neither could any man tame him. And always, night and day, he was in the mountains, and in the tombs, crying, and cutting himself with stones. But when he saw Jesus afar off, he ran and worshipped him, And cried with a loud voice, and said, What have I to do with thee, Jesus, thou Son of the most high God? I adjure thee by God, that thou torment me not. For he said unto him, Come out of the man, thou unclean spirit. And he asked him, What is thy name? And he answered, saying, My name is Legion: for we are many. And he besought him much that he would not send them away out of the country. Now there was there nigh unto the mountains a great herd of swine feeding. And all the devils besought him, saying, Send us into the swine, that we may enter into them. And forthwith Jesus gave them leave. And the unclean spirits went out, and entered into the swine: and the herd ran violently down a steep place into the sea, (they were about two thousand;) and were choked in the sea. And they that fed the swine fled, and told it in the city, and in the country. And they went out to see what it was that was done. And they come to Jesus, and see him that was possessed with the devil, and had the legion, sitting, and clothed, and in his right mind: and they were afraid. Mark 5:2-15

And at even, when the sun did set, they brought unto him all that were diseased, and them that were possessed with devils. And all the city was gathered together at the door. And he healed many that were sick of divers diseases, and cast out many devils; and suffered not the devils to speak, because they knew him. Mark 1:32-34

And he preached in their synagogues throughout all Galilee, and cast out devils. Mark 1:39

The woman was a Greek, a Syrophenician by nation; and she besought him that he would cast forth the devil out of her daughter. Mark 7:26

And he said unto her, For this saying go thy way; the devil is gone out of thy daughter. And when she was come to her house, she found the devil gone out, and her daughter laid upon the bed. Mark 7:29-30

Now when Jesus was risen early the first day of the week, he appeared first to Mary Magdalene, out of whom he had cast seven devils.
Mark 16:9

And in the synagogue there was a man, which had a spirit of an unclean devil, and cried out with a loud voice, Saying, Let us alone; what have we to do with thee, thou Jesus of Nazareth? art thou come to destroy us? I know thee who thou art; the Holy One of God. And Jesus rebuked him, saying, Hold thy peace, and come out of him. And when the devil had thrown him in the midst, he came out of him, and hurt him not.
Luke 4:33-35

And devils also came out of many, crying out, and saying, Thou art Christ the Son of God. And he rebuking them suffered them not to speak: for they knew that he was Christ. Luke 4:41

And certain women, which had been healed of evil spirits and infirmities, Mary called Magdalene, out of whom went seven devils. Luke 8:2

And as he was yet a coming, the devil threw him down, and tare him. And Jesus rebuked the unclean spirit, and healed the child, and delivered him again to his father. Luke 9:42

And he was casting out a devil, and it was dumb. And it came to pass, when the devil was gone out, the dumb spake; and the people wondered.
Luke 11:14

How God anointed Jesus of Nazareth with the Holy Ghost and with power: who went about doing good, and healing all that were oppressed of the devil; for God was with him. Acts 10:38

2. Disciples Casting Out devils

Heal the sick, cleanse the lepers, raise the dead, cast out devils: freely ye have received, freely give. Matthew 10:8

And he ordained twelve, that they should be with him, and that he might send them forth to preach, And to have power to heal sicknesses, and to cast out devils. Mark 3:14-15

And they went out, and preached that men should repent. And they cast out many devils, and anointed with oil many that were sick, and healed them. Mark 6:12-13

Then he called his twelve disciples together, and gave them power and authority over all devils, and to cure diseases. Luke 9:1

And the seventy returned again with joy, saying, Lord, even the devils are subject unto us through thy name. Luke 10:17

3. You Can Cast Out devils

And these signs shall follow them that believe; In my name shall they cast out devils; they shall speak with new tongues. Mark 16:17

Behold, I give unto you power to tread on serpents and scorpions, and over all the power of the enemy: and nothing shall by any means hurt you. Luke 10:19

Verily, verily, I say unto you, He that believeth on me, the works that I do shall he do also; and greater works than these shall he do; because I go unto my Father. John 14:12

4. Before Casting Out devils

And having in a readiness to revenge all disobedience, when your obedience is fulfilled. 2 Corinthians 10:6

Submit yourselves therefore to God. Resist the devil, and he will flee from you. James 4:7

Howbeit this kind goeth not out but by prayer and fasting. Matthew 17:21

Submit yourselves therefore to God. Resist the devil, and he will flee from you. James 4:7

> You have to say "yes" to God first before you can effectively say "no" to the devil. - Vance Havner

5. When Casting Out devils

a. Use the Name of Jesus, the Blood of Jesus, and the Sword of the Spirit (the Word of God).

Yet Michael the archangel, when contending with the devil he disputed about the body of Moses, durst not bring against him a railing accusation, but said, The Lord rebuke thee. Jude 1:9

Then he answered and spake unto me, saying, This is the word of the Lord unto Zerubbabel, saying, Not by might, nor by power, but by my spirit, saith the Lord of hosts. Zechariah 4:6

b. After you cast the devil out of someone, advise that person to receive Christ into their spirit and to study and obey God's Word.

When the unclean spirit is gone out of a man, he walketh through dry places, seeking rest, and findeth none. Then he saith, I will return into my house from whence I came out; and when he is come, he

findeth it empty, swept, and garnished. Then goeth he, and taketh with himself seven other spirits more wicked than himself, and they enter in and dwell there: and the last state of that man is worse than the first. Even so shall it be also unto this wicked generation.
Matthew 12:43-45

When the unclean spirit is gone out of a man, he walketh through dry places, seeking rest; and finding none, he saith, I will return unto my house whence I came out. And when he cometh, he findeth it swept and garnished. Then goeth he, and taketh to him seven other spirits more wicked than himself; and they enter in, and dwell there: and the last state of that man is worse than the first. Luke 11:24-26

Afterward Jesus findeth him in the temple, and said unto him, Behold, thou art made whole: sin no more, lest a worse thing come unto thee. John 5:14

Having therefore these promises, dearly beloved, let us cleanse ourselves from all filthiness of the flesh and spirit, perfecting holiness in the fear of God. 2 Corinthians 7:1

Occult, Witchcraft and Idolatry

And Moses and Aaron went in unto Pharaoh, and they did so as the LORD had commanded: and Aaron cast down his rod before Pharaoh, and before his servants, and it became a serpent. Then Pharaoh also called the wise men and the sorcerers: now the magicians of Egypt, they also did in like manner with their enchantments. For they cast down every man his rod, and they became serpents: but Aaron's rod swallowed up their rods. Exodus 7:10-12

Thou shalt not suffer a witch to live. Exodus 22:18

Regard not them that have familiar spirits, neither seek after wizards, to be defiled by them: I am the LORD your God. Leviticus 19:31

A man also or woman that hath a familiar spirit, or that is a wizard, shall surely be put to death: they shall stone them with stones: their blood shall be upon them. Leviticus 20:27

There shall not be found among you any one that maketh his son or his daughter to pass through the fire, or that useth divination, or an observer of times, or an enchanter, or a witch, Or a charmer, or a consulter with familiar spirits, or a wizard, or a necromancer. Deuteronomy 18:10-11

So Saul died for his transgression which he committed against the LORD, even against the word of the LORD, which he kept not, and also for asking counsel of one that had a familiar spirit, to enquire of it;
                                            1 Chronicles 10:13

And when they shall say unto you, Seek unto them that have familiar spirits, and unto wizards that peep, and that mutter: should not a people seek unto their God? for the living to the dead? Isaiah 8:19

Then the LORD said unto me, The prophets prophesy lies in my name: I sent them not, neither have I commanded them, neither spake unto them: they prophesy unto you a false vision and divination, and a thing of nought, and the deceit of their heart. Jeremiah 14:14

Therefore hearken not ye to your prophets, nor to your diviners, nor to your dreamers, nor to your enchanters, nor to your sorcerers, which speak unto you, saying, Ye shall not serve the king of Babylon: Jeremiah 27:9

For thus saith the LORD of hosts, the God of Israel; Let not your prophets and your diviners, that be in the midst of you, deceive you, neither hearken to your dreams which ye cause to be dreamed. Jeremiah 29:8

For the idols have spoken vanity, and the diviners have seen a lie, and have told false dreams; they comfort in vain: therefore they went their way as a flock, they were troubled, because there was no shepherd.
                                            Zechariah 10:2

And I will come near to you to judgment; and I will be a swift witness against the sorcerers, and against the adulterers, and against false swearers, and against those that oppress the hireling in his wages, the widow, and the fatherless, and that turn aside the stranger from his right, and fear not me, saith the LORD of hosts. Malachi 3:5

And when they had gone through the isle unto Paphos, they found a certain sorcerer, a false prophet, a Jew, whose name was Bar-jesus: Which was with the deputy of the country, Sergius Paulus, a prudent man; who called for Barnabas and Saul, and desired to hear the word of God. But Elymas the sorcerer (for so is his name by interpretation) withstood them, seeking to turn away the deputy from the faith. Then Saul, (who also is called Paul,) filled with the Holy Ghost, set his eyes on him, And said, O full of all subtilty and all mischief, thou child of the devil, thou enemy of all righteousness, wilt thou not cease to pervert the right ways of the Lord? And now, behold, the hand of the Lord is upon thee, and thou shalt be blind, not seeing the sun for a season. And immediately there fell on him a mist and a darkness; and he went about seeking some to lead him by the hand. Acts 13:6-11

BIBLICAL ECONOMICS

Tithes and Offerings

And all the tithe of the land, whether of the seed of the land, or of the fruit of the tree, is the Lord's: it is holy unto the Lord. And if a man will at all redeem ought of his tithes, he shall add thereto the fifth part thereof.
Leviticus 27:30-31

And it shall be, when thou art come in unto the land which the Lord thy God giveth thee for an inheritance, and possessest it, and dwellest therein; That thou shalt take of the first of all the fruit of the earth, which thou shalt bring of thy land that the Lord thy God giveth thee, and shalt put it in a basket, and shalt go unto the place which the Lord thy God shall choose to place his name there. Deuteronomy 26:1-2

And he hath brought us into this place, and hath given us this land, even a land that floweth with milk and honey. And now, behold, I have brought the firstfruits of the land, which thou, O Lord, hast given me. And thou shalt set it before the Lord thy God, and worship before the Lord thy God: And thou shalt rejoice in every good thing which the Lord thy God hath given unto thee, and unto thine house, thou, and the Levite, and the stranger that is among you. Deuteronomy 26:9-11

Will a man rob God? Yet ye have robbed me. But ye say, Wherein have we robbed thee? In tithes and offerings. Ye are cursed with a curse: for ye have robbed me, even this whole nation. Bring ye all the tithes into the storehouse, that there may be meat in mine house, and prove me now herewith, saith the Lord of hosts, if I will not open you the windows of heaven, and pour you out a blessing, that there shall not be room enough to receive it. Malachi 3:8-10

Not because I desire a gift: but I desire fruit that may abound: but I desire fruit that may abound to your account. But I have all, and abound: I am full, having received of Epaphroditus the things which were sent from you, an odor of a sweet smell, a sacrifice acceptable, well pleasing to

God. But my God shall supply all your need according to his riches in glory by Christ Jesus. Philippians 4:17-19

Sowing Seeds

For as the rain cometh down, and the snow from heaven, and returneth not thither, but watereth the earth, and maketh it bring forth and bud, that it may give seed to the sower, and bread to the eater: So shall my word be that goeth forth out of my mouth: it shall not return unto me void, but it shall accomplish that which I please, and it shall prosper in the thing whereto I sent it. Isaiah 55:10-11

He that goeth forth and weepeth, bearing precious seed, shall doubtless come again with rejoicing, bringing his sheaves with him. Psalms 126:6

Give, and it shall be given unto you; good measure, pressed down, and shaken together, and running over, shall men give into your bosom. For with the same measure that ye mete withal it shall be measured to you again. Luke 6:38

Sow your financial seeds as soon as you receive your increase. Faster sowers have a faster harvest. - Dr. John Avanzini

But this I say, He which soweth sparingly shall reap also sparingly; and he which soweth bountifully shall reap also bountifully.
2 Corinthians 9:6

Now he that ministereth seed to the sower both minister bread for your food, and multiply your seed sown, and increase the fruits of your righteousness. Being enriched in every thing to all bountifulness, which causeth through us thanksgiving to God. 2 Corinthians 9:10-11

Be not deceived; God is not mocked: for whatsoever a man soweth, that shall he also reap. Galatians 6:7

In the morning sow thy seed, and in the evening withhold not thine hand: for thou knowest not whether shall prosper, either this or that, or whether they both shall be alike good. Ecclesiastes 11:6

There is that scattereth, and yet increaseth; and there is that withholdeth more than is meet, but it tendeth to poverty. Proverbs 11:24

Cast thy bread upon the waters: for thou shalt find it after many days.
Ecclesiastes 11:1

Know the spirit of the person that toils the soil that you plant your seed into.

Reaping the Harvest

And let us not be weary in well doing: for in due season we shall reap, if we faint not. Galatians 6:9

And Jesus answered and said, Verily I say unto you, There is no man that hath left house, or brethren, or sisters, of father, or mother, or wife, or children, of lands, for my sake, and the gospel's. But he shall receive an hundredfold now in this time, houses, and brethren, and sisters, and mothers, and children, and lands, with persecutions; and in the world to come eternal life. Mark 10:29-30

> *The Dead Sea is a dead sea because it continually receives and never gives. - Anonymous*

The End-Time Transfer of Wealth to Christians

For I was envious at the foolish, when I saw the prosperity of the wicked. For there are no bands in their death: but their strength is firm. They are not in trouble as other men; neither are they plagued like other men. Therefore pride compasseth them about as a chain; violence covereth them as a garment. Their eyes stand out with fatness: they have more than heart could wish. They are corrupt, and speak wickedly concerning oppression: they speak loftily. They set their mouth against the heavens, and their tongue walketh through the earth. Therefore his people return hither: and waters of a full cup are wrung out to them. And they say, How doth God know? and is there knowledge in the most High? Behold, these are the ungodly, who prosper in the world; they increase in riches. Verily I have cleansed my heart in vain, and washed my hands in innocency. For all the day long have I been plagued, and chastened every morning. If I say, I will speak thus; behold, I should offend against the generation of thy children. When I thought to know this, it was too painful for me; Until I went into the sanctuary of God; then understood I their end. Surely thou didst set them in slippery places: thou castedst them down into destruction. How are they brought into desolation, as in a moment! they are utterly consumed with terrors. Psalms 73:3-19

This is the portion of a wicked man with God, and the heritage of oppressors, which they shall receive of the Almighty. If his children be multiplied, it is for the sword: and his offspring shall not be satisfied with bread. Those that remain of him shall be buried in death: and his widows shall not weep. Though he heap up silver as the dust, and prepare raiment as the clay; He may prepare it, but the just shall put it on, and the innocent shall divide the silver. Job 27:13-17

He that by usury and unjust gain increaseth his substance, he shall gather it for him that will pity the poor. Proverbs 28:8

For God giveth to a man that is good in his sight wisdom, and knowledge, and joy: but to the sinner he giveth travail, to gather and to heap up, that he may give to him that is good before God. This also is vanity and vexation of spirit. Ecclesiastes 2:26

If God can get it through you, God will give it to you. - E. V. Hill

Go to now, ye rich men, weep and howl for your miseries that shall come upon you. Your riches are corrupted, and your garments are motheaten. Your gold and silver is cankered; and the rust of them shall be a witness against you, and shall eat your flesh as it were fire. Ye have heaped treasure together for the last days. James 5:1-3

Loans

Owe no man any thing, but to love one another: for he that loveth another hath fulfilled the law. Romans 13:8

The rich ruleth over the poor, and the borrower is servant to the lender. Proverbs 22:7

For the Lord thy God blesseth thee, as he promised thee: and thou shalt lend unto many nations, but thou shalt not borrow; and thou shalt reign over many nations, but they shall not reign over thee. Deuteronomy 15:6

If thou lend money to any of my people that is poor by thee, thou shalt not be to him as an usurer, neither shalt thou lay upon him usury.
Exodus 22:25

Thou shalt not give him thy money upon usury, nor lend him thy victuals for increase. Leviticus 25:37

Thou shalt not lend upon usury to thy brother; usury of money, usury of victuals, usury of any thing that is lent upon usury: Unto a stranger thou mayest lend upon usury; but unto thy brother thou shalt not lend upon usury: that the Lord thy God may bless thee in all that thou settest thine hand to in the land whither thou goest to possess it.
Deuteronomy 23:19-20

The Lord shall open unto thee his good treasure, the heaven to give the rain unto thy land in his season, and to bless all the work of thine hand: and thou shalt lend unto many nations, and thou shalt not borrow.
Deuteronomy 28:12

The wicked borroweth, and payeth not again: but the righteous sheweth mercy, and giveth. Psalms 37:21

Co-Signing for Others

My son, if thou be surety for thy friend, if thou hast stricken thy hand with a stranger, Thou art snared with the words of thy mouth, thou art taken with the words of thy mouth. Do this now, my son, deliver thyself, when thou art come into the hand of thy friend; go, humble thyself, and make sure thy friend. Give not sleep to thine eyes, nor slumber to thine eyelids. Deliver thyself as a roe from the hand of the hunter, and as a bird from the hand of the fowler. Proverbs 6:1-5

He that is surety for a stranger shall smart for it: and he that hateth suretiship is sure. Proverbs 11:15

A man void of understanding striketh hands, and becometh surety in the presence of his friend. Proverbs 17:18

Take his garment that is surety for a stranger: and take a pledge of him for a strange woman. Proverbs 20:16

The rich ruleth over the poor, and the borrower is servant to the lender. Proverbs 22:7

Be not thou one of them that strike hands, or of them that are sureties for debts. If thou hast nothing to pay, why should he take away thy bed from under thee? Proverbs 22:26-27

Take his garment that is surety for a stranger, and take a pledge of him for a strange woman. Proverbs 27:13

God Wants You to Prosper Financially

But thou shalt remember the Lord thy God: for it is he that giveth thee power to get wealth, that he may establish his covenant which he sware unto thy fathers, as it is this day. Deuteronomy 8:18

For the Lord thy God blesseth thee, as he promised thee: and thou shalt lend unto many nations, but thou shalt not borrow; and thou shalt reign over many nations, but they shall not reign over thee. Deuteronomy 15:6

The Lord shall open unto thee his good treasure, the heaven to give the rain unto thy land in his season, and to bless all the work of thine hand: and thou shalt lend unto many nations, and thou shalt not borrow.
Deuteronomy 28:12

Thou preparest a table before me in the presence of mine enemies: thou anointest my head with oil; my cup runneth over. Psalms 23:5

Let them shout for joy, and be glad, that favour my righteous cause: yea, let them say continually, Let the Lord be magnified, which hath pleasure in the prosperity of his servant. Psalms 35:27

The biggest lie ever told is that God wants his children to be poor.

If they obey and serve him, they shall spend their days in prosperity, and their years in pleasures. Job 36:11

For the Lord God is a sun and shield: the Lord will give grace and glory: no good thing will he withhold from them that walk uprightly.
Psalms 84:11

That I may cause those that love me to inherit substance; and I will fill their treasures. Proverbs 8:21

I know that there is no good in them, but for a man to rejoice, and to do good in his life. And also that every man should eat and drink, and enjoy the good of all his labour, it is the gift of God. Ecclesiastes 3:12-13

Wherefore I perceive that there is nothing better, than that a man should rejoice in his own works; for that is his portion: for who shall bring him to see what shall be after him? Ecclesiastes 3:22

Fear not, little flock; for it is your Father's good pleasure to give you the kingdom. Luke 12:32

The thief cometh not, but for to steal, and to kill, and to destroy: I am come that they might have life, and that they might have it more abundantly. John 10:10

He that spared not his own Son, but delivered him up for us all, how shall he not with him also freely give us all things? Romans 8:32

And God is able to make all grace abound toward you; that ye, always having all sufficiency in all things, may abound to every good work.
2 Corinthians 9:8

Now unto him that is able to do exceeding abundantly above all that we ask or think, according to the power that worketh in us. Ephesians 3:20

For ye know the grace of our Lord Jesus Christ, that, though he was rich, yet for your sakes he became poor, that ye through his poverty might be rich. 2 Corinthians 8:9

According as his divine power hath given unto us all things that pertain unto life and godliness, through the knowledge of him that hath called us to glory and virtue. 2 Peter 1:3

> *God has given us two hands - one for receiving and the other for giving. - Billy Graham*

Giving in the Right Attitude

Every man according as he purposeth in his heart, so let him give; not grudgingly, or of necessity: for God loveth a cheerful giver.
2 Corinthians 9:7

Let each one [give] as he has made up his own mind and purposed in his heart, not reluctantly or sorrowfully or under compulsion, for God loves (that is, He takes pleasure in, prizes above other things, and is unwilling to abandon or to do without) a cheerful (joyous, prompt-to-do-it) giver– whose heart is in his giving. 2 Corinthians 9:7 AMP

He that observeth the wind shall not sow; and he that regardeth the clouds shall not reap. Ecclesiastes 11:4

He who observes the wind [and waits for all conditions to be favorable] will not sow, and he who regards the clouds will not reap.
Ecclesiastes 11:4 AMP

> *Self, service, substance is the Divine order and nothing counts until we give ourselves. - Vance Havner*

Take heed that ye do not your alms before men, to be seen of them: otherwise ye have no reward of your Father which is in heaven. Therefore when thou doest thine alms, do not sound a trumpet before thee, as the hypocrites do in the synagogues and in the streets, that they may have glory of men. Verily I say unto you, They have their reward. But when thou doest alms, let not thy left hand know what thy right hand doeth: That thine alms may be in secret: and thy Father which seeth in secret himself shall reward thee openly. Matthew 6:1-4

Take ye from among you an offering unto the Lord: whosoever is of a willing heart, let him bring it, an offering of the Lord; gold, and silver, and brass, Exodus 35:5

And they came, every one whose heart stirred him up, and every one whom his spirit made willing, and they brought the Lord's offering to the work of the tabernacle of the congregation, and for all his service, and for the holy garments. And they came, both men and women, as many as were willing hearted, and brought bracelets, and earrings, and rings, and tablets, all jewels of gold: and every man that offered an offering of gold unto the Lord. Exodus 35:21-22

The children of Israel brought a willing offering unto the Lord, every man and woman, whose heart made them willing to bring for all manner of work, which the Lord had commanded to be made by the hand of Moses. Exodus 35:29

True Riches

Lay not up for yourselves treasures upon earth, where moth and rust doth corrupt, and where thieves break through and steal: But lay up for yourselves treasures in heaven, where neither moth nor rust doth corrupt, and where thieves do not break through nor steal: For where your treasure is, there will your heart be also. Matthew 6:19-21

By humility and the fear of the Lord are riches, and honour, and life.
Proverbs 22:4

A faithful man shall abound with blessings. Proverbs 28:20

But thou shalt have a perfect and just weight, a perfect and just measure shalt thou have: that thy days may be lengthened in the land which the Lord thy God giveth thee. Deuteronomy 25:15

> *You really save in this life only that which you spend for the Lord. Under the guidance of the Holy Spirit every expenditure is an investment. The Bank of heaven is sound and pays eternal dividends. - Vance Havner*

Wisdom is good with an inheritance: and by it there is profit to them that see the sun. For wisdom is a defence, and money is a defence: but the excellency of knowledge is, that wisdom giveth life to them that have it.
Ecclesiastes 7:11-12

Do Not Put Your Trust or Hope in Money

For the love of money is the root of all evil: which while some coveted after, they have erred from the faith, and pierced themselves through with many sorrows. 1 Timothy 6:10

Charge them that are rich in this world, that they be not highminded, nor trust in uncertain riches, but in the living God, who giveth us richly all things to enjoy; That they do good, that they be rich in good works, ready to distribute, willing to communicate; Laying up in store for themselves a good foundation against the time to come, that they may lay hold on eternal life. 1 Timothy 6:17-19

They that trust in their wealth, and boast themselves in the multitude of their riches; None of them can by any means redeem his brother, nor give to God a ransom for him. Psalms 49:6-7

Trust not in oppression, and become not vain in robbery: if riches increase, set not your heart upon them. Psalms 62:10

Riches profit not in the day of wrath: but righteousness delivereth from death. Proverbs 11:4

He that trusteth in his riches shall fall: but the righteous shall flourish as a branch. Proverbs 11:28

> *Fortune does not so much change men as it unmasks them. - Anonymous*

There is that maketh himself rich, yet hath nothing: there is that maketh himself poor, yet hath great riches. Proverbs 13:7

He that loveth silver shall not be satisfied with silver; nor he that loveth abundance with increase: this is also vanity. When goods increase, they are increased that eat them: and what good is there to the owners thereof, saving the beholding of them with their eyes? The sleep of a labouring man is sweet, whether he eat little or much: but the abundance of the rich will not suffer him to sleep. Ecclesiastes 5:10-12

Two things have I required of thee; deny me them not before I die: **Remove far from me vanity and lies: give me neither poverty nor riches; feed me with food convenient for me:** Lest I be full, and deny thee, and say, Who is the Lord? or lest I be poor, and steal, and take the name of my God in vain. Proverbs 30:7-9

> *Money is a terrible master but an excellent servant. - P. T. Barnum*

Contentment

Better is little with the fear of the Lord than great treasure and trouble therewith. Proverbs 15:16

Labour not to be rich: cease from thine own wisdom. Wilt thou set thine eyes upon that which is not? for riches certainly make themselves wings; they fly away as an eagle toward heaven. Proverbs 23:4-5

Let your conversation be without covetousness; and be content with such things as ye have: for he hath said, I will never leave thee, nor forsake thee. Hebrews 13:5

Spreading the Gospel of Jesus Christ

And it shall come to pass in the last days, that the mountain of the Lord's house shall be established in the top of the mountains, and shall be exalted above the hills; and all nations shall flow unto it. Isaiah 2:2

And this gospel of the kingdom shall be preached in all the world for a witness unto all nations; and then shall the end come. Matthew 24:14

Go ye therefore, and teach all nations, baptizing them in the name of the Father, and of the Son, and of the Holy Ghost. Matthew 28:19

And he said unto them, Go ye into all the world, and preach the gospel to every creature. Mark 16:15

And they went forth, and preached everywhere, the Lord working with them, and confirming the word with signs following. Amen. Mark 16:20

> *We can go to the mission field in person, by prayer, by provision, or by proxy as we help send someone else. - Vance Havner*

Therefore said he unto them, The harvest truly is great, but the labourers are few: pray ye therefore the Lord of the harvest, that he would send forth labourers into his harvest. Luke 10:2

And the lord said unto the servant, Go out into the highways and hedges, and compel them to come in, that my house may be filled. Luke 14:23

And that repentance and remission of sins should be preached in his name among all nations, beginning at Jerusalem. And ye are witnesses of these things. Luke 24:47-48

And I, if I be lifted up from the earth, will draw all men unto me.
John 12:32

But ye shall receive power, after that the Holy Ghost is come upon you: and ye shall be witnesses unto me both in Jerusalem, and in all Judaea, and in Samaria, and unto the uttermost part of the earth. Acts 1:8

How then shall they call on him in whom they have not believed? and how shall they believe in him of whom they have not heard? and how shall they hear without a preacher? And how shall they preach, except they be sent? as it is written, How beautiful are the feet of them that

preach the gospel of peace, and bring glad tidings of good things!
Romans 10:14-15

But I say, Have they not heard? Yes verily, their sound went into all the earth, and their words unto the ends of the world. Romans 10:18

Preach the word; be instant in season, out of season; reprove, rebuke, exhort with all longsuffering and doctrine. 2 Timothy 4:2

Helping the Poor

For the poor shall never cease out of the land: therefore I command thee, saying, Thou shalt open thine hand wide unto thy brother, to thy poor, and to thy needy, in thy land. Deuteronomy 15:11

He that despiseth his neighbour sinneth: but he that hath mercy on the poor, happy is he. Proverbs 14:21

Blessed is he that considereth the poor: the Lord will deliver him in time of trouble. Psalms 41:1

Defend the poor and fatherless: do justice to the afflicted and needy. Deliver the poor and needy: rid them out of the hand of the wicked.
Psalms 82:3-4

Whoso stoppeth his ears at the cry of the poor, he also shall cry himself, but shall not be heard. Proverbs 21:13

And if thou draw out thy soul to the hungry, and satisfy the afflicted soul; then shall thy light rise in obscurity, and thy darkness be as the noonday. Isaiah 58:10

He answereth and saith unto them, He that hath two coats, let him impart to him that hath none; and he that hath meat, let him do likewise.
Luke 3:11

The Bible is very clear on the point that if we have money enough to live well, and do not share with others in need, it is questionable whether God's love is in us at all. - G. S.

Then said he also to him that bade him, When thou makest a dinner or a supper, call not thy friends, nor thy brethren, neither thy kinsmen, nor thy rich neighbours; lest they also bid thee again, and a recompence be made thee. But when thou makest a feast, call the poor, the maimed, the lame, the blind: And thou shalt be blessed; for they cannot recompense thee: for thou shalt be recompensed at the resurrection of the just.
Luke 14:12-14

If a brother or sister be naked, and destitute of daily food, And one of you say unto them, Depart in peace, be ye warmed and filled; notwithstanding ye give them not those things which are needful to the body; what doth it profit? Even so faith, if it hath not works, is dead, being alone. James 2:15-17

> *When you commit to giving finances for the spreading of the gospel of Christ and feeding the poor, God will supply all of your needs over and above.*

The Provisions of Christ

Love

The Lord openeth the eyes of the blind: the Lord raiseth them that are bowed down: the Lord loveth the righteous. Psalms 146:8

For as a young man marrieth a virgin, so shall thy sons marry thee: and as the bridegroom rejoiceth over the bride, so shall thy God rejoice over thee. Isaiah 62:5

The Lord hath appeared of old unto me, saying, Yea, I have loved thee with an everlasting love: therefore with lovingkindness have I drawn thee. Jeremiah 31:3

I will heal their backsliding, I will love them freely: for mine anger is turned away from him. Hosea 14:4

For God so loved the world, that he gave his only begotten Son, that whosoever believeth in him should not perish, but have everlasting life.
John 3:16

For the Father himself loveth you, because ye have loved me, and have believed that I came out from God. John 16:27

And the glory which thou gavest me I have given them; that they may be one, even as we are one: I in them, and thou in me, that they may be made perfect in one; and that the world may know that thou hast sent me, and hast loved them, as thou hast loved me. John 17:22-23

And I have declared unto them thy name, and will declare it: that the love wherewith thou hast loved me may be in them, and I in them.
John 17:26

But God commendeth his love toward us, in that, while we were yet sinners, Christ died for us. Romans 5:8

But God, who is rich in mercy, for his great love wherewith he loved us, Even when we were dead in sins, hath quickened us together with Christ, by grace ye are saved. And hath raised us up together, and made us sit together in heavenly places in Christ Jesus: That in the ages to come he might shew the exceeding riches of his grace in his kindness toward us through Christ Jesus. Ephesians 2:4-7

And to know the love of Christ, which passeth knowledge, that ye might be filled with all the fulness of God. Ephesians 3:19

Now our Lord Jesus Christ himself, and God, even our Father, which hath loved us, and hath given us everlasting consolation and good hope through grace, Comfort your hearts, and stablish you in every good word and work. 2 Thessalonians 2:16-17

Behold, what manner of love the Father hath bestowed upon us, that we should be called the sons of God: therefore the world knoweth us not, because it knew him not. 1 John 3:1

Beloved, let us love one another: for love is of God; and every one that loveth is born of God, and knoweth God. He that loveth not knoweth not God; for God is love. In this was manifested the love of God toward us, because that God sent his only begotten Son into the world, that we might live through him. Herein is love, not that we loved God, but that he loved us, and sent his Son to be the propitiation for our sins. Beloved, if God so loved us, we ought also to love one another. 1 John 4:7-11

And we have known and believed the love that God hath to us. God is love; and he that dwelleth in love dwelleth in God, and God in him.
1 John 4:16

We love him, because he first loved us. 1 John 4:19

Hope

To whom God would make known what is the riches of the glory of this mystery among the Gentiles; which is Christ in you, the hope of glory.
Colossians 1:27

Now our Lord Jesus Christ himself, and God, even our Father, which hath loved us, and hath given us everlasting consolation and good hope through grace. 2 Thessalonians 2:16

Let thy mercy, O Lord, be upon us, according as we hope in thee.
Psalms 33:22

For in thee, O Lord, do I hope: thou wilt hear, O Lord my God.
Psalms 38:15

The Provisions of Christ

And now, Lord, what wait I for? my hope is in thee. Psalms 39:7

Why art thou cast down, O my soul? and why art thou disquieted in me? hope thou in God: for I shall yet praise him for the help of his countenance. Psalms 42:5

Why art thou cast down, O my soul? and why art thou disquieted within me? hope thou in God: for I shall yet praise him, who is the health of my countenance, and my God. Psalms 42:11

For thou art my hope, O Lord God: thou art my trust from my youth.
Psalms 71:5

But I will hope continually, and will yet praise thee more and more.
Psalms 71:14

That they might set their hope in God, and not forget the works of God, but keep his commandments. Psalms 78:7

Let Israel hope in the Lord: for with the Lord there is mercy, and with him is plenteous redemption. Psalms 130:7

Let Israel hope in the Lord from henceforth and for ever. Psalms 131:3

Happy is he that hath the God of Jacob for his help, whose hope is in the Lord his God. Psalms 146:5

The Lord is my portion, saith my soul; therefore will I hope in him.
Lamentations 3:24

> *There is not enough darkness in all the world to put out the light of one small candle. - Anonymous*

The Lord also shall roar out of Zion, and utter his voice from Jerusalem; and the heavens and the earth shall shake: but the Lord will be the hope of his people, and the strength of the children of Israel. Joel 3:16

It is good that a man should both hope and quietly wait for the salvation of the Lord. Lamentations 3:26

And have hope toward God, which they themselves also allow, that there shall be a resurrection of the dead, both of the just and unjust. Acts 24:15

But sanctify the Lord God in your hearts: and be ready always to give an answer to every man that asketh you a reason of the hope that is in you with meekness and fear. 1 Peter 3:15

> *Hope means expectancy when things are otherwise hopeless.- G. K. Chesterton*

By whom also we have access by faith into this grace wherein we stand, and rejoice in hope of the glory of God. Romans 5:2

Wherefore gird up the loins of your mind, be sober, and hope to the end for the grace that is to be brought unto you at the revelation of Jesus Christ. 1 Peter 1:13

Joy

Then he said unto them, Go your way, eat the fat, and drink the sweet, and send portions unto them for whom nothing is prepared: for this day is holy unto our Lord: neither be ye sorry; for the joy of the Lord is your strength. Nehemiah 8:10

When the morning stars sang together, and all the sons of God shouted for joy? Job 38:7

Thou wilt shew me the path of life: in thy presence is fulness of joy; at thy right hand there are pleasures for evermore. Psalms 16:11

For his anger endureth but a moment; in his favour is life: weeping may endure for a night, but joy cometh in the morning. Psalms 30:5

Let them shout for joy, and be glad, that favour my righteous cause: yea, let them say continually, Let the Lord be magnified, which hath pleasure in the prosperity of his servant. Psalms 35:27

Restore unto me the joy of thy salvation; and uphold me with thy free spirit. Psalms 51:12

They that sow in tears shall reap in joy. Psalms 126:5

Let the saints be joyful in glory: let them sing aloud upon their beds.
Psalms 149:5

A man hath joy by the answer of his mouth: and a word spoken in due season, how good is it! Proverbs 15:23

It is joy to the just to do judgment: but destruction shall be to the workers of iniquity. Proverbs 21:15

Go thy way, eat thy bread with joy, and drink thy wine with a merry heart; for God now accepteth thy works. Ecclesiastes 9:7

And the ransomed of the Lord shall return, and come to Zion with songs and everlasting joy upon their heads: they shall obtain joy and gladness, and sorrow and sighing shall flee away. Isaiah 35:10

The Provisions of Christ

Therefore the redeemed of the Lord shall return, and come with singing unto Zion; and everlasting joy shall be upon their head: they shall obtain gladness and joy; and sorrow and mourning shall flee away. Isaiah 51:11

For ye shall go out with joy, and be led forth with peace: the mountains and the hills shall break forth before you into singing, and all the trees of the field shall clap their hands. Isaiah 55:12

And thou shalt have joy and gladness; and many shall rejoice at his birth.
Luke 1:14

And the angel said unto them, Fear not: for, behold, I bring you good tidings of great joy, which shall be to all people. Luke 2:10

Rejoice ye in that day, and leap for joy: for, behold, your reward is great in heaven: for in the like manner did their fathers unto the prophets.
Luke 6:23

Likewise, I say unto you, there is joy in the presence of the angels of God over one sinner that repenteth. Luke 15:10

And they worshipped him, and returned to Jerusalem with great joy.
Luke 24:52

These things have I spoken unto you, that my joy might remain in you, and that your joy might be full. John 15:11

Verily, verily, I say unto you, That ye shall weep and lament, but the world shall rejoice: and ye shall be sorrowful, but your sorrow shall be turned into joy. John 16:20

A woman when she is in travail hath sorrow, because her hour is come: but as soon as she is delivered of the child, she remembereth no more the anguish, for joy that a man is born into the world. And ye now therefore have sorrow: but I will see you again, and your heart shall rejoice, and your joy no man taketh from you. And in that day ye shall ask me nothing. Verily, verily, I say unto you, Whatsoever ye shall ask the Father in my name, he will give it you. Hitherto have ye asked nothing in my name: ask, and ye shall receive, that your joy may be full. John 16:21-24

And now come I to thee; and these things I speak in the world, that they might have my joy fulfilled in themselves. John 17:13

Thou hast made known to me the ways of life; thou shalt make me full of joy with thy countenance. Acts 2:28

And the disciples were filled with joy, and with the Holy Ghost.
Acts 13:52

And not only so, but we also joy in God through our Lord Jesus Christ, by whom we have now received the atonement. Romans 5:11

For the kingdom of God is not meat and drink; but righteousness, and peace, and joy in the Holy Ghost. Romans 14:17

Now the God of hope fill you with all joy and peace in believing, that ye may abound in hope, through the power of the Holy Ghost.
Romans 15:13

Not for that we have dominion over your faith, but are helpers of your joy: for by faith ye stand. 2 Corinthians 1:24

And having this confidence, I know that I shall abide and continue with you all for your furtherance and joy of faith. Philippians 1:25

And ye became followers of us, and of the Lord, having received the word in much affliction, with joy of the Holy Ghost. 1 Thessalonians 1:6

My brethren, count it all joy when ye fall into divers temptations.
James 1:2

And these things write we unto you, that your joy may be full. 1 John 1:4

Mercy

The Lord is longsuffering, and of great mercy, forgiving iniquity and transgression, and by no means clearing the guilty, visiting the iniquity of the fathers upon the children unto the third and fourth generation.
Numbers 14:18

And shewing mercy unto thousands of them that love me and keep my commandments. Deuteronomy 5:10

Know therefore that the Lord thy God, he is God, the faithful God, which keepeth covenant and mercy with them that love him and keep his commandments to a thousand generations. Deuteronomy 7:9

And he said, Lord God of Israel, there is no God like thee, in heaven above, or on earth beneath, who keepest covenant and mercy with thy servants that walk before thee with all their heart. 1 Kings 8:23

O give thanks unto the Lord; for he is good; for his mercy endureth for ever. 1 Chronicles 16:34

And that he would shew thee the secrets of wisdom, that they are double to that which is! Know therefore that God exacteth of thee less than thine iniquity deserveth. Job 11:6

Surely goodness and mercy shall follow me all the days of my life: and I will dwell in the house of the Lord for ever. Psalms 23:6

All the paths of the Lord are mercy and truth unto such as keep his covenant and his testimonies. Psalms 25:10

I will be glad and rejoice in thy mercy: for thou hast considered my trouble; thou hast known my soul in adversities. Psalms 31:7

Many sorrows shall be to the wicked: but he that trusteth in the Lord, mercy shall compass him about. Psalms 32:10

Thy mercy, O Lord, is in the heavens; and thy faithfulness reacheth unto the clouds. Psalms 36:5

The wicked borroweth, and payeth not again: but the righteous sheweth mercy, and giveth. Psalms 37:21

But I am like a green olive tree in the house of God: I trust in the mercy of God for ever and ever. Psalms 52:8

Also unto thee, O Lord, belongeth mercy: for thou renderest to every man according to his work. Psalms 62:12

For thou, Lord, art good, and ready to forgive; and plenteous in mercy unto all them that call upon thee. Psalms 86:5

For great is thy mercy toward me: and thou hast delivered my soul from the lowest hell. Psalms 86:13

But thou, O Lord, art a God full of compassion, and gracious, longsuffering, and plenteous in mercy and truth. Psalms 86:15

Justice and judgment are the habitation of thy throne: mercy and truth shall go before thy face. Psalms 89:14

The Lord is merciful and gracious, slow to anger, and plenteous in mercy.
Psalms 103:8

For as the heaven is high above the earth, so great is his mercy toward them that fear him. Psalms 103:11

Like as a father pitieth his children, so the Lord pitieth them that fear him. Psalms 103:13

But the mercy of the Lord is from everlasting to everlasting upon them that fear him, and his righteousness unto children's children.
Psalms 103:17

Help me, O Lord my God: O save me according to thy mercy.

Psalms 109:26

The earth, O Lord, is full of thy mercy: teach me thy statutes.

Psalms 119:64

The Lord is gracious, and full of compassion; slow to anger, and of great mercy. Psalms 145:8

Let not mercy and truth forsake thee: bind them about thy neck; write them upon the table of thine heart. Proverbs 3:3

He that despiseth his neighbour sinneth: but he that hath mercy on the poor, happy is he. Do they not err that devise evil? but mercy and truth shall be to them that devise good. Proverbs 14:21-22

He that followeth after righteousness and mercy findeth life, righteousness, and honour. Proverbs 21:21

He that covereth his sins shall not prosper: but whoso confesseth and forsaketh them shall have mercy. Proverbs 28:13

And therefore will the Lord wait, that he may be gracious unto you, and therefore will he be exalted, that he may have mercy upon you: for the Lord is a God of judgment: blessed are all they that wait for him.

Isaiah 30:18

For my name's sake will I defer mine anger, and for my praise will I refrain for thee, that I cut thee not off. Isaiah 48:9

Let the wicked forsake his way, and the unrighteous man his thoughts: and let him return unto the Lord, and he will have mercy upon him; and to our God, for he will abundantly pardon. Isaiah 55:7

Blessed are the merciful: for they shall obtain mercy. Matthew 5:7

As concerning the gospel, they are enemies for your sakes: but as touching the election, they are beloved for the fathers' sakes. For the gifts and calling of God are without repentance. For as ye in times past have not believed God, yet have now obtained mercy through their unbelief: Even so have these also now not believed, that through your mercy they also may obtain mercy. For God hath concluded them all in unbelief, that he might have mercy upon all. Romans 11:28-32

But God, who is rich in mercy, for his great love wherewith he loved us.

Ephesians 2:4

Not by works of righteousness which we have done, but according to his mercy he saved us, by the washing of regeneration, and renewing of the Holy Ghost. Titus 3:5

Let us therefore come boldly unto the throne of grace, that we may obtain mercy, and find grace to help in time of need. Hebrews 4:16

Behold, we count them happy which endure. Ye have heard of the patience of Job, and have seen the end of the Lord; that the Lord is very pitiful, and of tender mercy. James 5:11

Blessed be the God and Father of our Lord Jesus Christ, which according to his abundant mercy hath begotten us again unto a lively hope by the resurrection of Jesus Christ from the dead. 1 Peter 1:3

Which in time past were not a people, but are now the people of God: which had not obtained mercy, but now have obtained mercy.
1 Peter 2:10

Mercy unto you, and peace, and love, be multiplied. Jude 1:2

Peace

And, having made peace through the blood of his cross, by him to reconcile all things unto himself; by him, I say, whether they be things in earth, or things in heaven. Colossians 1:20

I will both lay me down in peace, and sleep: for thou, Lord, only makest me dwell in safety. Psalms 4:8

The Lord will give strength unto his people; the Lord will bless his people with peace. Psalms 29:11

Mark the perfect man, and behold the upright: for the end of that man is peace. Psalms 37:37

He hath delivered my soul in peace from the battle that was against me: for there were many with me. Psalms 55:18

In his days shall the righteous flourish; and abundance of peace so long as the moon endureth. Psalms 72:7

Lord, thou wilt ordain peace for us: for thou also hast wrought all our works in us. Isaiah 26:12

For ye shall go out with joy, and be led forth with peace: the mountains and the hills shall break forth before you into singing, and all the trees of the field shall clap their hands. Isaiah 55:12

He shall enter into peace: they shall rest in their beds, each one walking in his uprightness. Isaiah 57:2

To give light to them that sit in darkness and in the shadow of death, to guide our feet into the way of peace. Luke 1:79

Now the God of hope fill you with all joy and peace in believing, that ye may abound in hope, through the power of the Holy Ghost.
Romans 15:13

For God is not the author of confusion, but of peace, as in all churches of the saints. 1 Corinthians 14:33

And let the peace of God rule in your hearts, to the which also ye are called in one body; and be ye thankful. Colossians 3:15

Now the Lord of peace himself give you peace always by all means. The Lord be with you all. 2 Thessalonians 3:16

> *"There is no peace ....to the wicked." The world offers false peace to dull the senses, deaden the conscience, quiet the nerves, but it cannot give peace. - Vance Havner*

1. Peace Through Jesus Christ

But now in Christ Jesus ye who sometimes were far off are made nigh by the blood of Christ. For he is our peace, who hath made both one, and hath broken down the middle wall of partition between us. Having abolished in his flesh the enmity, even the law of commandments contained in ordinances; for to make in himself of twain one new man, so making peace. Ephesians 2:13-15

Therefore being justified by faith, we have peace with God through our Lord Jesus Christ. Romans 5:1

Peace I leave with you, my peace I give unto you: not as the world giveth, give I unto you. Let not your heart be troubled, neither let it be afraid.
John 14:27

These things I have spoken unto you, that in me ye might have peace. In the world ye shall have tribulation: but be of good cheer; I have overcome the world. John 16:33

Then said Jesus to them again, Peace be unto you: as my Father hath sent me, even so send I you. John 20:21

> *We will not have peace without righteousness. We will never get rested until we get right. - Vance Havner*

2. Peace from God's Word

My son, forget not my law; but let thine heart keep my commandments: For length of days, and long life, and peace, shall they add to thee.
Proverbs 3:1-2

Great peace have they which love thy law: and nothing shall offend them.
Psalms 119:165

And all thy children shall be taught of the Lord; and great shall be the peace of thy children. Isaiah 54:13

Let us therefore follow after the things which make for peace, and things wherewith one may edify another. Romans 14:19

And as many as walk according to this rule, peace be on them, and mercy, and upon the Israel of God. Galatians 6:16

Be careful for nothing; but in every thing by prayer and supplication with thanksgiving let your requests be made known unto God. And the peace of God, which passeth all understanding, shall keep your hearts and minds through Christ Jesus. Finally, brethren, whatsoever things are true, whatsoever things are honest, whatsoever things are just, whatsoever things are pure, whatsoever things are lovely, whatsoever things are of good report; if there be any virtue, and if there be any praise, think on these things. Those things, which ye have both learned, and received, and heard, and seen in me, do: and the God of peace shall be with you.
Philippians 4:6-9

Grace and peace be multiplied unto you through the knowledge of God, and of Jesus our Lord. 2 Peter 1:2

3. How to Have Peace

When a man's ways please the Lord, he maketh even his enemies to be at peace with him. Proverbs 16:7

For to be carnally minded is death; but to be spiritually minded is life and peace. Romans 8:6

Thou wilt keep him in perfect peace, whose mind is stayed on thee: because he trusteth in thee. Isaiah 26:3

For the kingdom of God is not meat and drink; but righteousness, and peace, and joy in the Holy Ghost. For he that in these things serveth Christ is acceptable to God, and approved of men. Let us therefore follow after the things which make for peace, and things wherewith one may edify another. Romans 14:17-19

And the work of righteousness shall be peace; and the effect of righteousness quietness and assurance for ever. Isaiah 32:17

Comfort

I, even I, am he that comforteth you: who art thou, that thou shouldest be afraid of a man that shall die, and of the son of man which shall be made as grass. Isaiah 51:12

To proclaim the acceptable year of the Lord, and the day of vengeance of our God; to comfort all that mourn. Isaiah 61:2

As one whom his mother comforteth, so will I comfort you; and ye shall be comforted in Jerusalem. Isaiah 66:13

Blessed are they that mourn: for they shall be comforted. Matthew 5:4

And I will pray the Father, and he shall give you another Comforter, that he may abide with you for ever. John 14:16

> *God does not comfort us to make us comfortable but to make us comforters. - J. H. Jowett*

Blessed be God, even the Father of our Lord Jesus Christ, the Father of mercies, and the God of all comfort; Who comforteth us in all our tribulation, that we may be able to comfort them which are in any trouble, by the comfort wherewith we ourselves are comforted of God. For as the sufferings of Christ abound in us, so our consolation also aboundeth by Christ. 2 Corinthians 1:3-5

Great is my boldness of speech toward you, great is my glorying of you: I am filled with comfort, I am exceeding joyful in all our tribulation.
2 Corinthians 7:4

Nevertheless God, that comforteth those that are cast down, comforted us by the coming of Titus; And not by his coming only, but by the consolation wherewith he was comforted in you, when he told us your earnest desire, your mourning, your fervent mind toward me; so that I rejoiced the more. 2 Corinthians 7:6-7

Finally, brethren, farewell. Be perfect, be of good comfort, be of one mind, live in peace; and the God of love and peace shall be with you.
2 Corinthians 13:11

Bear ye one another's burdens, and so fulfil the law of Christ.
Galatians 6:2

Comfort your hearts, and stablish you in every good word and work.
2 Thessalonians 2:17

God often comforts us, not always by changing the circumstances of our lives, but by changing our attitude toward them.
- S. H. B. Masterman

Deliverance

He shall deliver thee in six troubles: yea, in seven there shall no evil touch thee. Job 5:19

But know that the Lord hath set apart him that is godly for himself: the Lord will hear when I call unto him. Psalms 4:3

The angel of the Lord encampeth round about them that fear him, and delivereth them. Psalms 34:7

Many are the afflictions of the righteous: but the Lord delivereth him out of them all. Psalms 34:19

For the Lord loveth judgment, and forsaketh not his saints; they are preserved for ever: but the seed of the wicked shall be cut off. Psalms 37:28

He that believeth on him is not condemned: but he that believeth not is condemned already, because he hath not believed in the name of the only begotten Son of God. John 3:18

And ye shall know the truth, and the truth shall make you free. John 8:32

Knowing this, that our old man is crucified with him, that the body of sin might be destroyed, that henceforth we should not serve sin. Romans 6:6

For sin shall not have dominion over you: for ye are not under the law, but under grace. Romans 6:14

There hath no temptation taken you but such as is common to man: but God is faithful, who will not suffer you to be tempted above that ye are able; but will with the temptation also make a way to escape, that ye may be able to bear it. 1 Corinthians 10:13

Grace be to you and peace from God the Father, and from our Lord Jesus Christ, Who gave himself for our sins, that he might deliver us from this present evil world, according to the will of God and our Father:
Galatians 1:3-4

But the Lord is faithful, who shall stablish you, and keep you from evil.
2 Thessalonians 3:3

For in that he himself hath suffered being tempted, he is able to succour them that are tempted. Hebrews 2:18

For the eyes of the Lord are over the righteous, and his ears are open unto their prayers: but the face of the Lord is against them that do evil. And who is he that will harm you, if ye be followers of that which is good? 1 Peter 3:12-13

The Lord knoweth how to deliver the godly out of temptations, and to reserve the unjust unto the day of judgment to be punished: 2 Peter 2:9

Perseverance

DEFINITION: persistence; continued efforts; to stick to a task or purpose, no matter how hard or troublesome.

Know ye not that they which run in a race run all, but one receiveth the prize? So run, that ye may obtain. 1 Corinthians 9:24

The righteous also shall hold on his way, and he that hath clean hands shall be stronger and stronger. Job 17:9

I had fainted, unless I had believed to see the goodness of the Lord in the land of the living. Wait on the Lord: be of good courage, and he shall strengthen thine heart: wait, I say, on the Lord. Psalms 27:13-14

The Lord will perfect that which concerneth me: thy mercy, O Lord, endureth for ever: forsake not the works of thine own hands.
Psalms 138:8

But the path of the just is as the shining light, that shineth more and more unto the perfect day. Proverbs 4:18

For a dream cometh through the multitude of business. Ecclesiastes 5:3

Whatsoever thy hand findeth to do, do it with thy might; for there is no work, nor device, nor knowledge, nor wisdom, in the grave, whither thou goest. Ecclesiastes 9:10

> *When God sees someone who doesn't quit, He looks down and says, "There is someone I can use." - John Mason*

He giveth power to the faint; and to them that have no might he increaseth strength. Even the youths shall faint and be weary, and the young men shall utterly fall: But they that wait upon the Lord shall renew their strength; they shall mount up with wings as eagles; they shall run, and not be weary; and they shall walk, and not faint. Isaiah 40:29-31

Ask, and it shall be given you; seek, and ye shall find; knock, and it shall be opened unto you: Matthew 7:7

Wherefore seeing we also are compassed about with so great a cloud of witnesses, let us lay aside every weight, and the sin which doth so easily beset us, and let us run with patience the race that is set before us.
Hebrews 12:1

Therefore, my beloved brethren, be ye stedfast, unmoveable, always abounding in the work of the Lord, forasmuch as ye know that your labour is not in vain in the Lord. 1 Corinthians 15:58

And let us not be weary in well doing: for in due season we shall reap, if we faint not. Galatians 6:9

I press toward the mark for the prize of the high calling of God in Christ Jesus. Philippians 3:14

Thou therefore endure hardness, as a good soldier of Jesus Christ.
2 Timothy 2:3

Now the just shall love by faith: but if any man draw back, my soul shall have no pleasure in him. Hebrews 10:38

And whatsoever ye do, do it heartily, as to the Lord, and not unto men.
Colossians 3:23

And so, after he had patiently endured, he obtained the promise.
Hebrews 6:15

I have fought a good fight, I have finished my course, I have kept the faith: Henceforth there is laid up for me a crown of righteousness, which the Lord, the righteous judge, shall give me at that day: and not to me only, but unto all them also that love his appearing. 2 Timothy 4:7-8

Difficulties are stepping stones to success. - Anonymous

Let us hold fast the profession of our faith without wavering; for he is faithful that promised. Hebrews 10:23

Cast not away therefore your confidence, which hath great recompence of reward. For ye have need of patience, that, after ye have done the will of God, ye might receive the promise. Hebrews 10:35-36

Wherefore take unto you the whole armour of God, that ye may be able to withstand in the evil day, and having done all, to stand. Stand therefore, having your loins girt about with truth, and having on the breastplate of righteousness. Ephesians 6:13-14

Therefore, my brethren dearly beloved and longed for, my joy and crown, so stand fast in the Lord, my dearly beloved. Philippians 4:1

Rooted and built up in him, and stablished in the faith, as ye have been taught, abounding therein with thanksgiving. Colossians 2:7

Prove all things; hold fast that which is good. 1 Thessalonians 5:21

Watch ye, stand fast in the faith, quit you like men, be strong.
1 Corinthians 16:13

Of the Jews five times received I forty stripes save one. Thrice was I beaten with rods, once was I stoned, thrice I suffered shipwreck, a night and a day I have been in the deep; In journeyings often, in perils of waters, in perils of robbers, in perils by mine own countrymen, in perils by the heathen, in perils in the city, in perils in the wilderness, in perils in the sea, in perils among false brethren; In weariness and painfulness, in watchings often, in hunger and thirst, in fastings often, in cold and nakedness. 2 Corinthians 11:24-27

We are troubled on every side, yet not distressed; we are perplexed, but not in despair; Persecuted, but not forsaken; cast down, but not destroyed.
2 Corinthians 4:8-9

For which cause we faint not; but though our outward man perish, yet the inward man is renewed day by day. For our light affliction, which is but for a moment, worketh for us a far more exceeding and eternal weight of glory. 2 Corinthians 4:16-17

And we desire that every one of you do shew the same diligence to the full assurance of hope unto the end. Hebrews 6:11

SCRIPTURE REFERENCE LIST

Answered Prayer: *2 Chronicles 7:14; Psalm 145:18; Jeremiah 33:3; Matthew 7:7-8; Mark 11:24-25; John 14:13-14; James 5:16*

Assurance of Salvation: *Mark 5:16; John 3:16, 18, 36; John 5:24; John 6:39; John 10:27-29; Romans 10:9-10, 13; Ephesians 2:8-9; Philippians 1:6; 1 John 5:11-13*

Authority Over Satan: *Matthew 18:18; Mark 16:17; Luke 10:17-19; Ephesians 1:3; Ephesians 1:21-22; Ephesians 2:6; Ephesians 4:17; Ephesians 6:12, 16; Colossians 1:13; James 4:7; 1 Peter 5:7-9; 1 John 4:4; 1 John 5:18*

Believing God for a Mate: *Genesis 2:24; Proverbs 18:22; Matthew 6:33; 1 Corinthians 7:2, 9; 2 Corinthians 6:14-15*

Blessing: *Deuteronomy 11:26-27; Deuteronomy 28:2; Psalm 21:3-6; Galatians 3:14*

Blessing Upon Children: ***Isaiah 44:3; Isaiah 49:25; Isaiah 54:13; Isaiah 65:23-24***

Blessing Upon Home: *Psalm 4:8; Psalm 91:10; Psalm 112:1-3; Psalm 115:13-14; Psalm 122:7; Proverbs 3:33; Proverbs 12:7*

Child Discipline: *Leviticus 20:9; Deuteronomy 6:6-7; Deuteronomy 21:18-21; Proverbs 13:24; Proverbs 19:18; Proverbs 22:6, 15; Proverbs 23:13-14; Proverbs 29:15, 17; Matthew 15:4; Ephesians 6:4; Colossians 3:21*

Childbirth: *Genesis 29:31; Genesis 49:25; Exodus 23:26; Deuteronomy 7:13-14; Ruth 4:13; Psalm 113:9; Psalm 128:3*

Comfort: *Isaiah 51:12; Isaiah 57:18; Isaiah 66:13; Jeremiah 31:13; 2 Corinthians 1:3-5*

Controlling the Mind/Thought Life: Job 31:1; *Romans 8:6-7; 2 Corinthians 10:4-5; Philippians 4:8; Colossians 3:2; 2 Timothy 1:7; James 1:8*

Controlling the Mouth/Tongue: *Psalm 17:3; Psalm 34:13; Psalm 39:1; Psalm 141:3; Proverbs 10:19; Proverbs 13:3; Proverbs 15:4; Proverbs 16:24; Proverbs 18:21; 1 Peter 3:10*

Court Case: *Psalm 31:20; Psalm 91:1-3; Proverbs 6:19; Proverbs 8:8; Isaiah 43:2; Isaiah 49:25; Isaiah 54:14-15, 17; Luke 12:11-12; Colossians 4:6*

Direction/Guidance: *Psalm 16:11; Psalm 32:8; Psalm 37:5; Psalm 48:14; Proverbs 3:5-6; Proverbs 16:3, 9; John 16:13*

Divorce:

God Against Divorce: *Malachi 2:15-16; Matthew 19:3-12; Romans 7:1-3; 1 Corinthians 7:10-13*

Remarriage Allowed: *Deuteronomy 24:1-4; 1 Corinthians 7:27-28*

Employer/Employee Relations: *Matthew 5:41; Luke 16:10, 12; Ephesians 4:28; Ephesians 6:5-9; Colossians 3:22-25; 1 Thessalonians 4:11-12; 2 Thessalonians 3:10, 12; 1 Timothy 6:1; Titus 2:9; 1 Peter 2:18-23*

Enemies: *Exodus 23:22; Deuteronomy 20:4; Deuteronomy 28:7; 2 Kings 6:16; 2 Kings 17:39; Job 8:22; Psalm 27:5-6; Psalm 37:40; Psalm 41:11; Psalm 60:12; Psalm 112:8; Psalm 118:7; Psalm 125:3; Proverbs 16:7; Isaiah 54:15-17; Isaiah 41:11-12; Luke 1:71; Acts 18:10; Hebrews 13:6*

Faith/Believing God for the Impossible: *Numbers 23:19; Deuteronomy 7:9; Psalm 89:34; Isaiah 46:11; Jeremiah 1:12; Jeremiah 32:17; Ezekiel 24:14; Matthew 9:23, 29; Matthew 17:20; Matthew 19:26; Matthew 21:22; Mark 9:23; Mark 11:24; Luke 1:37; Luke 12:29; John 11:22; Romans 4:17-21; Romans 10:17; 2 Corinthians 1:20; Hebrews 6:12; Hebrews 10:23*

Favor: *Psalm 5:12; Psalm 41:11; Proverbs 3:1-4; Proverbs 8:34-35; Proverbs 11:27; Proverbs 12:2; Proverbs 14:9; Proverbs 16:7; Acts 2:47*

Forgiveness for Abortion: *Psalm 103:3-4; Psalm 127:3; Psalm 139:13-16; Isaiah 44:2; Jeremiah 1:5; Philippians 3:13-14; Hebrews 10:17; 1 John 1:9*

Guidance and Direction: *Deuteronomy 31:6; Psalm 16:11; Psalm 32:8; Psalm 37:23-24; Psalm 48:14; Psalm 121:8; Proverbs 3:5-6; Proverbs 16:3; Isaiah 48:17b; John 16:13a; James 1:5; 1 John 2:20*

Healing: *Exodus 15:26; Exodus 23:25-26; Deuteronomy 7:15; Psalm 30:2; Psalm 91:10; Psalm 103:2-3; Psalm 107:20; Proverbs 4:20-22; Proverbs 12:18; Isaiah 53:3-5; Nahum 1:9; Matthew 8:16-17; Matthew 9:35; Matthew 10:1; Mark 11:24; Acts 10:38; Galatians 3:13; Hebrews 13:8; James 5:14-15; 1 Peter 2:24*

How to Treat Your Enemies: *Proverbs 20:22; Proverbs 24:17; Proverbs 25:21; Matthew 5:44; Romans 12:20*

How to Treat Your Husband: *Proverbs 21:9, 19; Proverbs 31:10-12, 30; 1 Corinthians 11:3; Ephesians 5:22-23, 33; Colossians 3:18-19; 1 Corinthians 7:2-5, 10, 13-14; Titus 2:4-5; Hebrews 13:4; 1 Peter 3:1, 7b, 8-12*

How to Treat Your Wife and Children: *Proverbs 5:18-19; Proverbs 6:23-35; Proverbs 18:22; Ecclesiastes 9:9; Malachi 3:14-16; Matthew 19:5; 1 Corinthians 7:3-5; 1 Corinthians 13:4-8 AMP; Ephesians 5:23-33; Colossians 3:21; 1 Timothy 5:8; 1 Peter 3:7-12*

Joy: *Nehemiah 8:10c; John 15:11; John 16:24; John 17:13; Romans 14:17; Romans 15:13; James 1:2*

Living in the Present: *Psalm 46:1; Matthew 6:34; Philippians 3:13-14*

Long Life: *Psalm 91:16; Psalm 118:17; Proverbs 14:27; Ecclesiastes 7:17*

Love: *Matthew 5:44; Matthew 7:12; Mark 12:30-31; John 15:12-13; Romans 12:10; Romans 13:10; 1 Corinthians 13:4-8 AMP; 1 Peter 1:2; 1 John 2:10; 1 John 3:14, 18-19; 1 John 4:7-8, 20-21*

Old Age: *Genesis 15:15; Exodus 23:26; Job 5:26; Psalm 71:9, 18; Psalm 90:10; Psalm 92:14; Isaiah 46:4*

Overcoming Addictions, Bad Habits, Bondage: *Proverbs 11:19; Proverbs 12:28; Proverbs 28:13; John 8:3-6; Romans 8:11-14; Romans 8:2, 13, 37; 1 Corinthians 6:19-20; 1 Corinthians 9:27; 2 Corinthians 6:19-20; Galatians 6:8; James 4:7-8; 1 Peter 1:12; 1 John 5:4*

Overcoming Abusive Behavior (for Abusers):

- *Child Abuse – Matthew 18:6, 10; 1 Corinthians 6:10*

- *Domestic Abuse Against Wife – Malachi 2:14-16; Colossians 3:19-26*

- *For Those Who Have Suffered Abuse – Psalm 34:4-5; Romans 12:17-21; 1 Corinthians 7:15*

- *Physical Abuse – Psalm 58:2; Proverbs 28:17; Isaiah 59:6-8; Habakkuk 1:3*

- *Sexual Abuse – Deuteronomy 22:25-26; Judges 19:25*

- *Verbal Abuse – Psalm 140:11; Proverbs 10:6,11-14; Proverbs 13:2-3; 10; Proverbs 17:14; Proverbs 18:6; Colossians 3:8*

Overcoming Alcohol/Drugs/Substance Abuse: *Leviticus 10:9; Psalm 107:6, 26-29; Proverbs 20:1; Proverbs 21:17; Proverbs 23:19-20, 29-35; Isaiah 5:11, 22-23; Isaiah 28:1-4, 7-8; Isaiah 41:13; Habakkuk 2:15; Luke 1:34; John 8:36; Romans 14:21; 1 Corinthians 5:11; 1 Corinthians 6:9-11; Galatians 5:21*

Overcoming Anger, Hatred, Bad Temper: *Psalm 37:8; Proverbs 14:17, 29; Proverbs 15:1, 11, 18; Proverbs 16:32; Proverbs 19:11; Proverbs 21:19; Proverbs 22:24-25; Proverbs 25:21-22, 28; Proverbs 29:22; Ecclesiastes 7:9; Matthew 5:22; Romans 12:19-21; Ephesians 4:26-27, 29-32; Colossians 3:8; James 1:19-20*

Overcoming Backsliding: *Proverbs 28:13; Isaiah 55:7; Hosea 14:1; 1 John 1:9*

Overcoming Bad Habits/Sin: *Proverbs 28:13; Matthew 3:8; Romans 6:11-19; Romans 8:2, 13; Romans 13:14; 1 Corinthians 9:27; Genesis 5:16-17, 24; Galatians 16:7-8; Philippians 4:13; 1 Peter 4:1-3*

Overcoming Bitterness, Resentment: *Leviticus 19:17-18; Proverbs 10:12; Romans 12:14-21; Ephesians 4:31-32; Colossians 3:8; Hebrews 12:14-15; James 3:14-16, 18; 1 Peter 2:23; 1 John 2:9, 11; 1 John 4:20*

Overcoming Critical/Judgmental Attitude: *Matthew 7:1-5; Luke 6:37; Romans 2:1,3; Romans 12:10; Romans 14:10, 13*

Overcoming Depression/Discouragement/Disappointment: *Deuteronomy 31:6, 8; Psalm 31:24; Psalm 34:15, 19; Psalm 55:22; Psalm 107:19; Isaiah 41:10, 13; Isaiah 66:13a; Jeremiah 31:13; Matthew 6:33; John 14:1, 18; Romans 8:28; 2 Corinthians 1:4-5; 2 Corinthians 4:8-9; Philippians 1:6; Philippians 4:6,11; 1 Thessalonians 5:18; 2 Thessalonians 2:16; Hebrews 13:5; James 1:2-4; 1 Peter 4:12-13; 1 John 5:4*

Overcoming Envy/Jealousy: *Proverbs 10:12, 18; Proverbs 14:30; Proverbs 26:14; Proverbs 27:4; Song of Solomon 8:6; Matthew 5:43-44; Romans 12:17-21; Romans 13:13; Galatians 5:19-21, 26; James 3:14, 16; James 5:9; 1 Peter 2:1; 1 John 2:9; 1 John 3:15*

Overcoming Fear/Fear of People: *Exodus 14:13-14; Deuteronomy 31:8; Joshua 1:9; 2 Kings 6:16; Psalm 23:4; Psalm 27:1,3; Psalm 46:1; Psalm 56:4, 11; Psalm 112:7; Psalm 118:6; Proverbs 1:33; Proverbs 3:24-26; Proverbs 29:25; Isaiah 43:2; Isaiah 51:7; John 17:27; Romans 8:31; Timothy 1:7; Hebrews 13:6; 1 Peter 3:13-14; 1 John 4:18*

Overcoming Greed/Covetousness: *Proverbs 15:27; Proverbs 23:4-5; Matthew 6:21, 25-33; Matthew 16:26; Luke 12:15; Ephesians 5:5; Colossians 3:2, 5*

Overcoming Gambling Addiction: *Proverbs 1:19; Proverbs 15:27; Proverbs 21:25-26; Proverbs 23:4-5; Matthew 6:19-24; 2 Timothy 3:2*

Overcoming Grief/Bereavement: *Nehemiah 8:10, John 14:1-3; 2 Corinthians 1:3-5; Philippians 1:21-24*

Overcoming Guilt/God's Forgiveness: *2 Samuel 12:13; 2 Chronicles 30:9, 14; Psalm 32:1-2, 5; Psalm 85:2-3, 10; Psalm 86:5; Psalm 103:2-3, 12; Proverbs 28:13; Isaiah 43:25; Isaiah 44:22; Isaiah 55:7; Jeremiah 31:34; Jeremiah 33:8; Micah 7:18-19; Romans 8:1; Philippians 3:13; Colossians 1:14; Hebrews 8:12; Hebrews 10:17; 1 John 1:9; 1 John 2:12; 1 John 3:20-21*

Overcoming an Inferiority Complex/Building Self-Confidence: *Deuteronomy 28:13; Psalm 118:6; Proverbs 3:26; Proverbs 28:1; Romans 8:37; 2 Corinthians 2:14; Ephesians 2:10; Ephesians 3:12; Philippians 4:13; Hebrews 13:6; 1 John 4:4*

Overcoming Job/Work Pressures: Deuteronomy 20:4; *Deuteronomy 28:7; Psalm 75:6-7; Proverbs 21:2; Philippians 4:11-13; Colossians 3:17, 22-25*

Overcoming Laziness/Slothfulness: *Proverbs 6:6-11; Proverbs 10:4-5, 26; Proverbs 12:24, 27; Proverbs 13:4; Proverbs 15:19; Proverbs 18:9; Proverbs 20:13; Proverbs 21:5, 25, 29; Proverbs 24:30-34; Proverbs 28:19; Ecclesiastes 5:18-19; Ecclesiastes 10:18; Isaiah 56:10; Romans 12:11; Ephesians 4:28; 1 Thessalonians 4:11-12; 2 Thessalonians 3:10-12*

Overcoming Loneliness: *Psalm 34:18; Psalm 46:1; Isaiah 41:10; Jeremiah 23:23; John 14:18; Hebrews 13:5-6*

Overcoming Lust/Pornography: *Psalm 81:12; Proverbs 6:24-25; Matthew 5:28; John 8:44; Romans 1:24; Romans 6:12; Romans 13:14; 1 Corinthians 10:6; Galatians 5:24; Ephesians 4:22; Colossians 3:5; 2 Timothy 2:22; Titus 2:12; James 1:13-15; 1 Peter 2:11; 1 Peter 4:1-3*

Overcoming Lying: *Exodus 20:16; Exodus 23:1; Psalm 10:7; Psalm 12:2-3; Psalm 28:3; Psalm 52:2-5; Psalm 55:21,23; Psalm 62:4; Psalm 101:5, 7; Proverbs 6:16-29; Proverbs 12:22; Proverbs 13:5; Proverbs 14:5,25; Proverbs 19:5,9; Proverbs 24:28; Jeremiah 9:8; John 8:44; Ephesians 4:25, 29; Colossians 3:9-10; James 3:14; Revelation 21:8*

Overcoming Marital Problems: *Ephesians 4:32; Ephesians 5:21-33; 1 Peter 3:1-11*

Overcoming Overweight/Overeating: *Leviticus 3:17; Proverbs 13:25; Proverbs 17:1; Proverbs 18:20; Proverbs 19:15; Proverbs 23:1-2, 20; Proverbs 25:16, 27-28; Proverbs 28:1-3*

Overcoming Persecution: *Matthew 5:11-12; Luke 6:22-23; John 15:18-20; Romans 12:14; 2 Corinthians 4:8-12*

Overcoming Pride: *Job 40:12; Psalm 119:21; Psalm 138:6; Proverbs 8:13; Proverbs 16:18-19; Proverbs 21:4; Proverbs 26:12; Proverbs 28:25-26; Proverbs 29:23; Isaiah 5:21; Matthew 23:11-12; Mark 9:35; Luke 16:15; Romans 12:3, 16; 1 Corinthians 8:31; 1 Corinthians 13:4; 2 Corinthians 3:5; 2 Corinthians 10:17; Philippians 2:3; James 4:6-7, 10; 1 Peter 5:5*

Overcoming Profanity or Blasphemy: *Leviticus 19:12; Mark 7:21-23; Ephesians 4:29-31; Colossians 3:8; James 3:10*

Overcoming Racism and Prejudice: *Malachi 2:10; John 7:24; Acts 10:28, 34-35; Acts 17:26; Romans 2:11; James 2:1, 9; 1 Peter 1:17*

Overcoming Rejection: *Psalm 27:9-10; Psalm 147:3; Luke 4:18; Ephesians 4:32; Hebrews 4:15-16*

Overcoming Sexual Sins:

Adultery: *Exodus 20:14; Leviticus 18:20; Leviticus 20:10; Deuteronomy 5:18; Proverbs 6:26-32; Proverbs 30:20; Matthew 5:27-28; Mark 7:21; 1 Corinthians 6:9-10; Hebrews 13:4; Revelation 21:8; Revelation 22:15*

• **Fornication:** *1 Corinthians 5:1-5, 11; 1 Corinthians 6:9, 18-20; 1 Corinthians 7:1-2; 1 Corinthians 10:8; Galatians 5:19-21; Ephesians 5:3; 1 Thessalonians 4:3; Hebrews 13:4; Revelation 21:8*

• **Homosexuality/Lesbianism:** *Leviticus 18:22; Leviticus 20:13; Deuteronomy 23:17; 1 Kings 14:24; Romans 1:24-28, 31; 1 Corinthians 6:9-10; Galatians 5:19-21; Revelation 21:8*

• **Incest:** *Leviticus 8:6-30; Leviticus 20:11-17; Deuteronomy 27:20-23; 1 Corinthians 5:1-5*

• **Transvestites/Cross Dressing:** *Deuteronomy 22:5*

Overcoming Smoking: *Romans 6:12-22; 1 Corinthians 3:16-17; 1 Corinthians 6:20; 2 Corinthians 7:1; 1 Peter 4:1-3; 2 Peter 2:19*

Overcoming Strife: *Proverbs 15:18; Proverbs 16:28; Proverbs 20:3; Proverbs 22:10; Proverbs 26:17, 20-21; Proverbs 28:25; 1 Corinthians 3:1-3; James 3:14-16*

Overcoming Suicidal Thoughts/Tendencies: *Psalm 34:1,7; Psalm 42:11; Psalm 55:22; Psalm 91:14-16; Psalm 107:6; Psalm 116:1-9; Psalm 118:17-18; Isaiah 41:10, 13; Isaiah 43:2; Isaiah 54:14, 17; Jeremiah 33:3; John 10:10; Romans 8:37-39; Philippians 4:6-7;*
1 John 4:4

Overcoming Temptation: *Psalm 119:11; Luke 22:46; 1 Corinthians 10:13; James 1:2-3, 13*

Overcoming Trials & Tests/Endurance, Patience, Perseverance: *Psalm 27:13-14; Isaiah 40:29-31; 2 Corinthians 1:3-4, 7; Galatians 6:9; Hebrews 6:15; Hebrews 10:23, 35-36; James 1:2-4, 12-14; 1 Peter 1:6-7; 1 Peter 4:12-13; 2 Peter 2:9; 2 Peter 5:10*

Overcoming Unforgiveness: *Proverbs 19:11; Proverbs 20:22; Proverbs 24:17, 29; Proverbs 25:21-22; Matthew 5:43-44, 46; Matthew 6:12, 14-15; Matthew 18:21-22; Mark 11:24-25; Luke 6:35-37; Romans 12:14, 17, 19-20; Ephesians 4:32; Colossians 3:13; 1 Peter 3:9*

Overcoming Worry: *Psalm 34:4, 17; Psalm 37:5, 23-24; Psalm 55:22; Proverbs 16:3; Matthew 6:25-34; Philippians 4:6-7; 1 Peter 5:7-9*

Peace: *Psalm 4:8; Psalm 29:11; Psalm 37:37; Psalm 55:18; Psalm 85:8; Proverbs 3:1-2, 17, 24; Isaiah 26:3; Isaiah 32:17; John 14:27; John 16:33; Romans 5:1; Romans 8:6; Romans 15:13; Philippians 4:6-7; Colossians 3:15; 2 Peter 1:2*

Peaceful Sleep: *Psalm 3:5; Psalm 4:8; Psalm 127:2; Proverbs 3:24-26; Isaiah 29:10*

Prosperity: *Deuteronomy 8:18; Deuteronomy 29:29; Joshua 1:8; 1 Kings 2:3; 2 Chronicles 26:4-5; Job 36:!1; Psalm 1:2-3; Psalm 27:9-10; Psalm 35:27b; Psalm 84:11b; Psalm 112:1,3; Psalm 147:3; Proverbs 8;21; Proverbs 10:4; Proverbs 11:25; Isaiah 48:17b; Isaiah 55:11; Luke 4:18; 2 Corinthians 8:9; Ephesians 4:32; Philippians 4:19; 1 Timothy 6:17; Hebrews 4:15-16; 3 John 2*

Protection: *Deuteronomy 33:12; Job 11:18-19; Psalm 4:8; Psalm 5:12; Psalm 17:4; Psalm 31:19-20; Psalm 34:7; Psalm 46:1; Psalm 91:9-11; Psalm 97:10; Psalm 107:20; Psalm 112:7; Psalm 121:7-8; Psalm 145:18-20; Proverbs 1:33; Proverbs 3:24-26; Proverbs 30:5; Isaiah 32:18; Isaiah 43:1-2; 2 Thessalonians 3:3; 1 Peter 3:13*

Salvation: *John 3:3-12, 16; John 6:37; Romans 3:23; Romans 10:9-10; Ephesians 2:8-9; 2 Timothy 1:9; Revelation 22:17*

Salvation of Loved Ones: *Acts 11:14; Acts 16:31; Acts 26:18; Romans 10:13; Ephesians 1:17-18; 2 Peter 3:9*

Strength: *Deuteronomy 33:25; Joshua 1:9; 2 Samuel 22:40; Nehemiah 8:10; Psalm 27:1, 14; Psalm 28:7; Psalm 29:11; Psalm 46:1; Psalm 105:4; Psalm 138:3; Proverbs 24:5, 10; Isaiah 40:29, 31a; Isaiah 41:10; Ephesians 6:10; Philippians 4:13*

Successful Marriage: *Proverbs 18:22; Ecclesiastes 9:9; Mark 10:6-9; 1 Corinthians 7:1-5; Colossians 3:18-19; 1 Peter 3:7*

Trusting God: *Psalm 25:2; Psalm 37:5, 23-24; Psalm 55:22; Proverbs 3:5-6; Proverbs 16:3; Matthew 25:34; Philippians 4:6-7; 1 Peter 5:7-9*

Wisdom: *Psalm 111:10; 1 Corinthians 1:30; 1 Corinthians 2:6-7; Ephesians 1:8; Ephesians 3:10; Colossians 1:9; James 1:5*

Pneuma Life Publishing
12138 Central Ave, Suite 251,
Mitchellville, MD 20721
(301) 577-4052
(800) 727-3218
Website http://www.pneumalife.com

DEEPER WATERS

A Journey into the Heart of God

A 100-Day Devotional

"But when you ask, be sure that your faith is in God alone. Do not waver, for a person with divided loyalty is as unsettled as a wave of the sea that is blown and tossed by the wind." - James 1:6

PNEUMALIFE PUBLISHING

Pneuma Life Publishing books are available at discounted prices for bulk purchase for fund-raising, premiums, sales promotions.

For details, email your request to sales@pneumalife.com or write us at **Pneuma Life Publishing, 12138 Central Ave, Suite 251, Mitchellville, MD 20721**

Deep Waters: A Journey into the Heart of God
Published by Pneuma Life Publishing
Pneuma Life Publishing, 12138 Central Ave, Suite 251, Mitchellville, MD 20721
www.pneumalife.com

All rights reserved. No part of this publication may be reproduced, distributed, or transmitted in any form or by any means, including photocopying, recording, or other electronic or mechanical methods, without the prior written permission of the publisher, except in the case of brief quotations embodied in critical reviews and certain other noncommercial uses permitted by copyright law. For permission requests, write to the publisher, addressed "Attention: Permissions Coordinator," at the address below.

Unless otherwise noted, all Sciptures quotations are from the KJV of the Bible

Copyright © 2025 by Pneuma Life Publishing
All Rights Reserved
Printed in the United States of America

Table of Contents

Deep Waters Devotional

Section 1: WHO IS GOD?

Day 1: The God Beyond the Name	316
Day 2: Encountering the Invisible God	317
Day 3: The Personal Touch of the Almighty	318
Day 4: God: Sovereign, Yet Close	319
Day 5: Understanding the Unsearchable God	320
Day 6: The God Who Reveals Himself	321
Day 7: Knowing God as Father	323
Day 8: God: From Mystery to Mastery	324
Day 9: Face-to-Face with Holiness	325

Section 2: THE NATURE OF GOD

Day 10: Unfailing Love: The Heartbeat of God	327
Day 11: Holiness: Walking in the Light	328
Day 12: Righteous Judge, Merciful Savior	329
Day 13: Grace Beyond Measure	330
Day 14: The Faithfulness of God	331
Day 15: God's Eternal Patience	332
Day 16: Immutable: The Unchanging Nature of God	334
Day 17: Embracing the God of Justice	335
Day 18: The Compassionate Heart of God	336

Section 3: THE WISDOM OF GOD

Day 19: Wisdom From Above — 338
Day 20: Trusting the Divine Perspective — 339
Day 21: God's Wisdom in Our Waiting — 340
Day 22: Discerning His Voice — 341
Day 23: Wisdom for the Wilderness — 343
Day 24: The Wise Builder — 344
Day 25: Wisdom in Words and Deeds — 345
Day 26: Navigating Life with Godly Insight — 346
Day 27: The Secret of True Wisdom — 347

Section 4: UNDERSTANDING GOD

Day 28: Understanding God's Timing — 349
Day 29: Why God Allows Storms — 350
Day 30: Seeing God Clearly — 351
Day 31: God's Plan: Hidden Yet Revealed — 352
Day 32: The Mystery of His Ways — 353
Day 33: Understanding His Silence — 355
Day 34: Lessons from Divine Interruptions — 356
Day 35: Recognizing God in the Ordinary — 357
Day 36: Walking in Step with God — 358

Section 5: HOW TO LOVE GOD

Day 37: Love With All Your Heart	360
Day 38: The Language of Love for God	361
Day 39: More Than Feelings: True Love for God	362
Day 40: A Heart that Beats for God	363
Day 41: Loving God in Difficult Times	364
Day 42: The Sacrifice of Love	366
Day 43: Expressing Love through Obedience	367
Day 44: Cultivating Passion for God	368
Day 45: The Power of Undivided Love	369

Section 6: COMMITMENT TO GOD

Day 46: The Cost of True Commitment	371
Day 47: Committed in a Shallow World	372
Day 48: Anchored in Christ	373
Day 49: Wholehearted Devotion	374
Day 50: Keeping the Covenant	375
Day 51: Unwavering Faithfulness	377
Day 52: Beyond Convenience: Devoted to God	378
Day 53: Standing Firm in Commitment	379
Day 54: Faith that Endures	380

Section 7: LIVING FOR AND SERVING GOD

Day 55: Living Beyond Yourself	382
Day 56: Purpose-driven Living	383
Day 57: Called to Serve	384
Day 58: A Life that Honors God	385
Day 59: Serving with Gladness	386
Day 60: God's Hands and Feet	387
Day 61: Divine Assignment: Embracing Your Calling	389
Day 62: Serving God through Serving Others	390
Day 63: Active Faith, Visible Service	391

Section 8: DYING TO SELF

Day 64: The Power of Letting Go	393
Day 65: Crucified with Christ	394
Day 66: The Freedom of Surrender	395
Day 67: When Less is More	396
Day 68: Emptying Ourselves to Be Filled	397
Day 69: Choosing the Cross Daily	398
Day 70: Death to Self, Life in Christ	399
Day 71: Living Fully through Surrender	401
Day 72: Humility: The Pathway to Power	402

Section 9: PUTTING GOD FIRST

Day 73: First Things First	404
Day 74: Priority One: God	405
Day 75: Kingdom Priorities	406
Day 76: The First Fruit Lifestyle	407
Day 77: God Before Everything Else	408
Day 78: Reordering Your World	409
Day 79: The Blessings of Prioritizing God	411
Day 80: Daily Choices, Eternal Consequences	412
Day 81: Seeking God Above All	413

Section 10: NO MIDDLE GROUND: CHOOSE YOUR GOD

Day 82: No Room for Compromise	415
Day 83: Choose Today Whom You Will Serve	416
Day 84: The Danger of Lukewarm Living	417
Day 85: Absolute Allegiance	418
Day 86: Crossroads: Choosing Your Path	420
Day 87: When Faith Demands a Choice	421
Day 88: Breaking Free from Spiritual Neutrality	422
Day 89: The Courage to Commit	424
Day 90: All In: No Turning Back	425
Day 91: Beyond Surface Prayers	426
Day 92: Embracing Holy Disruption	428
Day 93: The Ministry of Presence	429

Day 94: Prophetic Living	430
Day 95: Stewarding Influence	431
Day 96: The Art of Spiritual Mentoring	433
Day 97: Cultivating Sacred Rhythms	434
Day 98: Intercession as Warfare	435
Day 99: Living as Kingdom Ambassadors	436
Day 100: The Eternal Perspective	438
FINAL BLESSING	439

Section 1: Who is God?

Day 1: The God Beyond the Name

"God said to Moses, 'I AM WHO I AM. This is what you are to say to the Israelites: I AM has sent me to you.'" - Exodus 3:14

When Moses stood before the burning bush, he encountered a revelation that would forever change humanity's understanding of the Divine. God didn't offer a title, position, or role—He declared His eternal existence. "I AM WHO I AM." This wasn't merely identification; it was a profound declaration of absolute, unchanging reality.

In our culture of labels and definitions, we struggle to grasp a God who transcends human categorization. We want to package Him neatly, reduce Him to concepts we can control. But the great I AM refuses our limitations. He exists beyond our need to understand, beyond our capacity to fully comprehend.

This God who spoke to Moses is the same God who speaks to you today. He is not bound by time, constrained by circumstances, or limited by your perception of Him. He simply IS—eternally present, eternally powerful, eternally personal.

When you face uncertainty, remember: you serve the God who IS. When circumstances threaten to overwhelm you, anchor yourself in His unchangeable nature. He was before your problem existed, He is present in your current situation, and He will be long after your trial has passed.

Reflection: How does knowing God as the eternal "I AM" change your perspective on current challenges?

Prayer: Father, I worship You as the God who simply IS. Help me rest in Your eternal presence and unchanging nature. Teach me to find security not in understanding You completely, but in trusting You completely. Amen.

Day 2: Encountering the Invisible God

"No one has ever seen God, but the one and only Son, who is himself God and is in closest relationship with the Father, has made him known." - John 1:18

The invisible God chose to make Himself visible through His Son. This divine strategy reveals the heart of our Creator—He desperately wants to be known. Despite His transcendence, He pursues intimacy with humanity. Consider the magnificent paradox: the God who inhabits eternity stepped into time. The One who cannot be contained by the universe confined Himself to human flesh. The invisible became visible, not to diminish His glory, but to display it in terms we could comprehend. In Jesus, we see God's character unveiled. His compassion for the broken, His intolerance of injustice, His tender care for children, His fierce love for the lost—all of these reveal the invisible God's heart. Every miracle Jesus performed was a window into heaven's values. Every word He spoke echoed the Father's voice.

But this revelation demands response. We cannot encounter the invisible God made visible and remain unchanged. When Philip asked Jesus to show them the Father, Jesus replied, "Anyone who has seen me has seen the Father." This wasn't merely theological instruction—it was an invitation to intimate relationship. Today, the invisible God continues to reveal Himself through His Word, His Spirit, and His people. He remains as eager to be known now as He was in the first century. The question is not whether God is revealing Himself, but whether we have eyes to see.

Reflection: Where do you most clearly see God revealing Himself in your daily life?

Prayer: Invisible God, thank You for making Yourself known through Jesus. Open my spiritual eyes to see You clearly in Your Word, in Your creation, and in the circumstances of my life. May I never become too familiar with the miracle of Your revelation. Amen.

Day 3: The Personal Touch of the Almighty

"Before I formed you in the womb I knew you, before you were born I set you apart; I appointed you as a prophet to the nations."

- Jeremiah 1:5

The God who numbers the stars and calls them by name also knows the intricate details of your existence. This isn't mere theological theory—it's transformational truth. The Almighty, who holds galaxies in His palm, holds you in His heart.

Jeremiah discovered that God's knowledge of him preceded his existence. Before his first breath, God had designed his purpose. Before his first step, God had prepared his path. This divine intentionality reveals something profound about our Creator—He doesn't deal in accidents or afterthoughts. Every person is a deliberate act of divine creativity.

This personal dimension of God's character shatters the myth of divine detachment. Our God is not the distant deity of philosophy, unmoved and uninvolved. He is the passionate Father who celebrates your victories, comforts your sorrows, and works continuously to fulfill His purposes in your life.

When you feel overlooked by the world, remember: you are seen by God. When you question your significance, remember: you were significant enough to be personally crafted by the Creator. When you wonder about your purpose, remember: God set you apart before you were even born. This personal touch of the Almighty should inspire both humility and confidence.

Humility, because you are known completely—flaws and all. Confidence, because the One who knows you completely has chosen to love you unconditionally.

Reflection: How does God's personal knowledge of you before your birth impact your sense of identity and purpose?

Prayer: Almighty God, I am amazed that You knew me before I existed and loved me before I could love You back. Help me live with the confidence that comes from being personally known and purposefully created by You. May my life reflect the personal touch of Your love. Amen.

Day 4: God: Sovereign, Yet Close

"'Am I only a God nearby,' declares the Lord, 'and not a God far away? Who can hide in secret places so that I cannot see them?' declares the Lord. 'Do not I fill heaven and earth?' declares the Lord."
— *Jeremiah 23:23-24*

Here lies one of faith's greatest mysteries: God is simultaneously sovereign over all creation and intimately close to each believer. He fills heaven and earth, yet dwells within the heart that invites Him. This paradox defies human logic but defines divine love.

God's sovereignty means nothing occurs outside His knowledge or beyond His control. Kingdoms rise and fall according to His purposes. Hearts beat by His permission. The winds obey His command. Yet this same sovereign God chooses to be accessible to a child's prayer, available in life's darkest moments, and present in the mundane moments of daily existence.

Many believers struggle with this duality. They either emphasize God's sovereignty to the point of making Him seem distant and unapproachable, or they focus on His closeness while diminishing His power and authority. But Scripture reveals both truths simultaneously. The God who commands the morning is the same God who walks with you through it.

This balance should produce both reverence and intimacy in our relationship with God. We approach Him with deep respect for His absolute authority, yet we come boldly because of His demonstrated love. We trust His sovereignty when circumstances overwhelm us, and we enjoy His closeness when life feels ordinary.

Understanding God as both sovereign and close transforms prayer from religious duty to relational dialogue, worship from performance to genuine adoration.

Reflection: How can embracing both God's sovereignty and closeness change your approach to prayer and worship?

Prayer: Sovereign Lord, I worship You as the King of all creation and thank You for choosing to be close to me. Help me maintain proper reverence for Your majesty while enjoying the intimacy You offer. Teach me to trust Your sovereignty and treasure Your presence. Amen.

Day 5: Understanding the Unsearchable God

"Oh, the depth of the riches of the wisdom and knowledge of God! How unsearchable his judgments, and his paths beyond tracing out!"
- Romans 11:33

Paul's exclamation emerges from wrestling with divine mysteries that stretch human understanding beyond its limits. Rather than frustration, he expresses wonder. Rather than defeat, he declares worship. This response models how believers should approach the unsearchable nature of God.

God's unsearchable character doesn't mean He cannot be known—it means He cannot be fully known. Like an ocean that can be entered and enjoyed but never fully explored, God invites relationship while maintaining mystery.

This divine hiddenness isn't cruel concealment but gracious preservation. If we could completely understand God, He would cease to be God. The temptation exists to reduce God to our level of comprehension, to create manageable versions of the Almighty that fit our theological boxes. But the moment we think we have God figured out, we're probably worshipping an idol of our own making rather than the living God who defies all categories.

Embracing God's unsearchable nature requires intellectual humility and spiritual maturity. It means being comfortable with questions that have no easy answers, mysteries that deepen rather than resolve, and truths that transcend human logic. This isn't anti-intellectual—it's acknowledging the limits of intellect when encountering the infinite. The unsearchable God invites us into lifelong discovery. Every prayer may reveal new dimensions of His character. Every Scripture may unveil fresh aspects of His nature. Every experience may deepen our appreciation for His complexity and beauty.

Reflection: Where in your spiritual journey do you need to embrace mystery rather than demand complete understanding?

Prayer: Unsearchable God, I praise You for being infinitely greater than my ability to comprehend. Grant me the humility to worship what I cannot fully understand and the wisdom to find security in Your mystery rather than my comprehension. Keep me always learning, always discovering, always marveling at who You are. Amen.

Day 6: The God Who Reveals Himself

"The secret things belong to the Lord our God, but the things revealed belong to us and to our children forever, that we may follow all the words of this law." - Deuteronomy 29:29

While God remains ultimately unsearchable, He is not unknowable. The same God who conceals certain mysteries simultaneously reveals essential truths. This divine balance ensures that we know enough to trust Him without knowing so much that we cease to need Him.

God's self-revelation is intentional and progressive. Through creation, He reveals His power and artistry. Through Scripture, He unveils His character and purposes. Through Christ, He demonstrates His love and justice. Through the Spirit, He provides personal guidance and confirmation. Each revelation builds upon previous ones, creating a comprehensive yet incomplete portrait of the Divine.

The purpose of God's revelation isn't merely informational—it's transformational. He doesn't reveal truth to satisfy curiosity but to facilitate relationship. Every divine disclosure carries an implicit invitation: "Now that you know this about Me, how will you respond?" Consider how God revealed Himself to different people throughout Scripture. To Abraham, He revealed His faithfulness through promises. To Moses, His holiness through the law. To David, His mercy through forgiveness. To Paul, His grace through calling. Each person received precisely the revelation they needed for their unique circumstances and calling.

God continues this pattern today. He reveals Himself to you in ways specifically designed for your spiritual development and life situation. The question isn't whether God is revealing Himself, but whether you're positioned to receive His revelation through consistent engagement with His Word, prayer, and spiritual community.

Reflection: What has God recently revealed to you about His character or will for your life?

Prayer: Revealing God, thank You for not leaving me to guess about Your nature or Your will. Open my heart to receive the truths You want to reveal to me today. Help me respond appropriately to every divine disclosure, growing closer to You through each revelation. Make me sensitive to the ways You speak. Amen.

Day 7: Knowing God as Father

"See what great love the Father has lavished on us, that we should be called children of God! And that is what we are!" - 1 John 3:1

The ultimate revelation of God's identity comes through the designation "Father." This title transcends mere description to become invitation—an invitation into family relationship with the Creator of the universe. What seemed impossible becomes reality: finite beings adopted into infinite love.

Jesus revolutionized spiritual understanding by consistently referring to God as "Father" and teaching His followers to pray, "Our Father." This wasn't merely religious language but relationship language. He was revealing that the transcendent God desires intimate, familial connection with humanity.

Understanding God as Father transforms every aspect of spiritual life. Prayer becomes conversation with a loving parent rather than petition to a distant deity. Obedience flows from relationship rather than fear. Provision becomes expected because good fathers care for their children. Discipline becomes developmental rather than punitive because it springs from love.

However, for those wounded by earthly fathers, this revelation may initially bring pain rather than comfort. God understands this struggle. He doesn't merely ask us to call Him Father—He demonstrates perfect fatherhood through His actions. His consistency heals our understanding of what true fatherhood means.

The love John describes isn't earned or temporary—it's lavished and permanent. God's fatherhood isn't conditional upon your performance but foundational to your identity. You are not hoping to become God's child; if you have trusted Christ, you already are His child. This reality should produce confidence, not insecurity; boldness, not timidity.

Reflection: How does understanding God as your perfect Father change your expectations in prayer and daily life?

Prayer: Father, I marvel that You would call me Your child and lavish Your love upon me. Heal any wounds from imperfect earthly relationships that hinder my ability to receive Your perfect fatherhood. Help me live with the confidence and security that comes from being Your beloved child. Amen.

Day 8: God: From Mystery to Mastery

"The mystery hidden for ages and generations but now revealed to his holy people. To them God has chosen to make known among the Gentiles the glorious riches of this mystery, which is Christ in you, the hope of glory." - Colossians 1:26-27

Paul identifies the ultimate mystery that has been revealed: Christ in you. This revelation transforms our understanding of God from abstract concept to indwelling reality. The goal isn't merely to understand God intellectually but to experience Him personally and practically.

The progression from mystery to mastery doesn't mean we master God—it means His presence masters us. As Christ dwells within believers through the Holy Spirit, His character begins to dominate our character. His perspectives shape our perspectives. His priorities become our priorities. This isn't achieved through human effort but through divine transformation.

"Christ in you" represents the pinnacle of God's self-revelation. He didn't merely want to be known from a distance—He chose to be experienced from within. This indwelling presence means God is not simply the object of our worship but the source of our transformation. This mystery-turned-reality should produce hope of glory. Glory here refers not to a future destination but to a present manifestation—

Christ's character becoming visible through your life. As others observe your love, joy, peace, and faithfulness, they witness the glory of the indwelling Christ.

The mastery aspect involves learning to cooperate with Christ's indwelling presence rather than resisting it. This requires daily surrender, consistent communion, and intentional alignment with His will. The mystery has been revealed; now comes the lifelong process of allowing that revelation to reshape every aspect of your existence.

Reflection: How are you actively cooperating with Christ's indwelling presence for your transformation?

Prayer: Indwelling Christ, I thank You for making Your home within me. Transform me from the inside out so that Your character becomes increasingly visible through my life. Help me cooperate with Your transforming work, surrendering every area of my life to Your lordship. May others see Your glory reflected in my daily living. Amen.

Day 9: Face-to-Face with Holiness

"In the year that King Uzziah died, I saw the Lord, high and exalted, seated on a throne; and the train of his robe filled the temple."
- Isaiah 6:1

Isaiah's encounter with God's holiness forever changed his understanding of both the Divine and himself. True knowledge of God must include recognition of His absolute holiness—His complete separation from all that is impure, imperfect, or corrupt. This holiness isn't merely moral perfection; it's divine otherness that demands response.

The seraphim's cry of "Holy, holy, holy" wasn't repetitive chanting but progressive recognition of God's infinite purity. Each declaration revealed deeper levels of divine holiness that creatures could only begin to comprehend. Their covered faces acknowledged the impossibility of looking directly upon such concentrated perfection.

Isaiah's immediate response reveals what happens when finite humanity encounters infinite holiness: conviction of sin and awareness of unworthiness. "Woe to me!" he cried, recognizing that God's holiness exposed his own spiritual poverty. This wasn't condemnation but revelation—seeing God clearly always reveals ourselves clearly.

Yet God's holiness doesn't repel; it purifies. The seraph touched Isaiah's lips with a coal from the altar, symbolically cleansing his impurity. God's holiness doesn't merely judge sin; it provides the solution for sin. His purity doesn't create distance; it makes intimacy possible by removing the barriers that separate.

Encountering God's holiness should produce both humility and hope. Humility because we recognize our desperate need for cleansing. Hope because God's holiness includes His power to make us holy. We don't merely admire His purity from afar; we participate in it through His grace.

Reflection: How does a deeper understanding of God's holiness impact your approach to sin and spiritual growth?

Prayer: Holy God, I stand in awe of Your absolute purity and perfection. Like Isaiah, I recognize my unworthiness in Your presence. Thank You for not leaving me in my impurity but providing cleansing through Christ's sacrifice. Continue to purify my heart and transform my character to reflect Your holiness. Amen.

Section 2: The Nature of God

Day 10: Unfailing Love: The Heartbeat of God

"The Lord your God is with you, the Mighty Warrior who saves. He will take great delight in you; in his love he will no longer rebuke you, but will rejoice over you with singing." - Zephaniah 3:17

God's love isn't merely one of His attributes—it's His essence. When Scripture declares "God is love," it reveals the fundamental nature of the Creator. This love isn't emotion-based or circumstance-dependent; it's character-based and eternally consistent. Understanding this truth revolutionizes your relationship with the Almighty.

Picture the scene Zephaniah describes: the mighty God of the universe singing over you with joy. This isn't the image many carry of a stern, distant deity keeping detailed records of failures. This is your Creator celebrating your existence, delighting in your potential, and rejoicing over your progress. His love isn't passive tolerance—
it's active celebration.

God's unfailing love means His affection never decreases. Your worst day cannot diminish it. Your greatest failure cannot exhaust it.
Your deepest doubt cannot shake it. This love remains constant because it flows from His unchanging character, not from your changing performance.

This truth should revolutionize how you face each day. When guilt whispers lies about your worthiness, remember God's unfailing love. When shame tries to convince you that you've gone too far, recall His relentless affection. When fear suggests that God might abandon you, anchor yourself in His promise to never leave or forsake you.

Reflection: How would your daily decisions change if you truly believed in God's unfailing love for you?

Prayer: Loving Father, I praise You for Your unfailing love that never changes based on my performance. Help me live with the confidence and security that comes from being unconditionally loved by You. Let Your love flow through me to others who need to experience this transforming truth. Amen.

Day 11: Holiness: Walking in the Light

"But just as he who called you is holy, so be holy in all you do; for it is written: 'Be holy, because I am holy.'" - 1 Peter 1:15-16

God's holiness isn't merely a characteristic He possesses—it's a calling He extends. When He commands us to be holy, He's not demanding perfection we cannot achieve. He's inviting us into a relationship that transforms us from the inside out.

Holiness begins with separation. God separates us from sin's power and sets us apart for His purposes. This separation isn't isolation from the world but distinction within it. We live differently not because we're trying to earn God's favor, but because His favor has already changed us.

Walking in the light means living with transparency before God and others. It means choosing truth over deception, integrity over convenience, and righteousness over popularity. This isn't religious performance—it's authentic living that reflects God's character.

The beautiful paradox of holiness is that we become holy by staying close to the Holy One. Just as spending time in sunlight produces a tan, spending time with God produces His character in us. We don't manufacture holiness through effort; we receive it through relationship. God's holiness should inspire both reverence and hope. Reverence because His purity demands our respect. Hope because His holiness includes His power to make us holy. We're not called to an impossible standard but to an incredible transformation.

Reflection: What areas of your life need to be brought into the light of God's holiness?

Prayer: Holy God, I thank You for calling me to holiness and providing the power to live it out. Search my heart and reveal anything that doesn't honor You. Transform me by Your Spirit so that my life reflects Your character in every relationship and circumstance. Amen.

Day 12: Righteous Judge, Merciful Savior

"Righteousness and justice are the foundation of your throne; love and faithfulness go before you." - Psalm 89:14

God's righteousness and mercy aren't opposing forces—they're complementary expressions of His perfect character. In Christ, we see both divine attributes perfectly united. The cross demonstrates God's righteous judgment of sin and His merciful provision for sinners simultaneously.

As a righteous judge, God cannot ignore sin or pretend it doesn't matter. His justice demands that wrongdoing be addressed. This aspect of God's character should bring comfort, not fear, to those who trust Him. In a world where injustice often seems to prevail, we serve a God who will ultimately make all things right.

Yet God is also merciful, choosing to extend compassion rather than punishment to those who turn to Him. His mercy doesn't compromise His righteousness—it fulfills it through Christ's sacrifice. Jesus absorbed God's righteous judgment so we could receive God's merciful forgiveness.

This dual nature of God's character should produce both gratitude and motivation. Gratitude for the mercy we've received instead of the judgment we deserved. Motivation to extend the same mercy to others who have wronged us.

Living in light of God's righteousness and mercy means pursuing justice while practicing forgiveness. It means standing against wrong while standing with those who have been wronged. It means reflecting both God's standards and His compassion in our daily interactions.

Reflection: How can you better balance pursuing justice and showing mercy in your relationships?

Prayer: Righteous and merciful God, I praise You for being perfectly just and perfectly compassionate. Thank You for satisfying Your justice through Christ's sacrifice and extending mercy to me. Help me reflect both Your righteousness and mercy in how I treat others. Make me an instrument of Your justice and grace. Amen.

Day 13: Grace Beyond Measure

"But because of his great love for us, God, who is rich in mercy, made us alive with Christ even when we were dead in transgressions—it is by grace you have been saved." - Ephesians 2:4-5

Grace is God's unmerited favor toward those who deserve His judgment. It's not merely forgiveness—it's divine generosity that gives us what we could never earn. Understanding grace correctly transforms both our relationship with God and our interactions with others.

Paul emphasizes that we were "dead in transgressions" when God's grace reached us. Dead people cannot contribute to their own resurrection. This truth humbles human pride and magnifies divine mercy. Grace isn't God's response to our goodness; it's His gift despite our badness.

God's grace is described as "rich," indicating its abundant and inexhaustible nature. You cannot use up God's grace or wear out His patience. His storehouse of mercy never runs empty. This abundance should eliminate any fear that you might exhaust His willingness to forgive and restore.

The purpose of grace extends beyond personal salvation to public testimony. We're saved by grace not just for our benefit but for His glory. As others observe the transformation grace produces in our lives, they glimpse the character of the gracious God.

Living in grace means extending grace. Those who have received unmerited favor from God should offer unmerited favor to others. Grace creates a cycle of generosity that reflects God's character and attracts others to His love.

Reflection: How has receiving God's grace changed your willingness to extend grace to others?

Prayer: Gracious God, I stand amazed at Your unmerited favor toward me. When I deserved judgment, You gave me salvation. When I deserved rejection, You offered acceptance. Help me live in the freedom of Your grace and extend that same grace generously to others. Amen.

Day 14: The Faithfulness of God

"Because of the Lord's great love we are not consumed, for his compassions never fail. They are new every morning; great is your faithfulness." - Lamentations 3:22-23

Jeremiah penned these words during one of Israel's darkest periods, proving that God's faithfulness shines brightest when circumstances appear bleakest. Divine faithfulness isn't dependent on human faithfulness or favorable conditions—it flows from God's unchanging character.

God's faithfulness means He keeps His promises regardless of external pressures or internal changes in our hearts. When we're unfaithful, He remains faithful. When we doubt, He stays true. When we waver, He stands firm. His consistency provides stability in an unstable world.

The prophet declares that God's compassions are "new every morning." This doesn't mean yesterday's mercy expires and must be renewed. Rather, it means God's mercy is so abundant that each day brings fresh expressions of His care. His love never grows stale or routine.

God's faithfulness should breed confidence in believers. If He has been faithful in the past, He will be faithful in the future. If He kept His promises to previous generations, He will keep His promises to this generation. His track record of faithfulness guarantees His future reliability.

This divine consistency should inspire human faithfulness. When we understand how faithfully God treats us, we're motivated to treat others with the same reliability. God's faithfulness becomes the model for our commitment to family, friends, and responsibilities.

Reflection: In what current situation do you need to trust God's faithfulness more completely?

Prayer: Faithful God, I praise You for Your unwavering consistency and reliable love. Thank You that Your compassions are new every morning and Your faithfulness endures forever. Help me trust Your promises when circumstances seem to contradict them. Make me a faithful reflection of Your character. Amen.

Day 15: God's Eternal Patience

"The Lord is not slow in keeping his promise, as some understand slowness. Instead he is patient with you, not wanting anyone to perish, but everyone to come to repentance." - 2 Peter 3:9

God's patience reveals His heart for humanity. What we sometimes interpret as divine delay is actually divine mercy. He withholds judgment not because He's indifferent to sin, but because He's passionate about salvation. His patience creates space for repentance. Human patience often wears thin when tested repeatedly. We reach breaking points where our tolerance expires. God's patience operates differently—it flows from His perfect love and endless mercy. He doesn't tire of extending second chances or grow weary of offering fresh starts.

Peter addresses those who questioned God's timing, wondering why promised judgment hadn't arrived. The apostle explains that perceived delay is actually demonstration of divine patience. God's timing reflects His values, not human expectations. He prioritizes salvation over swift judgment.

This truth should humble proud hearts and encourage broken ones. The proud should recognize that God's patience with their rebellion won't last forever. The broken should understand that God's patience creates opportunity for restoration and renewal.

God's patience toward us should cultivate patience within us. Those who have received divine longsuffering should extend human longsuffering to others. Patience becomes both a received gift and a given grace, flowing from God through us to those around us.

Reflection: How has God's patience with you influenced your patience with others?

Prayer: Patient God, I marvel at Your longsuffering toward me and all humanity. Thank You for not treating me as my sins deserve but extending opportunity for repentance and growth. Help me reflect Your patience in my relationships, especially with those who test my limits. Amen.

Day 16: Immutable: The Unchanging Nature of God

"I the Lord do not change. So you, the descendants of Jacob, are not destroyed." - Malachi 3:6

In a world of constant change, God's immutability provides unshakeable security. His character, promises, and purposes remain constant across time and circumstances. This unchanging nature isn't rigidity but reliability—the foundation upon which faith can safely rest.

God's immutability doesn't mean He's static or unresponsive. He interacts dynamically with creation while maintaining consistent character. His love doesn't fluctuate with our performance. His justice doesn't shift with cultural trends. His mercy doesn't diminish with repeated need.

The context of Malachi's declaration reveals why God's unchanging nature matters. Israel had been unfaithful, breaking covenant repeatedly. By human standards, they deserved complete destruction. But God's unchanging commitment to His promises preserved them despite their failures.

This divine consistency should produce both comfort and conviction. Comfort because God's love and grace toward you will never change. Conviction because His standards and expectations remain constant. You cannot manipulate or negotiate with the immutable God.

God's unchanging nature calls for unwavering faith. Since He remains the same, our trust in Him can remain steady regardless of shifting circumstances. His immutability becomes the anchor for our souls during life's storms and uncertainties.

Reflection: How does God's unchanging nature provide stability in your current circumstances?

Prayer: Unchanging God, I find great comfort in Your consistency and reliability. In a world of constant change, You remain my stable foundation. Thank You that Your love, promises, and character never waver. Help me build my life on the solid rock of Your unchanging nature. Amen.

Day 17: Embracing the God of Justice

"Learn to do right; seek justice. Defend the oppressed. Take up the cause of the fatherless; plead the case of the widow." - Isaiah 1:17

God's justice isn't merely punitive—it's restorative. He doesn't simply punish wrongdoing; He actively seeks to right wrongs and defend the defenseless. Understanding God's heart for justice should ignite our passion for fairness and compassion.

The Hebrew concept of justice encompasses both punishment of evil and protection of the innocent. God's justice judges oppressors while vindicating the oppressed. This dual aspect reflects His comprehensive concern for righteousness in all relationships and systems.

Isaiah's call to "learn to do right" suggests that justice must be both understood and practiced. It's not enough to appreciate God's justice theoretically; we must embody it practically. Those who worship the God of justice must pursue justice in their daily lives. The specific examples Isaiah provides—defending orphans and widows—represent the most vulnerable members of society. God's heart for justice particularly focuses on those who cannot defend themselves. This priority should shape our compassion and guide our activism.

Embracing God's justice means becoming agents of His righteousness in an unjust world. We stand against oppression, speak for the voiceless, and work toward fairness in our communities. God's justice flows through us to touch broken systems and hurting people.

Reflection: How is God calling you to be an agent of His justice in your community?

Prayer: God of justice, I praise You for Your perfect fairness and Your heart for the oppressed. Open my eyes to injustice around me and give me courage to stand for what is right. Use me as an instrument of Your justice and mercy in a world that desperately needs both. Amen.

Day 18: The Compassionate Heart of God

"When he saw the crowds, he had compassion on them, because they were harassed and helpless, like sheep without a shepherd."
- Matthew 9:36

Jesus' compassion reveals the heart of the Father. This wasn't casual sympathy but deep, motivated concern that moved Him to action. God's compassion doesn't simply feel for our struggles—it actively works to address them. His heart breaks for human brokenness.

The word "compassion" literally means "to suffer with." God doesn't observe our pain from a distance; He enters into it with us. Through the incarnation, He experienced human limitation, temptation, and suffering. His compassion is informed by personal experience.

Matthew describes the crowds as "harassed and helpless." These words paint a picture of people worn down by life's pressures and unable to find relief. God's compassion specifically targets those who feel overwhelmed and abandoned. His heart is drawn to the struggling. Jesus' compassion always led to action. He didn't simply feel sorry for people; He taught, healed, and delivered them. Divine compassion produces divine intervention. God's heart for humanity motivates His hands to help humanity.

This divine compassion should flow through believers to reach others. Those who have received God's compassionate care should extend compassionate care to those around them. Compassion becomes both a received gift and a given grace that reflects God's character.

Reflection: How can you more actively demonstrate God's compassion to those who are struggling around you?

Prayer: Compassionate God, thank You for Your tender heart toward my struggles and pain. Your compassion has rescued me countless times. Fill my heart with Your compassion for others who are hurting. Use me to be an expression of Your care to those who feel harassed and helpless. Amen.

Section 3: The Wisdom of God

Day 19: Wisdom From Above

"But the wisdom that comes from heaven is first of all pure; then peace-loving, considerate, submissive, full of mercy and good fruit, impartial and sincere." - James 3:17

James contrasts earthly wisdom with heavenly wisdom, revealing that God's wisdom operates by different principles than human reasoning. Divine wisdom isn't merely intellectual knowledge—it's practical understanding that produces godly character and righteous behavior. Earthly wisdom often promotes self-advancement through competition and manipulation. Heavenly wisdom pursues God's glory through service and sacrifice. The two approaches lead to vastly different outcomes in relationships, decisions, and life satisfaction.

The characteristics James lists aren't random traits but interconnected qualities that flow from divine wisdom. Purity leads to peace. Consideration produces mercy. Sincerity generates good fruit. God's wisdom creates a beautiful consistency in those who embrace it.
Notice that heavenly wisdom is "submissive." This doesn't mean weakness but willingness to yield to God's authority and timing. Human wisdom often demands immediate results and personal control. Divine wisdom trusts God's methods and timing even when they don't make sense.

Receiving wisdom from above requires humble dependence on God rather than proud reliance on human understanding. James promises that God gives wisdom generously to those who ask. The key is approaching Him with teachable hearts rather than know-it-all attitudes.

Reflection: In what current situation do you need to seek God's wisdom rather than rely on human reasoning?

Prayer: God of wisdom, I acknowledge that Your ways are higher than my ways and Your thoughts than my thoughts. Grant me wisdom from above to navigate the decisions and relationships in my life. Help me recognize and reject earthly wisdom that contradicts Your truth. Make me wise in Your sight. Amen.

Day 20: Trusting the Divine Perspective

"'For my thoughts are not your thoughts, neither are your ways my ways,' declares the Lord. 'As the heavens are higher than the earth, so are my ways higher than your ways and my thoughts than your thoughts.'" - Isaiah 55:8-9

God's perspective encompasses information we don't possess and understanding we cannot achieve. His viewpoint includes past, present, and future simultaneously. Trusting His perspective means acknowledging the limitations of our understanding while embracing the perfection of His knowledge.

The comparison between earth and heavens illustrates the vast difference between human and divine perspective. Just as we cannot fully comprehend the expanses of space, we cannot fully grasp the depths of God's wisdom. This isn't cause for frustration but invitation to trust.

Human perspective is limited by time, experience, and knowledge. We see portions of the picture while God sees the complete masterpiece. What appears to be a mistake from our viewpoint may be masterful design from His perspective. Our confusion doesn't indicate His confusion.

Trusting God's perspective requires surrendering our need to understand everything before we obey. Faith often means following divine direction that doesn't make sense to human logic.

Abraham didn't understand why God wanted him to sacrifice Isaac, but he trusted God's character despite confusing circumstances.

The divine perspective always includes redemptive purpose. God uses even difficult circumstances to accomplish His good plans. What Satan intends for evil, God transforms for good. This eternal perspective should comfort us during seasons of confusion or suffering.

Reflection: Where do you need to surrender your perspective and trust God's viewpoint more completely?

Prayer: All-knowing God, I confess that my perspective is limited and sometimes confused. Help me trust Your higher thoughts and ways even when I don't understand them. Give me faith to follow Your leading when it contradicts human logic. I rest in Your perfect knowledge and love. Amen.

Day 21: God's Wisdom in Our Waiting

"But those who hope in the Lord will renew their strength. They will soar on wings like eagles; they will run and not grow weary, they will walk and not be faint." - Isaiah 40:31

Waiting reveals whether we trust God's wisdom or demand our own timeline. Divine wisdom often includes divine timing that doesn't match human expectations. God's delays aren't denials—they're demonstrations of His perfect understanding of what we need and when we need it.

The progression Isaiah describes—soaring, running, walking—represents different seasons of spiritual life. Sometimes God's wisdom lifts us to soar above circumstances. Other times it gives us strength to run toward goals. Most often it provides endurance to walk faithfully through ordinary days.

Waiting periods aren't wasted time in God's economy. He uses delays to develop character, deepen faith, and prepare us for what He has planned. What feels like divine inactivity is often intensive preparation for future blessing. God's wisdom sees what waiting will produce.

Human nature resists waiting because it requires surrendering control. We want to force outcomes according to our schedules. Divine wisdom teaches us that the best gifts often require extended preparation periods. Premature answers might become permanent problems.

The promise attached to waiting is renewed strength. Those who wait on God don't just receive what they're waiting for—they're transformed by the waiting process. God's wisdom uses delays to develop patience, trust, and spiritual maturity that wouldn't develop otherwise.

Reflection: How is God using your current waiting season to develop your character and deepen your faith?

Prayer: Patient God, I confess that waiting is difficult for me. Help me trust Your wisdom in the timing of answered prayers and fulfilled promises. Use this waiting season to renew my strength and deepen my faith. Teach me to find You faithful even in the delays. Amen.

Day 22: Discerning His Voice

"My sheep listen to my voice; I know them, and they follow me."
- John 10:27

Jesus promises that His followers can recognize His voice among the many voices competing for their attention. This isn't mystical experience reserved for super-spiritual believers—it's normal Christian living available to every believer who desires to hear from God.

God's voice carries distinctive characteristics that set it apart from human voices or demonic deception. His voice produces peace rather than anxiety, builds up rather than tears down, and aligns with Scripture rather than contradicts it. Learning these qualities helps us discern divine communication.

The context of Jesus' statement involves distinguishing between shepherds and thieves. True shepherds call sheep by name and lead them to safety. Thieves use force and deception to steal and destroy. God's voice always leads toward life, health, and blessing.

Discerning God's voice requires developing spiritual sensitivity through regular prayer, Bible study, and worship. Like learning to recognize
a friend's voice on the phone, hearing God clearly improves with practice and familiarity. Consistent time in His presence sharpens
our spiritual hearing.

The sheep metaphor implies both relationship and responsibility. Sheep follow shepherds they know and trust. Similarly, we follow God's voice because we've learned to trust His character. Discernment isn't just about hearing correctly but responding obediently to what we hear.

Reflection: How can you become more sensitive to hearing God's voice in your daily decisions?

Prayer: Good Shepherd, I want to know Your voice and follow Your leading in every area of my life. Sharpen my spiritual hearing to discern Your voice from all the competing voices around me. Give me courage to obey when You speak, even when it's difficult. Lead me in Your paths of righteousness. Amen.

Day 23: Wisdom for the Wilderness

"Remember how the Lord your God led you all the way in the wilderness these forty years, to humble and test you in order to know what was in your heart, whether or not you would keep his commands."
- Deuteronomy 8:2

Wilderness seasons aren't punishment—they're preparation. God uses difficult circumstances to reveal character, develop faith, and prepare us for future responsibilities. His wisdom orchestrates challenges that produce spiritual growth we couldn't achieve in comfort.

The Israelites' wilderness experience taught them dependence on God for daily provision. Manna couldn't be stored overnight, forcing them to trust God's faithfulness each day. Modern wilderness seasons often serve the same purpose—breaking our self-reliance and building our God-reliance.

God's testing isn't designed to reveal character to Him—He already knows our hearts completely. Testing reveals character to us, showing us areas that need development and strengths we didn't know we possessed. Wilderness experiences function like spiritual X-rays, making the invisible visible.

The wilderness also serves to humble pride and develop patience. Instant gratification becomes impossible when God controls the timeline and supplies. We learn to wait on His provision rather than demanding immediate satisfaction of our desires.

Moses reminds the people to "remember" their wilderness experience because it's easy to forget God's faithfulness once circumstances improve. The lessons learned in difficulty should inform decisions made in prosperity. Wilderness wisdom provides guidance for seasons of blessing.

Reflection: What is God teaching you through your current or recent wilderness experience?

Prayer: Faithful God, I thank You for Your wisdom in allowing wilderness seasons in my life. Help me learn the lessons You want to teach me rather than simply endure the difficulty. Develop my character and deepen my faith through this experience. Let me never forget Your faithfulness in the wilderness. Amen.

Day 24: The Wise Builder

"Therefore everyone who hears these words of mine and puts them into practice is like a wise man who built his house on the rock."
- Matthew 7:24

Jesus concludes the Sermon on the Mount by contrasting two builders: one wise, one foolish. The difference isn't in their building materials or techniques but in their foundation choices. Wise builders understand that foundations determine whether structures survive storms.

Both builders in Jesus' parable faced identical storms—the same rain, floods, and winds tested both houses. External circumstances don't discriminate between wise and foolish choices. The difference appears when pressure reveals the stability of underlying foundations.

The wise builder represents those who not only hear God's Word but also practice it. Hearing without doing creates false confidence in spiritual knowledge that won't withstand life's storms. True wisdom transforms hearing into action, knowledge into obedience.

Building on rock requires more effort than building on sand. Rock must be cleared of debris and leveled carefully. Similarly, building life on God's truth requires more work than following cultural trends. But the extra effort produces structures that endure testing.

The foolish builder's house looked identical to the wise builder's house until the storm arrived. Appearances can be deceiving when foundations remain hidden. Only testing reveals the true stability of our spiritual foundations. Wise builders prepare for storms before they arrive.

Reflection: What areas of your life need to be rebuilt on the solid foundation of God's Word?

Prayer: Wise Master Builder, I want to build my life on the solid rock of Your truth rather than the shifting sand of cultural opinion. Help me not just hear Your words but put them into practice. Give me wisdom to invest in eternal foundations that will withstand every storm. Amen.

Day 25: Wisdom in Words and Deeds

"Who is wise and understanding among you? Let them show it by their good life, by deeds done in the humility that comes from wisdom."
- James 3:13

True wisdom manifests through consistent godly behavior rather than impressive spiritual vocabulary. James challenges those who claim wisdom to demonstrate it through transformed living. Actions validate or invalidate our claims to divine understanding.

The humility James mentions isn't self-deprecation but accurate self-assessment. Wise people understand their dependence on God for every good thing they accomplish. This humility protects against the pride that often accompanies increased knowledge or spiritual experience.

James contrasts divine wisdom with earthly wisdom earlier in the chapter. Earthly wisdom produces "bitter envy and selfish ambition." Heavenly wisdom produces "good fruit" and righteous behavior.

The fruit reveals the tree's true nature, regardless of its impressive appearance.

Wisdom affects both words and deeds. The wise person speaks truthfully but gently, offers correction but with compassion, and defends convictions but without arrogance. Their actions consistently reflect God's character rather than contradicting their spiritual claims. This passage challenges readers to examine the connection between their professed beliefs and actual behaviors. Do our deeds validate our declared faith? Does our lifestyle match our spiritual language?

Wisdom creates consistency between internal convictions and external conduct.

Reflection: How do your daily words and actions demonstrate the wisdom God has given you?

Prayer: God of wisdom, I don't want to be wise only in words but also in deeds. Help me live with the humility that comes from true understanding. Let my actions consistently reflect Your character and validate my faith. Make me wise in both speech and conduct. Amen.

Day 26: Navigating Life with Godly Insight

"In their hearts humans plan their course, but the Lord establishes their steps." - Proverbs 16:9

This proverb reveals the beautiful partnership between human responsibility and divine sovereignty. We're called to make thoughtful plans while remaining open to God's redirection. Godly insight helps us hold our plans loosely while holding our trust in God firmly.

Planning isn't unspiritual—it's wise stewardship of the mind God gave us. However, planning without seeking God's direction often leads to frustration when circumstances don't cooperate with our expectations. Divine insight transforms planning from control attempts into collaborative conversations with God.

The phrase "establishes their steps" suggests that God guides the specifics of our journey even when the general direction seems clear. His insight includes details we cannot anticipate and obstacles we cannot foresee. Trusting His step-by-step guidance prevents many wrong turns.

Navigating life with godly insight requires balance between preparation and flexibility. We should plan carefully but hold those plans with open hands. When God redirects our steps, we should respond with faith rather than frustration, recognizing His superior wisdom.

This principle applies to major life decisions and daily schedule management. Whether choosing a career or planning a day, we benefit from seeking God's insight and remaining open to His adjustments. His navigation system never fails, even when His route seems indirect.

Reflection: How can you better balance thoughtful planning with openness to God's redirection?

Prayer: Lord, I want to navigate life with Your wisdom rather than my limited understanding. Help me plan carefully while holding those plans loosely. Give me discernment to recognize when You're redirecting my steps and faith to follow Your leading. Guide my path according to Your perfect will. Amen.

Day 27: The Secret of True Wisdom

"The fear of the Lord is the beginning of wisdom, and knowledge of the Holy One is understanding." - Proverbs 9:10

True wisdom begins with proper relationship to God, not accumulation of information. The "fear of the Lord" isn't terror but reverent respect that acknowledges His authority and submits to His leadership. This foundational attitude opens our hearts to receive divine wisdom.

Many people pursue wisdom through education, experience, or spiritual practices while ignoring their relationship with the source of all wisdom. These approaches may increase knowledge but cannot produce the understanding that transforms life.

Wisdom without relationship to God lacks its essential foundation.

"Fear of the Lord" includes recognition of God's holiness, power, and justice. This healthy respect creates the humility necessary for learning. Pride prevents wisdom because it assumes we already know what we need to know. Reverent fear acknowledges our need for divine instruction.

Knowledge of God as "the Holy One" means understanding His character, not just His existence. Knowing about God differs from knowing God personally. True wisdom flows from intimate relationship with the One who embodies perfect wisdom and understanding.
This foundational principle explains why some highly educated people make foolish decisions while some simple believers demonstrate remarkable wisdom. Academic knowledge without reverential relationship to God cannot produce the insight needed for wise living. The secret isn't what you know but Whom you know.

Reflection: How does your reverent respect for God influence your daily decisions and relationships?

Prayer: Holy God, I acknowledge You as the source of all true wisdom and understanding. Create in me a heart that fears You properly—with reverent respect rather than paralyzing terror. Deepen my knowledge of Your character so that true wisdom can flow through my life. Be my teacher and guide. Amen.

Section 4: Understanding God

Day 28: Understanding God's Timing

"To everything there is a season, and a time to every purpose under the heaven." - Ecclesiastes 3:1

Solomon's famous words remind us that God operates according to perfect timing that often differs from human expectations. Understanding divine timing requires surrendering our schedules to His sovereignty and trusting His purposes even when His delays don't make sense.

God's timing considers factors we cannot see or understand. He coordinates circumstances, prepares hearts, and arranges opportunities according to His perfect knowledge. What appears to be delay from our perspective may be precise preparation from His viewpoint.

Human impatience often stems from limited perspective and desire for control. We want answers now, solutions immediately, and outcomes according to our timeline. Divine timing teaches us patience while developing faith and character through the waiting process.

The phrase "every purpose under heaven" suggests that God has specific intentions for each season of life. Times of planting serve different purposes than times of harvesting. Seasons of weeping accomplish different goals than seasons of laughing. Each has its place in God's plan.

Understanding God's timing doesn't mean passively waiting without action. Rather, it means actively trusting while consistently preparing. We remain alert to opportunities and faithful in responsibilities while allowing God to orchestrate the timing of outcomes.

Reflection: How is God using your current season to accomplish His purposes in your life?

Prayer: Sovereign God, I confess that Your timing often confuses me. Help me trust Your perfect schedule even when it conflicts with my desires. Teach me to find purpose in every season and to cooperate with Your work during waiting periods. Your timing is always perfect. Amen.

Day 29: Why God Allows Storms

"He stilled the storm to a whisper; the waves of the sea were hushed. They were glad when it grew calm, and he guided them to their desired haven." - Psalm 107:29-30

The psalmist describes God's power to calm storms, but the context reveals that He also allows storms to accomplish His purposes. Understanding why God permits difficulties helps us respond with faith rather than fear when storms arise in our lives.

Storms often serve to reveal our dependence on God rather than our self-sufficiency. When life becomes comfortable, we may begin trusting our own abilities more than divine provision. Storms remind us of our limitations and drive us back to the source of true security.

The psalm describes people who "cried out to the Lord in their trouble." Storms create desperation that produces authentic prayer. Sometimes God allows difficulties to restore proper communication patterns when our relationship with Him has become casual or neglected.

Storms also demonstrate God's power and faithfulness in tangible ways. When He delivers us from impossible circumstances, our faith grows stronger and our testimony becomes more powerful. What Satan intends for destruction, God transforms into demonstration of His character.

The "desired haven" represents more than physical safety—it symbolizes spiritual maturity and deeper relationship with God. Storms often transport us to levels of faith and intimacy with God we would never reach through easy circumstances.

Reflection: How has God used past storms in your life to develop your faith and character?

Prayer: Faithful God, I don't enjoy storms, but I trust Your purposes in allowing them. Help me respond to difficulties with faith rather than fear. Use every storm to draw me closer to You and develop spiritual maturity. Thank You for being my refuge and strength in every storm. Amen.

Day 30: Seeing God Clearly

"Blessed are the pure in heart, for they will see God." - Matthew 5:8

Jesus promises that heart purity produces spiritual vision. This isn't merely future hope but present reality—those with clean hearts can perceive God's presence and activity in daily life. Sin clouds our spiritual vision while righteousness clarifies our perception of divine truth.

Heart purity doesn't mean sinless perfection—it means sincere devotion without divided loyalties. The pure heart belongs fully to God rather than being torn between competing allegiances. This undivided commitment creates the clarity needed to recognize God's voice and presence.

Sin acts like fog on spiritual eyesight, making it difficult to discern God's will or recognize His work. Unconfessed guilt, unresolved anger, and unrepented disobedience all create barriers that prevent clear spiritual vision. Purification removes these obstacles.

Seeing God clearly affects every aspect of life. We recognize His hand in circumstances others attribute to coincidence. We discern His guidance in decisions others make through human wisdom alone. We perceive His love in experiences others view as random events.

The promise includes both present and future fulfillment. Pure hearts see God's activity now and will see His face eventually. This dual promise encourages both immediate obedience and eternal hope. Clear spiritual vision begins now but continues forever.

Reflection: What impurities in your heart might be hindering your ability to see God clearly?

Prayer: Pure God, I want to see You clearly in every aspect of my life. Search my heart and reveal anything that clouds my spiritual vision. Purify my motives and cleanse my conscience so that I can perceive Your presence and recognize Your work. Give me eyes to see You. Amen.

Day 31: God's Plan: Hidden Yet Revealed

"For I know the plans I have for you," declares the Lord, "plans to prosper you and not to harm you, to give you hope and a future." - Jeremiah 29:11

God's plans for our lives remain partially hidden to maintain our dependence on Him while being sufficiently revealed to provide hope and direction. This balance keeps us trusting rather than controlling while giving us enough information to move forward in faith.

Jeremiah delivered this promise to exiles who couldn't see how their current circumstances aligned with God's good intentions. Their situation appeared hopeless, yet God assured them of His beneficial plans. Sometimes His plans become clear only in retrospect.

The Hebrew word for "plans" suggests detailed blueprints rather than vague intentions. God hasn't casually considered your future—He's carefully designed it. His plans include specific provisions, protections, and purposes that reflect His intimate knowledge of your needs and potentials.

"Hope and a future" indicates that God's plans extend beyond immediate circumstances to encompass eternal purposes. Current difficulties don't negate future blessings. Temporary setbacks don't derail permanent plans. God's purposes transcend present troubles.
The tension between hidden and revealed plans teaches us to trust God's character when we can't trace His methods. We may not understand His strategies, but we can rest in His stated intentions to benefit rather than harm us.

Reflection: How does knowing God has good plans for you change your perspective on current difficulties?

Prayer: Faithful Planner, I thank You for having detailed plans for my life that are designed for my good and Your glory. Help me trust Your hidden purposes when I can't see the complete picture. Give me patience to wait for Your plans to unfold according to Your perfect timing. Amen.

Day 32: The Mystery of His Ways

"Oh, the depth of the riches of the wisdom and knowledge of God! How unsearchable his judgments, and his paths beyond tracing out!"
- Romans 11:33

Paul's exclamation emerges from wrestling with God's mysterious methods in salvation history. Rather than expressing frustration, he voices worship. This response models how believers should approach divine mysteries—with reverent wonder rather than demanding explanations.

God's ways remain mysterious not because He enjoys keeping secrets but because His thoughts operate on levels we cannot fully comprehend. The finite cannot completely grasp the infinite. Our limitations require faith to bridge the gaps in understanding.

The word "unsearchable" doesn't mean God's judgments are arbitrary or unreasonable. Rather, they reflect wisdom so profound that human investigation cannot fully penetrate their depths. Like an ocean that can be explored but never completely charted, God's ways invite discovery while maintaining mystery.

Paul's response to mystery is worship rather than worry. When confronted with divine methods that transcend human logic, he praises God's superior wisdom rather than demanding complete explanations. This attitude reflects mature faith that trusts character over comprehension.

The mystery of God's ways should inspire humility and deepen trust. We don't need to understand everything to believe Someone who understands everything. Sometimes the most spiritual response to confusion is worship that acknowledges God's superiority over our understanding.

Reflection: How can you respond with worship rather than worry when God's ways seem mysterious?

Prayer: Mysterious God, I praise You for wisdom that surpasses my understanding. When Your ways seem confusing, help me worship rather than worry. Increase my faith to trust Your character when I can't trace Your methods. Let mystery lead to deeper reverence rather than greater doubt. Amen.

Day 33: Understanding His Silence

"My God, my God, why have you forsaken me? Why are you so far from saving me, so far from my cries of anguish?" - Psalm 22:1

David's anguished cry, later echoed by Jesus on the cross, expresses the confusion and pain that accompany God's apparent silence. Understanding divine silence requires recognizing that God's quiet moments don't indicate His absence or indifference.

God's silence often serves purposes we cannot immediately understand. Sometimes He remains quiet to develop our faith, teach us patience, or prepare us for what He has planned. His silence doesn't mean He's not listening or working—it means He's working in ways we cannot detect.

The psalm that begins with desperate questions concludes with confident praise. David's initial confusion gives way to renewed trust as he remembers God's faithfulness. Divine silence often drives us back to proven truths about God's character when circumstances seem to contradict them.

Jesus' use of these words on the cross reveals that even the Son of God experienced the anguish of divine silence. This identifies Him with our struggles while demonstrating that God's silence doesn't indicate rejection. Sometimes silence precedes the greatest demonstrations of love.

God's silence calls us to faith rather than feeling, truth rather than emotion, and character rather than circumstances. When we cannot hear His voice, we can still trust His heart. Silence becomes a classroom for developing deeper faith.

Reflection: How has God used periods of silence in your life to develop your faith and character?

Prayer: Silent God, I confess that Your quiet seasons often confuse and discourage me. Help me trust Your heart when I cannot hear Your voice. Teach me that silence doesn't mean absence or rejection. Use these quiet times to deepen my faith and develop my character. I trust You even in the silence. Amen.

Day 34: Lessons from Divine Interruptions

"Many are the plans in a person's heart, but it is the Lord's purpose that prevails." - Proverbs 19:21

Divine interruptions often feel like divine interference, disrupting our carefully laid plans and forcing unexpected changes. However, God's interruptions usually redirect us toward better outcomes than our original plans would have produced. Learning to see interruptions as divine guidance transforms frustration into faith.

Human planning reflects wise stewardship of the resources and opportunities God provides. However, our plans are based on limited information and restricted perspective. God's purposes consider factors we cannot see and accomplish goals we haven't imagined.

The word "prevails" suggests that God's purposes will ultimately triumph, regardless of human planning. This doesn't negate the value of making plans—it puts planning in proper perspective. We plan carefully while holding those plans loosely, ready for divine redirection.

Divine interruptions often feel inconvenient because they disrupt our sense of control and predictability. Yet these interruptions frequently protect us from mistakes, prepare us for better opportunities, or redirect us toward God's preferred path. What seems like interference is often intervention.

Learning to recognize divine interruptions as divine guidance requires faith and flexibility. When circumstances force changes to our plans, we can respond with frustration or faith. Faith sees God's hand in the interruption and looks for His purposes in the redirection.

Reflection: How has God recently used interruptions to redirect your path in beneficial ways?

Prayer: Sovereign God, I confess that I often resist interruptions to my plans. Help me recognize Your hand in unexpected changes and trust Your purposes in divine redirections. Give me flexibility to adjust my plans when You have better ideas. Thank You for caring enough to interrupt when necessary. Amen.

Day 35: Recognizing God in the Ordinary

"Be still, and know that I am God; I will be exalted among the nations, I will be exalted in the earth." - Psalm 46:10

God often speaks most clearly in quiet moments rather than dramatic circumstances. Learning to recognize His presence in ordinary experiences prevents us from missing divine encounters while waiting for spectacular manifestations. He inhabits common moments as fully as miraculous ones.

The command to "be still" suggests that recognizing God requires intentional pause from life's constant activity. Our busy schedules and cluttered minds often prevent us from noticing God's subtle presence. Stillness creates space for awareness of divine activity in daily life.
God's exaltation "among the nations" and "in the earth" indicates His universal presence and activity. He's not confined to church buildings or special occasions—He's actively working in every situation and circumstance. This awareness transforms ordinary moments into opportunities for divine encounter.

Many believers expect God to communicate only through dramatic means—audible voices, miraculous signs, or supernatural experiences. While He certainly can and does use these methods, He more commonly speaks through Scripture, circumstances, other believers, and inner impressions during quiet reflection.

Recognizing God in ordinary moments requires developing spiritual sensitivity through consistent prayer, Bible study, and worship. Like tuning a radio to receive clear signals, we must adjust our spiritual frequency to perceive God's communication in everyday experiences.

Reflection: How can you become more aware of God's presence and activity in your ordinary daily experiences?

Prayer: Ever-present God, forgive me for often overlooking Your presence in ordinary moments while waiting for extraordinary experiences. Open my spiritual eyes to see You working in daily circumstances. Help me be still enough to recognize Your voice in quiet moments. Make me aware of Your constant presence. Amen.

Day 36: Walking in Step with God

"Since we live by the Spirit, let us keep in step with the Spirit."
- Galatians 5:25

Paul uses the metaphor of synchronized walking to describe how believers should live in harmony with the Holy Spirit. This imagery suggests both partnership and submission—we walk together with God while following His lead. Staying in step requires constant attention to His pace and direction.

Walking in step means matching God's rhythm rather than forcing Him to match ours. Sometimes He moves quickly, requiring us to accelerate our faith and obedience.

Other times He moves slowly, calling us to patience and trust. Staying synchronized requires flexibility and sensitivity.

The Spirit leads us according to Scripture, never contradicting God's written Word. This provides both guidance and protection—we can test our impressions against biblical truth to ensure we're following the Spirit rather than human desires or demonic deception.

Getting out of step happens gradually through small compromises rather than dramatic rebellions. We begin walking slightly behind God's pace or ahead of His timing. These minor misalignments compound over time until we find ourselves completely out of sync with His purposes.

Returning to step with God requires confession, correction, and renewed commitment to follow His lead. The Spirit is patient with our stumbling and gracious in helping us regain proper rhythm. He wants us in step more than we want to be in step.

Reflection: In what areas of your life do you need to adjust your pace to stay in step with the Spirit?

Prayer: Holy Spirit, I want to walk in perfect step with You rather than forcing You to follow my pace. Help me be sensitive to Your leading and quick to adjust when I get out of rhythm. Teach me to match Your timing and follow Your direction in every area of my life. Keep me in step with You. Amen.

Section 5: How to Love God

Day 37: Love With All Your Heart

"Love the Lord your God with all your heart and with all your soul and with all your mind and with all your strength." - Mark 12:30

Jesus identifies this as the greatest commandment, revealing that God desires comprehensive love that engages every aspect of our being. This isn't merely emotional affection but total life commitment that affects thoughts, choices, relationships, and actions.

"All your heart" represents the center of emotions and will. Heart love for God means our deepest affections and strongest desires focus on Him. This doesn't eliminate love for others but ensures that God receives the primary devotion from which all other loves flow.

The comprehensive nature of this love—heart, soul, mind, strength—indicates that loving God isn't compartmentalized to specific times or activities. It's a whole-life orientation that influences every decision, relationship, and responsibility. Love for God becomes the organizing principle of existence.

This complete love responds to God's complete love for us. He doesn't love us partially or conditionally—He gives His entire being to our relationship. Our response should match His commitment, offering our complete selves rather than selected portions of our lives.

Loving God with everything we are requires intentionality and discipline. Natural human tendency is to compartmentalize life, giving God access to some areas while maintaining control over others. Comprehensive love means surrendering every aspect of life to God's lordship.

Reflection: What areas of your life need to be more fully surrendered to your love for God?

Prayer: God of all love, I want to love You with my entire being—heart, soul, mind, and strength. Search my life and reveal any areas I'm withholding from You. Help me surrender completely to Your love and lordship. Make my love for You the organizing principle of my existence. Amen.

Day 38: The Language of Love for God

"If you love me, keep my commands." - John 14:15

Jesus reveals that obedience is love's primary language in our relationship with God. While emotions certainly play a role in loving God, actions demonstrate the authenticity and depth of our affection. Love that doesn't produce obedience remains incomplete.

Human relationships often emphasize verbal expressions of love—"I love you"—accompanied by emotional demonstrations. Divine relationship includes these elements but emphasizes behavioral proof. God reads our hearts through our choices, not just our declarations.

Obedience to God's commands isn't legalistic compliance that earns His favor. Rather, it's love's natural expression that flows from relationship. Just as children obey loving parents out of trust and affection, believers obey God because they know His commands reflect His character and care.

This principle helps evaluate the authenticity of our love for God. We can examine our patterns of obedience to measure the reality of our affection. Consistent disobedience in specific areas may indicate limited love rather than simple weakness.

The connection between love and obedience also reveals that growing in love for God will naturally increase our desire and ability to obey Him. As love deepens, obedience becomes less burdensome and more joyful. Commands become opportunities to express devotion.

Reflection: How does your pattern of obedience to God's commands reflect the depth of your love for Him?

Prayer: Loving Lord, I want my obedience to be the authentic expression of my love for You rather than mere religious duty. Help me see Your commands as opportunities to demonstrate my affection. Increase my love for You so that obedience becomes joy rather than burden. Amen.

Day 39: More Than Feelings: True Love for God

"Though you have not seen him, you love him; and even though you do not see him now, you believe in him and are filled with an inexpressible and glorious joy." - 1 Peter 1:8

Peter addresses believers whose love for God exists despite never seeing Him physically. This reveals that authentic love for God transcends emotional highs and sensory experiences. True love operates through faith rather than feelings, commitment rather than circumstances.

Feelings fluctuate based on circumstances, health, stress levels, and countless other variables. Love built on emotions alone becomes unstable and unreliable. God desires love that remains constant regardless of how we feel on any given day.

The "inexpressible and glorious joy" Peter mentions results from love that transcends circumstances. This joy doesn't depend on favorable conditions but flows from relationship with God that remains stable regardless of external pressures. Joy becomes love's fruit rather than love's foundation.

Faith provides the foundation for love that feelings cannot supply. We love God because of who He is and what He has done, not because of how we feel at any moment.

This faith-based love produces the stability needed for long-term relationship with God.

True love for God affects behavior more than emotions. While feelings may accompany genuine love, they don't validate or invalidate it. Our choices, priorities, and responses to difficulty provide more accurate measurements of love than emotional intensity.

Reflection: How can you love God more consistently regardless of your changing feelings?

Prayer: Faithful God, I don't want my love for You to depend on fluctuating emotions or changing circumstances. Build my love on the solid foundation of faith in Your character and truth. Help me choose love even when I don't feel love. Make my love stable and reliable like Yours. Amen.

Day 40: A Heart that Beats for God

"Above all else, guard your heart, for everything you do flows from it." - Proverbs 4:23

The heart represents the control center of human existence—the place where decisions are made, affections are formed, and priorities are established. A heart that beats for God produces a life that honors God. Protecting the heart's devotion to God becomes essential for spiritual health.

"Above all else" indicates the supreme importance of heart management. Nothing matters more than ensuring our deepest affections remain focused on God. Other responsibilities are important, but none surpass the necessity of maintaining heart purity and devotion.

The heart requires guarding because it faces constant assault from competing affections. The world, flesh, and devil all seek to redirect our love away from God toward lesser things. Without intentional protection, the heart gradually shifts its allegiance.

"Everything you do flows from it" reveals why heart condition matters so significantly. External behaviors reflect internal affections. Change the heart and you change the life. This is why God focuses on heart transformation rather than behavior modification.

A heart that beats for God demonstrates its affection through consistent choices that honor Him. It prioritizes His will over personal preferences, seeks His glory over personal gain, and treasures His approval over human recognition. Love becomes the heart's governing principle.

Reflection: What influences are you allowing to compete with God for your heart's affection?

Prayer: Heart-knowing God, I want my heart to beat primarily for You rather than divided among competing affections. Help me guard my heart from influences that would diminish my love for You. Create in me a pure heart that seeks You above all else. Let everything in my life flow from love for You. Amen.

Day 41: Loving God in Difficult Times

"And we know that in all things God works for the good of those who love him, who have been called according to his purpose."
- Romans 8:28

Paul's famous promise specifically addresses "those who love" God, suggesting that love for God enables us to trust His purposes even when circumstances seem to contradict His goodness. Love provides the foundation for faith during difficult seasons.

Difficult times test the authenticity and depth of our love for God. It's relatively easy to love God when life flows smoothly and prayers receive quick answers. True love emerges when circumstances challenge our faith and God's silence raises questions about His care.

The promise that God works "all things" for good doesn't mean all experiences are pleasant or that God causes all difficulties. Rather, it means God can weave even painful circumstances into patterns that ultimately benefit those who love Him. Love enables us to trust this process.

"Called according to his purpose" indicates that our love for God connects us to His larger plans that extend beyond our immediate comfort. Difficulties may serve purposes related to character development, ministry preparation, or testimony that we cannot see during the struggle.

Loving God in difficult times requires choosing trust over understanding, faith over feelings, and long-term perspective over immediate comfort. This mature love recognizes that God's love for us remains constant even when His methods seem confusing.

Reflection: How have difficult circumstances deepened or tested your love for God?

Prayer: Faithful God, I want to love You not just in easy times but especially during difficult seasons. Help me trust Your goodness when circumstances seem to contradict it. Strengthen my love for You through trials so that nothing can separate me from Your love. Work all things for good in my life. Amen.

Day 42: The Sacrifice of Love

"Greater love has no one than this: to lay down one's life for one's friends." - John 15:13

Jesus spoke these words shortly before demonstrating their truth through His crucifixion. His definition of greatest love involves self-sacrifice for others' benefit. This principle applies to our love for God—authentic love willingly sacrifices personal desires for divine purposes.
The sacrifice of love doesn't always require physical death. More commonly, it involves dying to selfish ambitions, comfortable routines, and personal preferences that conflict with God's will. Love sacrifices what we want for what God wants.

Jesus' sacrifice for us models the sacrifice He expects from us. He laid down His life for our benefit; we lay down our lives for His glory. This isn't a burden but a privilege—the opportunity to express love through meaningful sacrifice. Sacrificial love goes beyond emotional attachment to practical commitment. It's willing to pay costs, endure hardships, and surrender comforts for the sake of the beloved. This kind of love transforms both giver and receiver.

The sacrifice of love often involves small, daily choices rather than dramatic gestures. Choosing prayer over entertainment, service over comfort, or obedience over convenience demonstrates sacrificial love in practical ways. These small sacrifices accumulate into significant expressions of devotion.

Reflection: What sacrifices is God calling you to make as expressions of your love for Him?

Prayer: Sacrificial Savior, thank You for laying down Your life to demonstrate Your love for me. Help me respond with sacrificial love that willingly gives up personal desires for Your purposes.

Show me what sacrifices You want me to make and give me courage to make them joyfully. Let love motivate my sacrifices. Amen

Day 43: Expressing Love through Obedience

"Whoever has my commands and keeps them is the one who loves me. The one who loves me will be loved by my Father, and I too will love him and show myself to him." - John 14:21

Jesus connects obedience directly to love, revealing that our response to His commands demonstrates the authenticity of our affection. This isn't legalistic requirement but relational expression—we obey because we love, not to earn love.

The progression Jesus describes shows how obedience deepens relationship: obedience expresses love, love attracts God's love, and God's love produces greater revelation of Himself. Obedience creates an upward spiral of increasing intimacy with God.

"Whoever has my commands" suggests that knowing God's will is the first step toward loving obedience. We cannot obey commands we don't know or understand. This emphasizes the importance of Scripture study and spiritual education as foundations for loving response.

"Keeps them" indicates consistent, ongoing obedience rather than occasional compliance. Love-motivated obedience becomes a lifestyle pattern rather than sporadic behavior. It reflects changed character rather than temporary effort.

The promise that God will "show himself" to obedient believers reveals that love expressed through obedience increases our capacity to perceive God's presence and activity. Obedience doesn't earn God's love but positions us to experience it more fully.

Reflection: How has your obedience to God's commands affected your experience of His presence and love?

Prayer: Commanding Lord, I want my obedience to flow from love rather than duty. Help me know Your commands clearly and keep them consistently. Use my obedience to deepen our relationship and increase my awareness of Your presence. Show Yourself to me as I demonstrate my love through faithful obedience. Amen.

Day 44: Cultivating Passion for God

"As the deer pants for streams of water, so my soul pants for you, my God." - Psalm 42:1

David's metaphor captures the intensity of spiritual longing that should characterize mature believers. Like physical thirst drives us to seek water, spiritual passion should drive us to seek God. This passionate desire can be cultivated through intentional spiritual practices.

Passion for God often begins with recognition of our desperate need for Him. Just as deer pant for water when thirsty, we pursue God most earnestly when we realize our spiritual poverty without Him. Complacency diminishes passion while dependency intensifies it.
Regular exposure to God's presence through prayer, worship, and Scripture reading cultivates increasing appetite for more of Him. Like developing taste for fine cuisine, spiritual appetite grows through consistent experience of God's goodness and beauty.

Passion requires protection from competing affections that would diminish our desire for God. Entertainment, materialism, and human relationships can all become substitutes for God if we're not careful. Maintaining passion requires guarding against spiritual competitors.

The psalmist's longing led to action—he sought streams of water rather than simply talking about thirst. Similarly, spiritual passion motivates us to pursue God through prayer, study, worship, and service. Genuine passion produces corresponding behavior.

Reflection: What practices help cultivate and maintain your passion for God?

Prayer: God of my passion, I want to desire You like a deer pants for water. Increase my spiritual thirst and appetite for Your presence. Protect my heart from competing affections that would diminish my passion for You. Fan the flames of my love until it burns brightly for You alone. Amen.

Day 45: The Power of Undivided Love

"Give me an undivided heart, that I may fear your name."
- Psalm 86:11

David prays for heart unity that focuses entirely on God rather than being torn between competing loyalties. Divided hearts produce inconsistent behavior and spiritual instability. Undivided love concentrates all affection on God, creating power for consistent spiritual living.

The human heart naturally tends toward division, pulled in multiple directions by various desires and allegiances. Career ambitions, family relationships, financial goals, and personal pleasures all compete for our primary devotion. This division weakens our spiritual effectiveness.

"Fear your name" represents reverential respect that recognizes God's authority and submits to His leadership. Undivided hearts find it easier to maintain proper reverence because they're not constantly negotiating between God's will and competing desires.

Undivided love produces several benefits: clearer spiritual vision, more consistent obedience, greater peace, and increased power in prayer and ministry. When all our spiritual energy flows in one direction rather than being scattered among multiple focuses, it becomes more effective.

Achieving heart unity requires intentional effort to identify and eliminate competing loyalties that diminish our love for God. This doesn't mean neglecting responsibilities but ensuring they don't usurp God's rightful place as our primary affection.

Reflection: What competing loyalties are dividing your heart and weakening your love for God?

Prayer: God of unity, I confess that my heart is often divided among competing loyalties and desires. Give me an undivided heart that fears Your name and loves You supremely. Help me identify and surrender anything that competes with You for my primary affection. Unite my heart around love for You. Amen.

Section 6: Commitment to God

Day 46: The Cost of True Commitment

"Suppose one of you wants to build a tower. Won't you first sit down and estimate the cost to see if you have enough money to complete it?" - Luke 14:28

Jesus challenges potential followers to count the cost of discipleship before making commitment. True commitment to God requires understanding what discipleship involves and being willing to pay the price. Shallow commitment based on incomplete understanding often leads to spiritual failure.

The cost of commitment includes surrendering personal agenda for God's purposes, choosing obedience over convenience, and prioritizing eternal values over temporal pleasures. These prices aren't paid once but continuously throughout the Christian journey.

Jesus uses the building metaphor to illustrate the importance of finishing what we start. Incomplete commitment brings shame and represents poor stewardship of resources. God desires complete devotion rather than partial effort that never reaches its intended goal. Counting the cost doesn't mean calculating whether commitment is worthwhile—it means preparing for the sacrifices involved. The benefits of following Christ far outweigh the costs, but ignoring the costs leads to unrealistic expectations and eventual disappointment.

True commitment involves both initial decision and ongoing dedication. Like marriage vows that require daily renewal, commitment to God needs regular reinforcement through prayer, study, and intentional choice to prioritize His will over personal preferences.

Reflection: What costs of commitment to God are you currently finding most challenging?

Prayer: Worthy God, I want to follow You with full understanding of what commitment requires. Help me count the cost honestly and commit completely. Give me strength to pay the prices involved in true discipleship. Let my commitment to You be complete and lasting. Amen.

Day 47: Committed in a Shallow World

"But Daniel resolved not to defile himself with the royal food and wine, and he asked the chief official for permission not to defile himself this way." - Daniel 1:8

Daniel's commitment to God remained firm despite being immersed in a culture that opposed his values. His example shows that deep commitment can survive in shallow environments when believers maintain clear convictions and consistent practices.

The word "resolved" indicates deliberate decision-making rather than emotional response. Daniel didn't react impulsively to peer pressure—he had predetermined his standards based on God's commands. This advance decision-making protected him when temptation arose.

Living committed lives in shallow culture requires intentional resistance to prevailing values that contradict God's standards. This doesn't mean isolating ourselves from unbelievers but maintaining distinct lifestyle that reflects divine rather than cultural values.

Daniel's respectful approach to authority shows that commitment can be maintained without unnecessary offense. He didn't compromise his convictions but presented his request graciously. Commitment includes wisdom about how to express faithfulness in difficult circumstances.

The shallow world often interprets deep commitment as narrow-mindedness or legalism. However, commitment to God demonstrates loyalty to the highest values rather than restriction from lesser pleasures. True commitment chooses the better over the merely good.

Reflection: How can you maintain deeper commitment to God while living in shallow cultural surroundings?

Prayer: Faithful God, help me maintain deep commitment to You despite living in a shallow world. Give me Daniel's resolve to honor You regardless of cultural pressure. Show me how to stand firm in my convictions while showing grace to those who disagree. Keep me committed to Your standards. Amen.

Day 48: Anchored in Christ

"We have this hope as an anchor for the soul, firm and secure. It enters the inner sanctuary behind the curtain." - Hebrews 6:19

The author uses nautical imagery to describe how hope in Christ provides spiritual stability during life's storms. An anchor's purpose is to prevent ships from drifting when winds and currents threaten to carry them off course. Christ serves this function for believers' souls. Anchors work by connecting ships to something more stable than the surface conditions they're experiencing. Similarly, our anchor in Christ connects us to eternal realities that remain constant despite changing circumstances. This connection provides security when life feels unstable.

"Firm and secure" emphasizes the reliability of our anchor in Christ. Unlike human relationships or material possessions that can fail us, Christ provides absolutely dependable security. This anchor cannot drag, break, or lose its holding power.

The reference to "inner sanctuary behind the curtain" connects our hope to Christ's high priestly work in heaven. Our anchor doesn't just hold us steady—it connects us to the very presence of God where Christ intercedes on our behalf.

Being anchored in Christ affects how we respond to life's storms. Instead of being tossed about by circumstances, we remain stable because our security comes from unchanging source. This doesn't eliminate difficulties but prevents them from destroying our faith.

Reflection: How does being anchored in Christ provide stability during your current challenges?

Prayer: Anchoring Christ, thank You for being my firm and secure foundation when life's storms threaten to overwhelm me. Help me trust Your stability more than my circumstances. Keep me anchored in Your truth and love regardless of what winds are blowing around me. Be my soul's anchor. Amen.

Day 49: Wholehearted Devotion

"And you, my son Solomon, acknowledge the God of your father, and serve him with wholehearted devotion and with a willing mind, for the Lord searches every heart and understands every desire and every thought." - 1 Chronicles 28:9

David's charge to Solomon emphasizes that God desires complete devotion rather than partial commitment. Wholehearted devotion means holding nothing back from God but offering our entire selves to His service and glory.

"Wholehearted devotion" contrasts with halfhearted religion that gives God access to some areas of life while maintaining control over others. This divided approach weakens spiritual effectiveness and limits God's ability to work through us fully.

The phrase "willing mind" indicates that wholehearted devotion involves both emotional commitment and intellectual surrender. Our thoughts, as well as our feelings, must be submitted to God's authority. Mental reservation prevents complete devotion.

David reminds Solomon that "the Lord searches every heart." God sees past external religious performance to internal motivation and commitment. Wholehearted devotion cannot be faked or performed—it must be genuine.

"Understands every desire and every thought" reveals God's complete knowledge of our inner lives. This truth should both humble and encourage us. Humble because we cannot hide divided loyalties from God. Encourage because He loves us completely despite knowing us completely.

Reflection: What areas of your life still need to be surrendered for truly wholehearted devotion to God?

Prayer: Heart-searching God, I want to serve You with wholehearted devotion rather than holding back parts of my life. You know every desire and thought—purify my motives and unite my heart around love for You. Help me surrender every area to Your lordship. Accept my complete devotion. Amen.

Day 50: Keeping the Covenant

"But this is the covenant I will make with the people of Israel after that time," declares the Lord. "I will put my law in their minds and write it on their hearts. I will be their God, and they will be my people."
- Jeremiah 31:33

God's new covenant promise reveals His commitment to enabling our commitment to Him. Unlike external laws that we struggle to obey through human effort, the new covenant writes God's desires on our hearts, making obedience flow from transformed nature.

The contrast between law "in their minds" and "on their hearts" shows progression from intellectual knowledge to internal motivation. Covenant keeping becomes natural rather than forced when God's character is implanted within us through His Spirit.

"I will be their God, and they will be my people" describes mutual commitment that characterizes covenant relationship. God commits Himself to us and enables our commitment to Him. This isn't one-sided obligation but shared devotion between divine and human partners.

Keeping covenant requires ongoing attention to our relationship with God rather than simply avoiding major sins. It involves nurturing the internal transformation that makes obedience flow from love rather than duty. Heart change precedes behavior change.

The new covenant doesn't eliminate human responsibility but provides divine enablement for faithful response. We still must choose obedience, but God's Spirit within us makes that choice both possible and joyful rather than burdensome and impossible.

Reflection: How is God's Spirit helping you keep covenant with Him from internal motivation rather than external obligation?

Prayer: Covenant-keeping God, thank You for writing Your law on my heart and enabling my faithfulness to You. Help me nurture the internal transformation that makes obedience flow from love. Keep me faithful to our covenant relationship through the power of Your Spirit within me. Amen.

Day 51: Unwavering Faithfulness

"Let us hold unswervingly to the hope we profess, for he who promised is faithful." - Hebrews 10:23

The writer encourages believers to maintain steady faithfulness because it rests on God's unchanging character. Our faithfulness doesn't depend on our strength alone but finds support in His proven reliability. This partnership enables unwavering commitment even during difficult seasons.

"Hold unswervingly" suggests the kind of grip that doesn't loosen under pressure. Like rock climbers who maintain secure holds regardless of wind or fatigue, believers must maintain firm grasp on their faith regardless of circumstances that might encourage compromise.

"The hope we profess" refers to our public declaration of faith in Christ. This isn't private belief but openly declared allegiance that creates accountability. Public profession of faith creates expectation that our behavior will match our declaration.

"He who promised is faithful" provides the foundation for our unwavering faithfulness. We can remain steady because we're connected to One who never wavers. His faithfulness becomes the source and strength for our faithfulness in response.

Unwavering faithfulness doesn't mean never experiencing doubt or difficulty. Rather, it means maintaining commitment despite internal struggles and external pressures. Like marriage vows that survive rough seasons, spiritual faithfulness endures testing periods.

Reflection: What helps you maintain unwavering faithfulness to God during challenging seasons?

Prayer: Faithful God, I want to hold unswervingly to my faith because You are completely reliable. Strengthen my grip on hope when circumstances pressure me to compromise. Let Your faithfulness be the foundation and source of my unwavering commitment to You. Keep me faithful. Amen.

Day 52: Beyond Convenience: Devoted to God

"If anyone would come after me, let him deny himself and take up his cross daily and follow me." - Luke 9:23

Jesus defines discipleship in terms that transcend convenience and comfort. True devotion to God goes beyond what's easy or natural to embrace what's costly and transformational. This daily commitment shapes character and demonstrates authentic love.

"Deny himself" means saying "no" to selfish desires that conflict with God's will. This isn't self-hatred but self-discipline that chooses God's purposes over personal preferences. It's the deliberate choice to prioritize divine agenda over human agenda.

"Take up his cross daily" refers to the ongoing nature of sacrificial commitment. The cross represents death to self-will and acceptance of God's will even when it involves suffering. This isn't a one-time decision but daily choice to embrace God's purposes.

"Follow me" indicates that devotion involves active pursuit rather than passive observation. Following requires movement, adjustment, and ongoing attention to the leader's direction. It's dynamic relationship that affects every aspect of life.

Going beyond convenience means choosing God's will when it conflicts with personal comfort, popularity, or profit. It means serving when it's costly, obeying when it's difficult, and trusting when it's confusing.

This level of devotion reveals authentic spiritual maturity.

Reflection: Where is God calling you to move beyond convenience in your devotion to Him?

Prayer: Costly Savior, I want my devotion to You to go beyond what's convenient or comfortable. Help me deny myself, take up my cross daily, and follow You regardless of the cost. Transform my character through sacrificial commitment. Make me devoted rather than merely interested. Amen.

Day 53: Standing Firm in Commitment

"Therefore, my dear brothers and sisters, stand firm. Let nothing move you. Always give yourselves fully to the work of the Lord, because you know that your labor in the Lord is not in vain." - 1 Corinthians 15:58

Paul concludes his great resurrection chapter with a call to unwavering commitment based on eternal hope. Standing firm requires both defensive resolve that resists compromise and offensive dedication that pursues God's purposes regardless of obstacles.

"Let nothing move you" suggests the kind of stability that remains constant despite external pressures. Like buildings designed to withstand earthquakes, committed believers develop internal strength that enables them to remain steady when circumstances shake around them.

"Always give yourselves fully" indicates complete rather than partial dedication. This comprehensive commitment affects every area of life rather than being limited to religious activities. Full giving means holding nothing back from God's service.

"Your labor in the Lord is not in vain" provides motivation for sustained commitment. Knowing that faithful service produces eternal results encourages perseverance when immediate outcomes seem disappointing. Commitment becomes investment in permanent values. Standing firm often requires community support and mutual encouragement. Paul addresses "dear brothers and sisters," recognizing that individual commitment strengthens through corporate relationships. Isolated believers struggle more than connected ones to maintain firm commitment.

Reflection: What threatens to move you from firm commitment to God, and how can you stand stronger?

Prayer: Steadfast God, help me stand firm in my commitment to You regardless of what tries to move me from that position. Give me strength to give myself fully to Your work. Remind me that my labor for You is never in vain. Keep me committed through community with other believers. Amen.

Day 54: Faith that Endures

"Blessed is the one who perseveres under trial because, having stood the test, they will receive the crown of life that the Lord has promised to those who love him." - James 1:12

James describes faith that survives testing and emerges stronger rather than weaker. Enduring faith doesn't simply survive difficulties—it grows through them. This kind of faith demonstrates its authenticity by maintaining commitment when circumstances pressure it to quit.

"Perseveres under trial" indicates active resistance rather than passive endurance. Like athletes who push through fatigue to finish races, believers with enduring faith keep moving forward despite obstacles that would stop weaker commitment.

"Having stood the test" suggests that trials serve to prove and improve our faith rather than simply punish us. Like gold refined by fire, faith tested by difficulty becomes purer and more valuable. Testing reveals both the reality and quality of our commitment.

"Crown of life" represents the eternal reward for faithful endurance. This isn't earned salvation but recognition for persevering love that maintained commitment despite testing. The crown symbolizes victory over circumstances that tried to defeat faith.

"Those who love him" connects endurance to relationship rather than mere duty. Love provides motivation for perseverance when obedience alone might fail. Enduring faith flows from enduring love that refuses to quit despite difficulty.

Reflection: How have past trials strengthened your faith and commitment to God?

Prayer: Faithful God, I want faith that endures every test and emerges stronger. Help me persevere under trial with confidence that You're using difficulty to refine and strengthen my commitment. Let my love for You motivate endurance when circumstances pressure me to quit. Grant me faith that endures. Amen.

Section 7: Living for and Serving God

Day 55: Living Beyond Yourself

"For to me, to live is Christ and to die is gain." - Philippians 1:21

Paul's declaration reveals life purpose that transcends personal ambition and comfort. Living beyond yourself means finding identity, meaning, and satisfaction in Christ rather than in personal achievements or circumstances. This perspective transforms both life and death into opportunities for divine glory.

"To live is Christ" means that Christ becomes the organizing principle around which everything else revolves. Career, relationships, finances, and daily decisions all align with His purposes rather than personal preferences. Life finds its meaning in relationship with Him.

This Christ-centered living doesn't eliminate personality or individual gifts but channels them toward divine purposes. We don't become robots but become fully ourselves as God intended us to be. Living for Christ fulfills rather than restricts human potential.

"To die is gain" reveals that this perspective even transforms death from loss into benefit. When life centers on Christ, death becomes promotion rather than tragedy. This eternal perspective affects how we invest time, energy, and resources. Living beyond yourself requires daily choice to prioritize Christ's agenda over personal agenda. It means asking "What would honor Christ?" rather than "What would benefit me?" This mindset shift affects every decision and relationship.

Reflection: How can you more consistently organize your daily decisions around Christ rather than personal benefit?

Prayer: Life-giving Christ, I want to live beyond myself with You as my organizing principle. Help me find my identity, purpose, and satisfaction in You rather than in personal achievements. Transform my perspective so that both life and death serve Your glory. Make me truly alive in You. Amen.

Day 56: Purpose-driven Living

"For we are God's handiwork, created in Christ Jesus to do good works, which God prepared in advance for us to do." - Ephesians 2:10

Paul reveals that believers are God's artwork, created with specific purposes in mind. Purpose-driven living means discovering and fulfilling the good works God designed us to accomplish. This gives life meaning beyond personal satisfaction or worldly success.

"God's handiwork" translates a Greek word meaning "masterpiece" or "work of art." This reveals God's intentional creativity in designing each believer. We're not mass-produced but individually crafted for specific purposes that reflect God's creative genius.

"Created in Christ Jesus" indicates that our purpose flows from our relationship with Christ rather than from human planning. Salvation includes both forgiveness and purpose, both rescue from sin and assignment to service. Redemption restores both relationship and responsibility.

"Good works, which God prepared in advance" shows that our purposes aren't random or self-determined. God has specific assignments designed for our unique combination of gifts, experiences, and opportunities. Purpose-driven living means discovering and fulfilling these divine assignments. This perspective transforms work from mere career to calling, relationships from networking to ministry, and daily activities from routine to purpose. Every day becomes opportunity to fulfill God's creative intentions for our lives.

Reflection: What good works might God have prepared in advance for you to accomplish?

Prayer: Creative God, thank You for making me Your masterpiece with specific purposes in mind. Help me discover and fulfill the good works You prepared for me to do. Transform my perspective on work and relationships so I see them as opportunities to accomplish Your purposes. Live Your purpose through me. Amen.

Day 57: Called to Serve

"For even the Son of Man did not come to be served, but to serve, and to give his life as a ransom for many." - Mark 10:45

Jesus revolutionizes leadership by redefining greatness in terms of service rather than position. This principle applies to all believers—we're called to serve rather than to be served. Service becomes the measure of spiritual maturity and the means of following Christ's example.

Jesus contrasts His approach with worldly leadership that seeks personal benefit and recognition. Kingdom leadership inverts human expectations by prioritizing others' needs over personal comfort. This servant leadership reflects God's character and values.

"Give his life as a ransom" reveals that service sometimes requires sacrifice. True service may cost us time, energy, resources, or comfort. This sacrificial dimension distinguishes genuine service from self-serving acts disguised as service.

Being called to serve means every believer has ministry opportunities regardless of formal positions or titles. Service isn't limited to professional ministry but includes every act of love performed in Jesus' name. Daily life becomes arena for faithful service.

The call to serve should produce both humility and purpose. Humility because service requires putting others first. Purpose because service provides meaning and fulfillment that self-centered living cannot produce. Service becomes both calling and joy.

Reflection: How is God calling you to serve others in your current life circumstances?

Prayer: Serving Savior, thank You for demonstrating true greatness through service and sacrifice. Help me follow Your example by serving rather than seeking to be served. Show me opportunities to serve others in Your name. Make me willing to sacrifice for others' benefit. Use me as Your servant. Amen.

Day 58: A Life that Honors God

"So whether you eat or drink or whatever you do, do it all for the glory of God." - 1 Corinthians 10:31

Paul's instruction reveals that honoring God encompasses every aspect of life, not just religious activities. Eating, drinking, working, and playing can all glorify God when done with proper motivation and manner. This comprehensive approach transforms ordinary activities into worship.

"Whatever you do" indicates that no activity is too mundane to honor God. Changing diapers, filing reports, preparing meals, or mowing lawns can all bring glory to God when performed with proper heart attitude and excellence.

"For the glory of God" means seeking to display God's character and attract others to Him through our behavior. When people observe our work ethic, family relationships, or response to difficulty, they should glimpse something of God's nature.

Honoring God requires both internal motivation and external expression. Our hearts must desire His glory, and our actions must reflect His character. This alignment between inner devotion and outer demonstration creates authentic witness that honors God.

This principle affects daily decision-making by providing a filter for choices: "Will this honor God or bring shame to His name?" This question helps evaluate everything from entertainment choices to business practices to relationship dynamics.

Reflection: How can your daily activities more consistently bring glory to God?

Prayer: Glorious God, I want every aspect of my life to honor You rather than just my religious activities. Help me eat, drink, work, and play in ways that display Your character. Make my life a consistent testimony that attracts others to You. Let everything I do bring You glory. Amen.

Day 59: Serving with Gladness

"Serve the Lord with gladness; come before his presence with singing."
- Psalm 100:2

The psalmist connects service to God with joy rather than duty. Serving with gladness demonstrates that our service flows from love and gratitude rather than obligation or fear. This joyful attitude makes our service more effective and attractive to others.

"Gladness" suggests internal joy that affects external expression. Joyful service becomes a testimony to God's goodness and our appreciation for His blessings. Others notice when service flows from delight rather than duty.

The connection between serving and singing indicates that worship and service naturally flow together. When we serve God gladly, our work becomes worship. When we worship God sincerely, service becomes natural expression of our love.

Serving with gladness requires remembering what God has done for us. Gratitude for salvation, provision, and countless blessings motivates joyful service. When we lose sight of God's goodness, service becomes burden rather than privilege.

This joyful attitude is particularly important when serving others. People can sense whether we're helping them gladly or grudgingly. Cheerful service blesses both recipient and giver while grumpy service diminishes the value of our efforts.

Reflection: What helps you maintain gladness in your service to God and others?

Prayer: God of joy, I want to serve You with gladness rather than mere duty. Fill my heart with appreciation for Your goodness so that service becomes delight rather than burden. Help me maintain cheerful attitude in serving others. Let my joy in serving You be evident to all around me. Amen.

Day 60: God's Hands and Feet

"Now you are the body of Christ, and each one of you is a part of it."
- 1 Corinthians 12:27

Paul's metaphor reveals that believers collectively represent Christ's physical presence in the world. We become His hands to serve, His feet to go, His voice to speak, and His heart to love. This calling gives profound meaning to our service and witness.

Being part of Christ's body means our individual actions affect the whole church's reputation and effectiveness. When we serve faithfully, we enhance Christ's witness. When we fail, we damage the testimony of the entire body. This creates both privilege and responsibility.

The body metaphor emphasizes that every believer has essential functions regardless of prominence or recognition. Hands and feet are equally important for body function. Similarly, every Christian's service contributes to Christ's work in the world.

"Each one of you is a part of it" indicates that no believer is dispensable or unimportant. God designed the body to require every member's contribution. This should eliminate both pride in prominent positions and despair in humble roles.

Functioning as God's hands and feet requires staying connected to the Head, who is Christ. Disconnected body parts cannot function effectively. Our service must flow from ongoing relationship with Christ rather than independent effort.

Reflection: How is God using you as part of Christ's body to serve others and represent Him?

Prayer: Head of the body, thank You for making me part of Christ's presence in the world. Help me function faithfully as Your hands and feet to serve others. Keep me connected to You so my service flows from our relationship. Use me effectively as part of Your body. Amen.

Day 61: Divine Assignment: Embracing Your Calling

"But when God, who set me apart from my mother's womb and called me by his grace, was pleased to reveal his Son in me so that I might preach him among the Gentiles, I did not consult flesh and blood."
- Galatians 1:15-16

Paul describes his calling as divinely initiated and specifically designed. God set him apart before birth and called him at the appointed time for particular service. This pattern suggests that every believer has divine assignments tailored to their unique gifts and circumstances.

"Set me apart from my mother's womb" indicates that God's calling includes preparation that begins before we're aware of it. Our background, experiences, education, and even failures all become part of God's preparation for future service. Nothing is wasted in divine preparation.

"Called me by his grace" reveals that calling flows from God's favor rather than human merit. We don't earn our assignments through good behavior or spiritual achievement. God calls us because He chooses to use us, not because we deserve to be used.

"I did not consult flesh and blood" shows Paul's immediate obedience to divine calling without seeking human approval or advice. While wisdom normally includes seeking counsel, some divine assignments require faith that moves ahead of human understanding or support.

Embracing our calling requires both recognition and response. We must discern what God is calling us to do and then step forward in faith to do it. This often involves leaving comfort zones and risking failure for the possibility of divine purpose.

Reflection: What divine assignment might God be preparing you for through your current experiences?

Prayer: Calling God, thank You for setting me apart and preparing me for specific service. Help me recognize the divine assignments You have for me and respond with immediate obedience. Give me courage to embrace my calling without needing human approval. Use my background and experiences for Your purposes. Amen.

Day 62: Serving God through Serving Others

"Truly I tell you, whatever you did for one of the least of these brothers and sisters of mine, you did for me." - Matthew 25:40

Jesus reveals that service to needy people equals service to Him. This principle transforms acts of compassion from mere humanitarian efforts to worship expressions. When we help others, we're actually ministering to Christ Himself.

"The least of these" refers to people society often overlooks or dismisses—the poor, hungry, imprisoned, or marginalized. Jesus identifies with these vulnerable populations, making service to them a direct expression of love for Him.

This teaching elevates human dignity by revealing that every person bears Christ's image and deserves compassionate treatment. It also provides motivation for service that transcends mere social responsibility—we serve because we're serving Jesus.

"You did for me" indicates that Christ receives our service to others as personal ministry to Him. This should inspire excellence in our service and persistence in our compassion. We're not just helping people—we're ministering to our Savior.

The connection between serving God and serving others eliminates the false separation between spiritual and social ministry. Caring for physical needs becomes spiritual service. Meeting temporal needs expresses eternal love. Sacred and secular merge in compassionate service.

Reflection: How does seeing Christ in needy people change your motivation and approach to serving them?

Prayer: Compassionate Christ, help me see You in the faces of needy people around me. Transform my service to others into worship of You. Give me Your heart for the least and the lost. Let my compassion for others be an expression of my love for You. Use me to serve You through serving others. Amen.

Day 63: Active Faith, Visible Service

"In the same way, faith by itself, if it is not accompanied by action, is dead." - James 2:17

James insists that genuine faith produces corresponding action. Faith that doesn't result in service remains incomplete and ineffective. This principle challenges believers to move beyond intellectual belief to practical involvement in God's work.

"Faith by itself" describes belief that remains isolated from behavior. While faith begins with mental assent to truth, it must progress to lifestyle transformation that includes service to God and others. Inactive faith suggests incomplete faith.

"Accompanied by action" indicates that faith and works function as partners rather than competitors. Works don't earn salvation, but they demonstrate salvation. Service doesn't create faith, but it validates faith. Action accompanies authentic belief.

"Is dead" means that faith without corresponding action lacks the vitality of genuine spiritual life. Like a body without breath, faith without works appears lifeless and ineffective. Dead faith cannot produce the results that living faith produces.

Active faith expresses itself through visible service that others can observe and be influenced by. This creates credible witness that attracts people to Christ. Faith becomes convincing when it translates into consistent, compassionate action.

Reflection: How does your service to others demonstrate the reality of your faith in Christ?

Prayer: God of action, I don't want my faith to remain merely intellectual but to express itself through active service. Show me opportunities to demonstrate my faith through compassionate action. Make my faith visible through service that attracts others to You. Keep my faith alive through active obedience. Amen.

Section 8: Dying to Self

Day 64: The Power of Letting Go

"Then he said to them all: 'Whoever wants to be my disciple must deny himself and take up his cross daily and follow me.'" - Luke 9:23

Jesus reveals that discipleship requires releasing control over our lives to embrace His leadership. Letting go of self-determination enables us to receive God's direction and experience His power. This daily surrender transforms us from autonomous individuals into obedient disciples.

"Deny himself" means saying "no" to selfish desires that conflict with God's will. This isn't self-hatred but self-discipline that chooses divine purposes over personal preferences. Denial creates space for God's will to operate in our lives.

"Take up his cross daily" refers to the ongoing nature of self-surrender. Like the cross Jesus carried, our cross represents death to self-will and acceptance of God's will even when costly. This isn't a one-time decision but daily choice. The power of letting go lies in releasing burdens we were never meant to carry and control we cannot effectively exercise. When we stop trying to manage outcomes we cannot control, we're free to focus on obedience we can control.

Letting go requires both faith and courage. Faith to trust that God's plans are better than our plans. Courage to release familiar patterns of self-reliance and embrace dependence on divine guidance. This surrender leads to freedom rather than restriction.

Reflection: What areas of control do you need to surrender to experience greater freedom and power?

Prayer: Liberating Lord, I want to experience the power that comes from letting go of control and surrendering to Your will. Help me deny myself daily and take up my cross. Give me faith to trust Your plans and courage to release my plans. Free me through surrender. Amen.

Day 65: Crucified with Christ

"I have been crucified with Christ and I no longer live, but Christ lives in me. The life I now live in the body, I live by faith in the Son of God, who loved me and gave himself for me." - Galatians 2:20

Paul describes the spiritual reality that occurs at salvation—our old self dies and Christ's life begins operating through us. This crucifixion with Christ enables new life that operates by divine power rather than human effort. Understanding this truth transforms Christian living.

"I have been crucified" refers to past event with present implications. At salvation, our sinful nature received its death sentence through identification with Christ's death. This provides the foundation for freedom from sin's controlling power.

"I no longer live" doesn't mean Paul ceased existing but that his old self-centered life ended. The person controlled by selfish desires and worldly values died, making room for Christ-centered living. Death to self enables life in Christ.

"Christ lives in me" reveals the positive result of crucifixion with Christ. His life replaces our life, His power enables our service, and His character transforms our behavior. This indwelling presence makes Christian living possible rather than merely required.

"Live by faith" indicates that this new life operates through trust in Christ rather than self-effort. We believe that Christ's life in us produces the attitudes and actions that please God. Faith connects us to His power for daily living.

Reflection: How does understanding your crucifixion with Christ change your approach to overcoming sin and living righteously?

Prayer: Crucified and risen Christ, thank You for including me in Your death and resurrection. Help me live in the reality that my old self has died and You now live in me. Enable me to live by faith in Your indwelling presence rather than by self-effort. Transform me through Your life within me. Amen.

Day 66: The Freedom of Surrender

"Submit yourselves, then, to God. Resist the devil, and he will flee from you." - James 4:7

James reveals that submission to God provides strength for resistance to evil. This paradox of spiritual life shows that surrender to divine authority creates freedom from spiritual bondage. True liberty comes through yielding to God rather than asserting independence.

"Submit yourselves" means placing ourselves under God's authority voluntarily rather than reluctantly. This isn't forced compliance but willing cooperation with divine leadership. Submission flows from trust in God's character and wisdom.

The connection between submission to God and resistance to the devil shows that these actions work together. When we yield to God's authority, we gain power to resist Satan's temptations. Surrender to God strengthens us for spiritual warfare.

"He will flee from you" promises that sustained resistance will cause the devil to retreat. This doesn't mean temptation will cease, but it means Satan cannot force obedience from submitted believers. Resistance coupled with submission proves effective against spiritual attack. The freedom of surrender includes liberation from the exhausting effort of trying to control outcomes we cannot manage. When we surrender these burdens to God, we're free to focus on faithful obedience without anxiety about results.

Reflection: How has surrender to God's authority created greater freedom in your spiritual life?

Prayer: Sovereign God, I want to experience the freedom that comes through surrender to Your authority. Help me submit willingly rather than reluctantly to Your leadership. Use my submission to strengthen my resistance to temptation. Free me from burdens I cannot carry through surrender to You. Amen.

Day 67: When Less is More

"He must become greater; I must become less." - John 3:30

John the Baptist understood that his purpose was to point people to Christ rather than build his own following. This principle of decrease enabling increase operates throughout spiritual life—as self diminishes, Christ becomes more prominent through us. Less self means more of God.

"He must become greater" indicates John's intentional focus on Christ's prominence rather than his own recognition. This wasn't resignation to inevitable decline but purposeful choice to prioritize Christ's glory over personal acclaim. Humility becomes strategy for effective ministry.

"I must become less" doesn't mean John became less valuable or important as a person. Rather, his ego, personal agenda, and desire for recognition had to diminish so Christ could increase through his life and ministry. Self-promotion had to decrease for Christ-promotion to increase.

This principle applies to all believers. As our pride, self-will, and personal ambition decrease, Christ's character and purposes can increase through our lives. Others see more of Him and less of us when we practice this spiritual mathematics.

The beauty of "less is more" lies in discovering that decreasing self leads to increasing fulfillment. We find more satisfaction in Christ's prominence than in personal recognition. His increase becomes our joy rather than our threat.

Reflection: In what areas of your life does "less of you" need to happen so "more of Christ" can be seen?

Prayer: Great God, I want You to become greater in my life while I become less prominent. Help me decrease in pride, self-will, and personal ambition so You can increase through me. Let others see more of You and less of me in my attitudes and actions. Make less of me mean more of You. Amen.

Day 68: Emptying Ourselves to Be Filled

"In your relationships with one another, have the same mindset as Christ Jesus: Who, being in very nature God, did not consider equality with God something to be used to his own advantage; rather, he made himself nothing by taking the very nature of a servant."
- Philippians 2:5-7

Paul presents Christ's incarnation as the ultimate example of emptying oneself to accomplish divine purposes. Jesus voluntarily laid aside His heavenly privileges to serve humanity's needs. This pattern of self-emptying enables God's fullness to operate through us.

"Did not consider equality with God something to be used to his own advantage" reveals that Christ chose service over self-interest despite having every right to demand His own way. This choice demonstrates love that prioritizes others' welfare over personal benefit.

"Made himself nothing" doesn't mean Christ ceased being God but that He chose not to rely on His divine prerogatives for personal advantage. He emptied Himself of the use of divine privileges while retaining divine nature. This kenosis made incarnation possible. "Taking the very nature of a servant" shows that emptying enables filling with new purpose. Christ didn't become empty and remain empty—He filled the space left by relinquished privileges with servant character. Emptying creates capacity for divine filling.

This principle applies to believers who must empty themselves of selfish ambitions, prideful attitudes, and personal agendas to be filled with Christ's character and purposes. Self-emptying creates space for divine fullness.

Reflection: What do you need to empty from your life to create more space for God's presence and purposes?

Prayer: Self-emptying Christ, thank You for the example of laying aside Your privileges to serve others. Help me empty myself of selfish ambitions and prideful attitudes to create space for Your character and purposes. Fill the emptiness I create through surrender with Your presence and power. Amen.

Day 69: Choosing the Cross Daily

"And he said to all, 'If anyone wants to come after me, let him deny himself and take up his cross daily and follow me.'" - Luke 9:23

Jesus reveals that discipleship requires daily recommitment to self-denial and sacrifice. The cross represents ongoing choice to die to self-will and embrace God's will even when costly. This daily decision shapes character and demonstrates authentic discipleship.

"Take up his cross daily" emphasizes the ongoing nature of discipleship commitment. Like physical crosses that had to be carried continuously to their destination, spiritual crosses require daily choice to maintain sacrificial commitment to Christ's purposes.

The cross symbolizes death to self-interest and acceptance of God's will regardless of personal cost. Choosing the cross means prioritizing divine purposes over personal preferences, eternal values over temporal comforts, and Christ's glory over personal recognition.

"Daily" indicates that this isn't a one-time decision but recurring choice. Each day presents new opportunities to choose self or Christ, comfort or cross, easy path or narrow way. Daily cross-bearing shapes us progressively into Christ's image.

Choosing the cross produces both difficulty and reward. Difficulty because it requires ongoing sacrifice of personal desires. Reward because it aligns us with God's purposes and produces spiritual maturity that brings deep satisfaction and effectiveness.

Reflection: What does taking up your cross daily look like in your current circumstances?

Prayer: Crucified Savior, I want to take up my cross daily and follow You regardless of the cost. Help me choose sacrifice over comfort, Your will over my preferences, and eternal values over temporal pleasures. Shape my character through daily cross-bearing. Make me a faithful cross-bearer. Amen.

Day 70: Death to Self, Life in Christ

"For whoever wants to save their life will lose it, but whoever loses their life for me will find it." - Matthew 16:25

Jesus presents the paradox that losing life leads to finding it while trying to save life results in losing it. This principle governs spiritual transformation—death to self-centeredness enables life in Christ-centeredness. True life comes through surrender rather than self-preservation.

"Whoever wants to save their life" describes natural human instinct to protect and promote self-interest. This includes preserving comfort, reputation, resources, and personal agenda. While self-care is appropriate, self-absorption becomes spiritually destructive.

"Will lose it" indicates that self-centered living ultimately fails to produce the fulfillment it promises. Those who live only for themselves miss the joy, purpose, and satisfaction that come from God-centered living. Self-preservation leads to spiritual poverty.

"Loses their life for me" refers to voluntary surrender of self-interest for Christ's sake. This isn't physical martyrdom for most believers but daily choice to prioritize Christ's purposes over personal desires. Losing life for Christ means finding new life in Christ.

"Will find it" promises that self-surrender leads to discovering life's true meaning and purpose. Instead of losing everything, we gain everything worthwhile. Life in Christ provides fulfillment that self-centered living cannot produce.

Reflection: How has dying to self-interest enabled you to find greater life and fulfillment in Christ?

Prayer: Life-giving Christ, I want to find true life by losing my self-centered life for Your sake. Help me surrender personal agenda to embrace Your purposes. Show me that dying to selfishness leads to living in Your abundance. Let me find real life through losing my old life. Amen.

Day 71: Living Fully through Surrender

"I appeal to you therefore, brothers, by the mercies of God, to present your bodies as a living sacrifice, holy and acceptable to God, which is your spiritual worship." - Romans 12:1

Paul calls believers to present themselves as living sacrifices, combining the concepts of death and life in spiritual surrender. This paradox reveals that complete surrender to God enables fuller living than self-directed existence. True life comes through total consecration to divine purposes.

"By the mercies of God" indicates that surrender responds to God's grace rather than earning it. We don't sacrifice ourselves to gain God's favor—we sacrifice because we've already received His favor. Gratitude for mercy motivates surrender rather than desire for merit.

"Present your bodies" includes our entire physical existence—not just spiritual activities but daily choices about work, relationships, entertainment, and stewardship. Living sacrifice affects how we use our bodies as tools for God's glory.

"Living sacrifice" contrasts with Old Testament animal sacrifices that died completely. Believers remain alive but surrender control of their lives to God. We die to self-will while remaining alive to serve God's will through our ongoing existence.

"Which is your spiritual worship" reveals that surrender constitutes the most authentic form of worship. Beyond singing songs or saying prayers, offering our entire lives to God expresses the deepest reverence and devotion possible.

Reflection: How can you more completely present your body as a living sacrifice in daily decisions and activities?

Prayer: Merciful God, in response to Your grace, I want to present my body as a living sacrifice for Your service. Help me surrender every aspect of my physical existence to Your purposes. Make my daily choices acts of worship that honor You. Enable me to live fully through complete surrender to You. Amen.

Day 72: Humility: The Pathway to Power

"Humble yourselves, therefore, under God's mighty hand, that he may lift you up in due time." - 1 Peter 5:6

Peter reveals that humility provides the pathway to divine exaltation rather than human promotion. This counterintuitive principle shows that God lifts up those who lower themselves while resisting those who exalt themselves. Humility becomes strategy for receiving God's power and blessing.

"Humble yourselves" indicates that humility is both choice and action. We don't wait for circumstances to humble us—we actively choose humble attitudes and behaviors. This proactive humility positions us to receive God's grace and favor.

"Under God's mighty hand" suggests that humility means accepting God's authority and timing rather than asserting our own. His mighty hand can either discipline or bless, depending on our response to His authority. Submission to His hand brings blessing.

"That he may lift you up" promises divine promotion for those who humble themselves. This doesn't guarantee worldly success but ensures spiritual advancement and divine recognition. God's exaltation surpasses human promotion in value and permanence.

"In due time" reminds us that God's timing differs from human expectations. Humility includes patience with divine timing while maintaining faithfulness in current circumstances. Premature self-promotion often prevents divine promotion.

Reflection: How can you practice humility as a pathway to receiving more of God's power and blessing?

Prayer: Mighty God, I want to humble myself under Your authority rather than seek self-promotion. Help me accept Your timing and methods for any advancement in my life. Teach me that humility opens the door to Your power and blessing. Lift me up according to Your perfect timing. Amen.

Section 9: Putting God First

Day 73: First Things First

"But seek first his kingdom and his righteousness, and all these things will be given to you as well." - Matthew 6:33

Jesus reveals the priority principle that governs successful Christian living. When we put God's kingdom and righteousness first, He takes responsibility for providing everything else we need. This priority system transforms both our focus and our security.

"Seek first" indicates both priority and intensity. God's kingdom doesn't merely get included in our schedule—it receives primary attention and energy. This isn't casual interest but passionate pursuit that affects daily decision-making and resource allocation.

"His kingdom" refers to God's rule and reign in our lives and in the world. Seeking the kingdom means promoting God's values, submitting to His authority, and participating in His mission. Kingdom priorities supersede personal priorities.

"His righteousness" includes both right standing with God and right living before God. We seek justification through faith and sanctification through obedience. Both aspects of righteousness receive priority attention in kingdom living.

"All these things will be given to you" promises divine provision for those who maintain proper priorities. When we seek God first, He assumes responsibility for meeting our legitimate needs. This doesn't guarantee luxury but ensures sufficiency.

Reflection: How does putting God's kingdom first change your daily priorities and decisions?

Prayer: Kingdom God, I want to seek Your kingdom and righteousness first in every area of my life. Help me prioritize Your will over my wants and Your glory over my goals. Take responsibility for providing my needs as I focus on Your priorities. Make Your kingdom my primary pursuit. Amen.

Day 74: Priority One: God

"You shall have no other gods before me." - Exodus 20:3

The first commandment establishes God's rightful place as supreme priority in human life. This foundational principle affects every other relationship and responsibility. When God occupies first place, everything else falls into proper order and receives appropriate attention.

"No other gods" includes anything that receives the devotion, trust, or allegiance that belongs exclusively to God. Modern idols include career success, financial security, family relationships, personal comfort, or entertainment. These become gods when they take priority over the true God.

"Before me" literally means "in my presence" or "in front of my face." This suggests that God is always present and aware of our priorities. We cannot hide divided loyalties or compartmentalize our devotion. He sees what truly comes first in our lives. Making God priority one doesn't eliminate other responsibilities but arranges them according to His will and timing. We still care for family, work diligently, and manage resources, but these activities serve God's purposes rather than replacing His position.

The first commandment creates both freedom and responsibility. Freedom from the burden of serving multiple masters who make conflicting demands. Responsibility to order all of life according to God's revealed will and character.

Reflection: What "other gods" compete with the true God for first place in your priorities?

Prayer: One true God, I want to have no gods before You in my life. Help me identify and remove anything that competes with You for my primary devotion. Order my priorities according to Your will so that everything else serves Your purposes. Be my only God and supreme priority. Amen.

Day 75: Kingdom Priorities

"But he answered, 'It is written: Man shall not live on bread alone, but on every word that comes from the mouth of God.'" - Matthew 4:4

Jesus' response to Satan's temptation reveals that spiritual nourishment takes priority over physical nourishment. This doesn't diminish the importance of meeting physical needs but establishes the supremacy of spiritual needs. Kingdom priorities address eternal concerns first.

"Man shall not live on bread alone" acknowledges that humans need physical sustenance while emphasizing that we need more than physical sustenance. Bread represents all physical necessities that support temporal life. These are important but insufficient for complete living.

"Every word that comes from the mouth of God" represents spiritual nourishment that feeds the soul and provides guidance for life. God's Word contains truth, wisdom, comfort, and direction necessary for abundant living. Spiritual food enables meaningful existence.
Kingdom priorities mean seeking God's truth before pursuing worldly success, developing character before building reputation, and nurturing relationships with God and others before accumulating possessions. These priorities reflect eternal values over temporal concerns.

This principle challenges cultural priorities that emphasize material prosperity, physical pleasure, and social status. Kingdom citizens evaluate opportunities and investments according to eternal significance rather than temporary benefit.

Reflection: How do your daily choices reflect kingdom priorities versus worldly priorities?

Prayer: King of kings, I want to live by kingdom priorities that value eternal concerns over temporal ones. Help me seek spiritual nourishment before physical comfort and character development before material success. Align my priorities with Your kingdom values. Make me a true kingdom citizen. Amen.

Day 76: The First Fruit Lifestyle

"Honor the Lord with your wealth, with the firstfruits of all your crops; then your barns will be filled to overflowing, and your vats will brim over with new wine." - Proverbs 3:9-10

Solomon reveals that giving God the first and best of our resources demonstrates proper priorities and releases divine blessing. The firstfruit principle applies beyond finances to include time, energy, and attention. Priority giving reflects priority relationship.

"Honor the Lord with your wealth" indicates that how we handle money reveals our true priorities and loyalties. Money represents time, energy, and opportunity. Giving God first claim on our resources honors Him as the source of all provision.

"Firstfruits" refers to the first and best portion rather than leftovers or remainders. This requires faith because we give before knowing what remains. Firstfruit giving demonstrates trust in God's continued provision and priority relationship with Him.

The promise of overflowing blessing doesn't guarantee wealth but ensures sufficiency and satisfaction. God provides for those who prioritize Him in their stewardship. This isn't prosperity theology but providence theology—God cares for faithful stewards.

The firstfruit lifestyle extends beyond financial giving to include offering God the first part of each day through prayer and Scripture reading, the best of our energy through prioritized service, and the choicest of our time through worship and fellowship.

Reflection: How can you more consistently practice the firstfruit principle in your stewardship of time, money, and energy?

Prayer: Providing God, I want to honor You with my wealth and practice firstfruit giving in every area of life. Help me give You the first and best rather than the leftovers. Increase my faith to trust Your continued provision as I prioritize You in my stewardship. Bless my firstfruit lifestyle. Amen.

Day 77: God Before Everything Else

"And he said to another man, 'Follow me.' But he said, 'Lord, let me first go and bury my father.' Jesus said to him, 'Let the dead bury their own dead, but you go and proclaim the kingdom of God.'" - Luke 9:59-60

Jesus' seemingly harsh response reveals that following Him requires absolute priority even over important family responsibilities. This doesn't diminish family obligations but establishes that God's call takes precedence over every other claim on our lives.

"Follow me" represents immediate response to divine calling without delay or negotiation. Jesus expects prompt obedience when He calls, not extended deliberation about convenience or timing. Following Christ becomes the defining decision that affects all other decisions.

"Let me first go and bury my father" likely refers to waiting until his father died naturally rather than attending a funeral. This man wanted to delay obedience until family obligations were completed. His response shows how good things can compete with God things.

"Let the dead bury their own dead" means letting those who are spiritually dead handle temporal responsibilities while those who are spiritually alive focus on eternal purposes. Physical death isn't the only kind of death—spiritual deadness also exists.

This passage challenges us to examine what we put before God in our decision-making. Career advancement, family approval, financial security, or personal comfort can all compete with divine calling if we allow them priority over God's will.

Reflection: What legitimate concerns or relationships might be competing with God for first place in your life?

Prayer: Priority God, I want to put You before everything else in my life, even good things that compete with Your calling. Help me follow You immediately when You call rather than negotiating delays. Show me where I'm letting other priorities take precedence over Your will. Be my absolute first priority. Amen.

Day 78: Reordering Your World

"But godliness with contentment is great gain. For we brought nothing into the world, and we can take nothing out of it." - 1 Timothy 6:6-7

Paul reveals that contentment combined with godliness produces greater wealth than material accumulation ever could. This eternal perspective reorders our values and priorities, helping us invest in lasting treasure rather than temporary possessions.

"Godliness with contentment" describes character that finds satisfaction in relationship with God rather than in circumstances or possessions. This doesn't mean lacking ambition but finding primary fulfillment in spiritual rather than material progress.

"Great gain" indicates that this combination produces profit beyond financial measurement. Godly contentment provides peace, joy, security, and purpose that money cannot purchase. These spiritual riches outvalue material wealth.

"We brought nothing into the world" reminds us of our condition at birth—completely dependent and possessing nothing. This perspective humbles pride and reduces attachment to possessions that were never truly ours to begin with.

"We can take nothing out of it" points to our condition at death—leaving everything behind. Since we cannot take possessions beyond this life, wisdom invests primarily in relationships and character that survive death.

Reordering our world means evaluating everything according to eternal significance rather than temporal value. This transforms priorities, relationships, and resource allocation to reflect kingdom values.

Reflection: How does remembering that you brought nothing and can take nothing change your current priorities?

Prayer: Eternal God, help me reorder my world according to eternal values rather than temporal priorities. Give me godliness with contentment that finds great gain in relationship with You. Free me from excessive attachment to possessions and help me invest in lasting treasure. Order my priorities according to what survives death. Amen.

Day 79: The Blessings of Prioritizing God

"Delight yourself in the Lord, and he will give you the desires of your heart." - Psalm 37:4

David reveals that finding joy in God leads to fulfilled desires. This promise doesn't mean God grants every whim but that delighting in Him transforms our desires to align with His will. When our desires match His desires, fulfillment becomes inevitable.

"Delight yourself in the Lord" means finding genuine pleasure and satisfaction in relationship with God rather than in circumstances or possessions. This delight goes beyond duty to include joy, beyond obligation to include affection.

The progression is crucial: delight first, then desires granted. Many people reverse this order, seeking fulfilled desires first and offering delight as payment. God's method transforms desires while fulfilling them rather than simply satisfying unchanged desires.

"He will give you the desires of your heart" promises fulfillment but doesn't specify the method. Sometimes God grants what we desire. Sometimes He changes what we desire. Sometimes He shows us that what we thought we wanted isn't what we really needed.

The blessing of prioritizing God includes transformed desires that align with His will, fulfilled longings that satisfy deeply, and contentment that doesn't depend on circumstances. God becomes both the source and satisfaction of desire.

Reflection: How has delighting in God changed the desires of your heart?

Prayer: Delightful God, I want to find my primary joy and satisfaction in You rather than in circumstances or possessions. Transform the desires of my heart to align with Your will so that fulfillment becomes inevitable. Help me delight in You first and trust You to fulfill desires that honor You. Be my delight and my satisfaction. Amen.

Day 80: Daily Choices, Eternal Consequences

"Do not store up for yourselves treasures on earth, where moths and vermin destroy, and where thieves break in and steal. But store up for yourselves treasures in heaven, where moths and vermin do not destroy, and where thieves do not break in and steal."
- Matthew 6:19-20

Jesus contrasts earthly and heavenly treasure to help believers make wise investment decisions. Daily choices about time, money, and energy either accumulate earthly treasure that deteriorates or heavenly treasure that endures. Small decisions create eternal consequences.

"Do not store up for yourselves treasures on earth" doesn't prohibit saving money or acquiring possessions but warns against making earthly accumulation our primary focus and security. Earth-bound treasure becomes our master when it should be our tool.

"Moths and vermin destroy" reminds us that earthly treasure is vulnerable to deterioration, theft, and loss. Economic crashes, natural disasters, and personal crises can eliminate material wealth quickly. Building security on unstable foundation creates anxiety.

"Store up for yourselves treasures in heaven" encourages investment in eternal values—relationship with God, service to others, character development, and spiritual growth. These investments survive death and continue producing dividends forever.

Every day presents opportunities to choose between earthly and heavenly treasure through decisions about spending, serving, and prioritizing. Small choices accumulate over time to create significant eternal consequences.

Reflection: How are your daily choices accumulating treasures on earth or treasures in heaven?

Prayer: Eternal Treasurer, help me make daily choices that store up treasures in heaven rather than focusing exclusively on earthly accumulation. Give me wisdom to invest time, money, and energy in eternal values. Show me how small decisions create lasting consequences. Make me a wise eternal investor. Amen.

Day 81: Seeking God Above All

"Ask and it will be given to you; seek and you will find; knock and the door will be opened to you." - Matthew 7:7

Jesus encourages persistent pursuit of God through prayer and promises that sincere seeking produces spiritual results. This progression—asking, seeking, knocking—represents increasing intensity in spiritual pursuit. Seeking God above all else ensures finding what matters most.

"Ask" represents the beginning of spiritual pursuit through prayer. This includes requests for God's help, guidance, provision, and presence. Asking acknowledges our dependence on God and opens communication with Him. Prayer becomes the foundation for seeking. "Seek" indicates more intensive pursuit that goes beyond occasional requests to consistent spiritual discipline. Seeking includes studying Scripture, participating in worship, serving others, and ordering life according to divine priorities. Active pursuit demonstrates serious intent.

"Knock" suggests persistent effort that doesn't give up when doors seem closed. Some spiritual breakthrough requires sustained effort and faith that continues despite delays or obstacles. Knocking demonstrates determined faith that expects response.

The promise—"given," "find," "opened"—assures that sincere spiritual pursuit produces results. God rewards those who earnestly seek Him. This doesn't guarantee specific answers but promises meaningful spiritual encounter with the One we seek.

Reflection: How can you increase the intensity and consistency of your seeking after God?

Prayer: Seeking God, I want to pursue You above all else with increasing intensity and persistence. Help me progress from casual asking to serious seeking to determined knocking. Reward my sincere pursuit with deeper knowledge of You and stronger relationship with You. Let me find You as I seek You. Amen.

Section 10:
No Middle Ground: Choose Your God

Day 82: No Room for Compromise

"How long will you waver between two opinions? If the Lord is God, follow him; but if Baal is God, follow him." - 1 Kings 18:21

Elijah's challenge to Israel reveals that spiritual neutrality is impossible. We cannot serve two masters simultaneously or divide our allegiance between God and competing loyalties. The time comes when we must choose definitively whom we will serve. Compromise weakens commitment and confuses witness.

"Waver between two opinions" describes the exhausting attempt to maintain loyalty to contradictory authorities. This spiritual double-mindedness produces instability and prevents the peace that comes from clear commitment. Wavering between options often means choosing neither effectively.

Elijah's challenge forces decision rather than allowing continued indecision. He understood that avoiding choice is itself a choice—a choice for spiritual mediocrity and ineffectiveness. Sometimes love demands confrontation that forces clarity.

"If the Lord is God, follow him" calls for complete commitment based on God's identity rather than on convenience or cultural pressure. If we believe God is who He claims to be, then total allegiance becomes the only reasonable response.

The contest that followed this challenge demonstrated God's power and exposed Baal's impotence. Similarly, when we stop compromising and commit fully to God, His power becomes evident in ways that compromise prevents. Whole-hearted commitment releases
divine power.

Reflection: In what areas of your life are you still wavering between serving God and serving other masters?

Prayer: Uncompromising God, I don't want to waver between serving You and serving other masters. Help me recognize areas where I'm still trying to serve two authorities. Give me courage to choose You completely and abandon every competing loyalty. Make my commitment clear and total. Amen.

Day 83: Choose Today Whom You Will Serve

"But if serving the Lord seems undesirable to you, then choose for yourselves this day whom you will serve, whether the gods your ancestors served beyond the Euphrates, or the gods of the Amorites, in whose land you are living. But as for me and my household, we will serve the Lord." - Joshua 24:15

Joshua's famous declaration forces a decision that cannot be postponed indefinitely. Everyone serves someone or something—the question is whom or what we choose to serve. This decision affects not only personal destiny but also influences family and community.

"Choose for yourselves this day" emphasizes both personal responsibility and urgent timing. Others cannot make this choice for us, and we cannot delay indefinitely without consequences. Each day we live demonstrates our choice through actions and priorities.

Joshua presents three options: ancestral gods, cultural gods, or the true God. These represent past traditions, present pressures, and eternal truth. Every generation faces similar choices between inherited religion, cultural conformity, and authentic faith.

"As for me and my household" reveals that spiritual leadership includes making clear personal commitment and influencing others toward right choice. Leaders must choose first and choose publicly to provide direction for those who follow them.

The phrase "we will serve" indicates ongoing commitment rather than momentary decision. Serving the Lord requires daily renewal of commitment through consistent obedience, worship, and prioritizing His will over personal preferences.

Reflection: What choice are your daily actions and priorities demonstrating about whom you serve?

Prayer: Worthy God, I choose today to serve You rather than ancestral traditions or cultural pressures. Help me make this choice clear through consistent actions and priorities. Use my commitment to influence my household and community toward serving You. Renew this choice in me daily. Amen.

Day 84: The Danger of Lukewarm Living

"I know your deeds, that you are neither cold nor hot. I wish you were either one or the other! So, because you are lukewarm—neither hot nor cold—I am about to vomit you out of my mouth." - Revelation 3:15-16

Christ's message to Laodicea reveals His disgust with spiritual mediocrity. Lukewarm faith nauseates God because it represents the worst kind of spiritual condition—claiming allegiance without demonstrating commitment. Indifferent Christianity is more dangerous than honest rebellion. "Neither cold nor hot" describes spiritual temperature that lacks passion in either direction. Cold represents open rejection while hot represents fervent devotion.

Both have integrity that lukewarm living lacks. At least cold and hot are honest about their condition.

"I wish you were either one or the other" shows that God prefers honest opposition to dishonest profession. Cold people know they need salvation. Hot people serve with passion. Lukewarm people are deceived about their spiritual condition and resistant to change.

"I am about to vomit you out of my mouth" uses strong imagery to convey God's revulsion at halfhearted commitment. Lukewarm faith is unpalatable to God because it dishonors His character and weakens His witness in the world.

Lukewarm living often results from prosperity and self-sufficiency that reduce dependence on God. When life becomes comfortable, passion tends to cool and commitment becomes casual. Comfort can be more spiritually dangerous than crisis.

Reflection: How can you guard against lukewarm living and maintain spiritual passion for God?

Prayer: Hot-hearted God, I don't want to be lukewarm in my commitment to You. Keep my love fervent and my obedience passionate. Protect me from the spiritual dangers of comfort and self-sufficiency. Make me either fully committed or honestly seeking rather than deceived about my spiritual condition. Keep me hot for You. Amen.

Day 85: Absolute Allegiance

"No one can serve two masters. Either you will hate the one and love the other, or you will be devoted to one and despise the other. You cannot serve both God and money." - Matthew 6:24

Jesus reveals the impossibility of divided loyalty between competing authorities. Absolute allegiance means complete devotion to one master rather than attempting to serve multiple authorities with conflicting demands. This principle governs all spiritual commitment.

"No one can serve two masters" states a spiritual law as fixed as physical laws. Just as objects cannot move in opposite directions simultaneously, hearts cannot serve contrary masters effectively. Attempting divided service results in serving neither master well.

"Either you will hate the one and love the other" describes the inevitable result of trying to serve competing authorities. When masters make conflicting demands, we must choose one over the other. This choice reveals our true loyalty and ultimate commitment.

Jesus uses money as an example because it represents security, identity, and power that compete directly with God for human allegiance. Money becomes a master when it controls our decisions rather than serving as a tool for God's purposes.

Absolute allegiance to God doesn't eliminate other relationships or responsibilities but subordinates them to divine authority. We can love family, work diligently, and manage resources while maintaining God as supreme authority over all these activities.

Reflection: What competes with God for your absolute allegiance and how can you subordinate it to His authority?

Prayer: Supreme Master, I want to give You absolute allegiance rather than dividing my loyalty between You and competing authorities. Help me identify what competes with You for my devotion and subordinate everything to Your authority. Make You my only Master and supreme love. Amen.

Day 86: Crossroads: Choosing Your Path

"This is what the Lord says: 'Stand at the crossroads and look; ask for the ancient paths, ask where the good way is, and walk in it, and you will find rest for your souls. But you said, We will not walk in it.'"
- Jeremiah 6:16

God calls His people to pause at life's crossroads and choose paths that lead to spiritual rest rather than restlessness. The ancient paths represent time-tested ways of following God that produce peace and blessing. However, choosing right paths requires rejecting wrong ones. "Stand at the crossroads and look" suggests deliberate evaluation of options rather than rushing into decisions. Crossroads moments require careful consideration of where different paths lead and what consequences follow various choices. Wise people pause to evaluate before choosing.

"Ask for the ancient paths" means seeking wisdom from Scripture and spiritual tradition rather than following contemporary trends that lack proven results. Ancient paths represent biblical principles that have guided faithful people throughout history.

"Ask where the good way is" indicates that some paths are better than others. Not all options at crossroads are equally valid or beneficial. God's way leads to blessing while alternative paths lead to difficulty and disappointment.

"Walk in it, and you will find rest for your souls" promises that choosing God's path produces inner peace and spiritual satisfaction. Rest doesn't mean inactivity but contentment that comes from alignment with divine purposes.

"But you said, We will not walk in it" reveals the tragic response of people who recognize the right path but choose alternative routes anyway. Knowledge without obedience leads to spiritual disaster.

Reflection: What crossroads are you currently facing and how can you choose the path that leads to spiritual rest?

Prayer: Path-showing God, when I stand at crossroads in life, help me pause to seek Your guidance rather than rushing into decisions. Show me the ancient paths that lead to rest for my soul. Give me courage to choose Your way even when other paths seem easier or more popular. Guide my steps in Your paths. Amen.

Day 87: When Faith Demands a Choice

"And if it is evil in your eyes to serve the Lord, choose this day whom you will serve, whether the gods your fathers served in the region beyond the River, or the gods of the Amorites in whose land you dwell. But as for me and my house, we will serve the Lord." - Joshua 24:15

Joshua's challenge reveals that faith sometimes demands difficult choices between serving God and serving alternatives that appear more attractive or convenient. These decision moments test the authenticity and depth of our commitment to God. Faith matures through choosing God despite easier alternatives.

"If it is evil in your eyes to serve the Lord" acknowledges that serving God sometimes feels burdensome or restrictive compared to other options. Joshua doesn't minimize the cost of following God but insists that the choice must still be made.

The alternatives Joshua presents—ancestral gods or cultural gods—represent the pressures believers face in every generation. We must choose between family traditions that contradict Scripture and cultural values that oppose biblical truth.

"Choose this day" emphasizes the urgency of decision-making. We cannot postpone spiritual choices indefinitely without consequences. Delaying decision often becomes decision to reject God's way in favor of alternatives.

"But as for me and my house, we will serve the Lord" demonstrates personal commitment that influences others. Leaders must choose first and choose clearly to provide direction for those who look to them for guidance. When faith demands a choice, neutrality becomes impossible. We serve either God or alternatives but never both simultaneously. These choice moments reveal and develop the quality of our faith commitment.

Reflection: What choice is your faith currently demanding that you make between serving God and serving alternatives?

Prayer: Choice-demanding God, when faith requires difficult decisions between serving You and serving more convenient alternatives, give me courage to choose You. Help me recognize that neutrality is impossible and delayed decision often becomes wrong decision. Strengthen my faith through choosing You despite the cost. Amen.

Day 88: Breaking Free from Spiritual Neutrality

"So, because you are lukewarm—neither hot nor cold—I am about to vomit you out of my mouth." - Revelation 3:16

Christ's stark warning to the Laodicean church reveals the spiritual danger of neutrality. Lukewarm faith disgusts God because it represents the worst spiritual condition—claiming relationship while demonstrating indifference. Breaking free from neutrality requires honest evaluation and decisive commitment.

Spiritual neutrality often masquerades as wisdom or tolerance but actually represents unwillingness to commit fully to God's truth and authority. This position satisfies neither God nor world while deceiving us about our true spiritual condition.

"Lukewarm" describes spiritual temperature that lacks passion for God without honest acknowledgment of spiritual need. Cold people know they need salvation. Hot people serve with fervor. Lukewarm people are deceived about their condition.

"I am about to vomit you out of my mouth" uses vivid imagery to convey God's revulsion at halfhearted commitment. This strong language demonstrates how seriously God views spiritual indifference and the urgent need for change.

Breaking free from spiritual neutrality requires honest assessment of our commitment level, confession of spiritual indifference, and decisive choice to serve God wholeheartedly. Neutrality must give way to passionate commitment. The Laodicean church's problem was prosperity that bred self-sufficiency and reduced dependence on God. Comfort often produces spiritual complacency that appears harmless but actually represents dangerous spiritual drift.

Reflection: How can you break free from any spiritual neutrality in your relationship with God?

Prayer: Passionate God, I don't want to be spiritually neutral or lukewarm in my commitment to You. Help me honestly assess my spiritual temperature and make necessary changes to serve You with hot-hearted devotion. Break me free from any spiritual indifference or complacency. Make me passionately committed to You. Amen.

Day 89: The Courage to Commit

"And Elijah came near to all the people and said, 'How long will you go limping between two different opinions? If the Lord is God, follow him; but if Baal is God, follow him.' And the people did not answer him a word." - 1 Kings 18:21

Elijah's confrontation with Israel reveals that spiritual commitment requires courage to choose definitively between competing claims. The people's silence reflects the difficulty of making commitments that have serious consequences. However, courage to commit ultimately leads to spiritual clarity and power.

"How long will you go limping between two different opinions" describes the exhausting attempt to maintain loyalty to contradictory authorities. This spiritual double-mindedness produces instability and prevents effectiveness in serving either master.

Elijah forces decision by eliminating the option of continued indecision. He understood that refusing to choose is itself a choice—a choice for spiritual mediocrity and powerlessness. Sometimes love requires confrontation that demands clarity.

"The people did not answer him a word" reveals the uncomfortable silence that often follows challenges to make serious spiritual commitments. People recognize the implications of choosing but hesitate to accept the consequences of commitment.

The courage to commit means accepting responsibility for our choices and their outcomes rather than trying to keep all options open indefinitely. Commitment always involves risk, but it also enables the power and peace that come from decisive action. Following Elijah's challenge, God demonstrated His power in ways that eliminated doubt about who deserved exclusive allegiance. Similarly, when we find courage to commit fully to God, His power becomes evident in ways that hesitation prevents.

Reflection: What spiritual commitment is God calling you to make that requires courage to choose definitively?

Prayer: Courage-giving God, help me stop limping between competing loyalties and choose You decisively. Give me courage to make commitments that have serious consequences and accept responsibility for my choices. Show Your power when I commit fully to You. Amen.

Day 90: All In: No Turning Back

"Jesus replied, 'No one who puts a hand to the plow and looks back is fit for service in the kingdom of God.'" - Luke 9:62

Jesus uses agricultural imagery to illustrate the focused commitment required for kingdom service. Plowing demands forward focus because looking backward creates crooked furrows and poor results. Once we commit to following Christ, backward glances undermine our effectiveness and betray divided hearts.

"Puts a hand to the plow" represents beginning serious commitment to God's work and purposes. This isn't casual interest but active engagement that requires skill, effort, and persistence. Kingdom service demands more than good intentions—it requires dedicated action.

"Looks back" indicates divided attention that compromises performance and results. When plowmen glance backward while working, their furrows become crooked and their productivity decreases. Similarly, believers who keep looking at what they've left behind cannot serve effectively.

"Not fit for service in the kingdom" doesn't mean these people cannot be saved but that they cannot serve effectively while their hearts remain divided. Kingdom work requires undivided attention and wholehearted commitment to produce eternal results.

This principle challenges us to examine our own commitment level and identify what might be drawing our attention backward. Past comforts, abandoned ambitions, or former relationships can all compete with present obedience if we allow them to capture our focus.

Going "all in" with no turning back means burning bridges to alternatives and embracing God's path completely. This level of commitment brings both risk and reward—risk of leaving familiar behind, reward of discovering God's best ahead.

Reflection: What keeps pulling your attention backward from wholehearted commitment to following Christ?

Prayer: Forward-focused Lord, I want to go all in with no turning back in my commitment to You. Help me stop looking backward at what I've left behind and focus completely on following You forward. Make me fit for effective service in Your kingdom through undivided commitment. Keep my hand steady on the plow. Amen.

Day 91: Beyond Surface Prayers

"And when you pray, do not keep on babbling like pagans, for they think they will be heard because of their many words. Do not be like them, for your Father knows what you need before you ask him."
- Matthew 6:7-8

Jesus challenges us to move beyond superficial prayer patterns to authentic communication with God. Deep prayer emerges from relationship rather than religious routine. It focuses on communion rather than just petition, transformation rather than just transaction.

Surface prayers often consist of repetitive phrases, familiar requests, and predictable patterns that require little heart engagement. While God hears all prayers, He desires conversations that reflect genuine relationship rather than mechanical repetition.

"Your Father knows what you need before you ask" reveals that prayer's primary purpose isn't informing God about our needs but aligning our hearts with His will. Deep prayer changes us more than it changes circumstances. It transforms our desires to match His desires. Moving beyond surface prayers requires honest self-examination, vulnerable confession, and patient listening for God's response. It means praying Scripture back to God, wrestling with difficult questions, and remaining silent long enough to hear His voice.

Deep prayer also includes intercession that goes beyond our immediate circle to embrace God's global purposes. It involves spiritual warfare that confronts evil forces and claims victory through Christ's authority. This level of prayer requires spiritual maturity and persistent faith.

Reflection: How can you move beyond surface prayers to deeper, more authentic communication with God?

Prayer: Deep-hearing God, I want to move beyond surface prayers to authentic conversation with You. Teach me to pray with honesty, vulnerability, and patient listening. Transform my prayer life from religious routine to relationship reality. Draw me into the depths of communion with You. Amen.

Day 92: Embracing Holy Disruption

"And Jesus entered the temple and drove out all who sold and bought in the temple, and he overturned the tables of the money-changers and the seats of those who sold pigeons." - Matthew 21:12

Jesus' cleansing of the temple demonstrates that spiritual maturity sometimes requires disrupting comfortable patterns that dishonor God. Holy disruption challenges systems, relationships, and habits that compromise our devotion to God, even when they appear religious or beneficial.

The money-changers weren't necessarily evil people—they provided services that worshippers needed. However, their activities had transformed God's house into a marketplace rather than a place of prayer. Sometimes good activities become barriers to God's best purposes.

Holy disruption begins with allowing God to overturn the tables in our hearts—challenging priorities, relationships, and activities that crowd out authentic worship and service. This process often feels uncomfortable because it requires changing familiar patterns.
This principle applies to church practices that have become more traditional than transformational, relationships that encourage spiritual compromise, and career paths that conflict with God's calling.

Sometimes love requires confrontation that others may misunderstand. Embracing holy disruption requires wisdom to distinguish between human preferences and divine purposes. Not every disruption is holy, and not every comfortable pattern needs changing. Spiritual discernment helps us cooperate with God's transforming work while resisting mere change for change's sake.

Reflection: What comfortable patterns in your spiritual life might need holy disruption to honor God more fully?

Prayer: Disrupting God, I invite You to overturn any tables in my heart that dishonor You or crowd out authentic worship. Give me courage to embrace holy disruption when You challenge comfortable patterns. Help me distinguish between Your transforming work and mere human change. Cleanse my spiritual temple. Amen.

Day 93: The Ministry of Presence

"And surely I am with you always, to the very end of the age." - Matthew 28:20

Jesus' final promise to His disciples emphasizes presence over programs, relationship over resources. The ministry of presence means offering others the gift of attentive, caring availability that reflects God's constant accessibility to us. This often ministers more powerfully than words or solutions.

Our culture emphasizes doing over being, achievement over availability. However, many people need someone to be with them in their struggles more than they need someone to fix their problems. Presence communicates value, love, and support in ways that advice cannot match.

The ministry of presence requires laying aside our agenda to enter someone else's experience with empathy and attention. This means listening without immediately offering solutions, sitting with people in their pain without trying to eliminate it quickly.

Jesus demonstrated this ministry by being fully present with individuals He encountered. He gave them His complete attention, entered their world of need, and offered His presence as the primary gift. His solutions flowed from relationship rather than distance.
Developing this ministry requires slowing down enough to be truly present rather than just physically available.

It means turning off distractions, making eye contact, and offering the gift of undivided attention that has become rare in our multitasking world.

Reflection: How can you better offer the ministry of presence to those around you who need attentive, caring availability?

Prayer: Ever-present God, thank You for Your constant availability and attentive presence in my life. Help me offer others the same gift of presence that You give me. Teach me to be fully present rather than just physically available. Use my presence to minister Your love to hurting people. Amen.

Day 94: Prophetic Living

"But the one who prophesies speaks to people for their strengthening, encouraging and comfort." - 1 Corinthians 14:3

Paul reveals that prophetic ministry focuses on building others up rather than tearing them down. Prophetic living means allowing God to speak His truth through our lives in ways that strengthen, encourage, and comfort those around us.
This lifestyle reflects God's heart for His people.

Prophetic living doesn't require dramatic supernatural experiences or public platforms. It begins with listening carefully to God through Scripture and prayer, then speaking His truth appropriately into situations and relationships where we have influence.

"Strengthening, encouraging and comfort" describes the fruit of authentic prophetic ministry. If our words consistently tear down rather than build up, we're not operating in true prophetic anointing regardless of how spiritual we sound or how accurate our observations may be.

This ministry requires spiritual sensitivity to discern when to speak and when to remain silent, what to say and how to say it. Timing, tone, and relationship all affect whether prophetic words accomplish their intended purpose of blessing rather than burden.

Prophetic living also means allowing our lifestyle to speak God's truth about His character, values, and priorities. Sometimes our actions prophesy more powerfully than our words, demonstrating God's love, justice, and mercy through consistent Christian behavior.

Reflection: How is God calling you to speak His strengthening, encouraging, and comforting truth into the lives around you?

Prayer: Prophetic God, I want to live in ways that speak Your truth for strengthening, encouraging, and comforting others. Give me spiritual sensitivity to know when and how to speak Your words. Let my lifestyle prophesy Your character to those who observe my daily choices. Use me prophetically for blessing. Amen.

Day 95: Stewarding Influence

"From everyone who has been given much, much will be demanded; and from the one who has been entrusted with much, much more will be asked." - Luke 12:48

Jesus reveals that influence carries corresponding responsibility. Every believer possesses some degree of influence—in family, workplace, community, or church. Stewarding influence means using it intentionally to advance God's kingdom rather than merely personal interests.

Influence operates through relationships, resources, skills, knowledge, and position. Whether our influence seems large or small, God holds us accountable for how we use it to impact others for His glory and their benefit.

"Much will be demanded" indicates that greater influence brings greater responsibility. Leaders, parents, teachers, and others with expanded influence cannot use it carelessly without consequence. Their choices affect more people and carry weightier results.

Stewarding influence requires recognizing its source in God rather than claiming it as personal achievement. All influence ultimately comes from opportunities, abilities, and relationships that God provides. Humility about influence's source guides its proper use.

This stewardship includes using influence to mentor others, promote justice, encourage faith, and model Christian character. It means speaking up for those who have no voice and using our platform to advance causes that matter to God.

Reflection: How is God calling you to more intentionally steward the influence He has given you?

Prayer: Influence-giving God, help me recognize and steward the influence You've entrusted to me. Show me how to use it for Your kingdom rather than just personal benefit. Give me wisdom to handle greater influence with greater responsibility. Make me a faithful steward of every opportunity to impact others. Amen.

Day 96: The Art of Spiritual Mentoring

"The things you have heard me say in the presence of many witnesses entrust to reliable people who will also be qualified to teach others."
- 2 Timothy 2:2

Paul presents the multiplication principle of spiritual mentoring—investing in others who will invest in others. This creates spiritual legacy that extends far beyond our personal ministry to impact generations. Mentoring becomes essential for kingdom advancement and personal spiritual growth.
Spiritual mentoring means sharing not just information but transformation through intentional relationship. It involves walking alongside others in their spiritual journey, providing guidance, encouragement, and accountability that facilitates their growth in Christ.

"Reliable people who will also be qualified to teach others" describes the multiplication effect of effective mentoring. We don't just transfer knowledge—we develop character and calling that enables others to pour into additional lives. This creates exponential kingdom impact.
The art of mentoring requires wisdom to know when to speak and when to listen, when to challenge and when to comfort, when to direct and when to allow discovery. Different people need different mentoring approaches at different stages of growth.

This ministry doesn't require perfection from mentors—it requires authenticity, availability, and commitment to others' spiritual development. Our own growth continues through the mentoring process as God uses our investment in others to deepen our own faith.

Reflection: Who has God placed in your life to mentor, and who do you need as a mentor for your continued growth?

Prayer: Mentoring God, thank You for those who have invested in my spiritual growth. Show me who You want me to mentor and help me be faithful in that investment. Connect me with mentors who can guide my continued development. Use mentoring relationships to multiply Your kingdom impact. Amen.

Day 97: Cultivating Sacred Rhythms

"Be still, and know that I am God; I will be exalted among the nations, I will be exalted in the earth." - Psalm 46:10

The psalmist reveals that knowing God requires intentional stillness that counteracts life's constant activity. Sacred rhythms create space for spiritual formation that busy schedules crowd out. These patterns become channels through which God's grace flows into our daily existence.

Sacred rhythms include regular practices like daily prayer, weekly Sabbath, seasonal retreats, and annual spiritual assessments. These aren't legalistic requirements but gracious opportunities to encounter God consistently rather than sporadically.

"Be still" doesn't mean inactivity but focused attention that eliminates distractions preventing spiritual awareness. In our hyperconnected culture, stillness requires intentional discipline to create space for God's voice to be heard above life's noise.

Cultivating these rhythms requires planning and protection. Sacred time must be scheduled and defended against competing demands. Without intentional rhythm, spiritual practices become irregular and ineffective for sustained growth.

Different people need different rhythms based on personality, season of life, and spiritual maturity. The goal isn't conformity to external patterns but consistency in practices that facilitate authentic encounter with God and spiritual transformation.

Reflection: What sacred rhythms do you need to establish or protect to create more consistent space for spiritual formation?

Prayer: Rhythm-establishing God, help me cultivate sacred patterns that create consistent space for encountering You. Show me the rhythms that fit my life and personality while serving my spiritual development. Give me discipline to establish and protect these practices from competing demands. Meet me in the stillness. Amen.

Day 98: Intercession as Warfare

"For our struggle is not against flesh and blood, but against the rulers, against the authorities, against the powers of this dark world and against the spiritual forces of evil in the heavenly realms."
- Ephesians 6:12

Paul reveals that believers engage in spiritual warfare that requires different weapons than physical battles. Intercession becomes our primary weapon against spiritual forces that oppose God's kingdom and attack His people. This prayer ministry engages in cosmic conflict for eternal stakes. Intercessory warfare goes beyond personal prayer requests to engage spiritual forces that influence individuals, families, communities, and nations.

It requires understanding that many problems have spiritual roots requiring spiritual solutions rather than just natural remedies.

"Not against flesh and blood" reminds us that people aren't our enemies even when they oppose us. Behind human conflict often lie spiritual forces using people to accomplish dark purposes. Intercession targets these spiritual enemies rather than human opponents.

This warfare requires spiritual armor described in Ephesians 6—truth, righteousness, peace, faith, salvation, and God's Word. Intercession without proper spiritual protection becomes vulnerable to counterattack from forces that don't surrender territory easily.

Effective warfare intercession often involves identifying specific spiritual strongholds, claiming biblical promises, and persisting until breakthrough occurs. This isn't formulaic but relational—partnering with God's Spirit to accomplish His purposes through prayer.

Reflection: How is God calling you to engage in intercessory warfare for specific people, situations, or spiritual strongholds?

Prayer: Warrior God, I want to engage in effective intercessory warfare against spiritual forces that oppose Your kingdom. Teach me to pray with spiritual authority and persistence. Show me specific battles where You want me engaged. Protect me with Your armor as I fight through prayer. Give victory through intercession. Amen.

Day 99: Living as Kingdom Ambassadors

"We are therefore Christ's ambassadors, as though God were making his appeal through us. We implore you on Christ's behalf: Be reconciled to God." - 2 Corinthians 5:20

Paul reveals that believers serve as official representatives of heaven's kingdom on earth. Ambassadors don't operate by their own authority but represent their sovereign's interests in foreign territory. This calling transforms how we view our role in the world and our responsibility to others.

Kingdom ambassadors live with dual citizenship—citizens of heaven currently stationed on earth. This perspective affects our values, priorities, and responses to earthly circumstances. We represent eternal interests while engaging temporal responsibilities.

"As though God were making his appeal through us" indicates that our lives and words carry divine weight when we fulfill our ambassadorial role properly. People encounter God's invitation to relationship through our authentic testimony and consistent character.

Ambassadors require training in their sovereign's will, values, and purposes. We cannot represent God effectively without intimate knowledge of His character and clear understanding of His kingdom principles. This requires ongoing study and spiritual formation.

This calling also includes immunity from earthly citizenship conflicts—we answer to higher authority than cultural or political pressures. Kingdom ambassadors maintain loyalty to heaven's values even when they conflict with earthly expectations.

Reflection: How does understanding your role as Christ's ambassador change your approach to daily relationships and responsibilities?

Prayer: Sovereign King, I accept my calling as Your ambassador in this world. Help me represent Your kingdom faithfully through my words and actions. Give me intimate knowledge of Your will and wisdom to apply kingdom principles in earthly situations. Use me to make Your appeal to others. Amen.

Day 100: The Eternal Perspective

"So we fix our eyes not on what is seen, but on what is unseen, since what is seen is temporary, but what is unseen is eternal."
- 2 Corinthians 4:18

Paul's final principle for this devotional journey centers on eternal perspective that transforms how we evaluate everything else. Living with eternity in view affects our priorities, decisions, relationships, and resource allocation. This perspective produces wisdom that temporal viewpoints cannot provide.

"Fix our eyes" requires intentional, sustained focus rather than casual glance. Eternal perspective doesn't develop accidentally—it requires deliberate choice to evaluate circumstances through the lens of everlasting rather than immediate consequences.

"What is seen is temporary" includes everything visible in this world—possessions, positions, problems, and pleasures. While these aren't necessarily evil, they're all transitional. Wisdom invests primary attention in realities that survive temporal changes.

"What is unseen is eternal" encompasses spiritual realities—God's character, kingdom purposes, transformed lives, and relationships that continue beyond physical death. These invisible realities carry more weight than visible circumstances because they endure forever.

Living with eternal perspective doesn't eliminate concern for temporal responsibilities but subordinates them to eternal priorities. We still work diligently, love deeply, and serve faithfully, but we do so with awareness that eternal results matter most.

As you conclude this 100-day journey, carry this eternal perspective forward. Let it guide every decision, relationship, and investment of your time and energy. The deeper waters you've entered lead ultimately to the eternal ocean of God's glory.

FINAL BLESSING

May the God who called you into deeper waters continue to reveal Himself to you in ever-increasing measures of love, wisdom, and power. May the insights you've gained transform not only your own life but ripple outward to touch countless others who need to discover that deeper relationship with the living God is possible.

May you never again be satisfied with surface-level Christianity but continue diving deeper into the inexhaustible depths of God's character and purposes. And may others, observing the transformation in your life, be drawn to their own journey into the deeper waters where God's glory dwells.

The journey continues. The deeper waters beckon. And the One who is deeper still awaits your continued discovery of His infinite love. "Now to him who is able to do immeasurably more than all we ask or imagine, according to his power that is at work within us, to him be glory in the church and in Christ Jesus throughout all generations, for ever and ever! Amen." - Ephesians 3:20-21

www.ingramcontent.com/pod-product-compliance
Lightning Source LLC
Chambersburg PA
CBHW071355300426
44114CB00016B/2076